STEREO: COMPARATIVE PERSPECTIVES ON THE SOCIOLOGICAL STUDY OF POPULAR MUSIC IN FRANCE AND BRITAIN

Stereo: Comparative Perspectives on the Sociological Study of Popular Music in France and Britain

Edited by

HUGH DAUNCEY
Newcastle University, UK

PHILIPPE LE GUERN
University of Avignon and CNRS-EHESS-UAPV, France

ASHGATE

Published by
Ashgate Publishing Limited
Wey Court East
Union Road
Farnham
Surrey, GU9 7PT
England

Ashgate Publishing Company
Suite 420
101 Cherry Street
Burlington
VT 05401-4405
USA

www.ashgate.com

British Library Cataloguing in Publication Data
Stereo : comparative perspectives on the sociological study of popular music in France
    and Britain. – (Ashgate popular and folk music series)
    1. Popular music – France – Analysis, appreciation.
    2. Popular music – Great Britain – Analysis, appreciation.
    3. Popular music – Research – Cross-cultural studies.
    I. Series II. Dauncey, Hugh, 1961– III. Le Guern, Philippe.
    306.4'8424'072'041–dc22

Library of Congress Cataloging-in-Publication Data
Stereo : comparative perspectives on the sociological study of popular music in France
and Britain / [edited by] Hugh Dauncey and Philippe Le Guern.
        p. cm.—(Ashgate popular and folk music series)
    Includes bibliographical references and index.
    ISBN 978-1-4094-0568-9 (hardcover : alk. paper)
    1. Popular music—Social aspects—France. 2. Popular music—Social aspects—Great
Britain. I. Dauncey, Hugh, 1961- II. Le Guern, Philippe.
    ML3918.P67S74 2010
    306.4'84240941—dc22

                                                            2010025099

ISBN 9781409405689 (hbk)
ISBN 9781409419501 (ebk)

Mixed Sources
Product group from well-managed
forests and other controlled sources
www.fsc.org Cert no. SA-COC-1565
© 1996 Forest Stewardship Council
FSC

Printed and bound in Great Britain by
MPG Books Group, UK

Contents

List of Figures

List of Contributors

Martin Cloonan is Professor of Popular Music Politics and Convener of Postgraduate Study in the Department of Music at the University of Glasgow. His research interests lie in the politics of popular music with particular reference to policy issues and questions of freedom of expression. His most recent work is a co-authored book with Bruce Johnson (University of Turku) *Dark Side of The Tune: Popular Music and Violence* (Ashgate, 2008). Previous works have included *Popular Music and the State in the UK* (Ashgate, 2007) and *Policing Pop* (co-edited with Reebee Garofalo, Temple University Press, 2003). Martin is also chair of Freemuse, the World Forum on Music and Censorship (www. freemuse.org).

Hugh Dauncey is Senior Lecturer in French Studies at Newcastle University, UK and associate member of the CNRS/Paris 1 Sorbonne University Georges Friedmann research laboratory. He teaches and researches French and francophone popular culture – particularly music and sport – and has edited a number of studies, such as (with S. Cannon) *Popular Music in France from* Chanson *to Techno: Culture, Identity, Society* (Ashgate, 2003), (with G. Hare) *The Tour de France, 1903–2003: A Century of Sporting Structures, Meanings and Values* (Frank Cass, 2003) and *French Popular Culture* (Arnold, 2003). He is currently working on a monograph study of cycling in France as leisure and sport and various studies of French sporting and musical culture. In 2003 he was decorated by the French state with the order of the *Palmes Académiques*, in recognition of 'services to French Culture'.

Simon Frith is Tovey Professor of Music at the University of Edinburgh. He trained as a sociologist and was previously Professor of English Studies at Strathclyde University and Professor of Film and Media at the University of Stirling. His academic career was paralleled by a career as a rock critic, writing for various magazines in the UK and USA before becoming rock critic of the London *Sunday Times* and a columnist for the *New York Village Voice*. A collection of his academic articles was recently published as *Taking Popular Music Seriously* (Ashgate, 2007). He is chair of the judges of the Mercury Music Prize.

Hervé Glevarec is a researcher at the CNRS research laboratory 'Communication et Politique'. His research interests focus principally on the sociology of cultural and media practices in the context of the cultural industries. In particular he looks at the media practices of children and adolescents. He also works on radio audiences in France, having studied, particularly, radio production at the French national cultural radio station France-Culture. Recent publications include (with Michel Pinet) *La culture de la chambre. Pré-adolescence et culture contemporaine dans l'espace familial* (La Documentation française, 2010), *La radio et ses publics. Sociologie d'une fragmentation* (Irma/Mélanie Séteun, 2009), and (co-edited with Eric Mace and Eric Maigret) *Cultural Studies. Anthologie* (Colin/INA, 2008).

Gérôme Guibert has a PhD in Sociology and is Senior Lecturer at the University of Paris III (Sorbonne-Nouvelle). He is general editor of the periodical *Volume!* a French research journal devoted to popular music. Amongst other work, he has notably published *La production de la culture. Le cas des musiques amplifiées en France. Genèse, structurations, industries, alternatives* (Paris, Mélanie Seteun/Irma, 2006). A former musician, he is now a music critic.

Fabien Hein is Senior Lecturer in Sociology at the Université Paul Verlaine in Metz, and is a member of the research team Erase (anthropology and sociology of expertise) within the Lorraine research laboratory in Social Sciences 2L2S. His research interests lie principally in popular culture, the cultural industries and employment in culture. Recent publications include *Le monde du rock. Ethnographie du réel* (Mélanie Séteun/Irma, 2006) and *Rock & Religion. Dieu(x) et la musique du Diable* (Autour du Livre, 2006). He is also a practising musician and music critic.

Mike Jones is Course Director for the MA in Music Industry Studies at the Institute of Popular Music in the University of Liverpool, before this he was Course Director for the MBA in Music Industries. Mike's interest and understanding of music industries developed through his membership of the band Latin Quarter. Best known for the hit single 'Radio Africa' and the album 'Modern Times', Latin Quarter released seven albums for major and independent labels between 1985 and 1997. He is currently writing a monograph *Managing Popular Music* and co-editing 'Positive Response', a collection of essays on HIV/AIDS and popular music.

Dan Laughey is Senior Lecturer in Media and Popular Culture at Leeds Metropolitan University, UK. He is the author of *Music and Youth Culture* (Edinburgh University Press, 2006), *Key Themes in Media Theory* (Open University Press/McGraw-Hill, 2007) and *Media Studies: Theories and Approaches* (Kamera Books, 2009), as well as numerous articles on everyday music and media use. His research interests are cross-cultural and interdisciplinary: music and media audiences; sport and fan cultures; cultural histories of everyday life; dance cultures; media and cultural theory; popular anthropology. He is also interested in the social theory of Michel de Certeau and Erving Goffman.

Philippe Le Guern is Professor of Sociology of Culture at the University of Avignon, member of the Centre Norbert Elias research laboratory (CNRS-EHESS-UAPV), France, and associate member of the Georges Friedmann research laboratory (Paris 1-CNRS). He has edited a number of studies on popular culture including *Les cultes médiatiques. Oeuvres cultes et culture fan* (PUR, 2002) and (with J. Migozzi) *Production(s) du Populaire* (PULIM, 2004). He has worked to encourage dialogue between French and British researchers studying popular music through ventures such as the special number (Vol. 25, 141–2, 2007) of the French journal *Réseaux* (co-edited with S. Frith) available on-line at http://reseaux.revuesonline.com, and the recent creation of the webjournal *Cultures sonores* (www.culturessonores.org). Current work covers music and everyday life, the impact of digital technologies on work practices in the music and film industries and trends towards considering popular music as 'heritage'. He is principal investigator in a French national research council project on the effects of digital technologies on work in cultural industries.

J. Mark Percival is Programme Leader for Media at Queen Margaret University, Edinburgh. His 2007 doctoral thesis *Making Music Radio*, focused on the social dynamics of the relationship between record industry pluggers and music radio programmers in the UK. He has analysed Scottish indie music production in *Popular Music History* (2009) and contributed chapters on popular music and identity in I. Brown (ed.), *From Tartan to Tartanry: Scottish Culture, History and Myth* (Edinburgh University Press, 2010) and A. Bennett and J. Stratton (eds), *Britpop and the English Music Tradition* (Ashgate, 2010). Mark is a member of the Radio Studies Network and has been a Mercury Music Prize judging committee member (1999–2000) and DJ for BBC Radio Scotland (1988–2000).

Josie Robson has had a varied music industry career. She began singing in local Sheffield bands in the 1980s and secured a record and publishing deal with Chrysalis records and music. When the label was bought by EMI in 1991, Josie and her band Respect were 'dropped', along with one third of the roster. This encouraged her to find out what the industry was all about and she enrolled on a Communication Studies course at Sheffield Hallam University. She went on to design and deliver the first popular music course at the university and began her ten year PhD on the gender dynamics of Sheffield's music scenes. Currently, she runs her own business, Harmony Training, which provides music industry training, work experience and business support for women and other under-represented communities in South Yorkshire.

Dominique Sagot-Duvauroux is Professor of Economics at Angers University, and Director of the Granem research grouping. He specializes in research into the economics of culture, and has published widely on the subject, including *'La propriété intellectuelle, c'est le vol!' Les majorats littéraires de Proudhon et autres textes* (Dijon, 2002). Recent publications include (with N. Moureau) *Le Marché de l'art contemporain* (La Découverte, 2006), and as part of his work advising the Ministry of Culture (with F. Benhamou) 'La place du droit d'auteur dans la rémunération de la création artistique, une synthèse', *Culture Études*, 16 (2007/2008), (*Ministère de la Culture et de la Communication*, 2008).

Philippe Teillet is Senior Lecturer in Political Science at the Institut d'études politiques Grenoble (Université de Grenoble Pierre Mendès-France) and a member of the CNRS research laboratory Pacte. His research focuses principally on cultural policies, and more specifically, on changing forms of state intervention in the cultural domain, as well as the political dimensions of cultural policies. Recent research publications include (with E. Négrier) 'La montée en puissance des territoires: facteur de recomposition ou de décomposition des politiques culturelles?', in J.-P. Saez (ed.), *Culture et société* (L'Attribut, 2008), and 'Le "secteur" des musiques actuelles', *Réseaux* 25/141–2 (2007): 269–96.

Simon Warner is Lecturer in Popular Music Studies in the School of Music and was Director of PopuLUs, the Centre for the Study of the World's Popular Musics, from 2004–2008. His principal research interests lie in the relationship between the Beat Generation writers and subsequent rock culture reflected in his edited collection *Howl for Now: A Celebration of Allen Ginsberg's epic protest poem* (Route, 2005) and his chapter on Ginsberg's 1965 Liverpool visit for *Centre of the Creative Universe: Liverpool and the Avant Garde* (University of Liverpool Press, 2007). His 75th birthday portrait of British Beat poet Michael Horovitz was broadcast on BBC Radio 4 in 2010. Recent publications include the co-edited volume *Summer of Love: The Beatles, Arts and Culture in the Sixties* (WVT, 2008) and an essay on Manchester and Liverpool's sporting and musical rivalries for *Soccer & Society* (2011). His live rock reviews and obituaries have appeared in *The Guardian* and he is presently developing Beat-linked recording projects with the US producer Jim Sampas.

General Editor's Preface

The upheaval that occurred in musicology during the last two decades of the twentieth century has created a new urgency for the study of popular music alongside the development of new critical and theoretical models. A relativistic outlook has replaced the universal perspective of modernism (the international ambitions of the 12-note style); the grand narrative of the evolution and dissolution of tonality has been challenged, and emphasis has shifted to cultural context, reception and subject position. Together, these have conspired to eat away at the status of canonical composers and categories of high and low in music. A need has arisen, also, to recognize and address the emergence of crossovers, mixed and new genres, to engage in debates concerning the vexed problem of what constitutes authenticity in music and to offer a critique of musical practice as the product of free, individual expression.

Popular musicology is now a vital and exciting area of scholarship, and the *Ashgate Popular and Folk Music Series* presents some of the best research in the field. Authors are concerned with locating musical practices, values and meanings in cultural context, and draw upon methodologies and theories developed in cultural studies, semiotics, poststructuralism, psychology and sociology. The series focuses on popular musics of the twentieth and twenty-first centuries. It is designed to embrace the world's popular musics from Acid Jazz to Zydeco, whether high tech or low tech, commercial or non-commercial, contemporary or traditional.

Professor Derek B. Scott
Professor of Critical Musicology
University of Leeds

Acknowledgements

Many thanks to Niall Mercer, who has doubtless forgotten more about popular music than we will ever know.

Thanks also to Andy Simpson, for his unstinting work translating the chapters originally written in French.

Chapter 1

Top of the Pops, or Gilbert and Maritie Carpentier? Ways of Doing and Thinking Popular Music in Britain and France

Hugh Dauncey and Philippe Le Guern

This volume is the most recent result of some ten years or so of research collaboration between the editors. Whereas the British editor is a specialist in French Studies in the UK interested in a variety of forms of French popular culture – music and sport in particular, the French editor is a French academic specializing in the sociology of music and popular culture, principally in France, but also in Britain as well. Early in our working together, we quickly realized that some of our own preconceptions about the politics, economics and sociology of what we were studying in the other's country were perhaps not quite as accurate as they should be, and that work on teasing out the actual realities of music and popular culture was of particular usefulness to us as partners in research projects focusing either on the UK or on France or comparatively. Moreover, talking to colleagues in France and Britain about these kinds of subjects convinced us that there was an equally important operation to be undertaken of explaining and deconstructing many of the ways of thinking about music and popular culture in France held by British academics, and equally, the understandings and misconceptions of British popular culture cherished by French researchers.

It was thus that after an initial volume edited on French popular music from *chanson* to techno published by Ashgate in 2003,[1] ongoing discussions between us and other colleagues about cultural policies in our two countries regarding

---

[1]   Hugh Dauncey and Steve Cannon (eds), *Popular Music in France from* Chanson *to Techno* (Aldershot, 2003). A number of chapters in particular in this volume are likely to help inform readers interested in the themes and issues covered here in *Stereo*. These are Philippe Le Guern, 'The Study of Popular Music between Sociology and Aesthetics', pp. 7–26; David Looseley, 'In from the Margins: Chanson, Pop and Cultural Legitimacy', pp. 27–40; Hugh Dauncey, 'The French Music Industry: Structures, Challenges and Responses', pp. 41–56; Geoff Hare, 'Popular Music on French Radio and Television', pp. 57–76; and finally Philippe Teillet, 'Rock and Culture in France: Ways, Processes and Conditions of Integration', pp. 171–90. Other chapters deal with the popular music press, with music and cinema, with politically-engaged *chanson*, with Edith Piaf, with hip hop and electronica and other topics.

popular music and the differing ways in which this particular form of popular culture was perceived by academia led to the constitution of a small team of French and British researchers commissioned to produce a collection of expert survey-analyses describing and reflecting upon the ways in which popular music has been studied in academic research on both sides of the Channel since the 1950s also including where relevant, some more practical considerations of developments in politics, mediation or other topics. These individual studies – with those originally written in English translated into French and organized in pairs of chapters to provide a comparative perspective – formed the basis of the edited volume *Stéréo: Sociologie comparée des musiques populaires France/G.-B.* published in France in late 2008 by the *Centre d'information et de ressources pour les musiques actuelles* (Irma)[2] in partnership with the specialized music-publisher Mélanie Seteun.[3] This volume has been extremely well received in France where – although much research on popular culture in general and on music in particular is often inspired by American and British authors, the fact that these studies are available only in their original versions poses difficulties of access and fine understanding – the possibility of reading in *version française* how the study of popular music has been 'done' in the UK was a considerable advantage. Moreover, the 'French' half of the volume provided a very useful survey of the development over recent decades of a field of academic study in France which has for a long time struggled to achieve credibility in an environment of research where the 'popular' in all its forms was for a long time disqualified as a subject for serious academic inquiry, and by bringing together a number of summary-analyses of how music has been studied, the book provided something of an *aide-mémoire* for French researchers themselves on the development of their field. Successful in France, the volume was however the object of frustration in the UK, where the British contributors – although several were able to read the insights of their French counterparts in the language of Molière – were keen to see the volume translated into English in order to better understand the differences and similarities between their approaches to the study of popular music and those characteristic of French research. It was thus that the current volume saw the light of day, generously recognized by Ashgate as a

---

[2]   Irma is a non-profit-making organization located in central Paris. It is supported by: the French Ministry for Culture (Department for Music, dance, theatre, and live performances), by the French ministry for Youth and Sports (NGO Department); by the FCM (Fonds à la Création Musicale – Fund for Musical Creativity); by the SACEM (Société des Auteurs, Compositeurs et Editeurs de Musique – Author, Composer and Publisher's Society); by the ADAMI (Société pour l'Administration des droits des Artistes et Musiciens Interprètes – Artists' and Performing Artists' Rights' Administration Body), by the SPPF (Société civile des Producteurs de Phonogrammes en France – Record Industry Syndicate). See http://www.irma.asso.fr/About-IRMA. Irma is the subject of a forthcoming study by Hugh Dauncey and Philippe Le Guern.

[3]   Hugh Dauncey and Philippe Le Guern (eds), *Stéréo. Sociologie comparée des musiques populaires France/G.-B.* (Paris, 2008).

worthwhile contribution to the better comprehension – through the Franco-British comparative perspective – of popular music in France, in Britain, and in general.

The work of translation of the French contributions, although ultimately successful in rendering both the content and the tenor of the original French texts, has been challenging, and merits perhaps a brief note of explanation here. One of the stereotypes of French academic writing held by British and American researchers – or as the French tend to call them, the 'Anglo-Saxons' – is that French texts tend to be abstruse, complicated, wordy and circumlocutory, with their expression verging on the obscurantist. Unfortunately, the experience of working together on this current book has led the editors to conclude, regretfully, that in this case at least, the stereotype is not too far from the truth. Whereas translation of most French texts into English often results in savings of 10 per cent of total word length (in reflection of the 'wordiness' of French and the 'concision' of English!), here we have been unable to find such economies of conversion, such has been the necessity to make meanings as clear as possible for an Anglophone and UK/US readership unaccustomed to the specific debates and issues in question. Moreover, the frequent need to gloss organizations, principles and mechanisms specific to the French institutional and academic context of popular music has created extra material without which the messages of our French authors might have failed to be properly communicated. The translations are not works of art; but they do render faithfully as many of the subtleties of the analysis as possible, while at the same time retaining enough of a taste of the undoubted complexity of expression of our Gallic contributors.

Many French academics have for a long time suffered from something of an inferiority complex concerning their own abilities to say anything new about popular culture, such as has seemed to be to them the volume and quality of research produced, for decades, by American and British scholars. This point is touched upon and discussed more fully by a number of the French contributors to this volume, who explain how French research on popular culture in general and popular music in particular has often suffered from a kind of double disqualification both by an academic and intellectual system which has traditionally favoured 'élite' cultural forms and practices, and by the perceived backwardness and simplicity of French conceptualizations and research methods compared with those – imported slowly and late in translation or received more quickly but perhaps more imperfectly in the original English – of British and American specialists. Additionally, and it is another point which arises in various chapters, where French research on popular culture and popular music did occur, it was disappointing to many more sociologically-inspired academics for its general and 'philosophical' approaches, thought to be lacking in the social-science seriousness of UK/US ethnographic or more quantitative investigations. But whatever their insecurities (and some compensating elements of self-satisfaction) *vis-à-vis* 'Anglo-Saxon' research, the French have remained durably intrigued both by UK/US traditions of research into popular music and by the musical, cultural, social, political and economic practices which they take as their subject matter.

To adopt for a short while a specifically French perspective, and consider the introductory remarks made in the French version of this current volume, only ten years or so ago, the idea that a young aspiring academic could make a career in the French university system on the basis of a PhD on popular music was extremely brave, naive, or simply unrealistic. Such a post grad student would have looked enviously at the situation which appeared so much more favourable in the UK, where university lecturers were free and happy to write on the Pet Shop Boys or the Clash, to muse on the respective merits of technologies such as the Roland TR 808 or the Akaï S1000 and their significance for techno or electronic genres, or even, study entirely seriously the social meaning of Madonna. Inhibited by the theories of cultural legitimacy propounded by Pierre Bourdieu which constrained the intellectual space available for the study of the 'popular', and having so efficiently internalized the hierarchies of intellectually acceptable subjects of academic study, French researchers saw such British studies as astonishingly novel and risky initiatives to undertake in their own professional universe. Another feature of British academia which surprised, even shocked French researchers some ten years ago was the dual status of some of their UK colleagues who were simultaneously extremely well-known rock critics[4] as well as university researchers, or who were practising or past musicians.[5] In traditional French university terms, such a status was indicative of lack of distance and objectivity from the subject of study, as was indeed the way in which French researchers perceived the tone and nature of much of 'Anglo-Saxon' rock/popular music criticism and academic research as being 'disinhibited' and closer to the idea of listening pleasure contained within the experience of popular music. In general, French academia saw British and US research as more free to tackle subjects of significance whatever their place in a cultural hierarchy, and their desire to follow suit was particularly strengthened by the contributions of Cultural studies perspectives, as they fed into French research in the late 1970s, 1980s and 1990s.

However, although many of these French inhibitions were actually the case, in various ways, recent studies have demonstrated that the sociology of popular music is not an entirely new invention in France after all.[6] As we shall see in detail in subsequent chapters of this volume, French research has developed in a dialogue between 'Anglo-Saxon' theoretical and methodological influences imported into France either quickly in English, or much more slowly in translation, and existing French structures of academia and intellectual values. The first studies of yé-yé music and its stars appeared at the end of the 1960s, and during the 1970s, in a

---

[4]   The 'best' example is of course Professor Simon Frith .

[5]   Such as Fabien Hein, Josie Robson, J. Mark Percival, Philippe Le Guern, Hervé Glevarec and others amongst the contributors to this current volume. The fact that French researchers are now able to be both involved in musical practice and analysts of popular music reflects recent changes in French academia which are detailed throughout the 'French' chapters here.

[6]   As explained by Philippe Le Guern in Chapter 3.

period of considerable socioeconomic and sociocultural change, the links between 'youth' and popular music began to be explored using a variety of analytical and ideological perspectives, with, interestingly, Marxist interpretations failing to gain the same hold on the study of popular music as they did on literature at the same time.[7] During the 1970s, French studies began to draw parallels between life-styles and genres of music, somewhat in the same way that Hebdige was able to define meanings of style for mods and rockers towards the end of the decade. In the 1980s, French research developed to take account of 'work' in the cultural sector, analysing musicians' careers – in amateur or 'professional' music – and undertaking ethnographic studies of rehearsals or live performances. Also during the 1980s, other French researchers – using the recently invented term of 'amplified musics' as the basis for their focuses, stressed the inseparability of musical practice and listening to music from the physical and material conditions of their production and dissemination. This strand in analysis attached central importance to musical instruments, to amplifiers and to sound systems, giving them a significance sufficient to justify their inclusion in the seriously thought-out museum exhibitions. Simultaneously, researchers such as Antoine Hennion reconsidered issues of taste and of individuals' passionate enthusiasm for the musics they like, examining fan behaviour and attempting to pull the centre of ideological and theoretical gravity for studies of music away from the gravitational pull of Bourdieu's notions of cultural legitimacy. Although French sociological studies of popular music have indeed come a long way since the 1960s in terms of their freedom to address a wider variety of issues and in terms of the abilities of individual researchers to actually build careers within French academia on popular culture and popular music, there is still an enduring suspicion that the lesser exposure of 'Anglo-Saxon' researchers to restrictive hierarchies of cultural values (for cultural consumption and for academic study) makes their studies somehow different and more valuable than those produced in France. This current volume should hopefully go some small way, at least, towards enabling music-loving sociologists of culture on either side of the Channel to better decide for themselves on the relative merits of Gallic and UK/US approaches.

A concrete example of what French people in general and French researchers into popular music tend to see as the fundamental difference between popular music in the UK and in France is furnished by the contrast perceived between the one British television programme relating to music that is almost universally known in France – *Top of the Pops* – and the presenters of numerous French television shows on music produced during the 1960s, 1970s and 1980s, known by almost no-one outside of France and in France by few under the age of 40: the married duo Maritie et Gilbert Carpentier. The famous French rock critic Jérôme Soligny once remarked to the French author of this introduction that it is the difference between *Top of the Pops* – a symbol of youth and change and revolt and popular culture – and the bland, traditional, culturally conservative, linguistically

---

[7]   These issues are discussed in detail in Chapter 3.

protective, musically unadventurous style of programmes and music showcased by the Carpentiers that summarizes the gulf between French and British/American popular music.[8] Quite how far this example of a difference between programmes presenting French 'variété' music in the 1960s and 1970s can really illustrate an overall trend is debatable, but Soligny's quip does serve to exemplify the enduring French inferiority complex about music and popular culture that can so undermine both practice and academic analysis. And the concept of 'variété' as a genre leads us to another consideration, that of the dominant influence of *chanson* over much of French music, especially 'variétés' in the period when the Carpentiers held sway over music on French television but also in more contemporary times, where enduring concern over 'text' and lyrics and the use of the French language has led to one of the features of French popular music and broadcasting that is – unlike the Carpentiers – generally known to analysts in the UK/US, namely the quotas imposing minimum volumes of French music on French radio stations.[9] These quotas imposed from 1994 and adapted in various ways since the late 1990s have been an example of what stereotypical interpretations of French cultural and broadcasting policies would see as statist intervention typical of a volontarist state aiming to protect national culture against globalized commercial culture. We shall see in later discussions in various chapters how simplistic views held on either side of the Channel about French interventionism and British cultural and commercial *laisser-faire* need to be nuanced and qualified, and this kind of cliché is but one of many which this volume hopes to be able to dispel.

We do not propose here in this introductory chapter to present summaries of the individual contributions provided by our team of authors, hoping that the analyses themselves will speak sufficiently clearly for themselves, and certain as we are that each reader will find differing elements of each chapter more significant or intriguing than others. On the other hand, however, it seems necessary that mention should be made here of a number of studies undertaken by British academics of French popular culture which have provided in a number of ways, the inspiration for a comparative project of the kind which this current volume aspires to be itself.

---

[8]   The Carpentiers' programmes, notably a series of 'specials' devoted to individual artists were highly popular, but focused on French musicians and genres which were essentially main-stream and uncontroversial such as: Jane Birkin, Charles Aznavour, Sacha Distel, Claude François, Chantal Goya, Johnny Hallyday, Sylvie Vartan, Mireille Mathieu, Thierry Le Luron, Eddy Mitchell, Dalida, Alain Souchon or Joe Dassin. It is in this sense that – more narrowly – Jérôme Soligny's sarcasm about French inability to produce a different kind of popular music is most pertinent. Hugh Dauncey and Philippe Le Guern are currently working on a study of the role played by the Carpentier duo in French music in the 1960s and 1970s.

[9]   A very helpful and comprehensive discussion of French *chanson* can be found in Peter Hawkins, *Chanson. The French Singer-Songwriter from Aristide Bruant to the Present Day* (Aldershot, 2000). And the work of Chris Tinker on figures such as Brel, Brassens and other major singers of this genre is highly useful: Chris Tinker, *Georges Brassens and Jacques Brel: Personal and Social Narratives in Post-war Chanson* (Liverpool, 2006).

An early example of this kind of cultural 'intercession' between French and British cultures and French and British academia was the work of Brian Rigby. Although his work is not specifically referenced by the French contributors to this volume, his ground-breaking study of French popular culture published in 1991 marked the evolving development of research and some teaching in a number at least of French departments in British universities towards an interest in the popular cultural dimensions of French civilization, rather than the traditional disciplines of literature (conceived as 'the canon' and its various derivatives, but always high literary culture) and language.[10] And subsequent research by Rigby on, for example, the reception of the ideas of Richard Hoggart in France and the ways in which British cultural studies perspectives interacted with the structures and practices of French academia anticipated more contemporary attempts to build conceptual and disciplinary bridges between schools of research into popular culture and popular music on both sides of the Channel.[11]

Another significant figure of cultural relations in academia in the field of popular culture and popular music is David Looseley, whose work is referred to on numerous occasions in this current volume. David Looseley is another major figure in British 'French Studies' whose research interests – in the popular and particularly in French popular music – have helped to foster a diversity of approach in departments of French in UK universities. His two major books on popular culture and music in France have informed the thinking of numerous analysts of French cultural policy and culture.[12] Highly respected in France as well as in the UK for the expertise and knowledge he has accumulated about French popular music in all of its cultural, social, political, institutional and other dimensions, as well as for the enviable clarity with which he communicates his findings, Looseley is a prime example of a British academic who has been able to explain French popular culture to UK researchers and students.[13]

---

[10]   Brian Rigby, *Popular Culture in Modern France: A Study of Cultural Discourse* (London, 1991).

[11]   See for example Brian Rigby, 'La "culture populaire" en France et en Angleterre: la traduction française de The Uses of Literacy' in Jean-Claude Passeron (ed.), *Richard Hoggart en France* (Paris, 1999), and 'The Hidden Selves of Scholars and Teachers', *French Cultural Studies*, 10 (1999): pp. 241–53.

[12]   David Looseley, *The Politics of Fun: Cultural Policy and Debate in Contemporary France* (Oxford, 1995), and *Popular Music in Contemporary France: Aunthenticity, Politics* (Oxford, 2003).

[13]   Amongst numerous other publications by David Looseley, we should mention: 'In from the Margins: Chanson, Pop and Cultural Legitimacy', in Steve Cannon and Hugh Dauncey (eds), *Popular Music in France from* Chanson *to Techno* (Aldershot, 2003), pp. 27–39; 'Naming the Popular: Youth Music, Politics and Nation in Contemporary France', in J. Marks and E. McCaffrey (eds), *French Cultural Debates* (Newark, 2001), pp. 109–20; 'Conceptualising Youth Culture in Postwar France', *Modern and Contemporary France*, special issue 'Youth Cultures in the Fifth Republic' (eds), Chris Tinker and Wendy Michallat, 15/3 (2007): pp. 261–75; 'Intellectuals and Cultural Policy in France: Antoine Hennion

Other work on French music being undertaken by British researchers that can be mentioned here includes forthcoming projects by Chris Tinker on links between popular music and concepts of 'youth' in 1960s and 1970s France, looking in particular at how music and youth issues were represented in the iconic music magazine *Salut les copains*[14] and a volume edited by the French researcher Barbara Lebrun (who has perhaps significantly, in light of the barriers to working on the 'popular' existing in places still in France) chosen to work mainly in the UK on the body and music in contemporary French culture.[15] Barbara Lebrun is already the author of a growing corpus of work on French music which is playing a useful role in facilitating exchange between French and British researchers focusing on popular music.[16]

While anticipating future work together which will build on some of the themes discussed in this present volume, we hope that the discussions here of doing and studying music in France and Britain will meet with the same interest they stimulated in France. There is much further investigation to be done of how approaches differ (and coincide) in our two countries, and the linkages and partnerships of authors established by this project of common reflection

---

and the sociology of music', *International Journal of Cultural Policy*, November (2006), pp. 341–54; 'The Return of the Social: Thinking Postcolonially about French Cultural Policy', *International Journal of Cultural Policy*, July (2005): pp. 145–55; 'Fabricating Johnny: French Popular Music and National Culture', *French Cultural Studies*, 16/2, (2005): pp. 191–203; 'The Development of a Social Exclusion Agenda in French Cultural Policy', *Cultural Trends*, 13/2 (2004), pp. 15–27; 'Frères ennemis'? French Discourse on Jazz, Chanson and Pop', in 'Jazz Adventures in French Culture'; J. Dutton and C. Nettelbeck (eds), *Nottingham French Studies*, 43 (2004): pp. 72–9; 'Back to the Future: Rethinking French Cultural Policy, 1997–2002', *International Journal of Cultural Policy*, 9/2 (2003): pp. 227–34; 'Cultural Democratisation and Popular Music', in David Looseley and Phil Dine (eds), 'Cultural Practices and Policies: Democratisation Reassessed', special issue of *Modern and Contemporary France*, 11 (2003): pp. 45–55.

[14]   Chris Tinker, *'Salut les copains' (1962–76) Interrogating Culture and Youth* (forthcoming 2010). and also see by Tinker: 'Jacques Brel is Alive and Well: Anglophone Adaptations of French Chanson', *French Cultural Studies*, 16/2 (2005): pp. 179–90; 'Shaping Youth in Salut Les Copains', *Modern and Contemporary France*, 15/3 (2007): pp. 293–308.

[15]   Barbara Lebrun (ed.), *Corps de chanteurs. Performance et présence dans la chanson française et francophone* (forthcoming, 2011).

[16]   See Barbara Lebrun: 'René, Ginette, Louise et les autres: nostalgie et authenticité dans la chanson néo-réaliste', *French Politics, Culture and Society*, 27/4 (2009): pp. 47–62; '"Le bruit et l'odeur ... du success" Contestation et contradictions dans le rock métis de Zebda', *Modern and Contemporary France*, 15/3 (2007): pp. 325–37; 'Charity and Political Protest in French Popular Music', *Modern and Contemporary France*, 13/4 (2005): pp. 435–47; 'Mind over Matter. The Under-performance of the Body and Gender in French Rock Music of the 1990s', *French Cultural Studies*, 16/2 (2005): pp. 205–21; and 'A Case Study of Zebda: Republicanism, Métissage and Authenticity in Contemporary France', *Copyright Volume!*, 1/2 (2002): pp. 59–69.

should help to take this investigation forward. On a practical note, at the end of the book is to be found a very substantial Bibliography bringing together all of the material referred to by French and British contributors alike. As a further element for the consideration of cultural differences between French and British academia, it is perhaps interesting to point out that in many equivalent volumes published in France, there would be no such overall bibliography (indeed, there is often no bibliography accompanying individual chapters, with readers being expected to follow the references in the notes alone). Be this as it may, however, our bibliography exists, and constitutes a very useful compendium of academic resources for anyone wishing to undertake further research either on French popular music/popculture, on the shifting relations between French and British/American research on popular music/popculture, or on the politics, economics and sociology of popmusic in the UK. Likewise – and it only merits mention because once again it is something which is often lacking in French academic works – the Index has been drawn up in the hope that it will rapidly guide readers to those aspects of our comparative and contrastive endeavour which intrigue them the most, serving in this humble way to facilitate and accelerate Franco-British intellectual exchange in the way that our whole project has aimed to do from the start.

Vive l'Entente musicale!

Chapter 2
Writing the History of Popular Music

Simon Frith

Does any other nation take pop as seriously as we Britons do? Are Korean and Latvian broad-sheets full of handwringing closely argued think pieces about the death of the 7in single and the demise of TV pop shows? I doubt it. Other countries worry about the GDP and food and military might. We worry about our sitcoms, our house prices and our rock'n'roll.[1]

In an article in *Popular Music* in 1990 Sarah Thornton noted that:

> One of the things that distinguishes music from other forms of popular culture is that its consumption is accompanied by so much comment. Neither TV nor film, for instance, has incurred the volume, diversity and specialisation of the books and magazines devoted to music and read by people without a professional investment. This literature poses particular problems for historians of rock'n'roll, rock and pop.[2]

For Thornton the problems here concerned historical data: many of the 'facts' of pop music history are embedded in mediated narratives which are partial, self-serving or straightforwardly ideological; which are, in short, for a variety of reasons, unreliable. For Keith Negus, writing a few years later, these narratives had distorted academic popular music studies too, leading to the unself-reflective use of historical clichés (about 'the rock era', for example).[3]

Ten years on it is clear that the problems described here have intensified. 'The history of popular music' has become, in itself, a commodity, a form of intellectual property which for television and film companies, for magazines and photographic agencies and, indeed, for musicians and their managers is as valuable a source of income as the back catalogue for record companies. Pop music programmes featuring archive footage are now a routine part of the television schedule; the most acclaimed British film of 2007 was *Control*, Anton Corbijn's loving reconstruction of the life and death of Joy Division; among the books pushing for Christmas 2007 sales were the autobiographies of Eric Clapton, Jules Holland and Blur's Alex James, competing for space with coffee table collections of the best of *Jackie*

---

[1]   Stuart Maconie, 'The Golden Age of Pop', *Times Online* (2008), January 11.

[2]   Sarah Thornton, 'Strategies for Reconstructing the Popular Past', *Popular Music* 9/1 (1990), pp. 87–95.

[3]   Keith Negus, 'Histories' in *Popular Music in Theory* (Cambridge, 1996).

and *Smash Hits*; retrospective exhibitions of such music photographers as Harry Hammond are now a familiar feature of the provincial art gallery calendar. This is not the contemporary pop comment that Sarah Thornton described as a problem for historians but, rather, the cacophony of pop history itself, history being constructed and sold with little respect for the niceties of academic methodology or the dignity of the past. Amidst this din how can scholarly historians of popular music in Britain make themselves heard?

I have to answer that I do not know. There aren't any. Perhaps for the reasons already outlined, academic historians have not been drawn to the field of 'popular music studies'.[4] And while there are admirable social histories of British popular music these do not extend into the 1950s.[5] This is not to say, of course, that popular music scholars do not pay attention to history but that this involves either what one might call do-it-yourself history, the past approached through the lens of other kinds of social scientific methodology,[6] or, more commonly, and certainly in terms of any grand historical narrative, that writers more or less critically use non-scholarly accounts.[7] All of which is to say that to understand how the history of popular music is written in Britain we have to understand *popular* historical discourse.

Last night I began a series called *Pop on Trial* on BBC4, the aim of which is to decide which has been the most exciting, fertile, significant and entertaining decade in the short, colourful life of pop so far. 'Oh, that's obvious', say friends when I mention this premise to them. They then go on to cite, say, the Fifties for their primal rawness, the Sixties for their revolutionary glee or the Seventies for the dizzying diversity of their classic records. During the course of the series, cases are made strongly for both the Eighties and the Nineties and, indeed, right up to the present day. But the hand-me-down wisdom is that, the odd great band or golden moment aside, be it Britpop and Jarvis showing his bum to Wacko Jackson or Dancepop and Kylie nearly showing her bum in microscopic golden shorts, the music we love is in terminal decline.[8]

---

[4] Which means that even good social histories of postwar Britain have inadequate accounts of musical experience. See, for example, Dominic Sandbrook, *Never had it so good* (London, 2005) and *White heat* (London, 2006).

[5] See, for example, Derek Russell, *Popular Music in England 1840–1914. A Social History* (Manchester, 1987); Derek Scott, *The Singing Bourgeois. Songs of the Victorian Dining Room and Parlour* (Milton Keynes, 1989); James Nott, *Music for the People. Popular Music and Dance in Interwar Britain* (Oxford, 2002).

[6] For recent excellent examples see Sara Cohen, *Beyond the Beatles: Decline, Renewal and the City in Popular Music Cultures* (Aldershot, 2007), which provides, among other things, an ethnomusicology of a city drawing on its local history, and Jason Toynbee, *Bob Marley* (Cambridge, 2007), which provides, among other things, a political economy of reggae drawing on its global history.

[7] This is most obvious in textbooks. See, for example, Brian Longhurst, *Popular Music and Society* (Cambridge, 2007).

[8] Maconie, 'The Golden Age of Pop'.

My proposal here is that five narrative models are commonly deployed in the popular understanding of popular music history. One implies, superficially at least, that popular music evolves, gets better; four imply that, at least in the longer term, it does not. I will proceed by examining each approach in turn.

The Business Model

By this I mean the model used both to make sense of the history of popular music as an industry and deployed by the industry itself as part of its sales process. In this model popular music does get better but this sense of progress derives from the combination of two rather different kinds of argument, the first about *technology*, the second about *fashion*.[9]

The history of popular music is obviously implicated in the history of technology (and vice versa) and technological history is almost always understood in terms of progress. We therefore take it for granted that each new device for carrying or mediating music is better than (and effectively replaces) that which has gone before. Phonography gave way to electrical recording which gave way to analogue tape recording which gave way to digital recording which will doubtless give way to something else in the years to come. Each new method of recording is sold and often, indeed, experienced as better than what went before: offering a better sound and better 'fidelity' to the original performances that are being recorded; each new playback method is more convenient to use and manipulate, increases both the producer's and listener's abilities to achieve sonic perfection. That such changes in the ways in which music is produced/stored and retrieved/heard are changes for the better is a matter of common sense. To suggest otherwise (to prefer vinyl to CDs or MP3s, as I do) is regarded as eccentric. Richard Osborne quotes Compton Mackenzie's 1925 objection in *The Gramophone* (which he edited) to the replacement of acoustic by electrical recording:

> The exaggeration of sibilants by the new method is abominable, and there is often harshness which recalls some of the worst excesses of the past. The recording of massed strings is atrocious from an impressionistic standpoint. I don't want to hear symphonies with an American accent. I don't want blue-nose violins and Yankee clarinets. I don't want the piano to sound like a free-lunch counter.[10]

---

[9]   For an early exemplar of this sort of history see George Martin, *Making Music* (London, 1983). In this book the record producer George Martin solicited articles by a variety of big-name musicians, producers, and technicians to describe how their music making activity had evolved in the previous 30 years. I supplied the introductory overview, 'Popular Music, 1950–1980', a relentlessly optimistic account.

[10]   Compton Mackenzie, 'Where We Stand', *The Gramophone*, III/6 (November 1925): pp. 254–60 (p. 267). Quoted in Richard Osborne, 'The Label' *Reseaux* 25/141–2 (2007): pp. 67–96 (p. 88).

As Osborne suggests, this kind of argument (like those resisting the replacement of 78s by long-playing records, turntables by CD players, or CD collections by iPods) quickly becomes, as each new technology is rolled out, incomprehensible.

Perhaps this is, at least in part, a result of the second sort of industry argument, about the effects of fashion. Like any other commodity producer, the music industry has to persuade consumers to keep acquiring new goods (and music, unlike food or clothes, is not obviously used up). The popular recording industry, then, has traditionally marketed its wares with an emphasis on the new, 'the latest thing', with the implication that a new product, a new release, is a better product, will replace the old – in the shops, on radio playlists, in people's private listening habits. This is to reinforce the argument from technology. Popular music progresses. Each new record by an artist is better than the one before; each new technology of sound production/reproduction offers a better listening experience. Old sounds are 'out of date'.

Such marketing discourse has been familiar for a hundred years or more and the subject of academic disdain for almost as long (as in T.W. Adorno's account of the culture industry, for example). But today it is not clear whether anyone (even in the industry) really believes it! There are a number of points to be made here. To begin with, technological changes in how sounds are carried do not necessarily impinge on people's understanding of the *musical* experience involved. It is, in fact, noteworthy how little popular musical principles have changed since the onset of recording. Just as the 'classical' music repertoire with which most people engage is much the same now as it was a hundred years ago, so most basic pop forms (if not their degree of amplification) would still be recognizable to an early twentieth-century listener. In the digital age, certainly, the success of new technological devices has been as dependent on the reselling of old sounds as the launching of new ones. The percentage of old to new product in sales figures has risen steadily since the launch of CDs (now more than 50 per cent) and even such a fashion object as the iPod is (like the original 78 gramophone record) more significant for enabling individual consumers to listen on demand to music with which they are already familiar than as a device for downloading/hearing new or unfamiliar sounds.

At the same time, even more paradoxically, it is certainly arguable that 'anachronistic' music technologies continue to set the standards against which new devices are measured – the vinyl record did not disappear but remains as a kind of reproof to the over-bright, over-compressed sound of digital playback, just as acoustic instruments are still the musical tools to whose subtlety and character digital instruments aspire. Indeed (and this is why even the music business belief in progress has become more complicated), one of the most significant effects of digital recording, as I have already noted, has been to freeze history. Old records going back to the origins of recording can be retrieved and remarketed; sound archives plundered more profitably and less riskily – by record company and iPod user alike – than new acts launched or listened to. The new still matters to the music industry but less so than it has ever done before. As many commentators have noted, if digital technology has meant a sales crisis for record companies and retailers, it has also led to a boom in the live music market, in the sales possibilities for 'unique' musical events. And who was the biggest live music act of 2007? The Police! Who staged the most in-demand performance? Led Zeppelin!

The Musicological Model

One common way of understanding popular music is as a field made up of a number of genres – rock'n'roll, heavy metal, punk, reggae, Britpop, soul, grunge, rap, techno, progressive rock itself, and so on. I do not want to go into the finer points of genre theory (and its problems) here but just note its historical assumptions, its account of how musical styles emerge, develop and decline. Genre theory is primarily concerned with popular music's formal qualities (which is why I call this model musicological, though the formal description involved is not just musical but may cover aspects of visual and performing style too).

Again this is a familiar discourse (commonly used in the music press, for example). In this historical narrative new genres are taken to emerge through the interstices of existing genres, or in the coming together of elements from previously separate kinds of music. Each new genre takes on its own characteristic form until it is 'perfected' (in some arguments this ideal form is immanent in its origins). Thereafter it decays, is corrupted, loses audience interest and musical power, becomes 'a parody of itself', and so on. Such critical clichés are well enough known and I do not need to say any more about them here. This is the normal historical narrative for all popular music genres (I cannot think of any exceptions) and has two characteristics that are therefore worth noting.[11]

First, although what we have here is very clearly an organic or biological account of birth, development and decline, in music criticism the period of ageing/decline always seems to be much longer than the period of youth/growth or, at least, gets far more attention. Indeed, it sometimes seems as if a musical genre reaches self-consciousness – is recognized by performers and audiences as a new genre – at precisely the moment when arguments begin as to whether or not it is now in decline.

Second, while the replacement of one genre by another is seen as inevitable, natural even, the overall history of genres (unlike the history of species) is not seen as cumulatively progressive, with each genre superior, richer, better adapted to the world than what went before. Rather, the model is Buddhist in its implications: popular music as an endlessly repeated cycle of genre birth/life/death.

In short, the genre model (the most common historical discourse among popular music devotees) feels like an argument about the inevitability of decay. Whatever

---

[11] The best current source for such genre debates is probably Simon Reynolds' blog: http://blissout.blogspot.com.

the sense of progress such a narrative must at moments assume, its general sense is that music does not – cannot – progress for very long.

The Sociological Model

From a sociological point of view the history of music must be understood as an aspect of social history; musical changes reflect changes in society. We could expect then, that when a society is 'progressing' (in terms of technology, affluence, health and education, leisure time, social structures, human rights) its popular music would be progressive too. But in practice the issue is *how* society is taken to influence and shape popular music and this makes the story more complicated.

In Western capitalist countries since 1945 the social variable taken to be most significant for the sound and meaning of popular music has been age. The history of Western popular music has been related to demographic factors (such as the post-war baby boom) and the social role of popular music has been related to the growing up (or ageing process) and, in particular, to the social construction and experience of *youth*. Young people are thought to have the most emotional investment in music and popular music is believed to have its most significant impact on people's lives, on their identities, social networks, moral values and so forth when they are young.[12] This means, paradoxically, that for grown-ups popular music always seems best to express the past, the sense of possibility that they no longer have. From this perspective, popular music cannot be heard to progress because its value is essentially a matter of memories. Hence the common sociological observation that people value most highly the music to which they were committed in their teens and early twenties; hence too the widely shared popular belief that new music gets worse as one gets older: young people today just cannot play or sing or write tunes or even enjoy themselves on the dance floor as *we* used to do! In short, even if people's lives do get better as they get older, even if they believe they have, indeed, 'progressed', popular music is not included in the narrative of what such progress means.

Two other sociological arguments are familiar. The first understands musical change in terms of population movement – migration, urbanization, globalization, and so forth, changes that undermine 'traditional' or customary or established ways of doing things. Again, what is striking here is that whatever the overall material consequences of such change, in terms of such things as improved quality of life or greater opportunities for women or better conditions of childhood, musically such changes tend to be regarded negatively. There are familiar critical tropes here: describing, for example, how local, traditional, 'folk' music is commercialized, standardized, turned into something simply quaint. More

---

[12]   For early and recent academic versions of this position see, for example, Beatrice Martin, 'Rock' in her *A Sociology of Contemporary Cultural Change* (Oxford, 1981), pp. 153–84, and Andy Bennett, *Popular Music and Youth Culture* (Houndmills, 2000).

generally, socio-musical history describes minority, marginal, idiosyncratic music moving into the international commercial mainstream, losing its specific regional or national character. In short, whatever the realities of social progress (not least for musicians), discursively such change is almost always described negatively (hence the elaborate mechanisms for concealing such processes in the marketing of so-called world music). This is where the recurring concept of *authenticity* comes into critical play. The 'authentic' describes a musical form before 'progress' happens to it.[13]

Another sociological approach is rather different. This suggests that what one might call the ideology of popular music – its account of how music should sound, what it is for – is related to broader cultural and aesthetic arguments. To put this more simply, it is a matter of historical record that musical *tastes* change. This is perhaps most obvious in performing styles. What seems sincere (or authentic) in one era can seem exaggerated and insincere in another. In the 'high' performing arts, good acting or opera singing or instrumental playing are judged differently now than even 30 years ago. Popular music similarly can and does simply sound old-fashioned (and in popular music this can be a matter too of recording sound, of changing studio conventions and technologies and instruments). Now it might seem to be necessarily the case that as accounts of musical excellence or correctness change so ways of doing things in the past will sound inadequate. But in the digital age the argument is not so clear-cut. The classical music world's exploration of 'authentic' historical instruments and performing styles is now echoed by suggestions in the popular music world that digital remixes of classic jazz and rock albums do not change them for the better. I would argue, indeed, that digital technology has confused the once taken-for-granted relationship of taste and history. Popular music is no longer rooted in a particular time and place but continually revived, remixed and re-released and until it occupies a kind of virtual, history-less space.[14] For many of their listeners, the Beatles are as much a 1990s group (when the various digitally remixed anthology albums were released) as a 1960s one. In fact, it is hard now, in the CD age, to determine exactly what the Beatles' 1960s sound was. There is a kind of musical progress here but by default and without any real sense of history. Old music is continuously being made new.[15] One can no longer straightforwardly root the meaning of a piece of popular music in the circumstances (or sound) of its first performance.

---

[13]   For such rhetoric see, for example, reviews and correspondence in the magazine, *fRoots* – http://www.-frootsmag.com.

[14]   As Richard Osborne remarks, while a vinyl record carries visible and audible traces of the history of its use (the marks of wear and tear), digital information is essentially immaterial. See Osborne, 'The Label'.

[15]   A recent concert fad in Britain is for bands to reproduce live their 'classic' albums.

The Historical Model

Popular music histories have two main concerns: origins and lives. By *origins* I mean the search for a founding moment of whatever musical world or genre is being studied: the first be-bop gig, the first rock'n'roll record, the first punk act. (This obviously relates to the kind of genre analysis that I've already discussed.) This approach is common in TV music history programmes, and the tone of such programmes, whatever their chronological narrative, is that the excitement of popular music history comes from moving backwards from the present music (which is familiar) to its origins (which are not). Every TV series on popular music history I have ever watched gets duller, the nearer it gets to the present.

In print, most popular music history is written through *lives*, in the form of biographies; as any visit to a large bookstore will confirm, biographies dominate the popular music shelves. The dynamic of the pop or rock biography is fairly consistent. Even if the life does not end literally in early death or burn out, the narrative convention is the *decline* of creativity as the artist's will and imagination are sapped by too much success (or too little), by wealth (or continued poverty), by personal and commercial pressures, by boredom, falling sales, rising sales, shooting up, settling down.[16] Pop and rock are unusual artistic forms in that it is widely assumed that performers get less interesting as they get older (and increasingly play only their old numbers anyway). Is there any significant rock artist whose work is thought to have got steadily better? Even the positive reviewers of the last Bob Dylan album took it for granted that his new music was not – could not be – as important, startling or inspiring as the music he made that really mattered, in the 1960s. And this relates to the final model, that I will mention, if briefly.

The Art History Model

By this I mean the Romantic (nineteenth century) suggestion that there are some artists who can be removed from, *transcend* history; their value is timeless. Such artists' works are canonical; they reach 'humanity', generally defined, rather than audiences defined historically, by market or social forces. Popular music *en bloc* has, of course, been defined as outside this history-less history by the ideology of classical music; pop is too obviously functional, commercial, and crowd-pleasing to express eternal values. Nevertheless rock and other popular musical forms (jazz, country) have developed their own canons, halls of fame, and 'classic' works. What they have not done successfully (jazz comes closest) is establish cultural traditions in institutional terms, in the form of conservatories, formal qualifications and master/pupil relations. And, for this reason, and unlike art music, pop and rock have not established an institutionalized dialectic of tradition/innovation. A new

---

[16]   For a recent example, touching on almost all these issues, see Paolo Hewitt, *Paul Weller. The Changing Man* (London, 2007).

band like the Arctic Monkeys is not difficult to place in rock stylistic terms but whether the group is valued by its fans as a 'traditional' or 'innovative' British indie rock band is much less easy to determine. By and large, though, over the last 40 years of rock music, new bands have been as often acclaimed for returning to the essence of rock'n'roll as for developing something new.

Most discourses through which people understand popular music do not make sense of its history in terms of development. Those that do (the industrial model, for instance) are treated with suspicion. What this perhaps surprising finding reflects, I believe, is the truism that popular music is rooted in people's sense of time passing, whether their own time (ageing, social change) or at the instant of hedonism as in dance music, and that time passing is mostly an occasion for regret. Regret, one could say, has been the essence of popular music (whatever its use for social excess and celebration) since its emergence as a commodity form in the context of industrial capitalism in the nineteenth century, from the Irish song through the blues and old-time country music and Tin Pan Alley pop through to their various offspring.

For rock fans (and academics) of a certain age (50+) this is not how rock music was initially understood. The word 'progressive' has been deployed in various musical genres – progressive country music, progressive jazz, progressive folk. But as a genre label it was most significantly used in rock. *The Guardian* headlined its obituary of the musician, Pip Pyle (20 September 2006), 'Innovative drummer at the heart of progressive rock', and suggested that he 'encapsulated all that was groundbreaking in British progressive music in the shakeout from the 1960s'. But what is clear in the paper's account of Pip Pyle's career – as a member of Hatfield and the North, Gong, National Health and numerous other bands – is that 'progressive rock' was not, in the end, a stage pop music moved through on its way to somewhere else but, rather, describes a particular musical genre, whose popularity was small scale and short lived (and, quite soon, rooted in France and Germany rather than the UK). In the dominant discourse of both rock criticism and popular music studies since the mid-1970s, 'progressive rock' has been more often used negatively than positively as if, by its nature, popular music is something that should not 'progress'. For most contemporary popular music critics 'progressive rock' describes a historical genre that is nowadays heard as rather ridiculous.

I started my rock writing career in the heyday of progressive rock, the early 1970s. At the time my response to this kind of music was muddled, a confusion of admiration (for its ambition) and irritation (with its pretension). Looking back at progressive rock now, from an academic perspective, I find it easier to disentangle the arguments. On the one hand, 'progressive rock' described various musical elements that were clearly emerging from the newly established, late 1960s distinction between rock and pop. Progressive rock thus involved, above all, complexity; this was music with complex melodic structures and time signatures, with constant rhythmic and narrative shifts. Progressive rock numbers tended to foreground the instrumental rather than lyrical aspects of songs, but the lyrics too aspired to complexity, complexity of language and mood, the poetic use of symbolism and word games, a deliberate pursuit of the opaque. Complex musical arrangements meant, in turn, particularly on stage, foregrounding band members' musicianship and technique, the control and display of sonic invention and instrumental virtuosity. The most obvious distinction between a progressive rock and a pop track was thus scale: a twenty-minute musical epic *versus* a three-minute pop song.

It was from this perspective that progressive rock could be heard to develop both the musical and cultural tendencies that had in the latter half of the 1960s begun to differentiate rock from pop, its consciously arty seriousness and self-importance. In this, progressive rock clearly drew conventions and practices from non-popular musical forms: from jazz (as is obvious in Pip Pyle's career) in terms of virtuosity and improvisation; from classical or, rather, contemporary academic or art music, in terms of instrumentation and scoring. And certainly for some progressive rock musicians, 'progress' meant moving out of pop/rock into the jazz and/or academic *avant-garde* worlds. Part of the thinking here (to which I was sensitive as a would-be rock critic) was that to be appreciated, progressive rock needed the right kind of audience. Listeners had to 'progress' too, in terms of what they wanted from music, how and where they listened, with what listening equipment. If rock defined itself against pop as 'commercial music', progressive rock defined itself against pop as 'easy listening'. It offered, rather, difficult listening and so called forth a new audience of progressive rock listeners, who equally saw themselves as *moving on* from pop.

On the other hand, though, to go back to my critical confusion in the 1970s, 'progressive rock' was still recognizably rock, and not jazz or art music. It still drew on obvious pop elements in its use of the song form; it still deployed blues structures and explored the sonic potential of amplified guitars/drums. Above all, its performance style and stage display of musical personas were still rooted in showmanship. Compared to most 1970s jazz and art musicians, progressive rockers were deliberately humorous and self-mocking, playing with the trappings of stardom and, if not exactly crowd-pleasing, complicit with their audiences in the way their shows were mounted. Think, for example, of such pioneers of progressive rock as Frank Zappa, Soft Machine and Can.

In retrospect, then, I think it can be argued that if 'progressive rock' was a significant moment in rock history, its effects were felt along divergent historical paths. On the one hand, as a musical genre, progressive rock fed into the successful commercial stylization of 'heavy rock'. The key bands here (following different musical routes) were Led Zeppelin and Pink Floyd, from which all stadium rock bands, from U2 to Muse, could be said to descend. On the other hand, as an attitude and aspiration, the legacy of progressive rock can be traced in an *avant-garde* sensibility that has, on occasion, emerged in all subsequent rock genres. Progressive rock, to put this another way, left *avant-garde* artists of all sorts a model for the use of rock/pop elements in their work. This lineage is traceable in such postpunk bands as Pere Ubu and Public Image, but also in electronic, techno and other dance music forms throughout the 1980s.[17]

Whatever its historical importance and continuing influence, however, the central conceit of progressive rock – its notion that popular music could and should indeed progress – quickly became problematic. In the late 1960s it was widely argued that popular music was getting ever more interesting as a variety of musicians developed pop forms to explore unexpected musical, lyrical, cultural and political issues. By the mid-1970s such explorations seemed self-indulgent and wrong headed. The value of popular music was once more heard to lie in its simplicity and directness. And, as I have suggested, however this argument has gone since, there certainly is no consensus that popular music now is any better than it was 40 years ago, that its language, techniques or expressive principles have in any way 'progressed'. In fact, such an assertion would nowadays seem silly – this is no longer how rock is conceptualized.

To put this another way, the issue here is not whether or not popular music at a particular moment is thought to 'progress' (as a verb) but how popular music became, in day-to-day terms, the art form that best expresses the people's uneasy experience of 'progress' (as a noun), their doubts about the relentless effects of modernism and capitalism. Our understanding of nostalgia – as a feeling characteristic of modern life – is, I believe, defined musically, and that feeling is, in turn, central to the ways in which popular music is used and heard. Thus 'progressive rock' itself became eventually the object of an intensely nostalgic cult, a continuous search for listening experiences past, conducted on the internet, at fan conventions and in the classroom by teachers. Even in the academy, that is to say, 'the history of popular music' is not something we do, but something in which we indulge, according to our age, for comfort.

---

[17]   For this history see Simon Reynolds, *Rip It Up and Start Again: Post-punk 1978– 1984* (London, 2005).

Chapter 3

Charting the History of Amplified Musics in France

Gérôme Guibert and Philippe Le Guern

Research focusing on the music industry, musical entertainment, or practices related to rock or other forms of amplified musics over the long term is recent in France. Musical genres termed rock, rap, reggae, punk, metal or techno for example, were for a long time perceived as phenomena imported from the US or the UK both by the media as well as by researchers or other key players on the cultural scene. Over the course of several decades, it was believed that such forms of music had nothing to do with French culture and that there was no national history of such phenomena to be studied. These phenomena were considered as the consequence of commercial processes aimed at selling music to younger generations.[1] It is moreover within this utilitarian perspective that professionals who focused their efforts on France were to view such phenomena for a long time.[2] It was thus not by chance that, at the start of the 1980s – some years before pioneering field studies by Catherine Dutheil in Nantes, Jean-Maris Seca in Paris (Parking 2000) or Norbert Bandier in Lyon – the first research undertaken on the subject, albeit isolated and fragmented, aimed to shed light on these new music genres and the development of society.[3] As indicated by Danièle Pistone[4] in 2000,

---

[1]   Eric Maigret and Eric Macé , *Penser les médiacultures* (Paris, 2005).

[2]   Fabrice Ferment, 'Interview Jean-Marie Perrier par Gilles Verlant', in Fabrice Ferment, *40 ans de tubes, 1960–2000, les meilleures ventes de 45 tours et CD singles* (Paris, 2002).

[3]   Jean Charles-Lagrée, 'Rock'n'roll, pop music et folk de la fin des années 1950 aux années 1970' in Jean-Charles Lagrée, *Les Jeunes chantent leur culture* (Paris 1982); Paul Yonnet, 'Rock, pop et punk', in Paul Yonnet, *Jeux, modes et masses* (Paris, 1985).

[4]   Danièle Pistone, 'De l'histoire sociale de la musique à la sociologie musicale: bilans et perspectives', in Anne-Marie Green, *Musique et sociologie. Enjeux méthodologiques et approches empiriques* (Paris, 2000), pp. 75–94. The author notably underlines the contributions made by social analyses of musicology whilst championing the fact that, as a sociological production of music is constructed, this becomes detached from possible contributions from musicology. Regrettably, she gives scarce consideration to recent research, particularly into amplified musics.

and by Philippe Le Guern[5] in 2003, the social history of contemporary/amplified musics thus appeared rather late in French academia and extremely infrequently: the central database of French theses shows that it was not until the mid-1980s that the word 'rock' appeared in the title of any work of research.[6]

Whilst many researchers writing about rock in the 1980s never obtained a post lecturing in this specific subject area[7] – arguably considered as lacking the seriousness required for a career in the French universities – the 1990s witnessed however the arrival of a new generation, carrying the torch for the study of contemporary music through sociology, anthropology, musicology, information and communication sciences, and social geography, the characterizing feature of this new generation being that it was composed of people from the world of rock (musicians, concert organization association members etc); this giving these researchers the status and skills of 'insiders' and additionally, views no doubt tinged by the dominant musical ideology of students in the 1980s and 1990s, that of the independent music scene. It should thus be clear that the history of contemporary/amplified musics written in France is significantly influenced by the history of French academia itself.

This chapter will initially highlight precisely which epistemological and structural obstacles confronted the history of rock in France. By focusing primarily on the history of techniques and of mediation, we will secondly consider the co-existence of histories written by researchers and those written by learned music lovers.

The Difficulties of Charting a History of Amplified Musics: The Failures of Disciplinary Divisions

In France, research dealing with the history of music has persistently been compartmentalized according to its various 'aesthetics', that is to say by musical genres, just as it has been separated by differing academic disciplines or specialisms. In addition to this double tying up of the field came a lack of communication between researchers, on the one hand, and journalists and music-loving 'experts' on the other; each side defending their own domain after exclusively defining

---

[5]   Philippe Le Guern, 'The Study of Popular Music Between Sociology and Aesthetics. A Survey of Current Research in France', In Hugh Dauncey and Steve Cannon (eds), *Popular Music in France from* Chanson *to Techno: Culture, Identity and Society* (London, 2003), pp. 7–26.

[6]   For example, Jean-Marie Seca, *L'État acide. Analyse pyscho-sociale des minorités rock*, doctoral thesis supervised by Serge Moscovici (Paris, 1987). One of the first PhD theses produced on amplified musics is the work of Lagrée, *Les Jeunes*.

[7]   This is for instance the case of Patrick Mignon, whose 'conversion' to the sociology of sport led to working at the Insep national sports centre, after publishing his thesis *La Production sociale du rock* (Paris EHESS, 1996).

the outline of their particular subject of study. The significance of the absence in mutual interest between these different niches of knowledge has only become debated in recent years. The question of reflexivity[8] leads us to reflect on the extent to which research on music is influenced by the dual statuses of some academics who are also musicians, and furthermore, the gradual arrival into the study of popular musics of different academic disciplines (the latest arguably being geography)[9] has raised problems of competition and different methodologies. This often leads to constructive debate, albeit rather unproductive in terms of creating results in an institutional context of research where the isolation of disciplines is implicitly favoured. Whereas in England, the simultaneous position of academic theorist and rock journalist, as held by Simon Frith, is valued and even considered appropriate,[10] in France, it is clear that this dual status is best hidden. Indeed, such a position is deemed as indicating a lack of critical distance, or worse, of lack of objectivity.

However, although now prolific and stimulating, academic work on popular musics has, for a long time, produced results marked by the way it is shaped by intra-disciplinary expertises and the specific analytic tools linked to them.

The first theoretical work on jazz was written by a French ethnologist, André Schaeffner – a student of Marcel Mauss – and published as early as 1926.[11] The author, using the expertise gained from his particular research field, believed he could reveal the roots of what he called jazz in African musics, both in terms of *instrumentarium* and the ways in which the music was performed. Issues of Afro-American culture and the conditions of artistic production related to this culture, notably in terms of economics and sociology, were absent from this book. It should also be noted that, in 1935, the work of Hugues Panassié entitled *le Jazz Hot*, a subjective study aiming to define what should be understood by the term 'jazz',[12] although helping the formation and gradual officialization of groups of jazz music lovers, simultaneously prepared the ground for subsequent 'academic infighting', given the exclusion of *bebop* from the definitions outlined by its author. By declaring what 'true jazz' should be, and by essentializing and reifying generic labels, French specialists opened the door to struggles for symbolic power which often seemed incomprehensible to American musicians performing such music[13]

---

[8]   Philippe Le Guern, 'Sociologues et musiciens: usages de la réflexivité en sociologique de la culture', *Copyright Volume!*, 4/1 (2005).

[9]   Inaugural symposium 'Géographie et musiques: quelles perspectives?', Paris IV Sorbonne, 8 June 2006 and the study 'Géographie et musiques', *Géographie et cultures*, 59 (2007).

[10]   The same can be said regarding the interdisciplinary confrontation within culture, through writings in the field of 'cultural studies'.

[11]   André Schaeffner, *Le Jazz* (Paris, 1926), republished Paris, 1988.

[12]   Hugues Panassié, *Le Jazz Hot* (Paris, 1934).

[13]   Ludovic Tournès, *New Orleans sur Seine. Histoire du jazz en France* (Paris, 1999).

and which were furthermore devoid of interest for many British and American researchers involved in ethnomethodology or pragmatics inspired by the work of John Dewey.

When we reflect upon the creation and development of music and its practices and uses, it becomes clear that theorizing musical trends from a structuro-functionalist viewpoint which is additionally specialized by different academic disciplines is a tendency which is particularly well-developed in France. Jacques Chayronnaud[14] demonstrates for example the long-term trend in France towards the dividing up of the study of popular music by academic specialism according to repertoires and traditions, but also through the diverging definitions given to musical works and to their originators. According to Chayronnaud, in the 1990s, sociology thus appropriated rap and rock, ethnomusicology took for itself the study of traditional musics (from France or elsewhere), history primarily focused its study on music halls and *chanson*, whilst research and studies into jazz were anthropological or musicological.

This resulted in the formation of a *corpus* of data collected in parallel but with very little cross-referencing, caused equally by lack of awareness of other work and by institutional, strategic or political structural constraints. An example of this are the extensive works on *chanson* of Claude Duneton, *Histoire de la chanson française*, a work in two volumes each of 800 pages; or that of Louis Jean Calvet, *Cent ans de chanson française*, which both consider musical repertoires in a typological perspective,[15] far removed from consideration of local town bands, jazz orchestras or rock groups. Other examples relating to traditional musics is the overview article by J. Chayronnaud in the journal *Ethnologie Française*[16] and this journal's thematic issue on music from 1984.[17] Such writing followed in the wake of works started in the 1920s by folklore analysts such as A. Van Gennep, themselves based on the earliest collections of material made some decades before in the French regions.[18] Mention should also be given to work focusing on jazz, which after studies by Ludovic Tournès[19] and Denis-Constant Martin and Olivier Roueff,[20] was continued by a very comprehensive special edition of the

---

[14]   Jacques Cheyronnaud, *Musique, politique, religion. De quelques menus objets de culture* (Paris, 2002).

[15]   Some explanation can be found in Marie Naudin, *Évolution parallèle de la poésie et de la musique en France. Rôle unificateur de la chanson* (Paris, 1968).

[16]   Jacques Cheyronnaud, 'Ethnologie et musique: l'objet en question', *Ethnologie française*, 27/3, (1997).

[17]   Jacques Cheyronnaud, *Ethnologie et musique*, 14/3.

[18]   Jean-Marie Privat, *Chroniques de folklore d'Arnold Van Gennep. Recueil de textes parus dans le Mercure de France 1905–1949* (Paris, 2001).

[19]   Tournès, *New Orleans*.

[20]   Denis-Constant Martin and Olivier Roueff, *La France du jazz. Musique, modernité et identité dans la première moitié du xxe siècle* (Marseille, 2002).

anthropology journal *L'Homme*.[21] Contributing to this journal, Patrick Williams demonstrated for instance that gipsy jazz, far from being a long-standing tradition, was in fact the style of a sole individual, Django Reinhardt.[22] Following the politically engaged work by Carles and Comolli,[23] which interpreted free jazz in an international perspective from its origins in the realities of black life in the US, the adoption of free jazz by French musicians was dealt with in several research works which considered the relationship of this mode of musical expression to revolutionary countercultures and the Afro-American community. And finally, following the works of musicologist Vincent Cotro,[24] one should also note the recent study by Jedediah Sklower.[25] Regarding rock, many sociologists have investigated various musical styles and genres.[26]

The Difficulties of Charting a History of Amplified Musics (Continued): The Failure of Populist and Miserabilist Standpoints

Yet, throughout all of these works, little space was devoted to amplified musics. It would not be until the twenty-first century that the first works appeared[27] which considered the historical particularities of such musics in France. Before then, research works which considered these musics merely pigeonholed them into pre-existing categories, focusing more on the content of the musical works than on the periodization of their social uses.

It was in this manner that, in the 1980s, specialists in working-class culture established a link between the birth of rock and the history of popular urban songs, on occasions highlighting rock's revolutionary aspect[28] and its linkages

---

[21] 'Jazz et anthropologie', *L'Homme*, 158–9 (2001).

[22] Patrick Williams, 'Un héritage sans transmission: le jazz manouche', *Ethnologie française*, XXX/3 (2000), pp. 409–22.

[23] Philippe Carles and Jean-Louis Comolli, *Free Jazz, Black power* (Paris, 2000).

[24] 'Champs libres: le free-jazz en France, 1960–1975' (Paris, 2000).

[25] *La Catastrophe féconde. Une histoire du monde éclaté du jazz en France 1960–1982* (Paris, 2007).

[26] For example, we can mention, for a history of metal in France, Fabien Hein, *Hard-rock, heavy metal, metal* (Paris, 2003).

[27] Marc Touché, 'Mémoire Vive', volume 1 (Annecy, 1998) and Patrick Mignon, 'Évolution de la prise en compte des musiques amplifiées par les politiques publiques', in Gema/Adem-Florida, *Politiques publiques et musiques amplifiées* (Paris, 1997), pp. 23–31 and Gérôme Guibert, *La Production de la culture. Le cas des musiques amplifiées en France* (Paris, 2006).

[28] Here for example, Laurent Marty, 'De la chanson ouvrière du xixᵉ siècle au rock. Une approche socio-anthropologique de l'histoire de la chanson française', in Dietmar Rieger (ed.), *La Chanson française et son histoire* (Tubingen, 1988) as well as Caroline Doublé-Dutheil, 'Le rock est-il une musique populaire?', in Joëlle Deniot and Caroline

to working class audiences. Inversely, some authors, in trying to sort the 'wheat from the chaff', and echoing standpoints adopted after May '68 by pop musicians, underlined the features of rock allowing it to be considered as more culturally legitimate, emphasizing the awareness of some musicians of the conceptual dimensions of their activities.[29] In part inspired by Adorno, and often trained in art history, these researchers highlighted what they considered to be works of rock worthy of interest, describing the rest merely as commercial,[30] doing so with the ideological objective of acknowledging the value of particular groups.

But, from the 1960s to the 1990s, for many researchers at a time when Marxist paradigms were influential, rock – and its history – was merely an illustration of the dominant ideology and an avatar of the superstructure of the capitalist production.[31] It was a product of alienating mass consumption which had to be analysed as such.[32] It seems from this point that the 'Gramscian turn',[33] visible among English theorists at the CCCS who studied rock during the 1970s, did not occur amongst French researchers, notably because Bourdieusian paradigms favoured structuralist perspectives based on the concept of domination.[34] One might, however, be able

---

Dutheil, *Métamorphoses ouvrières* (Paris, 1994) and Michel Verret, *La Culture ouvrière* (Paris, 1988) who says notably that 'Doubtless, the classic age of fanfares and town bands is behind us and "rock groups" who replaced these have come to the fore. ... playing to large-working class publics however, particularly amongst young people': p. 88.

[29]   Denys Lemery, 'Musique contemporaine, pop music et free-jazz, convergences et divergences', *Musique en jeu*, 2 (1971): pp. 80–86.

[30]   See for example, Marie-Pierre Bonniol, 'Sonic Youth, du style au geste ou la prétention esthétique d'un groupe de rock', *Copyright Volume!*, 1/1 (2002). In this perspective we can also consult the work of Pascal Bussy, notably in his work on Kraftwek and Can published by Camion Blanc.

[31]   The Marxist analysis of rock can potentially inspire two types of socio-economic readings of the world: either rock is perceived – positively – as a means of contesting and refusing the dominant social order through its forms of 'adolescent' rebellion; or it can be identified – negatively – as a vector assisting the dissemination of capitalism, in its ideological and commercial form. This possible contradictory reading is embodied in the history of rock, where the criticisms and reforming ideas carried by music leading counter-culture are subsequently recuperated and transformed by the recording industry as 'international variety' (compared to ballroom music or *chanson* as expressions of 'authentic' working-class tradition).

[32]   Péron R., Cottereau J. and Huet A., 'Le disque', in *La Marchandise culturelle* (Paris, 1978) or Daufouy P. and Sartron J.-P., *Pop music rock* (Paris, 1972), or even Jacques Attali, *Bruits, essai sur l'économie politique de la musique* (Paris, 1978).

[33]   Eric Maigret, *Sociologie de la communication et des médias* (Paris, 2001).

[34]   The same can be said for the idea of 'legitimisable' which allows musical strands such as jazz to be placed in between two middle-classes ('the lower middle class') or serves to characterize the 'counter-culture' of the 1970s, as symbolized *inter alia* by the journal *Actuel*. See Pierre Bourdieu, *La Distinction* (Paris, 1979).

to detect in some works following Bourdieusian hypotheses, key ethnographic elements regarding practices of working-class youth with relation to music.[35]

Consequently, students wishing to undertake research relating to issues of the sociology of art or culture were dissuaded,[36] which prevented the development of studies in this field. Active researchers themselves encountered some difficulties. We can cite the case of Marc Touché who, working for the MNATP,[37] was for over ten years, until the mid-2000s, attached to the 'leisure' department of the Museum: for his management, amplified musics had no place in the 'music' department of that institution.[38]

Following Jean-Claude Passeron and Claude Grignon, it can be said that research into the history of amplified musics was for a long time inspired and limited by two extremes: 'populism' and 'miserablism'.[39] To escape this double constraint, it was necessary that the musics which interest us here should no longer be simply described 'by default'. There were in fact many examples of definitions of 'popular music' which were a 'neither/nor' refusal of both of these extremes as the only possible compromise locating an area in which such music perceived as imported from outside France could be placed.[40] For example, for many key players in the field of rock, the genre was for a long time defined as being 'neither classical, nor variety, but everything between the two'.[41]

This is why Marc Touché's report following his study into repetition/rehearsal which proposed employing the terms 'amplified musics' or 'electro-amplified musics' was so useful.[42] He considered such musics from a constructive, and no

---

[35]   Gérard Mauger, *Hippies, loubards, zoulous. Jeunes marginaux de 1968 à aujourd'hui* (Paris, 1992).

[36]   Regarding this one can consult the account by Brice Couturier, *Une Scène-jeunesse* (Paris, 1983).

[37]   Musée national des Arts et Traditions populaires.

[38]   Marc Touché, dissertation as part of a Masters Programme, 'Équipements culturels et politique de loisir', supervised by Stéphane Dorin (Paris, 2005).

[39]   Claude Grignon and Jean-Claude Passeron, *Le Savant et le populaire* (Paris, 1985).

[40]   It is symptomatic that in their history of rock, Benetollo A. et Le Goff Y., regarding the period 1966–76, write that it 'is important not to overestimate the importance of French rock; rock remains and will remain an Anglo-Saxon genre …'. To explain this problem, others take up the hypothesis of Paul Yonnet in *Jeux, modes et masses. 1945–1985* according to which the particularly dense occupation of the French music scene held by *chanson* during the 1950–60s may have for a long time sterilized all possibility of an independent French rock music. See Anne Benetollo and Yann Le Goff, 'Historique (aspects politique, économique et social)', in Anne-Marie Gourdon, *Le Rock. Aspects esthétiques, culturels et sociaux* (Paris, 2000), pp. 11–53.

[41]   Interview with Dominique Marie, president of the Férarock network of radios, in *Musique info hebdo,* 19, 6 February 1998.

[42]   Marc Touché, *Connaissance de l'environnement sonore urbain. L'exemple des lieux de répétitions* (Vaucresson, 1994) and for an overview, Marc Touché, 'Les lieux

longer negative viewpoint, 'by default'. He furthermore proposed examining the history of uses of these musics in France in terms of technology, an important aspect for understanding the rapid developments in such musics. More generally, Touché emphasized the significance of recording and storing data at the very heart of what he termed the 'culture of the variable resistor',[43] intended to move analysis of music beyond the dialectic oral/written through the study of the recording of sound on tape. In our view, these works echoed those undertaken elsewhere, notably in the UK and the US on popular musics.[44] However, in France (where, as we know, the reading of English-language research untranslated is rather haphazard), the position adopted by Touché was important in that, previously, the orality was inevitably related to the notion of popular or working-class culture raised earlier; whilst the written dimensions led to comparison of these musics with 'culturally legitimate musical forms', often negatively highlighting their simplicity or basic nature.[45] Recently, many researchers have thus considered the failure arguably represented in France during several decades of 'graphocentrism' in music.[46] This term implies the compulsory use of the musical score and, at the same time, the shortcomings of so doing in understanding timbres, sound effects or cultural particularities of performance in popular musics. The issue of the musical score additionally brings us to that of materiality in music prior to the advent of recording. In the view of O. Roueff, it is this very reason which led Schaeffner to focus on musical instruments themselves from the 1930s onwards, an acceptable compromise, at the time, for the study of other musics within graphocentric institutions.[47]

History Charted by Historians

Musical research undertaken by French historians followed a particular development, reflecting the extent to which the study of media and mediations of music gathered significance. From the beginning of the twentieth century until the 1950s, research focused primarily, as part of events-based approaches to history,

---

de répétition des musiques amplifiées', *Les Annales de la recherche urbaine*, 70 (1996), pp. 58–67.

[43]   Marc Touché, 'La culture du potentiomètre est-elle soluble dans les clichés?', *Fusible*, 4 (1996).

[44]   Gérôme Guibert, *La Production*.

[45]   Marc Touché was moreover the first chair of the Gema (amplified musics study group) which brought together professionals from the music industry and researchers and which, as early as 1994, was responsible for an historical reading of music in the town of Agen *via* this notion of technology of 'amplified musics'.

[46]   'Musique et sciences humaines. Rendez-vous manqués?', *Revue d'histoire des sciences humaines*, 14 (2006).

[47]   Olivier Roueff, 'L'ethnologie musicale selon André Schaeffner: entre musée et performance', *Revue d'histoire des sciences humaines*, 14 (2006): pp. 71–100.

on the most culturally legitimate forms of music or on major music media figures. Related to this, in the 1960s and 1970s, was a history of the media focusing on the concept of 'serious' content.[48] The second phase reflects an interest shown in content and cultural uses of culture (Rioux, Sirinelli, Lemonnier) prior to reflection on a socio-economic history of culture (Kalifa). The most recent phase of this history analyses technological developments adopted by industries and their impact on audiences (Tournès, Farchy, Méadel).[49]

However, the historical gaze on mass culture in France has gradually enabled a break with a long tradition of suspicion: the contribution of sociological reception theory, taking the opposite view to that of works inspired by the Frankfurt School or Bourdieu's theory of domination strongly fuelled this new history of cultural industries. The interchange between audiences – progressively more urban, more educated, more prosperous – and the development of new production methods and of distribution of culture – whose expansion would be supported by industrialization and development as commercial activity – constitute the central thread of analyses undertaken by historians which have developed in France since the mid-1980s, written by specialists in modern history (notably Roger Chartier) and contemporary history (Dominique Kalifa, Jean-Yves Mollier, Pascal Ory, Jean-François Sirinelli, Jean-Pierre Rioux etc.).[50] We can thus note how, as early as the 1830s, conditions for a quantitatively and qualitatively modified supply of culture were established,[51] even if it was essentially a question of popular newspapers and reading rather than music, in these pioneering times. As neatly summarized by Dominique Kalifa, the *café-concert*, which was well-established in urban areas as early as the Second Empire, marked the birth of the musical performance industry; no fewer than 274 *café-concerts* existed in Paris alone in 1900, producing over 10,000 new songs annually. The expansion of this type of activity can be gauged notably by the growth in turnover which, from 32 million francs in 1893, rose to 69 million in 1913. Some venues became famous and remain

---

[48] For example, Pierre Miquel, *Histoire de la radio et de la télévision* (Paris, 1972).

[49] See for example the study 'L'enregistrement sonore', edited by Ludovic Tournès in *XXᵉ siècle*, 92 (2006) as well as his 'Jalons pour une histoire internationale de l'industrie du disque: expansion, déclin et absorption de la branche phonographique de Pathé (1894–1936)', in *Histoire des industries culturelles en France xixᵉ et xxᵉ siècles* (Paris, 2002). See also Joëlle Farchy, *La Fin de l'exception culturelle?* (Paris, 1999) and Cécile Méadel, *Histoire de la radio des années trente. De l'auditeur au sans-filiste* (Paris, 1994). One can also consult the article by Marc Savev, 'Deux exemples de presse musicale jeune en France, de 1966 à 1969: *Salut les copains* et *Rock & folk*', *Copyright Volume!*, 3/1 (2004).

[50] By favouring the analysis of methods of mediation and reception of cultural goods, French history of culture is involved in social history and its dialogue with sociology has been particularly useful: see Roger Chartier, Pierre Bourdieu and Robert Darnton, *Pratiques de la lecture* (Paris, 2003) or Roger Chartier, *Au bord de la falaise: l'histoire entre certitudes et inquiétude* (Paris, 1998).

[51] See Dominique Kalifa, *La Culture de masse en France, 1860–1930* (Paris, 2001).

so to this day, such as the Olympia, the Alcazar and the Bataclan, to name but a few. But, as historians have demonstrated, the music hall would replace the *café-concert* at the dawn of the twentieth century. The layout of the venue (with rows of seats in place of tables) contributed to the 'domestication' of audience members; the role of the orchestra – and thus rhythm – became preponderantly important at the expense of the songs themselves; major stars (such as Tino Rossi, Mistinguett, Maurice Chevalier) who performed in venues such as the Folies-Bergères or the Moulin Rouge personified the middle-class craze for this type of entertainment. Generally, this expansion in mass-audience musical performance as well as its economic rationalization – in 1926 takings for all Parisian shows were 2.5 billion francs – went hand in hand with the creation of structures in this sector. Thus the first unions for performers were created and, in 1851, the SACEM (Union for Music Writers, Composers, and Producers).

In parallel to the success of *chanson* as the popular genre – confirmed from the mid-nineteenth century by the large scale print runs and sales of music and lyrics of successful songs – the recorded music industry failed to find its mark and become established. Although Charles Cross and Thomas Edison had invented the gramophone in 1877, it reached the general public after 1910, and even then was only available to the wealthy classes, as the cost of acquiring such technologies placed them beyond reach for the middle and working classes. Records would not be mass produced until the second half of the twentieth century, and it was instead radio broadcasting which was to undertake the large-scale 'musicalization' of France, with rapid growth in numbers of homes owning a radio (between 1920 and 1940 there was a tenfold increase, one in two households owning a radio in 1940).

In order to analyse the origins of the music industry, historians had to consider the intricate relationships between various factors: companies, artists and professions, audiences, and technologies. But it was arguably the desire not to understate the role played by technological developments – both in terms of production of content and its reception by audiences – which constituted one of the striking features of French cultural historiography of music. Thus when Jean-François Sirinelli described the cultural practices of baby-boomers between 1945 and 1969,[52] he highlighted the massive impact of radio or records on the development of their generationally-specific cultural behaviour. It is indeed a fact that the availability of musical culture and broadcasting technologies to the first groups of baby-boomers was enabled by increases in their purchasing power or by the realization by this age group of its own social status. But it nonetheless remains that it was the mass culture of music which best expressed the aspirations of this generation, and thus, in the late 1950s, there was a move away from the family wireless towards individual transistor radios: '... the independence henceforth acquired by the young generation – who often now had "their own" room – did not

[52]   Jean-François Sirinelli , *Les Baby-boomers. Une génération, 1945–1969* (Paris, 2003).

result solely in increasing privacy. This independence would result, culturally, in a true process of independence'.[53] Technological development was, therefore, the condition rendering possible the proliferation of sound which would characterize the late 1950s and 1960s. Similarly, the advent of the LP – appearing in France after 1951 and replacing the 78rpm in just a few years – as well as that of portable record players, would make the record an influential tool in defining the identity of 'youth'.

Social History, History of Musical Techniques

It is doubtless this interest paid to technical developments which, in France, enabled the failings in academic study outlined at the outset of this chapter to be surpassed. At first glance, taking interest in record formats or in the development of amplifiers, to take just two examples, might seem trivial; in reality, the technological perspective is particularly heuristic insofar as it shows the totality of the social world, that of both material and sound cultures. As observed by Edgar Morin about the large music festival held on 22 June 1963 at Place de la Nation in Paris, which brought together 150,000 young people at the behest of the pop magazine *Salut les Copains*, rituals of 'rock' culture (parties, concerts, adoration of singer idols, collections of singles and star photos etc.) were, also, made possible by these transistor radios, vinyl records, and electric guitars to which young people had access. From his *Journal de Californie*, a veritable socio-biographical UFO in French academia of the early 1970s, we can mainly take from Edgar Morin his descriptions of the youth revolution and counterculture which had just shaken America, followed by its repression and decline. Without equivalent, at that time, in the French sociological scene,[54] in this study one could read about concerts ('At the *Matrix,* temple of rock. The Sons of Champlin played the other night. There was something mystic and religious in this music which reaches sublime moments of hysteria'),[55] about counterculture ('… a cultural totality which has its own lifestyle, its own sacraments (drugs, sex, rock-festival …)'),[56] about the hippie movement, or about sociability in festivals ('What happens in the stadium, from the first notes played by the bands which do not yet lead to any group fervour, it is exactly this: being *ensemble*, together').[57] Yet, there is less of a tendency to highlight what runs through all Morin's text, which is the technical progress which can transform concerts into vast liturgies of decibels ('For a moment,

---

[53]   Sirinelli , *Les Baby-boomers*, p. 143.

[54]   On another level – that of the rock press – as early as 1967 articles on counter culture could be seen in the US: see Alain Dister in *Rock & folk*, 11 and subsequent numbers (1967).

[55]   Edgar Morin, *Journal de Californie* (Paris, 1970), p. 140.

[56]   Ibid., p. 136.

[57]   Ibid., p. 114.

I moved closer to the band, where the wild people are gathered, dancing shoulder to shoulder, in the deafening racket of 16 six-speaker amplifiers placed in line'),[58] or which sometimes makes the sensory experience of listening to music at home literally gripping ('At Crichton's house. He gave me some amazing, enormous, padded stereophonic earphones. It was not a flood of music which rushed into my ears; it was a streaming galaxy of harmonies which entered my head, flooding the inside of my body, all the way to my feet. As if I was possessed!').[59]

Marc Touché, a pioneering researcher albeit isolated for a long time, is arguably the individual who took the history of rock in France the furthest and with the greatest consistency in the importance accorded to technical and sound cultures.[60] On the one hand, this was achieved for example by taking interest in the concrete conditions of musical practice in a town such as Annecy since the 1960s.[61] On the other hand, this was done by telling the story of a family of instrument makers famous for their French-made electric guitars, the Jacobacci family, as well as by studying the small universe of microphone or amplifier manufacturers at the time.[62] The key concept for Touché concerned electro-amplification; this notion, directly linked to the arrival of electricity in the world of sound, represented a particularly significant marker in the history of changes in music. The changes in instruments – the movement from acoustic to electric guitars providing the best illustration – did indeed directly affect playing styles and consequently the production of styles and genres, the division of roles and hierarchies within orchestras or groups, the practical conditions for rehearsal and concerts, the means of purchasing or learning instruments, or even the symbolic value of instruments which carried along with them an array of imaginary symbolism. The notion of 'amplified musics' forged by Touché therefore has the virtue of characterizing not the product of social construction ('contemporary musics', a catch-all ahistoric generic administrative category referring to the subsidization of musics outside of classical music by the State) but all of those musics which use electricity and amplification. Herein we can find a typical Beckerian style – that of 'worlds of art' – of seeing things, whereby it is the forms of cooperation between key players and also the entirety

---

[58]   Ibid., p. 114–15.

[59]   Morin, *Journal de Californie,* p. 230.

[60]   On a clearly different level, due to being inspired more philosophically or ethonomusically than sociologically, one can find other works which closely articulate the significance of instruments and musical practices, and for which the notion of 'types of instrument' is a good descriptive term: see for example André Schaeffner, *Origine des instruments de musique. Introduction ethnologique à l'histoire de la musique instrumentale* (Paris, 1936), or Nicolas Donin and Bernard Stiegler , 'Le tournant machinique de la sensibilité musicale', in Nicolas Donin and Bernard Stiegler (eds), 'Révolutions industrielles de la musique', *Cahiers de médiologie/IRCAM,* 18 (2005): pp. 7–17.

[61]   Marc Touché, *Mémoire vive # 1* (livre + 2 CDs) (Paris, 1998).

[62]   Marc Sabatier, Stanislas Grenet, Marc Touché, Marie-Claire Lory, *Guitares Jacobacci, un atelier de lutherie à Paris, 1924–1994* (Paris, 2007).

of material conditions involved in the mediation of these musics which are taken into consideration.[63] What also adds to the specific nature of Touché's work is the fact that it forms part of a museographic project (that of the Montluçon Museum of Popular Musics on the one hand, and also that of the National Museum of Arts and Popular Traditions and subsequently the Museum of European and Mediterranean Civilizations), concerned with creating collections of amplified musics which avoid 'telling their story' merely on the basis of broad categories and periodizations – often debatable – elaborated by the key players in the media-cultural industries. All things considered, this deconstruction of the historical mythemes of which rock is a vast supplier has today paved the way in France for a large research area where almost everything remains to be examined. For the moment, Marc Touché's works have allowed significant advances; in taking an opposite stance to the official history of rock, he has seemingly undertaken a more modest history, that of amateur musicians, mere extras typically overshadowed by the major figures. Moreover, he has placed an emphasis on aspects which have for a long time been important for cultural history (the price of instruments, the material, ordinary, and everyday conditions involved in musical practice for example) but which the sociology of amplified musics had ignored. All of this has led him to dispel a number of clichés, notably relating to the complete separation between rock music and variety or ballroom dance music, whose shared boundaries are historically considerably more porous than might be expected; or even, relating to the dependent allegiance of the first French rock scenes on Anglo-Saxon models, which were in fact rapidly able to show a degree of typically French originality and inventiveness, and whose imitation/distance relationship with British or American rockers required closer analysis. However, in the context of the relative scarcity of socio-historical studies of music, it is not surprising that researchers who are themselves performing (or former) musicians, have found in the self-ethnographic and introspective studies a path into this history yet to be charted. This was the case with Touché, himself when he recounts, with photographic evidence, his past as a bassist in the 1970s,[64] or with Philippe Le Guern considering a career stemming from learning how to listen through the self-teaching of an instrument – in a social background where nothing predisposed this – to signing with Virgin Music.[65] In reality, where historians have studied amplified musics, it is essentially

---

[63]   For a detailed explanation of his work, see Marc Touché, 'Muséographier les "musiques électro-amplifiées". Pour une sociohistoire du sonore', in Simon Frith and Philippe Le Guern, 'Sociologies des musiques populaires', *Réseaux*, 141–2 (2007): pp. 97–141.

[64]   Fabien Hein and Gerome Guibert, 'Metal. Une culture de la transgression sonore, entretien avec Marc Touché', in *Copyright Volume!, Les scènes métal. Sciences sociales et pratiques culturelles radicales*, 5/2 (2006): pp. 137–52.

[65]   Philippe Le Guern, 'Quand le sociologue se raconte en musicien. Remarques sur la valeur sociologique de l'autobiographie', in *Copyright Volume!, Musiciens sociologues. Usages de la réflexivité en sociologie de la culture*, 4/1 (2005): pp. 25–55.

because this music reflects social changes in the late 1950s and they do not make these musics an object of analysis in themselves: it is essentially only in recent work undertaken by students in MA dissertations, and to a lesser extent in PhDs, that we can note work specifically on amplified musics.[66]

Whereas until now we have primarily discussed those socio-historical studies focusing on instruments and practice, it should be underlined that people's relationship with music is also enabled through access to records and other recording media and listening to them, a process which is neatly encapsulated by the notion of 'recording-inspired changes in taste',[67] which highlights the conjoined development of technologies and tastes. In this way, the history of recording media – particularly of records – has demonstrated the close relationship existing between ways of listening to music and the material mechanisms which structure this listening and which construct auditory schema on the basis of context (on the car radio, on the radio alarm clock, in a disco, at a rock festival, on headphones or in the street with a walkman etc.) and medium (vinyl, CD, iPod etc.). But, in French research dealing with listeners and their progressive social construction, it should be noted that more interest has been paid to the consequences of the arrival of the record from the end of the nineteenth century than to 'rock' audiences since the 1950s. This is doubtless because researchers understood the invention of the record player as the generating matrix of contemporary musical culture, without considering the influence of their own social origins which may have led them to focus on classical musics or early forms of mediation of music through records and record players, rather than on more popular and more recent forms of music. The work of Sophie Maisonneuve on the invention and development of records as a 'new' medium has demonstrated just how this constituted a profound revolution of accessing music as well as ways of listening to music (and also of musical performance). For instance, Maisonneuve has showed how changing formats are influenced by increase in possible recording duration, from two minutes at the end of the nineteenth century to 30 minutes in the 1950s, or how developments in sound (from mechanical gramophones, to the 'electrical revolution'[68] in the 1920s, up until stereo recording) have adequately served a particular musical instrument or enhanced the value of one repertoire over another. This reveals the abilities of listeners for what they really are, that is to say social constructions; for

---

[66]   Consult, for example, the numerous Masters programme dissertations on amplified/ contemporary musics in the cultural history area. An example can be seen at Versailles-Saint-Quentin University http://www.chcsc.uvsq.fr/-soutenances/DEA.html. Two from 15 dissertations are on music in 2007 (without however a direct link to amplified musics) and two from 27 in 2006 (one on *Woodstock* in France and the other on the TV programme 'Les enfants du rock').

[67]   See Antoine Hennion, Sophie Maisonneuve and Emilie Gomart, *Figures de l'amateur* (Paris, 2000).

[68]   The expression was coined by Sophie Maisonneuve, 'Du disque comme médium musical', in Donin and Stiegler, *Révolutions industrielles*, p. 40.

example, recordings on record would for instance enable understanding or taste for comparing different versions of a work, but also the learned analysis of the sound parameters of recording (notably with the development of the 'hi-fi' from the 1930s and especially from the 1970s).[69] In the end, this type of research into the historical origins of the record shows just how technical developments, emotional aesthetics and critical competencies are hinged on one another, and just how listening to music is in reality the product of a slow process of incorporation.[70]

Parallel Histories

One of the handicaps that the historicization of contemporary musics in France has had to overcome was the importance – whether real or imagined – attached to Anglo-Saxon culture as the original birthplace of rock culture. This often led to French rock being considered as a pale ersatz of American rock or British pop, lacking individuality. The exhibition organized by the Cartier Foundation for Contemporary Art in 2007 was a clear display of such an historical eclipse: it presented the roots of rock between 1939 and 1959 without the slightest space for French rock,[71] the sole French figure cited being Line Renaud due to her ties with Elvis Presley. A further example comes from the work of Touché, when he highlights the generalized ignorance by the Art-world encompassing of French rock which nevertheless came into being very early, with its groups, instrument makers, and performance venues.

On the peripheries of research by practising historians, for whom contemporary musics however remain a subject rarely discussed, there do exist parallel histories charted by enthusiasts which also research rock in France. Amongst this work can be found, with clearly varying concerns for methodological accuracy, (auto)biographies of artists or key players in the musical sector, journalistic writings, and studies undertaken by knowledgeable spectators generally coming from a local scene. The recent increase in local histories of rock, moreover, leads us to think that the interest in this type of music is today part of a renewed interest in new forms of cultural heritage and more generally in the activity of commemoration. Indeed, rock bands or 'rock' towns are attaining the dignity of being new 'realms of memory'. And, judging by the periods concerned – the 1950s and 1960s, the mid-1970s and the 1980s – it might be thought that we are dealing

---

[69]   Maisonneuve, ibid.

[70]   See also Sophie Maisonneuve, 'La constitution d'une culture et d'une écoute musicale nouvelles: le disque et ses sociabilités comme agents de changement culturel dans les années 1920 et 1930', *Revue de musicologie*, 88/102/1 (2002): pp. 43–66 and 'De la "machine parlante" à l'auditeur: le disque et la naissance d'une culture musicale nouvelle dans les années 1920 et 1930', *Terrain*, 37 (2001): pp. 11–28.

[71]   See the brochure for this exhibition by the Fondation Cartier pour l'art contemporain, *Rock'n'roll 39–59* (Paris, 2007).

with two distinct generations of 'amateur historians'; firstly the baby-boomers who grew up listening to rock music and secondly those who were influenced more by the development of an alternative French music scene where different musical genres are, moreover, linked to specific towns.[72] From the early 2000s, as a consequence of the enhanced visibility of this new musical heritage and of the crystallization of local scenes (cf. Chapter 15 in this study), books summing up the local histories of rock have been published for an increasing number of towns and cities (Annecy, Toulouse, Brest, Rennes, Bordeaux, Saint Germain en Laye etc.). These show how, in contradiction of what is often maintained by national media and recording industry professionals concentrated in Paris,[73] French rock does indeed exist. The authors of such books are almost always involved in a local music scene and are often members of associations which aim at helping understanding of amplified musics in a given area (by publishing, for instance, compilations). In general, it is from their domains of expertise that these writers begin their work before widening their research to other periods and genres. The documents used are gathered via appeals for individual accounts or for documents, posted in the local press,[74] to which people generally respond with much enthusiasm. The interest of such works is that they highlight the importance of amplified music cultures in addition to stressing the impressive numbers of people concerned. For example, these books always have anecdotes relating to politicians, academics, business leaders, or well-known local traders, linking such people to their past and hitherto unknown adventures in rock music. From this point of view, such writings often hold an informative value; due to their very existence, they contribute towards the specific character of local culture and its representation. Such works are of course not exempt from criticism. First of all, their subjective nature – primarily due to the aesthetic preferences of the authors in addition to an inevitably fragmented understanding of dynamics and activities, by their very definition small-scale and little-known (how is it possible to list every band having rehearsed or played, especially if no recordings were produced?) – should be underlined. Additionally,

---

[72]   For contemporary musics in the provinces, see notably: Christophe Brault, *1978–1988: 10 ans de rock à Rennes* (self-published, 1988); Roland Bougain and Bruno Rotival, *Photo music, Lyon 1975–76* (self-published, 1976); Pierre Favre and Christian Pirot, *Bourges, histoire d'un printemps 1977–1986* (Paris, 1986); Stéphane Davet and Frank Tenaille, *Le Printemps de Bourges: chroniques des musiques d'aujourd'hui* (Paris, 1996); Daniel Colling, Philippe Magnier, *Le Printemps de Bourges: scènes, rues et coulisses* (Paris, 2003); L'Association Dingo, *10 ans de musiques amplifiées à Angoulême* (Angoulême, 1998); Thierry Liesenfeld, *Le Temps des copains, rock twist. Alsace années 1960* (1996) (+ 1 CD 25 tracks of Alsace rock groups from 1960 to 1969); Thomas Hirsh and Grégory Tuban, *Perpignan rock: 1960–2000* (2000) (+ 4 CD box set) ; Laurent Charliot, *La Fabuleuse histoire du rock nantais de 1960 à nos jours* (2003); Richard Louapre, *Les Années rock en Haute-Normandie: 1958–1968* (2002).

[73]   Gérôme Guibert, *La Production*.

[74]   Requests nowadays posted on internet sites, as is the case the work currently underway into rock in Laval (http://www.MySpace.com/rockinlaval).

they frequently describe the careers of artists without truly contextualizing their actions in relation to the more theoretical issues of the period in question. For example, a band which played on the radio between 1982–83 for example, benefitted from a structural effect caused by the legalization of independent radio stations, in the same fashion as in the early 1970s, musicians who played in rock bands were often also involved in dance hall groups for financial reasons (this allowed them to use relatively costly musical equipment as well as earning money at a time when the social security regime of *intermittence* was underdeveloped and when, on the other hand, dance halls were a lot more common – discos and DJs being yet underdeveloped). It is such aspects that are often missing from these studies.

Taking one example from many local rock histories, it is interesting to note the beginnings of rock in Haute-Normandie. Richard Louapre viewed the presence of American NATO bases and geographic proximity with England as two principal factors of the spread of rock culture in Normandy. Language trips to the southern counties of England coupled with receiving English radio broadcasts from 1958 increased awareness of rock music, in addition to the Le Havre-New York sea route, which enabled import of records and symbols of American youth culture. Similarly, it would seem that bars which welcomed NATO soldiers based in Evreux, contributed – via jukeboxes – to the dissemination of rock music.[75] Louapre also unveils the origins of the first French rock groups with 'Danny Boy et les Pénitents', the American-sounding stage name of singer Claude Piron, who recorded a first single in 1958 on the Ducretet-Thomson label. A further example is Little Bob, a celebrity in Le Havre and subsequently national star in France, who demonstrated how in the 1960s, dance halls were one of the most favoured performance venues for rock musicians. The first rock festival in the region was held in 1963, and it is clear that from the early 1960s, several possibilities for socialization were established in the area: concert venues, record and instrument stores, and music magazines. However, despite the undeniable contribution it makes, some of the implicit methodologies of this work merit some further detailed study, to guard against a 'history which is self-evident'. Moreover, work in progress by Marc Touché focusing on the first rock bands in the centre of France – a region theoretically less favourably exposed to the rock contagion than those towns and cities studied by Louapre – seems to indicate this music spread very rapidly, via multiple channels which still remain to be studied, but whose effectiveness is unquestionable.

At a different level, rock journalists and critics have also contributed towards the historic knowledge of rock, such as Jean-Noël Coghe, Claude Barsamian,

---

[75] A detailed description can for instance be found of bar-dancing – and the social make-up of the clientele, French people and GIs – in Louapre, *Les Années rock*, pp. 13–16.

Christian Eudeline and François Jouffa, etc.[76] Christophe Quillien, for example, in a work on *Rock&Folk*, one of the principal French rock magazines, established in 1966, showed how the magazine recruited its contributors, the transformations in the practice and the discourse of rock journalism, and more generally how such a discourse contributed to the social construction of rock itself through the years,[77] with a body of work, a history, key players, and audiences. It was thus able to participate in the birth of *Rock&Folk*, the first edition being a summer supplement of the *Jazz Hot* magazine suffering plummeting sales. The taxonomies and generic boundaries continued to remain unclear – in Quillien's view, the term 'pop' was not yet in use – and under the term 'folk-rock', the likes of Chuck Berry or the Animals rubbed shoulders with Hugues Aufray or Eddy Mitchell. Right from the start, the problem of creating a definition and a history of rock are key challenges is obvious: this first issue included a lengthy article by Kurt Mohr entitled 'Rock Story', which placed the origin of rock adjacent to jazz, and which made 1955 the pivotal year for the recognition of this music. The problem resurfaced in the seventh issue, with Sylvie Vartan appearing on the cover to pose the question 'am I rock?'. Finally, it is possible to trace the reaction of the public through the readers' letters column which deplored, for example in 1966, the sheer rarity of Parisian clubs and venues where rock music was played, or indeed the rock wilderness of provincial France, or even the difficulty for musicians in finding places to perform aside from '*parties*':[78] 'What's left for us to do? Play at dancehalls and stupid dances. With idiots drinking their wine, we've seen it a thousand times and we'll keep on seeing it ... Apart from a few reasonably civilised clubs, all we've got ahead of us are difficult kilometres driving through the snow, playing for audiences who treat us like queers.'[79] The usefulness of this type of approach can be found primarily in that it displays, through the testimony of insiders from rock journalism, the fashion in which aesthetic choices and a discourse regarding this music were elaborated, unveiling the inner workings of the construction of rock as a social object. It additionally displays the way in which a constant exchange

---

[76]   Notably François Jouffa and Jacques Barsamian, *Vinyl fraise: les années 1960* (Paris, 1993); Jean-Noël Coghe, *Autant en emporte le rock: 1960–2000* (Paris, 2001); Christian Victor and Julien Regoli, *Vingt ans de rock français* (Paris, 1978); Christophe Quillien, *Génération Rock & folk. 40 ans de culture rock* (Paris, 2006).

[77]   Social construction is summarized by comments from Philippe Garnier, US correspondent of the magazine: 'What are we talking about? It's we rock critics who have invented most of these stories! Captain Beefheart the genius and Patti Smith the poet, Keith Richards the most elegantly ravaged of human beings and Syd Barrett the dead king of Pink Floyd ... these are the pure inventions of critics!', in Quillien, *Génération Rock*, p. 9. Also consult Philippe Teillet, 'Les cultes musicaux, la contribution de l'appareil de commentaires à la construction de cultes, l'exemple de la presse rock', in Philippe Le Guern (ed.), *Les Cultes médiatiques. Culture fan et œuvres cultes* (Rennes, 2002), pp. 309–42.

[78]   Quillien, *Génération Rock*, p. 67.

[79]   *Rock & folk*, 40 (1970).

operates between rockers and rock critics; it is precisely via this exchange of adjustment between these two bodies that generic categories were established, with rock becoming however increasingly difficult to define from the 1980s.

More generally, journalistic hagiographies of rock began to appear in France in the 1970s, at a time when the *Folk&Rock* magazine which wanted to 'take rock seriously',[80] established a series of books with Albin Michel – edited by Jacques Vassal – which primarily published French authors.[81] But these writers spoke little of French music history,[82] rather specializing in artists who, in their view were influential for music from an international perspective.[83] However, electro-amplified musics gradually became the 'common culture' in France, as shown for example by the statistics produced by surveys of 'cultural trends of the French' undertaken by the Culture Ministry's research department.[84] In addition to countless numbers of works on individual artists,[85] a certain number of anthologies compiling several years of music criticism began to appear, and it became progressively clear that electro-amplified musics henceforth held significant historical substance.[86]

For journalistic writing to be able to study the history of popular music in France over the last half-century in a more thorough manner, and analyse comprehensively the way in which artists lived and worked, a new element was required, in the form of the translation of American and English music critics. This literature grew exponentially in France from the late 1990s among a number of publishers, the largest of which was Allia.[87] In 1998, a 'Secret History of the 20th Century', with the subtitle *Lipstick Traces* by Greil Marcus was revealed to the French public. Many authors followed in its wake and began writing closely documented studies based on interviews, relying upon their own domains of expertise, and revealing

---

[80]   *Rock & folk*, special edition ' Trente ans de rock et de folk' (1996), p. 115.

[81]   We can also note a two volume translation of the history of rock'n'roll (*Sound of the city*) by Charlie Gillett in 1986 which had far-reaching effects.

[82]   As an exception, we can quote Christian Victor and Julien Regoli, *Vingt ans de rock français* (Paris, 1978).

[83]   The place of French artists compared with international artists is ambiguous, as demonstrated, for example, by the book – which is very relevant moreover by Michka Assayas, *Dictionnaire du rock* (Paris, 2000).

[84]   Pierre Mayol, 'Les pratiques musicales des jeunes, *Note de synthèse d'après les enquêtes Pratiques culturelles des Français 1973–1989*', DEP DT 1078 (Paris, 1991) and the figure 'genre de rock écouté le plus souvent selon les générations des personnes écoutant du rock' in Olivier Donnat, *Les Pratiques culturelles des Français* (Paris, 1997).

[85]   Notably publications by Librio Musique (Gainsbourg, Brassens, Les musiques celtiques, etc.) and Camion Blanc (Bérurier Noir, Noir Désir, Téléphone, etc.).

[86]   For example, Gilles Verlant (ed.), *Le Rock et la plume, le rock raconté par les meilleurs journalistes (1960–1975)* (Paris, 2000) or François Jouffa, *La Culture pop des années 70* (Paris, 1994), (Reedited version of 'Pop-notes' from the journal *Pop Music 1970–72*).

[87]   Which translated notably Nick Kohn, Greil Marcus, Nick Tosches, Jon Savage and Simon Reynolds.

previously little known facts. The work of Christian Eudeline studying the first wave of French punk[88] or the underground bands performing in France during the 1960s[89] can be cited as examples of this movement, and recent works focusing on alternative rock from the 1980s[90] is also worthy of mention.

To the overview presented in this chapter, it is also necessary to add the autobiographies written by key players in the French music sector which allow us to recollect and better understand the different contexts over the periods covered. In this respect, we can mention the works of journalists, such as J.N. Coghe, formerly of *Disco-Revue, Rock&Folk* and *Extra*, or additionally those emanating from many artists of rock, *chanson*, and variety.[91]

---

[88]   Christian Eudeline, *Nos années punk, 1972–1978* (Paris, 2002).

[89]   Christian Eudeline, *Anti yé-yé. Une autre histoire des sixties* (Paris, 2006).

[90]   Rémy Pépin, *Rebelles. Une histoire du rock alternatif* (Paris, 2007) and Arno Rudeboy, *Nyark-nyark. Rock alternatif 1976–1989* (Paris, 2007).

[91]   As early as the 1970s, we can mention the collection entitled 'Vécu' by Robert Laffont who published autobiographies of Joséphine Baker (1976) and Jean Sablon (1979).

Chapter 4
Popular Music Policy in the UK

Martin Cloonan

In recent years the UK government has taken an increasing interest in the fate of its popular music industries. Having previously been somewhat loath to become involved in what has often been seen as a free market form *par excellence*,[1] the UK government has been called upon to help its popular music industries and has increasingly reacted to such calls. Why those calls were made and the reactions which followed form the basis of this chapter, which falls into five parts. First a brief overview of developments in the changing relationship between the state and popular music in the UK is provided. Secondly I introduce two key arguments, before looking at some of the reasons why government and industry began to get closer. The fourth part looks at developments under the New Labour government from 1997, before I conclude with a critique of recent developments. The chapter does not generally discuss broadcasting as while still vitally important to the fate of popular music, there is not space to do justice to such a complex issue here.

Government and Pop, 1954–1997

While the topic of what is popular music has filled volumes of debate[2] this chapter is concerned with those forms of music which can be seen as flowing out of the arrival of rock and roll into the British mainstream from late 1954 onwards. Importantly it is from this point onwards that governmental interest in popular music begins. When it does, three things can be discerned. The first is general political indifference. The second is an occasional need for the state to *react* to popular music and the third is examples of attempts by leading politicians to associate themselves with pop's populism.

In fact governmental interest in popular music was rather slow to develop and in the 1950s was almost nil. The arrival of rock and roll did see some political interest but this was generally limited to MPs' expression of 'outrage' at the antics

---

[1] For example following a speech to the Conservative Party conference in 1985, Miles Copeland, owner of IRS records, called pop 'free enterprise at its best', See Robin Denselow, *When the Music's Over* (London, 1989), p. 223.

[2] See for example: Brian Longhurst, *Popular Music and Society* (Cambridge, 1995); Richard Middleton, *Studying Popular Music* (Milton Keynes, 1990) and Roy Shuker, *Understanding Popular Music* (London, 2nd edition 2001).

of Teddy Boys. However these were somewhat isolated concerns – such as that of Conservative MP Robert Boothby calling for the film *Rock Around The Clock* to be banned following press exaggerations of disturbances involving Teddy Boys and the film – rather than any united response.[3] While the extent of Teddy Boys' violence is debated,[4] the linking of rock and roll with juvenile delinquency was quickly established[5] and was to become a recurring theme in some political circles.[6]

The 1960s saw the development of government and pop interaction. At one level there was an attempt by some politicians to come to terms with the new form of consumerism which was evidenced by Beatlemania. This included courting its populism as was most famously shown by Labour Prime Minister Harold Wilson awarding the band MBEs for services to exports.[7] However, the band was also courted by the Conservatives.[8]

Elsewhere a somewhat harder political approach was adopted to one facet of pop's new found appeal: pirate radio. Popular music's increasing popularity took place at a time when the BBC was the UK's only legitimate radio broadcaster. However its somewhat rigid three station format did not allow it to respond flexibly to the new phenomena. A gap in the broadcasting market was filled by the pirates, the first of which, Radio Veronica, began broadcasting in 1961.[9] Figures of 20 million listeners a day have been claimed for the pirates.[10] However, their existence was a direct challenge to the state's authority in controlling its airwaves. The result was the passing of the *Marine, &c., Broadcasting (Offences) Act* which came into law on midnight of 14 August 1967. This outlawed broadcasting from offshore rigs and supplying goods to them. The BBC established Radio 1 as its popular music stations six weeks later and this station became the *de facto* voice of UK pop for its residents.

While it was punk which attracted most attention as a political phenomenon in the 1970s, it is important to note that the central state did not intervene. The BBC *did* ban some punk records,[11] but independently of government. The main attacks on punk came from the media, politicians such as Labour's Marcus Lipton and *local* authorities which were able to ban punk bands from the venues which they

---

[3]   See Chris Salewicz, 'Thorpe: Victim of the Curse of Rock 'n' Roll?', *NME*, 19 February (1977), p. 11, and Ian Whitcomb, *After the Ball* (New York, 1994), p. 227.

[4]   See for example Dave Harker, *One for the Money* (London, 1980), p. 75.

[5]   See Dick Bradley, *Understanding Rock 'n' Roll* (Milton Keynes, 1992), p. 56.

[6]   See Martin Cloonan, *Banned! Censorship of Popular Music in Britain; 1967–1992* (Aldershot, 1996).

[7]   Andrew Blake, *The Land Without Music: Music, Culture and Society in Twentieth Century Britain* (Manchester, 1997), p. 93.

[8]   Peter Laurie, *The Teenage Revolution* (London, 1965), p. 23.

[9]   Harker, *One for the Money*, p. 79.

[10]   Iain Chambers, *Urban Rhythms* (Basingstoke, 1985), p. 54.

[11]   Cloonan, *Banned!*, pp. 116–77.

owned.[12] Thus the reaction to punk was a mixture of national media, individual MPs and the *local* state.

What is largely forgotten – but politically more important in the longer term – was the reaction to the free festivals movement which had begun to stage festivals without the necessary licences and permissions. Matters here came to a head around the People's Free Festival (PFF), held annually from 1972 in Windsor Great Park without the permission of its controllers, the Crown Commissioners. In 1974 the festival was invaded by police after five days and fighting took place with some attendees. Press reports of police violence made the festival's fate a key political issue.[13] The following year the government provided an alternative site at Watchfield in Oxfordshire.

Harder economic times meant that this funding was not repeated. However, the festivals issue was given continued government attention. In 1972, the Conservative government established an Advisory Committee which reported in a generally pro-festival way and produced a Code of Practice (*Advisory Committee on Pop Festivals 1973*). Following Windsor 1974, the then Labour administration set up a Working Group which produced two reports *(Working Group on Pop Festivals* 1976, 1978). Although no legal changes followed, the fact that these reports were more about *how* to have festivals rather than *whether* they should take place meant that in the longer term festivals could become an established part of the UK's cultural scene.

Official politics were absent from what was arguably the peak of 1980s political pop – Live Aid. Here was an event which urged human compassion and therefore stood in direct contrast to the individualism of Thatcherism, although it could also be seen as making compassion an act of consumerism. However it was kept at arm's length by the Conservative government of the time, which now stands in marked contrast to the way in which New Labour embraced Live 8, 20 years later.

By the late 1980s raves were becoming a political issue. A number of laws and issues were involved here – safety at unlicensed venues, the act of illegally staging unlicensed events, illegal drug usage (especially ecstasy) and disturbance in the countryside. Raves thus had all the makings of a traditional moral panic[14] and, indeed, the press did make them a political issue. But it should also be noted that when a reaction came it was via a Private Member's Bill, rather than via a government bill (although it was clear that the government would offer support). Graham Bright, MP for Luton, introduced what became *Entertainments (Increased Penalties) Act* in 1990. This introduced fines and prison terms for organizing unlicensed events.[15] However it had little effect and in 1994 the battle against

---

[12]   Ibid., pp. 174–80, pp. 261–5 and pp. 280–81.

[13]   Ibid., p. 202.

[14]   Stanley Cohen, *Folk Devils and Moral Panics* (London, 1973).

[15]   Steve Redhead, 'Rave off: Youth, Subcultures and the Law', *Social Studies Review*, January (1991): pp. 92–4 (p. 93).

raves did become part of government policy when a Criminal Justice Act included provisions to counter raves. The Act allowed the police to seize equipment being used in unlicensed raves and to stop people within a five mile radius of a rave. Those ignoring police demands not to proceed to a site or to leave it faced three months imprisonment and a £2,500 fine. The number of raves went into decline after this, although the simultaneous liberalization of nightclub opening hours might have played the most important role in this.

The 1980s also witnessed a hitherto unprecedented wave of local government support for popular music. Local authorities such as such as Norwich, Cambridge, Liverpool, Manchester and Sheffield and the Greater London Council began initiatives which sought to use popular music for a mixture of political populism and economic development.[16] The Councils involved were all Labour-controlled and sought to use popular culture at a local level in ways which the Party's absence from national power (1979–97) prevented it from doing on a larger scale. Importantly these initiatives legitimized government intervention in popular music in the eyes of many Labour politicians who would be influential when the party came to power nationally.

By the early 1990s then it was clear that behind the scenes some tentative exchanges between the music industries[17] and government were taking place. The recording industry had been concerned by proposed changes to copyright in the late 1980s, although the *Copyright, Designs and Patents Act* (1988) which followed largely met its requirements. Nevertheless key record industry personnel now saw that government could affect it – for better or worse – and that if it wanted this to be for the good then it had to lobby.

This was particularly the case as the industry was being attacked for high CD prices, about which a House of Commons Select Committee produced a damning report in 1993.[18] While a subsequent wide-ranging Monopolies and Mergers Commission report on CD prices was to largely exonerate record companies and retailers from any wrongdoing,[19] it was clear that political and public confidence

---

[16]   See for example John Street, 'Making Fun: The Local Politics of Popular Music', paper presented at Political Studies Association conference, York, 1995; Sara Cohen, 'Popular Music and Urban Regeneration: The Music Industries of Merseyside', *Cultural Studies*, 5/3 (1991): pp. 332–46, and Adam Brown, Justin O'Connor and Sara Cohen, 'Local Music Policies within a Global Music Industry: Cultural Quarters in Manchester and Sheffield', *Geoforum*, 31 (1998): pp. 437–51.

[17]   I use the term music industries – plural – rather than music industry – singular – for reasons which are explained fully in John Williamson and Martin Cloonan, 'Rethinking the Music Industry', *Popular Music*, 26/2 (2007): pp. 305–22.

[18]   National Heritage Committee, *The Price of Compact Discs Volume I* (London, 1993a), and National Heritage Committee, *The Price of Compact Discs Volume II* (London, 1993b).

[19]   Monopolies and Mergers Commission, *The Supply of Recorded Music* (London, 1994).

had to be rebuilt. The response was for the industries to show their economic value in a report they commissioned called *The Overseas Earnings of the Music Industry*. This produced a figure which was to become widely quoted – that the music industry's annual net earnings were £571 million, which, as another oft-quoted point noted, was 'similar to the net overseas earnings of the steel industry'.[20]

Significantly the report was launched by Trade and Technology Minister Ian Taylor, whose presence marked confirmation of a new concordat between government and parts of the music industries. Further evidence of this was shown when leading politicians were invited to industry ceremonies – where they could be lobbied. Thus Kenneth Clarke as Chancellor of the Exchequer attended the British Phonographic Industry (BPI)-sponsored Brits awards in 1989 and the BPI's AGM in 1994 (Spence 1996b).[21] The Brits were also attended by Norman Tebbit (Conservative Party Chairman, 1986), Lord Baker (former Education Secretary, 1989) and Virginia Bottomley (Heritage Secretary, 1996). Tony Blair went as Leader of the Opposition in 1996 and also attended the BPI's AGM in July 1995 and two successive *Q* magazine awards (1994 and 1995).

Heritage Secretary Virginia Bottomley invited representatives from the music industries to a reception in early 1996.[22] On 6 November 1996 her department issued a press release which said that: 'London is universally recognized as a centre of style and innovation. Our fashion, music and culture are the envy of our European neighbours. This abundance of talent, together with our rich heritage makes "Cool Britannia" an obvious choice for visitors from all over the world'.[23] 'Cool Britannia' soon became associated with the early days of the first Blair administration,[24] but it was actually a Tory invention.

Meanwhile the national scene had received a boost from the success of 'Britpop'. While the nationalistic tint given to this movement[25] was later to be blamed for the lack of success in the USA for UK acts,[26] in the short term its populism appealed to New Labour which courted its leading acts such as Blur and Oasis.[27] In the case of Oasis this led to overt support from Noel Gallagher who in autumn 1996, in the run

[20] See British Invisibles, *The Overseas Earnings of the Music Industry* (London, 1995), pp. 4–5.

[21] N. Spence, 'Britpop's Morning Glory', *Observer*, 30 June 1996, p. 15.

[22] John Harris, *The Last Party: Britpop, Blair and the Demise of English Rock* (London, 2003), p. 304.

[23] Harris, *The Last Party*, 2003, p. 328.

[24] Sean O'Hagan, 'Labour's Love Lost', *Guardian*, 13 March (1998), part two, pp. 12–13.

[25] Martin Cloonan, 'State of the Nation: "Englishness", Pop and Politics in the mid-1990s', *Popular Music and Society*, 21/2 (1997): pp. 47–70.

[26] Doug D'Arcy and Paul Brindley, *Make or Break: Supporting UK Music in the USA* (London, 2002), p. 12.

[27] Harris, *The Last Party*.

up to a general election, appeared on the cover of the Labour Party's *New Labour New Britain*.

In February 1996 Labour received a boost from the setting up of an organization called Rock The Vote (RTV).[28] Its aim was to encourage young people to vote in a context where youth voting was in decline. To this end it organized a comedy tour, issued CDs and staged club nights which all encouraged voter registration. While voting amongst all groups fell it was clear that it was part of a reconfiguration of the new concordat between industries and government.[29] The music industries saw that New Labour was 'business friendly' and RTV's protestations in its literature that it was 'apolitical' should be treated with caution. It was always clear that Labour would be the beneficiary of any increase in youth voting; there were clear links between the Party and RTV and Kane's 1996 description of RTV as 'thinly disguised Blairite organisers'[30] has a ring of truth, an example of this is Darren Kalynuk, who moved from working in Labour Deputy Leader John Prescott's office to work for RTV which was chaired by BPI's chair John Preston, a confidant's of Blair's.

Again the context is important. The industries were keen to enlist political support following the NHC and MMC reports and by 1996 it was clear that Labour would be in power the following year. Once it was, the necessary links were already in place. Thus RTV can be seen as not so much an attempt to engage young people in politics, as to engage political elites with the music industries. It was to prove to be far more successful in the latter than in the former.

Thus by the mid-1990s the music industries had countered official suspicion by making the case for their economic value and thus for government to assist a vital industry. They had also begun to lobby. In the case of the former this was to be via a raft of reports which outlined the value of the industries,[31] in the latter it was via lobbying efforts which will be outlined below. Both were to continue once New Labour assumed power.

Two Arguments

The theorization of what happened from the mid-1990s onwards requires the introduction of two key arguments. The first is that in terms of popular music policy the UK has moved from being a benign state to being a promotional one. In previous work I examined the relationship between nation states and popular music, suggesting that these could be characterized as falling into three types of

---

[28]   Martin Cloonan and John Street, 'Rock The Vote: Popular Culture and Politics', *Politics*, 18/1 (1998): pp. 33–8.

[29]   David Butler and David Kavanagh, *The British General Election of 1997* (Basingstoke, 1997).

[30]   Pat Kane, 'Don't Rock the Vote', *Guardian*, 19 January 1996, part two, p. 13.

[31]   See Martin Cloonan, *Popular Music and the State in the UK* (Aldershot, 2007).

relationship – benign, authoritarian and promotional.[32] Benign states tend not to interfere and to generally let the market take its course, authoritarian states tend to want to control the production and dissemination of music, while promotional might want to promote certain forms of popular music. Between 1955 and 2007 it is clear that the UK went from being 'benign' to being 'promotional'. However, what is more important was the *type* of promotion that was taking place and this will be returned to later.

The second argument is that there is no such thing as a single 'music industry'. This again builds on previous work which was primarily motivated by a sense of frustration that when commentators referred to 'the music industry' they often actually meant the *recording* industry and in particular the machinations of the big four record companies (Universal, Sony/BMG, Warners and EMI).[33] Our research found examples of such references in the proclamations of various industries' organizations, in the media, in various official reports, and amongst academics. From our Scottish base this made no sense as we were located in a place where there were certainly music industries, but *not* major record companies. Thus in order to develop an argument which highlighted the non-recording sectors, we began to speak of the music industries – plural. The implications of this are more fully developed elsewhere[34] and below.

New Labour's Reasons to Support the Music Industries

The Labour Party elected on 1 May 1997 was branded as 'New' Labour – avowedly pro-business and committed to a Third Way between Thatcherite free markets and old style state interventionism. Nevertheless this government came to intervene more in popular music than any previous UK one. There are at least three overlapping reasons for this apparent paradox. The first was the new government's belief that the creative or cultural industries – it tended to use the terms interchangeably – were a vital part of the economy in an era where the traditional heavy industries had declined and the service sector was now the main provider of jobs. If this was the case, it was inevitable that popular music would also come into consideration. This was made when the new Culture Secretary Chris Smith quickly said that the government wanted to 'do all it can to create the right environment for the music industry to flourish'.[35]

The inevitability of new links had been bolstered by the music industries' decision in the mid-1990s to counter its somewhat tawdry image through commissioning reports which stressed the economic value of the industries. As

---

[32] Martin Cloonan, 'Popular Music and the Nation-State: Towards a Theorisation', *Popular Music*, 18/2, (1999): pp. 193–207.

[33] Williamson and Cloonan, 'Rethinking the Music Industry'.

[34] Ibid.

[35] Chris Smith, *Creative Britain* (London, 1998), p. 82.

noted above, a key text here was the *The Overseas Earnings of the Music Industry* and its success is illustrated by the fact that its figure of £571m in export earnings was quoted in a newspaper article byelined by the new Prime Minister soon after he came into office.[36]

The second reason was that, as noted earlier, some music industries' personnel had come to see the necessity of courting government which had the power to pass laws which could affect those industries. While the new *Copyright Act* in 1988 had largely benefited the recording industry, its introduction again alerted many music industries' figures to the potential dangers of legislation being passed without the music industries being consulted. Some began to envy the closer relationship which the film industry enjoyed with government and to begin a charm offensive, in which the various reports played a key part.

In addition, the recording industry was not only seeking to improve its image but it was also under threat from the rise of 'illegal' downloading and the rise of piracy (which it often equated). While the highest profile case, Napster, was eventually to become a legal service and other services such as Grokster and Kazaa were effectively seen off, the industry also resorted to law to prosecute uploaders. Here the support of government was vital in the public image battle and New Labour Ministers obliged with quotes outlining their opposition to 'illegal' filesharing and piracy.[37]

The third factor was the populist dimension of New Labour. This was evidenced in their courting of Britpop bands in the run up to the 1997 general election. Following Labour's victory there was an infamous party at Number 10 on 30 July 1997 with Noel Gallagher, his record company's owner and Labour donor, Alan McGee, and the Pet Shop Boys. While the support of popular musicians and other celebrities is always a double-edged sword, at least in its first years the New Labour government mouthed music industries' arguments while those industries seemed largely supportive of the party's modernization agenda.

New Labour in Power

Chris Smith was appointed as Secretary of State in the new Department of Culture, Media and Sport (DCMS), which replaced the Department of National Heritage. Importantly Smith was from a local government background and so knew all about the legacy of the GLC and other attempts to use popular culture/music for urban regeneration. He was also part of the generation who saw no contradiction in providing government support for popular music.

Smith set up a Cultural Industries Task Force which commissioned a mapping exercise of all the cultural industries. This *Cultural Industries Mapping Document* (DCMS 1998) brought together a lot of existing data, but lacked any primary

---

[36]   Tony Blair, 'Britain Can Re-make It', *Guardian*, 22 July 1997, p. 17.

[37]   For example see Cloonan, *Popular Music and the State*, p. 51.

research.[38] A follow up was published in 2001 (DCMS 2001).[39] Smith argued that some statistics were needed in order to convince the Treasury that the cultural industries were worth supporting *economically*.[40] Stressing common interests between those industries and government, Smith spoke of the music industries as a 'high risk' one in which 80–90 per cent of artists signed to record companies do not succeed[41] and said that: 'The British music business ... invests heavily in new talent.'[42] However, not only did Smith simply equate the music industry with the recording sector, he also presented ideas which were actually part of a mantra which the major record companies were repeatedly using in their campaigns to counter allegations that CD prices were too high and to end so-called illegal downloading. This mouthing of a form of music industries' commonsense was something which other ministers were soon to follow. In fact the primary concentration henceforth was on meeting the needs of bigger business. This can be illustrated by examining four areas: the Music Industry Forum, increasing professionalization and lobbying by the music industries, the Live Music Forum, and various sorts of ongoing support.[43]

The Music Industry Forum (MIF)

In January 1998 the DCMS established a Music Industry Forum (MIF) as a sounding board via which the music industries could lobby government. Its setting up was a response to concerns emanating from the recording industry's association, the BPI, that responsibility for the music industries had moved within government from the long-established – and large – Department of Trade and Industry to the newer – and much smaller – DCMS.[44] In order to counter this Smith established and chaired, as Minister, the MIF. This enabled him to show that government was being serious about helping popular music because whereas previously music industries' personnel tended to meet DTI officials or junior ministers on an *ad hoc* basis, they now had scheduled meetings with the Minister.

The MIF was also a result of industries' personnel being seconded into government as civil servants. This also started under the Tories, but was expanded under New Labour and included the appointment of Sara John, formerly head of

---

[38]   Department for Culture, Media and Sport (DCMS), *Creative Industries Mapping Document 1998* (London, 1998).

[39]   Department for Culture, Media and Sport (DCMS), *Creative Industries Mapping Document 2001* (London, 2001).

[40]   Chris Smith. (former Secretary of State for Culture, Media and Sport), personal interview, Glasgow, 14 April 2005.

[41]   Ibid.

[42]   Ibid.

[43]   In fact New Labour has done more than this and for a fuller account see Cloonan, *Popular Music and the State*, pp. 39–65.

[44]   Chris Smith, personal interview, Glasgow, 14 April 2005.

Legal Affairs at the BPI, as a DCMS special adviser in early 1998; it was John who drew up a list of members of the MIF.[45]

The MIF's official role was to act as an 'informal channel of communication'.[46] It discussed such things as copyright, provision of youth music, live music, exports, and support for small businesses. The latter resulted in a commissioned report which is actually amongst the better of such reports.[47] Another report – on new technologies – was less successful.[48] However, the meetings became less regular, especially after Smith was replaced by Tessa Jowell as Minister following the 2001 general election. After a couple more low key meetings, the MIF effectively fell into abeyance.

Professionalization

Emerging from the MIF came the Music Business Forum (MBF). This was born from MIF pre-meetings of music industries' personnel and it is now the MBF which lobbies government and meets with the DCMS. Thus the net effect of the MIF was to spur the music industries into becoming more professional and adept at lobbying. In fact this can be seen as having been one notable effect of Labour's initiatives. According to one insider whom I interviewed, when the music industries found that they finally had a government which would listen to them, they also found that they were not able to articulate their arguments.[49] The need to do so eventually led to the formation of the MBF and one obvious effect of New Labour's policies has been to induce more professionalism within the industries and the MBF is an example of this.

Perhaps the other most important example has been the formation of British Music Rights which was formed in 1996 by the leading rights collections agencies and has continually lobbied government for the extension of copyright. Its main success was in being part of a lobbying process which led the government to set up a Committee of Inquiry into intellectual property known as the Gowers Committee. However Gowers failed to provide what parts of the music industries wanted as it went against a campaign to copyright sound recordings beyond 50 years.[50] This was despite an intense campaign coordinated by Phonographic Performance

---

[45]   Sarah John (Vice President, Government Affairs, with EMI), phone interview, 26 January 2006.

[46]   Cloonan, *Popular Music and the State*, p. 46.

[47]   Nicolas Wilson, David Stokes and Robert Blackburn, *Banking on a Hit: The Funding Dilemma for Britain's Music Business* (London, 2001).

[48]   Department for Culture, Media and Sport (DCMS), *Consumers Call the Tune: The Impact of New Technologies on the Music Industry* (London, 2000).

[49]   Martin Mills (Chair of Beggars Banquet), phone interview, 15 November 2005.

[50]   Andrew Gowers, *Gowers Review of Intellectual Property* (London, 2006).

Limited.[51] As yet the government has not responded to Gowers, but here it seems as if the limits of New Labour's generosity towards the music industries has been reached.

Meanwhile the closeness of the relationship can be shown by the fact that a former junior culture minister, Estelle Morris, joined the board of the PRS – one of the collecting agencies – after ceasing to be a minister. In addition the industry is able to lobby government via the All Party Music Group, a cross party group set up in 2002 which has held the first ever parliamentary debates on popular music and puts on charity and other events at which MPs can be lobbied by industries' representatives. It is thus another example of both increased political interest in the fate of popular music *and* of increased professionalization of the industries.

The Live Music Forum

Labour also sought to reform the somewhat archaic licensing laws in England and Wales via a Bill which was initially introduced into parliament in November 2002. This was headlined in the press as the arrival of round-the-clock drinking in the UK, while the potential impact on live music was much less widely reported. Here the main concern was that under the previous licensing system, up to two musicians could play in pubs without the pub needing a licence, under what was known as the 'two in a bar' system. However the new regulations meant that with the exception of a limited number of special events each year, virtually *all* music events would need a licence. The Musicians Union dubbed the legislation 'none in bar'.[52]

Such was the concern expressed in various circles, that the government set up a Live Music Forum to advise on the legislation and monitor the new law's impact. A report produced for the Forum on the state of live music was a pretty bland document which tried to show how healthy things were and produced a headline figure of 1.7 million gigs a year in England and Wales.[53] However, there were a series of questions about how live music was defined, what the likely impact of the Act was, and so on.[54]

By the time the Forum issued its report another issue in live music had come to prominence – online ticket touting. A campaign led by the Concert Promoters Association sought a clampdown, arguing that concert tickets be covered by laws similar to those which restrict the resale of football tickets. While the government also rejected this after a series of meeting with ministers, it was noticeable that all of this was done *outside* of the Live Music Forum. Thus a Forum which had

---

[51]   See *Music Week*, 16 December and 23 December 2006, and PWC, *Music Collection Societies: Evolution or Regulation* (London, 2006).

[52]   Cloonan, *Popular Music and the State*, p. 54.

[53]   MORI, *A Survey of Live Music Staged in England and Wales in 2003/4* (London, 2004).

[54]   Cloonan, *Popular Music and the State*, pp. 56–7.

been established to monitor live music was been excluded from possibly the most significant development in live music.

Meanwhile the Act came into force in November 2005 and the Forum published a report into its effects[55] which, along with a Musicians' Union survey,[56] suggested that the Act has had little impact on the total number of gigs. This at least belied Ministers' claims that the Act would help the live scene flourish. While the Forum's concentration on smaller venues has meant that it has not simply served the interests of big business, its narrow focus has meant that it has ignored issues such as the impact of consolidation within the live music sector. Thus, for example, it has ignored the machinations of Clear Channel which has been buying up large sections of the UK live industry under its Live Nation trading arm. In fact ignoring the machinations of multinational corporations is typical of New Labour. In the case of the Live Music Form this has meant that a body which has been set up to safeguard live music has been resolutely silent on patterns of ownership and exclusive deals with agents such as Ticketmaster, which impact on millions of fans. It has also meant silence on such issues as key venues closing. Thus when the important Hammersmith Palais venue was closed in April 2007 to make way for blocks of flats, the LMF was silent.

Ongoing Support

New Labour has also tried to provide ongoing support for the music industries. This comes via such things as the Department of Trade and Industry giving support for British companies wishing to attend international trade fairs such as MIDEM and SXSW and via UK Trade and Investment (UKTI) which funds music industries trade missions to such places as India, China, Germany, Japan, the US and Australia. In order to do this UKTI has seconded an employee from AIM – the Association of Independent Music – which is effectively the independent label's association. This employee, Phil Paterson, described his role as being a translator. By this he meant that he translated music industries speak to government and *vice versa*.[57]

In fact what UKTI offers is the kind of support which other industries have used for years – trade missions, support for showcases, and so on. This activity predates New Labour, but it has really taken off under it. This has met a longstanding demand from the music industries, to treat them as seriously as other industries are treated. Paterson's view was that what mattered was not so much financial support, but opening doors via such things as holding events in ambassadors' houses and so on.

---

[55]   Caroline Callahan, Andy Martin and Anna Piece, *Licensing Act 2003* (London, 2006).

[56]   Neil Crossley, 'Survey success', *The Musician*, Spring (2007): pp. 20–21.

[57]   Phil Paterson, Export Promoter for the British Music Industry within UK Trade and Investment), personal interview, London, 25 November 2005.

Meanwhile the Foreign and Commonwealth Office has published a document called *Music* which highlights British music and mentions UK acts and UK *signed* acts[58] while simultaneously highlighting globalization as a threat to the distinctiveness of British music. The British Council, which was set up in 1934 to promote the British way of life overseas, also supports pop in various ways such as publishing and began to publish an overview of British music called *New Routes*, a formatted radio programme, *The Selector*,[59] putting guides to UK music on its website and publishing another report which called for the setting up of an office in New York to promote UK music.[60]

Following this, in March 2006 the Trade and Industry secretary Alan Johnson announced increased support for UK music in the US such as market research, training for commercial officers in US diplomatic posts to help them understand the needs of the music industries and the creation of a music portal showcasing latest UK acts. Overall there are thus a number of ongoing initiatives, which provide further evidence of a move from benignly indifferent state to a more active promotional one.

New Labour: A Critique

Under New Labour two things came together. The first was a government which was comfortable in helping popular music and was keenly aware of the populist potential this had. The second was a recording industry which was concerned with declining sales which it attributed to a combination of increased international competition and the rise of 'illegal' downloading. It also saw the government as a means by which is could counter this via 'improved' copyright legislation. They appeared to be perfect bedfellows.

But what emerged from all this was actually an attempt to re-assert UK hegemony in the international music market. Thus in 1996 just before he became Prime Minister, Tony Blair spoke of putting 'British music back once again in its right place, at the top of the world'.[61] Once in government New Labour took the view that in order to do that it had to implement policies broadly in line with what the music industries needed. However, there were always tensions here and three should be noted.

The first of these goes back to the notions of 'the music industry'. If, as argued earlier, it is hard to talk of a single 'music industry', it is even more difficult to demonstrate the existence of a *British* music industry. Indeed this is one of the things which the various reports on 'the music industry' show – complex, cross-national patterns of ownership across a number of diverse sectors. If at a

58   Paul Sexton, *Music* (London, 2002).
59   www.britishcouncil.org/arts-music.htm.
60   D'Arcy and Brindley, *Make or Break.*
61   Harris, *The Last Party*, p. 273.

national level 'British' artists can be born or resident in the UK, in reality the *ownership* of music that is being produced often lies with multinational corporations whose first allegiance lies with their shareholders, rather than to their geographic location. The point here is not to be narrowly nationalistic, but simply to point out that initiatives which are done in the name of the *British* music industry and paid for by UK taxpayers actually went to serve the interests of international capital.

This is compounded by a second problem which is that Ministers wanted to treat 'the music industry' as being a unified body which has the same interest. Differences between, for example, the record companies and artists, or record companies and retailers, found no expression in ministerial pronouncements where simplicity was required. In fact the complexity of the music industries was openly resented. Thus as junior Culture Minister, Estelle Morris told the Radio Conference that 'the music industry' needed to 'give the government one point of contact' as 'what I find difficult is that it is such a diverse industry. There are so many organizations representing so many aspects of the music industry. In other sectors there is one focal point'.[62] Such wishful thinking – that a complex industry could be simplified to suit the needs of ministers – shows that there is some way to go in pop's relationship with official politics.

A third problem was that New Labour has absolutely *no* critique of business practices. It is very easy to gather examples of ministers praising 'the music industry', quoting figures about its value and repeating the industries' *own* analysis of the issues they face; it was much harder to finder any critiques from ministers. In part New Labour's acquiescence to the whims of big business was due to a change in attitude towards cultural policy. Previously cultural policy might have been about protecting those artforms which struggled in the market and, of course, some of that continued. However, elsewhere the state has intervened to protect indigenous cultures or national cultures. But as Marion Leonard has noted, under New Labour: 'The introduction of new policy strategies might still be labelled "protectionist" but they are not concerned with protecting an indigenous culture under threat from globalization. Instead (they have been) a series of measures designed to protect market share and to compete with the ways in which other countries are marketing their music output.'[63]

The reluctance of ministers to delve too deeply into the internal affairs of the music industries is made all the more glaring as it coincided with a range of illicit or dubious practices within those industries being increasingly revealed. In January 2004 the independent Consumers' Association reacted to a deal between the BPI and the retailer CD-WOW! which prevented the latter from importing cheap non-EU CDs and selling them in the UK by saying that 'the UK music industry

---

[62]   Estelle Morris, in *Music Week*, 3 May 2004: p. 3.

[63]   Marion Leonard, '"We're in it for the art, but we'd like to see it chart in the Billboard Hot 100": Promoting UK music in the US', paper presented at 12th International IASPM conference, Montreal, 2003.

has been ripping off customers for years ... [their] arrogance ... is staggering'.[64] Soon after this, Camden Council in London, home of many important venues, found itself having to resort to the law in a successful effort to prevent flyposting by major record companies. One, Sony/BMG, narrowly avoided having an anti-social behaviour order placed on it.[65] The Council complained that the flyposting was costing it an annual £250,000 to clear up. It commented that while the major record companies were flouting the law it was hard to have much sympathy for their campaign against 'illegal' downloading. Such sentiments were certainly *not* being expressed by government ministers.

The same month, Sony BMG in the USA was found guilty of payola by Attorney General Eliot Spitzer. They paid $10 million in compensation with a full agreement between the Federal Communications Commission and broadcasters to stop payola following in April 2007. Back in the UK the Office of Fair Trading has launched further inquiries into CD prices and also into ticket prices for gigs. In January 2006 the National Consumer Council expressed concern about Sony BMG marketing CDs which used virus-like techniques to hide itself and called for new laws to protect users of digital music and movies.

But while sharp practice with the music industries was continually being exposed, ministerial pronouncements on such events were noticeable by their absence. Thus the government increasingly colluded with the music industries at *exactly* the same time as others were trying to call constituent parts of those industries to account for their practices. It is important to recognize that via such things as investment in music in schools and the New Deal for Musicians scheme for unemployed musicians,[66] New Labour has made some attempts to help those at the lower end of the scale, but it has generally helped those already in power within the music industries.[67]

Moreover a myopic view of the industries – generally involving simply responding to industries' demands – has meant that New Labour's interventions in popular music can be characterized as being a series of initiatives rather than a coherent policy. Thus there is, for example, little if any link up between the NDfM and trade promotions or the Live Music Forum. There is no real oversight or joined up thinking. In terms of popular music, there is a little cultural policy, but more economic reaction.

In essence when Ministers have met the music industries it has been in order to find out what they want, rather than to articulate a view of what a progressive popular music policy might look like. Therefore the problems caused by lacking a

---

[64] Independent Consumers' Association, press release 21 January 2004.

[65] Steven Morris, 'Song Promises to Stop Flyposting after Court Threat', *Guardian*, 15 June 2004; John Oates, 'London Council Clamps Down on Sony and BMG', *The Register*, 3 June 2004.

[66] Cloonan, *Popular Music and the State*, pp. 44–6 and pp. 103–17.

[67] Mike Jones, 'Changing Slides – Labour's Music Industry Policy under the Microscope', *Critical Quarterly*, 41/1 (1999): pp. 22–31 (p. 28).

definition of the national and a tendency to see as unified that which is fractured, are exacerbated by a lack of critique of existing industries' practices.

Conclusion

The main thing which emerges when popular music initiatives undertaken by New Labour are reviewed is that the government has tried to help multinational corporations which are branded as being 'British' restore competitive advantage in the international music market. However, it is still important to recognize that a major shift has taken place. Previously it was common for commentators to argue that popular music was a free-market form *par excellence*. Now it is almost taken for granted that it is legitimate for the government to take an interest in popular music. For example in March 2005 there was a debate in the Scottish Parliament celebrating the success of Franz Ferdinand. During this, representatives from Labour, the Conservatives, the Scottish National Party, the Liberal Democrats and the Scottish Socialist Party *all* proclaimed not only that they were fans of the band, but also that the government should support popular music. What then becomes important is the *form* which that interest takes.

But we are a long way from 1955. In just over 50 years the UK has moved from benign indifference to myopic promotion. This may not be progress, but it is undoubtedly change. The question is no longer *whether* to support popular music, but *how*. Thus far a concern for the economic has resulted in those near the top of the tree receiving most help. The battle remains for a more *cultural* approach which attends to the needs of those lower down the scale.

Chapter 5

Cultural Policies and Popular/Contemporary/ Amplified Musics in France

Philippe Teillet

The small-scale government subsidies which popular musics[1] have received from the French state since the early 1980s have carried with them an implicit criticism of previous cultural policies and their restrictive conceptions of 'culture'.[2] Presenting political initiatives in this domain requires us to also provide a general review of the ways in which cultural policies have been analysed and understood.[3]

This early government intervention in the 1980s had more symbolic than financial importance.[4] And in 1997, the money allocated to this nevertheless extremely vast domain was still only comparable to that received by the pension fund of the Paris Opera alone.[5] It was instead municipal authorities which funded

---

[1]   Here we shall use the expression 'popular music' to distance ourselves from exclusively French terminology, notably the term of 'contemporary music'. However, 'popular music' shall cover exactly the same field (*chanson*, jazz, rock, rap, electronica, traditional music and world music). The use of the expression 'contemporary music' signifies an explicit reference to public policies implemented in France.

[2]   Philippe Teillet, 'Sur une transgression: la naissance de la politique du rock', *L'Aquarium*, 'Musique et politique', 11/12 (1993): pp. 73–85, and Philippe Teillet, 'Publics et politiques des musiques actuelles', in Paul Tolila and Olivier Donnat, *Le(s) Public(s) de la culture* (Paris, 2003), pp. 155–80.

[3]   Due to the heavy and direct involvement of French public authorities in this field (Philippe Poirrier, *État et culture en France au xxe siècle* (Paris, 2000); Guy Saez, 'Les politiques de la culture', in Jean Leca and Madeleine Grawitz (eds), *Traité de science politique*, vol. 4 (Paris, 1985), pp. 387–422), this research comes chiefly from political experts, sociologists of political organizations or political historians. I. Popa recently (May 2006) undertook a summary presentation for the Observatoire des mutations des industries culturelles entitled 'Approches politistes des politiques culturelles', http://www. observatoire-omic.org.

[4]   David Looseley, *Popular Music in Contemporary France: Authenticity, Politics, Debate* (Oxford and New York, 2003); David Looseley, 'In from the Margins: Chanson, Pop and Cultural Legitimacy', in Hugh Dauncey and Steve Cannon (eds), *Popular Music in France from* Chanson *to* Techno (Aldershot, 2003), pp. 27–39.

[5]   Since the publication of the report undertaken by the National commission for contemporary musics established by Catherine Trautmann as Minister for Culture, in 1998, state aid has grown by 1 million euros annually, but contemporary musics are still in a

rehearsal and concert venues and subsidies for the organization of festivals.[6] Initially the ways in which they were produced and distributed, in addition to their relationship with cultural industries and the media, pitted these musics against the customs and values of traditional cultural sectors and led to specific measures being envisaged for them alone. However, two decades later, the subsidies allocated to these musics have drawn closer to conventional patterns of public cultural policy.[7]

These initiatives were also contemporaneous with serious criticisms of cultural policies implemented since 1981,[8] as well as of questions regarding their purpose[9] and their implementation (whether local authorities should play a dominant role in funding cultural life). Such initiatives additionally accompanied and contributed to the production of a phenomenon which Guy Saez has described as 'cultural insecurity',[10] that is, the questioning of the legitimate culture which cultural policies intended to bring to audiences.[11] Measures taken in favour of popular musics found themselves at the centre of all these concerns, seemingly exemplifying both necessary changes in cultural policies and an embodying of a number of the criticisms made of them.

---

marginal position with 18 million euros of budgetary resources in total – 2005 figures – or 2.7 per cent of Ministry funding for live performance. See Michel Berthod and Anita Weber, *Rapport sur le soutien de l'État aux musiques dites actuelles* (Paris, 2006).

[6]   The Berthod-Weber report (2006) estimated that state subsidy of the 140 SMAC (contemporary music scenes) averaged 20 per cent of their total funding. Local authorities provided 55 per cent, with regions and local councils providing 11 and 12 per cent each. See Philippe Teillet, 'Éléments pour une histoire des politiques publiques en faveur des musiques amplifiées', in Philippe Poirrier (ed.), *Les Collectivités locales et la culture. Les formes de l'institutionnalisation, xixe et xxe siècles* (Paris, 2002), pp. 361–93.

[7]   Philippe Teillet, 'Le "secteur" des musiques actuelles. De l'innovation à la normalisation … et retour?', *Réseaux*, 25/141–142 (2007): pp. 269–296.

[8]   Alain Finkielkraut, *La Défaite de la pensée* (Paris, 1987); Marc Fumaroli, *L'État culturel* (Paris, 1991); Michel Schneider, *La Comédie de la culture* (Paris, 1993).

[9]   Jean Caune, *La Culture en action. De Vilar à Lang: le sens perdu* (Grenoble, 1991); Jacques Rigaud, *Rapport pour la refondation de la politique culturelle de l'État* (Paris, 1996).

[10]   Guy Saez, 'Le modèle culturel français face à la mondialisation', in Guy Saez (ed.), *Institutions et vie culturelles* (Paris, 2004), pp. 119–23.

[11]   Olivier Donnat, *Les Français face à la culture. De l'exclusion à l'éclectisme* (Paris, 1994); Bernard Lahire, *La Culture des individus: dissonances culturelles et distinction de soi* (Paris, 2004).

Policies for Popular Musics and Conventional Cultural Policies: Initial Differences

In 2006, two chief inspectors of the Culture Ministry[12] summarized the initiatives taken by the French State in favour of 'contemporary' musics (the term which finally became accepted). Rather than offering a résumé of this report,[13] we shall examine the State initiatives from the perspective of conventions developed by traditional cultural policies, notably in the field of live performance.

Two decades ago, policies for contemporary musics treated them differently to other cultural domains. Such departures from conventional practices were justified by the concern placed on avoiding the institutionalization of forms of musical expression which, it was claimed, could only flourish outside of officialization. The distrust of government departments with respect to their own practices will be of little surprise to public policy observers accustomed to such contradictions. But, across all fields of artistic creativity, artistic activity is pitted against *managerial*, bureaucratic or economic rationalities.[14] In truth, such sensitivities were explained by the fact that the ministry officials involved (small in number as they were) lacked sound knowledge of these musics, and of rock in particular. More than any other type of music, rock symbolized the transgression of the normal boundaries of cultural intervention. Jazz, *chanson*, and traditional musics had already undergone a certain degree of legitimation, but contemporary rock was seen by ministry officials as unknown territory. The successive waves of different genres – the 'waltz of musical labels' – whose endlessly changing classifications had exerted a powerful effect of superannuation'[15] had been highly effective in making previous generations feel out of date, and Ministry expertise in this area was inoperative, instead replaced by that of its opposite numbers from 'rock' associations. To escape the (undeniable) difficulty posed by classifying this new area, the ministry decided to deal with aggregated groupings of genres. Rock, *chanson*, jazz, and traditional musics were thus combined, despite the various differences advanced by their representatives.[16] But this aggregated grouping still required a name. Following the attempted 'music of today', it was not until the mid-1990s that the term 'contemporary musics' became current, despite its many drawbacks. The

---

[12]   Berthod and Weber, *Rapport sur le soutien de l'État aux musiques dites actuelles.*

[13]   Downloadable on the site of the Ministry at: http://www.culture.gouv.fr/culture/actualites/index–rapports.htm.

[14]   Eve Chiapello, *Artistes versus managers* (Paris, 1998).

[15]   François Ribac, *L'Avaleur de rock* (Paris, 2004).

[16]   The latter would progressively see the strategic interest in collaboration allowing larger pressure groups to be established. Thus, since 2006, Fédurok, the association of venues for amplified musics, and the federation of jazz scenes have shared a common internet site following several years of joint activities.

term 'amplified musics', more restrictive yet also more precise,[17] met with some success but it limited the possibility of establishing alliances between the ministry and representatives of musical aesthetics who rejected it (jazz and traditional musics). The term 'popular musics' never became established, for at least two reasons; if such musics were popular already, then this state encouragement was no longer justified; and furthermore, the term 'popular' is laden with burdensome symbolic and political connotations.[18]

The frustration felt by ministry officials faced with artistic productions whose classifications and hierarchies they were unsure of was intensified by the confusing location within government of public support offered to these musics. The creation of the Ministry for Culture in 1959 led to new distinctions between education, popular education and cultural intervention, which progressively fell under the responsibility of three distinct ministries.[19] Departments of the Ministry for Culture, backed by professionals in the fields for which they had charge, constantly worked to confirm the boundaries of these administrative divisions. Excluded from the field of cultural policies and their facilities, key players in the local rock scenes had sought refuge in 'sociocultural' infrastructures and started careers in this sector. But others preferred to demand their integration within overall cultural policies. The recognition of these musics as the preferred music of young people only accentuated these ambiguities. Supported by the Minister for Culture, Jack Lang in the 1980s, this recognition turned its back on two decades of intervention from its departments when youth issues had been referred to ministries of 'Youth and sports'. Finally, the report established by J. Hurstel on youth relations with cultural and sociocultural infrastructures[20] encouraged central government to support those cultural spaces favoured by young people independently of their geographic and administrative location. Further still, the amplification of these musics and the behaviour of their audiences necessitated suitably adapted venues which ignored existing definitions of different types of infrstructure.

---

[17]   Resulting from research by the sociologist Marc Touché, this designates music characterized by electro-amplification techniques and materials in their production, playing, and in the life of of their musicians.

[18]   Pierre Bourdieu, 'Vous avez dit "populaire"?', *Actes de la recherche en sciences sociales*, 46 (1983): pp. 98–105.

[19]   A similar division existed in Germany between *Kulturpolitik* and *Sozialkultur*, alternative form of official culture. This two-tier organisation, just as the cultural and the sociocultural in France, however followed relatively different workings and trajectories. See Vincent Dubois and Pascale Laborier, 'Le "social" dans l'institutionnalisation des politiques culturelles locales en France et en Allemagne', in Richard Balme, Alain Faure and Albert Mabileau (eds), *Les Nouvelles Politiques locales* (Paris, 1999), pp. 253–69). See also Philippe Urfalino, *L'Invention de la politique culturelle* (Paris, 1996); Vincent Dubois, *La Politique culturelle – Genèse d'une catégorie d'intervention publique* (Paris, 1999).

[20]   Jean Hurstel, *Jeunes au bistrot, cultures sur macadam* (Paris, 1984).

Such confusion between the administrative fields of previous state policy further presented itself through the issue of professionalization. The existing dichotomy between cultural and sociocultural was constructed around the distinction between professional and amateur work. Yet, within the scope of these musics, such distinctions were blurred by the ways people learned their trade and quite how they were paid. Educational qualifications in music, hierarchies and programmes of music education had no meaning (with the arguable exception of jazz) in these musics and in no sense affected recruitment into bands, nor decisions taken by concert hall managers or recording labels. The amount of remuneration, moreover, counted less than the amount of time dedicated to musical activities.[21] Furthermore, the unemployment benefits system for occasional workers termed *intermittence*, which was of wider application than merely in music,[22] tended to establish as 'professionals' those who accessed the state unemployment insurance scheme. Poorly regulated by a decree dated December 1953 (modified in 2007), the work of amateurs in live performance represented a subject of tension for artists' unions who were constantly watchful over the defence of professionals' rights. And, despite the reference made to artistic practices (meaning: amateurs) in the brief of the Ministry of Culture after 1997, state departments were characterized, for a long time, by their exclusive interest in professional artists. It could further be added that within many facilities devoted to contemporary musics, insecure and subsidized employment and voluntary work occupy a much greater place than within other types of cultural infrastructures. The 'long-term fragility' of these teams of workers[23] goes hand in hand with that of commercial entertainment production businesses which, in this sector, are often very small scale structures and function even more intermittently than the artists they employ.[24] It is for this very reason that, although professionalization has constituted a major strand of State policy since the 1960s,[25] the sector of popular musics remained relatively isolated from this concern.

Finally, whilst democratization of legitimate culture was the credo of cultural administrations, popular musics, and particularly those considered as being the expression of youth, embodied another normative and intellectual framework,

---

[21]   Marc Perrenoud, *Les Musicos: enquête sur des musiciens ordinaires* (Paris, 2007).

[22]   The occupation of 'musical performer' is dominated by the intermittent nature of employment. But this situation is most characteristic of those specializing in popular musics. See 'Les musiciens interprètes', *Développement culturel*, 140 (2003).

[23]   Established in 1994, Fédurok is a federation of facilities for performance and support of artists in amplified/contemporary musics. This federation today brings together 64 facilities across France and has a determining role in the artistic and cultural sectors, locally and nationally. Cf. http://www.la-fedurok.org.

[24]   Berthod and Weber, *Rapport sur le soutien de l'État aux musiques dites actuelles*, p. 18.

[25]   Dubois, *La Politique culturelle*, p. 239 and following.

that of 'cultural democracy'.[26] This was not, however, without contradictions, as cultural democracy implies attention to practices and values already existing within social groups,[27] whereas in many cases it was a question, even for 'popular' musics, of introducing to the public new or key artists whose value was fixed by 'experts' (venue managers, show producers, specialist associations, journalists etc.). Cultural democracy was only marginal within cultural policies overall. Only *Arts et Traditions Populaires* and eco-museums illustrated such a strand of thinking. It made a return as the government reflected on social issues in under-privileged urban areas. To confront these, the French government, in taking control of urban problems left largely to the attention of local authorities since the early 1980s, would at the end of that decade, create a 'national policy for urban areas'. As part of an action programme cutting across government departments, it mobilized funds from various government bodies, notably cultural. Simultaneously the musical practices of 'youths' in disadvantaged areas – often second generation immigrants – received greater visibility in the media with the commercial success of French rap, and services of the Ministry for Culture, encouraged by the minister's cabinet, invented 'musical cafés' in the early 1990s. But, the split created 30 years earlier between cultural and sociocultural activities made cultural aspects of the plan for urban areas a battlefield between 'legitimate and relativist culture, between republican integration and promotion of specific expressions of cultural identity, between culture and cultures'.[28] For example, hip hop could be considered either as a means of social integration and prevention of delinquency, or used to attract 'youths' towards artistic forms considered as more 'noble'[29] or envisaged as an element of contemporary creativity reflective of people's identities at levels below the national.[30]

---

[26]   On this distinction see: Raymonde Moulin, *L'Artiste, l'institution et le marché* (Paris, 1997), p. 90 and following.

[27]   Jean-Claude Passeron, *Le Raisonnement sociologique* (Paris, 1991), p. 293 and following.

[28]   Philippe Chaudoir and Jacques de Maillard (eds), *Culture et politique de la ville* (Paris, 2004), p. 23.

[29]   Vincent Dubois, 'Action culturelle/action sociale: les limites d'une frontière', *Revue française des Affaires sociales*, 48/2 (1994); Loïc Lafargue de Grangeneuve, 'L'ambivalence des usages politiques de l'art. Action publique et culture hip-hop', *Revue française de science politique*, 56/3 (2006): pp. 457–77.

[30]   Virginie Milliot, 'Culture, cultures et redéfinition de l'espace commun: approche anthropologique des déclinaisons contemporaines de l'action culturelle', in Jean Métral (ed.), *Cultures en ville ou de l'art et du citadin* (Paris, 2000), pp. 143–68.

A Gradual Shift towards Conventional Treatment: Convergence

Over the long term, structures devoted to contemporary musics drew closer to existing norms of public support for live performance.[31] The anti-institutional mood of the early 1980s was replaced by strong demand for government subsidies, and in such a context, it was unsurprising to see the tools of state cultural intervention in live performance gradually being deployed for contemporary musics.[32] This standard cultural intervention has chiefly been one of infrastructures and support for artistic creation.

The need to build or adapt specific premises for 'young people's' music, or more generally amplified music, led to investment policies (initially polarized between small venues and large concert halls with capacities of several thousands, Zéniths) and the implementation of all the resources, procedures, and know-how previously gained in the cultural aspects of regional development policies. Gradually, however, medium capacity venues (between 500 and 1000 seats) began to join the mainstream of cultural infrstructures, whose construction cost – increasingly substantial[33] – then led to increased running cost subsidies. In this way, the need for specific venues led support for popular musics to create investment policies and subsequently operational cost support – can be termed a 'logic of infrastructure development' – which has strongly marked cultural policies, particularly at the level of towns and cities.[34]

Key players in the domain of contemporary musics shared concerns about issues around creativity with professionals in the cultural sector. On the lookout for new talent, they shared the fear both of academicism and of constraints commercial imperatives place upon artistic work. These concerns are typical of the major characteristics of cultural policies in France since André Malraux, and it is, arguably, no longer believed that only rare individuals have the ability to create art, but rather that innovation can originate from 'below', from the street or from people on the margins of society. But, not all things are yet equal: the lack of cultural value granted to the most commercial musical productions reflects the existence of cultural values independent of the market. What is created or invented remains central to the concerns of many key players or venues, thus sharing the value of identity with all cultural sectors.

At the very beginnings of public support allocated to these musics, a kind of 'cultural gap' afflicting state decision makers and civil servants deflected them from a type of support (subsidies for creation or production) which has a long-standing tradition in relations between public authorities and artists. Whereas, jazz

---

[31]   Teillet, 'Le 'secteur' des musiques actuelles'.

[32]   In terms of public policy instruments, cf. Pierre Lascoumes and Patrick Le Gales, *Gouverner par les instruments* (Paris, 2005).

[33]   11.7 million euros for the Cartonnerie opened in Reims, February 2005.

[34]   Guy Saez, 'La politique culturelle des villes', in Guy Saez (ed.), *Institutions et vie culturelles* (Paris, 2004), pp. 44–9.

and *chanson* gradually began to benefit from measures of this nature, amplified musics remained neglected for a long time. Their being treated as an exception began to disappear following the growth of the 'artistic residency' programme which offered a venue for performance as well as means of promotion. The support measures made available to this type of artistic project developed through the involvement of experts (internal or external to ministerial departments) whose opinions 'informed' official decision makers, just as was happening in other cultural policy domains. Within the field of vocational training in the arts, Mr Fleuret had striven to diversify the genres of musics taught in state-run educational institutions, but faced with cultural and professional obstacles, this initiative had mixed benefits for contemporary musics. Whereas teaching of jazz and traditional musics was adopted quickly – even if only as 'window dressing' and variably from one institution to another – training in rock, rap and electronic musics remained provided by other structures, such as the *Studio des Variétés* (established in 1983 by the Ministry for Culture and the SACEM),[35] a number of schools run by associations federated within the FNEIJMA,[36] as well as by concert venues which developed supportive training. The planned integration of these musics into specialist musical education institutions continued to inform Ministry initiatives, leading to the creation of a teaching aptitude certificate (*certificate d'aptitude de professeur*) in 2001 and a State teaching diploma. Despite the meagre results achieved, caused by various misgivings noted in the Berthod-Weber report, the authors of this study call for continued integration of such musics into specialist teaching programmes.

State-controlled regulation of relationships between live performance, the recording industry and the media is a specific dimension of policies encouraging contemporary musics.[37] The Berthod-Weber report recommends policy uniting the three sectors of the industry (performing arts – through the CNV,[38] the recording industry, and the media). Because the other domains of 'live performance' do not

---

[35]   Société des auteurs, compositeurs et éditeurs de musique, established in 1850 and responsible for collectively managing musical royalties.

[36]   National federation of jazz and contemporary music schools.

[37]   Hugh Dauncey, 'The French Music Industry: Structures, Challenges and Responses', in Dauncey and Cannon (eds), *Popular Music in France*, pp. 41–56.

[38]   The CNV (National centre for chanson, variety and jazz music), a public body created in 2002, took over from the Support fund for chanson, variety and jazz music itself established in 1986. It receives the tax levied on concert tickets and redistributes this to businesses having paid it in the form of a proportional automatic aid – or selective aid – following advice proposed by a commission. In 2004 the total amount of aid stood at 10,265,000 euros with 57 per cent of this being automatic. Constructed on the model of the Centre national de la cinématographie and the Centre national des lettres it is however far from generating the amounts equivalent to those granted to these two public bodies, See Berthod and Weber, *Rapport sur le soutien de l'État aux musiques dites actuelles*, p. 11.

have any equivalent relationships with cultural industries, it is a matter of inventing entirely new policy. But this is more for the future than a current reality.

To understand why this overall shift in interventions towards norms of intervention already established in other cultural fields has occurred, two primary explanations can be advanced. The first is suggested by Path Dependency analysis.[39] Tried and tested mechanisms and recognized support had the advantage of saving learning costs for new measures. Furthermore, the repetition of the term 'recognition' in demands made by stakeholders in these musical domains indicated an aspiration to be treated in the same way as other cultural forms, and the deployment of these aid models constituted a good sign of recognition. Secondly, and conversely, keeping special and different policies for the support of these musics was not an option in that to do so would amount to denying them the same cultural dignity attributed to other musics, and would imply that their audiences were less important. It is in this sense at least that policies benefitting contemporary musics demonstrate a logic of cultural recognition.[40]

Policies for Popular Music: Symptoms of/Remedies to the Cultural Policies Crisis

It was precisely during the period (the 1990s) when cultural polices began to be increasingly questioned, that they took an interest in popular music. Considered as symptomatic of this phase, initiatives in favour of these musics can also be envisaged as having introduced new ways of conceiving and undertaking cultural policies.

Crisis? What Crisis?

The inventory established by Berthod and Weber clearly outlines the policy implemented in the field of contemporary musics and draws up an overall assessment but does not clearly present the overall framework within which all the mechanisms operate. In this sense, this assessment reflects the situation of cultural policies as a whole, as events taking place during the last Presidential campaign in 2007 bear witness.

In 2007, the cultural sectors were concerned by the silence of political parties concerning the future of cultural policies. However, in their manifestos, the main candidates formulated responses to their expectations, or at least to the most

---

[39]   Paul Pierson, 'Path Dependence, Increasing Returns, and the Study of Politics', *American Political Science Review*, 94/2 (2000): pp. 251–67.

[40]   Charles Taylor, *Multiculturalisme, différence et démocratie* (Paris, 1994); Axel Honneth, *La Lutte pour la reconnaissance* (Paris, 2002); Nancy Fraser, *Qu'est-ce que la justice sociale? Reconnaissance et redistribution* (Paris, 2005).

fundamental of them.[41] But, beyond the promise of specific measures, what workers in these sectors were hoping for was what Malraux had succeeded in achieving in the early 1960s: 'a successful, that is to say accepted, representation of the role that the State would like art to play in changing or consolidating society, coherently linked with a programme of state initiatives (appointments, funding, creation of various mechanisms and institutions)'.[42] Whereas Jack Lang had echoed this by linking his initiatives in culture with French governments' overall plans of action, subsequent Ministers of Culture merely restricted themselves to their own affairs. Although urban social problems and questions of cultural globalization (GATT and WTO negotiations, UNESCO work) led ministers to adopt some ideological stands, the lack of overall meaning and rhetorical support for culture is nowadays patently obvious and goes some way towards explaining the disappointment, even the nostalgia, felt by cultural sectors.

Indeed, the disappearance of a 'coherent and socially ambitious conception of State-led cultural initiatives'[43] represents a phenomenon of which the measures benefitting contemporary musics appear symptomatic. Ministerial services under Malraux's charge represented a restricted field of culture, and Jack Lang can be credited with having attempted to harmonize fields of intervention with a wider understanding of culture involving cultural forms hitherto not considered as legitimate. Alongside circus skills, strip cartoons, culinary arts, fashion, and science and technology, popular musics and rock in particular have frequently appeared as the most significant elements of this widened definition, but such a vast domain requires diversified initiatives difficult to integrate within a major political project.

This scattering of initiatives is also an important contributor to the 'overpopulation' of cultural policies involving local government bodies, central government actors, concert hall or rehearsal venue staff, amateur or semi-professional musicians, multiple associations, (micro) businesses in the recording, musical production and media fields: the crowding of the contemporary music sector highlights the situation particularly well. This manifests itself through multiple, under-coordinated, even competing initiatives which public authorities attempted to regulate, all the while finding these initiatives almost impossible to manage satisfactorily.

Finally, this overpopulation is directly linked to the lack of a reference of cultural policies. Some analyses of public policies – using cognitive approaches – have illustrated that any given package of measures is all the more likely to constitute a policy that it is directed by a social grouping possessing a clear vision of its place and role in society. It is around this intellectual and practical matrix, described as

---

[41]   Philippe Teillet, 'Culture et présidentielles: demandez-le(s) programme(s)!', *L'Observatoire*, 31 (2007): pp. 9–13.

[42]   Philippe Urfalino, 'Après Lang et Malraux, une autre politique culturelle est-elle possible?', *Esprit* (2004): p. 55.

[43]   Urfalino, 'Après Lang et Malraux, p. 56.

a 'reference point'[44] that a policy can organize itself, establishing the leadership of the group responsible for directing the policy. From this perspective, the difficulties experienced today by many public policies can be explained by the absence of such leadership. This, in particular, is what is happening in the cultural domain; the widening of intervention has occurred in parallel with the diversification of groups involved, some of which come from public administrations, others from the non-profit private sector, more still from the commercial private sector, some of whom have recognized professional qualifications, while others have expertise which is unclear or gained 'through experience'. This has led to a fragmented situation, where no group is able to propose a vision of the entire cultural sector capable of uniting all the others. Even within the (sub)sector of contemporary musics, the divergences between genres, between profit-making activities or not in the domain of performing arts, recording or media, the aspirations to professionalism or the amateurism cherished by others, even political colouring, constitute so many differences which, without altogether preventing cooperation, make it difficult to construct shared values around which a public policy can be defined. The establishment of the *Conseil Supérieur des Musiques Actuelles* (Superior Council of Contemporary Musics) in late 2005, following a national dialogue between the majority of national and regional organizations operating in this sector, represents a means of bringing together the positions of these various organizations and has made visible the major gaps which continue to separate them. Thus, in light of this dispersion, both the difficulty for cultural leaders of constructing coherent policy, and the difficulty for analysts in identifying political choices of which such policies could be the expression can be understood. The contemporary music sector is, as we have seen, a prime example of this situation.

A Representative Sector in What Ways?

However, it is possible to find more positive aspects in the difficulties of cultural policy towards contemporary music and even to consider what happens in this domain as a potential way forward for all public policies relating to culture.

Firstly, initiatives in favour of contemporary musics demonstrate a new age of cultural policies henceforth focused around towns and cities. Cultural decentralization has favoured multi-level governance which obscures the key roles played by towns and cities. Their financial resources, cultural departments and local cultural professionals allow them to hold responsibilities which reach beyond their own borders. It is in conurbations that most large-scale cultural infrastructures and events are located. These conurbations have heavily involved themselves in contemporary musics. Rock, rap, and electronic are historically and aesthetically associated to the urban world, and the vitality of local music scenes is additionally linked to the presence of universities and necessary population

---

[44]   Bruno Jobert and Pierre Muller, *L'État en action* (Paris, 1987).

thresholds. Furthermore, social problems in urban areas have numerous local governments to use culture for redevelopment and to grant it significant importance in urban regeneration strategies.[45]

France's centralizing tradition, the administrative fragmentation of national space and conflicts between levels of political responsibility (towns, *départements*, regions, intermunicipal structures) tends to inhibit towns and cities' power to act and prevents the awareness of their strengths to which, generally speaking, the 'rebirth of towns and cities in Europe' should lead.[46] Moreover, key players in cultural policies, including those in contemporary musics, are sometimes concerned at city-led developments from which they are actually the first to benefit. This concern can partly be explained by French national Jacobin culture (a desire to standardize development of all regions), but, these fears are caused chiefly by the fact that the rebalancing of power between the centre and the peripheries necessitates similar reconfiguring of professional and sectoral bodies to allow them to benefit from government at all levels, just as they previously benefitted principally from the centralized state.

Secondly, policies benefitting popular musics were founded on the principle of cultural recognition of minorities. Although this orientation remained implicit because of the way it can contradict the Republican model of integration,[47] this recognition did, however, appear in cultural policies following the 1970s, through claims to legitimacy of regional cultures and then, particularly, through debates over immigration.[48] Rather ambivalent policies resulted from this situation which did not strictly reflect ethnocultural criteria, but which within the framework and the logic of urban development policies, addressed issues of cultural difference via socio-spatial mapping.

The promotion of cultural diversity is an escape from this ambivalence. In order to break free from this and lay down new cultural policy perspectives, the academic Jean-Michel Lucas – a former member of Lang's ministerial team and former Regional Director of Cultural Affairs – published, under the pseudonym of Dr Kasimir Bisou, a series of stimulating texts.[49] Underlining the doublespeak of a country which now makes cultural diversity a priority, but where cultural policies are still essentially restricted to cultural values defined by experts convinced of

---

[45]   Franco Bianchini and Michael Parkinson (eds), *Cultural Policy and Urban Regeneration* (Manchester, 1993); Chris Gibson and Shane Homan, 'Urban Redevelopment, Live Music and Public Space', *International Journal of Cultural Policy*, 10/1 (2004): pp. 67–84.

[46]   Le Gales, *Le Retour des villes en Europe*.

[47]   Guy Saez, 'Le modèle culturel français face à la mondialisation', in Guy Saez (ed.), *Institutions et vie culturelles* (Paris, 2004), pp. 119–23.

[48]   David Looseley, 'Thinking Postcolonially about French Cultural Policy', *International Journal of Cultural Policy*, 11/2 (2005): pp. 145–55.

[49]   These texts can be found on the site of the Irma: http://www. irma.asso.fr/spip. php?article4236.

the necessity to make them accessible to as many people as possible, the work of J.M. Lucas aims primarily to render public initiatives coherent with the principles on which they are based.[50] His reflections draw from UNESCO declarations and conventions, work undertaken by *Cités et Gouvernements Locaux Unis* (CGLU) – the world organization of local governments signatory to Cultural Agenda 21 in May 2004 in Barcelona[51] – research on social and community economics (so as to give some reality to the much challenged notion of cultural exception and remove culture from free market forces of a capitalist economy), as well as the work of the legal expert P. Meyer-Bisch (Freiburg University) on cultural rights, which were the basis for the Freiburg declaration on cultural rights adopted in May 2007.[52]

As a learned equivalent of grass-roots cultural activism, this thinking confronts political leaders with documents they had themselves adopted (such as those of UNESCO) and provide some cultural key players with an intellectual grounding allowing them to challenge interpretations of policies unfavourable to them. This explains the interest shown in his work by the contemporary music sector,[53] despite some contradictions. The overall critique made by Bisou is not uncritical of these individuals, to the extent that he is critical of the long-term initiatives in favour of these musics and the practices of a number of professionals in the sector which – as we have seen – have progressively drawn closer to conventions of cultural policies. Conversely, the adoption of participatory practices (as advocated by Cultural Agenda 21) implies a profound transformation of values and working methods, including in the field of contemporary musics. Particularly, the notion of cultural identity – figuring at the heart of UNESCO declarations – is not unproblematic. As far as various forms of rock, rap or electronica and their variant forms are concerned, unless one adopts an overly-simplistic approach, it is difficult to relate these musics to any particular social groups. From this perspective, the Freiburg Declaration on cultural rights seems more suitable, considering cultural rights as being linked to individuals rather than groups.

Yet beyond these ambivalences, the underlying logic of state support to contemporary musics is very much that of recognition, which is somewhat innovative in France. It is not a question here of considering differences in terms of ethnicity, religion, gender, sexual orientation or differences of any other nature likely to distinguish specific groupings from the whole of society. If differences between groupings are not to be considered as natural, but as never-ending processes

---

[50]   Jean-Michel Lucas (Doc. Kasimir Bisou), *Culture universelle et diversité culturelle: reconstruire la politique culturelle* (Paris, 2007).

[51]   For information on the work of CGLU, see: http://www.agenda21culture.net/docs/.

[52]   http://www.aidh.org/ONU_GE/Comite_Drtcult/decla–fribourg.htm.

[53]   Knowing, furthermore, that Lucas in his various previous responsibilities initiated consideration of and institutional support in favour of these musics.

of 'decomposition and recomposition',[54] a cultural policy of recognition should, in accordance with the contribution of Cultural Studies[55] approaches, take account of cultural dynamics which are not merely vertical (top-down) but also horizontal and thus relatively independent of norms of cultural legitimacy. It is, therefore, a question of cultural policy giving recognition to the ability of social groups outside the cultural elite to produce symbolic forms and works which are representative of the culture of our times, and able to function in the construction and recomposition of our identity, whilst also responding to a plurality of aesthetic norms. In the case of contemporary musics, this means establishing different conceptions of musical work, of relationships with musical creations, even of the ways in which people are involved in musical activities. Although the challenges are significant, what has taken place in the field of contemporary musics is representative of trends which, for all that they are new, are no less necessary for the future of all cultural policies and for the harmonization of their content with their principles.

Conclusion

This chapter reflects the ways in which issues of culture can be unendingly politicized. The standpoints of cultural key players and the work produced by researchers represent material just as likely to contribute towards a greater understanding of these policies and bring changes in them, as they are to fuel controversy. Moreover, the deep-rooted and direct involvement of government means that any such debate calls government into question. Whereas the rhetoric of French 'public service' had relatively neutralized and de-politicized this issue, today issues of legitimacy and cultural diversity are re-politicizing it once again. Measures in favour of popular musics are thus at the core of these developments and their accompanying conflicts.

Meanwhile, musicians continue to play, rehearse and record. France enjoys a long-standing tradition of rock criticism and has – although only very recently – seen international approval of its artists (via the so-called French Touch and its place in world musics). But public policies are not behind such achievements.

The successes of public policy have been more at the local level. Government support for popular music is not a French particularity.[56] In France, as elsewhere,

---

[54]   Michel Wieviorka, 'Culture, société et démocratie', in Michel Wieviorka (ed.), *Une société fragmentée? Le multiculturalisme en débat* (Paris, 1997), p. 28.

[55]   Eric Maigret and Eric Macé (eds), *Penser les médiacultures* (Paris, 2005).

[56]   Simon Frith, 'Popular Music and the Local State', in Tony Bennett (ed.), *Rock and Popular Music* (New York, 1993), pp. 14–24; Paul Rutten, 'Popular Music Policy: a Contested Area – The Dutch Experience', in Bennett (ed.), *Rock and Popular Music*, pp. 37–51; Peter Wicke and John Sheperd, '"The Cabaret is Dead": Rock Culture as State Enterprise. The Political Organization of Rock in East Germany', in Bennett (ed.), *Rock and Popular Music*, pp. 25–36; John Street, *Politics and Popular Culture* (Cambridge, 1993).

it largely depends on 'well-trodden paths' of cultural policies. It is in the areas where they have the least legitimacy, and therefore autonomy, for example in the prevention of delinquency or in economic development, that popular music will be the most supported by government.[57] Data collected by Simon Frith[58] suggests also that policies of local government in various countries are converging. This hypothesis is yet to be proved, but it is in part coherent with what can be observed in France where local government initiatives aim, in the long run, to support local music scenes under threat from the globalization of the music industry.[59]

---

[57]　Simon Frith, ibid., pp. 14–24; Paul Rutten, ibid., pp. 37–51.

[58]　Simon Frith, ibid., pp. 14–24.

[59]　On these issues, for the case of France, see Gérôme Guibert, *La Production de la culture – Le cas des musiques amplifiées en France* (Paris, 2006).

Chapter 6

The UK Music Economy

Mike Jones

An 'economy' is, effectively, a collective noun. It stands for a complex series of decisions involved in the satisfaction of needs and wants through the allocation of scarce resources – where needs, wants and access to resources all differ on an individual and group basis. The total of decisions is expressed as the production, distribution, sale and consumption of commodities, where differentials in needs, priorities and access affect bargaining power in each of these dimensions. The total of these differentials is then captured in the expression 'market forces' and bear on decision making in all phases of the supply of, and demand for, products. In discussing the current condition of the UK *music* economy, limitations of space prevent a full engagement with each of these dimensions; rather, what I hope to achieve is the identification of a series of challenges faced by the domestic music economy at the time of writing. Many of these challenges are not specific to the UK; they are, to use a loose term loosely, 'global' in their origin as a borderless 'digital economy' in recordings begins to emerge. Even so, it is worth considering how the UK is experiencing upheavals in the music economy in general, in order to evaluate how, if at all, these challenges are being met.

When discussing the music economy of any nation state we need to be able to separate the sales of goods or services manufactured *within* a nation state from those imported from other countries. Further, we need to recognize that 'home' originated music may not be intended for purely domestic consumption, it may also be exported to countries from which other musical goods and services are imported. Ultimately the 'health' of a music economy is judged quantitatively, in terms of monetary value: do 'we' export more than 'we' import; are 'we' more or less competitive than 'we' used to be; do 'we' earn as much as 'we' need to in order to provide a return on investment in music?

Framed in these quite dull and quantitative terms much of the glamour of music making and music use – music of any type, style or genre – seems diminished. Further, none of the complexity and richness of music as a sense-making practice can either be captured by or reflected in sales figures. Music is a cultural activity. The pleasure taken in music derives from the meanings its experience provokes. To discuss music 'economically' is to intrude on its sensuality; to encroach on individual personality itself. Yet, the 'bottom line' is that there is no 'we' in music, although to make this assertion is to fly in the face of much of the recent representation of UK music. Increasingly, and overwhelmingly in the form of reports commissioned by the government or by various national organizations connected to music in some way,[1] music made in the UK is praised as if it is some collective treasure, a naturally-occurring and common resource; but while music may well be experienced collectively it is made and more pertinently *owned* privately. Most music is made to yield a profit, at the very least so that musicians can remain musicians; but much more than this almost all music (whether on record, on license, or 'live') is supplied by companies who operate, as all companies do, to yield a profit on capital invested in making music products – a reality as apparent in classical music, in jazz, in folk and in 'world' music as it is in the 'pop' music so readily dismissed as 'commercial'.

The making, marketing and promotion of recordings has to be paid for; the staging, marketing and promotion of live events is costly; payments are made and costs borne only when investors believe that there is likely to be a return on investment.[2] In this way, what music attracts investment is music considered 'marketable' – music that appears to demonstrate an ability to be taken to market and sold there. This is why, when there is so much popular music made, only *some* pop acts succeed when so many are consigned to history; but it is also why *some* jazz acts prosper while others fight for air, why only *some* of the classical repertoire is performed while, for example, a once obscure Mahler becomes ubiquitous; why *some* African acts continue to tour Europe while other former favourites now languish, and so on. Music does not sell itself; music does not attract market attention to itself. The types of market success musicians require to continue to be musicians has (at least until now) been beyond their economic and organizational reach. For this reason, musicians and the music they make rely on the intervention of intermediary figures and their businesses. Consequently, what has distinguished the 'known' from the 'unknown'; the 'talented' from 'the others' in all music genres is the degree to which an investor can argue successfully the distinctiveness of particular music in the face of market competition – where this runs counter to the commonsense notion that music declares its *own* distinctiveness, and is rewarded correspondingly.

---

[1]   Cloonan lists the following: National Heritage Committee: *Inquiry into CD Prices* [1993]; Monopolies and Mergers Commission: *The Supply of Recorded Music* [1994]; British Invisibles: *Overseas Earnings of the Music Industry* [1995]; The National Music Council: *The Value of Music* [1996]; Department of Culture Media and Sport: *Creative Industries Mapping Document* [1998]; The National Music Council: *A Sound Performance* [1999]; Department of Culture, Media and Sport: *Consumers Call the Tune* [2000]; Department of Culture, Media and Sport: *Creative Industries Mapping Document* [2001]; Department of Culture, Media and Sport: *Banking on a Hit* [2001]; the British Council: *Make or Break: Supporting UK Music in the USA* [2002]; The National Music Council: *Counting the Notes* [2002]; Office of Fair Trading: *Wholesale Supply of Compact Discs* [2002]; Office of Fair Trading: *Ticket Agents in the UK* [2005]; Department of Culture, Media and Sport: *SME Music Businesses* – all in Martin Cloonan, *Popular Music and the State in the UK* (Aldershot/Birmingham USA, 2007).

[2]   *Fan-Based Funding for New Bands: Alamo Records as an Alternative Business Model*, S. Harrison, University of Liverpool, unpublished MA Dissertation, 2007.

The bulk of economic information and theory is expressed in numbers – whether as sets of formulae that yield figures for the 'performance' of an economy, or as masses of statistics that allow economists and media commentators to compare such performance over time and between firms, industries and entire economies. Unfortunately for these purposes, the discourse of numbers ends before an analysis of a music economy can begin. Taken as a whole, current figures for the consumption of *records* make for bleak reading, whether in the UK or beyond. The recording industry is clearly in crisis but the economy of music seems as buoyant as ever. Consequently, the question of an economy *in* music needs to be separated from the supply and demand of recordings on physical formats and needs also to be extended into two further economic realms – into a consideration of an economy of signs and into the economy of the senses. Considered as three economies, the UK music economy would seem to be both weak *and* strong; turbulent *and* prosperous; it would seem, therefore, to be both meeting challenges and falling short of them. To understand why and how we need to consider each economy in turn.

Music as an Economy of Numbers

One method of attempting to gauge economic activity in music is to consult a 'listings' magazine. Here, no distinction is made between music products (whether records or live events) that make profit for UK companies and those for companies beyond the nation-state. What we are presented with is the huge scale and range of such products which, regardless of point of origin, are on offer at any one time. For example, in the summer months, there are abundant music festivals to attend while throughout the year there are rock and jazz 'gigs', classical concerts and dance 'club' nights in every major city (and, to some degree, in most towns) on every night of the week; large numbers of records continue to be released; multi-channel, predominantly commercial, radio offering the widest range of music together with digital audio and 'freeview' radio channels delineated by music genre; musicians on TV in dedicated programmes (with music on television in every ad, every film and as a theme for every show), together with, again, genre-based channels on cable and satellite TV. Further, we could readily find evidence of musicians celebrated in newspapers on a daily basis; we could enjoy music magazines dedicated to a range of styles and we would be aware, from frequent news reports, of enormous numbers of individuals buying music online, whether as mail order CDs or as downloads, and of huge numbers participating in 'social networking' sites such as MySpace, Facebook and Bebo in which musicians are active in self-promotion and through which non-musicians create new friendships substantially by identifying their tastes in music. Further still, the soundscape of any journey by public transport susurrates with leakage from MP3 players and is jolted by the persistent clash of musical ringtones; many passengers and passers-by identify themselves by wearing the logos or album artwork of popular music acts on garments; smoking is banned in enclosed public spaces but music suffuses almost all of them; karaoke is a staple of a 'night out', voting for fame-hungry young singers on 'reality' TV shows is a staple of a 'night in'.

If music is economically active and vibrant in the UK, the UK music economy is perhaps less robust than data on the consumption of music might suggest. In what has been a turbulent year for UK music businesses there is evidence of much upheaval. For example, at the time of writing, EMI, the UK's one 'major' record company, has passed into the hands of the private equity firm Terra Firma. It is too soon to assess the impact of the transition from a PLC to a private firm but private equity has become synonymous with 'corporate raiding' – with large-scale sackings to create immediate cost savings and with 'asset stripping' to produce immediate profit. A 'worst case' scenario for EMI would be that its record division was either closed entirely or sold as a newly-profitable 'going concern' – that is only after significant reduction in staff employed and acts signed. Under these circumstances a likely buyer might be Warner Music. In this way the UK would lose its one 'major' to a US company and Robbie Williams would go on to earn for the US music economy what he does currently for the UK, regardless of whether Americans buy his records.

Also in 2007, music retail began to demonstrate evidence of severe crisis. In January, Music Zone closed all 103 of its stores. Up to that point Music Zone had been one of the great success stories of the UK music economy. Its chain grew rapidly to become the third largest UK music retailer at the time of closure. This growth was driven through the simple, though comparatively high-risk, strategy of offering CDs [as well as DVDs and computer games] at very low prices. Its main rival, Fopp, bought over half of Music Zone's stores from the administrators. Fopp had also enjoyed spectacular growth and also through offering low prices to customers, although in its case, Fopp offered low cost 'catalogue' albums the chain purchased cheaply and in bulk as deletions made by overseas divisions of major record companies. Yet, despite the elimination of its nearest rival, Fopp entered administration just five months later, in June 2007, with the closure of 105 stores. In the same month, HMV, the UK's largest music retailer announced that annual profits would be half those of the previous year. This 'profit warning' was then followed by Virgin's abandonment of record retailing in their sell-out to Zavvi in September 2007. Taken together, while the extreme difficulties faced by the record-retailing sector of the music economy are reliably an indicator only of changing buying habits (rather than diminished interest in purchasing music *per se*), the sheer intensity of change can only register as negative disturbance within that economy in the short term.

It could be argued that the fortunes of the UK music economy do not need to be presented in so bleak a fashion; for example, 'live' music is argued to be growing in significance. Yet, here again, it is not entirely the case that live music in the UK earns money for the UK economy – for example Prince played 21 dates at the O2 arena (formerly Millennium Dome) in London in September 2007, but the Arena is US-owned and the concerts were promoted by the Arena's owners, Anschutz

Entertainment Group (AEG) of Los Angeles. Equally, much of the UK live music industry is US-owned, formerly by Clear Channel and latterly by their live music 'spin off', Live Nation. None of this means that there are no UK employees of the US businesses, or that no significant UK businesses exist in live music, but simply celebrating a vibrant 'live' sector of the UK music economy is to miss the point that only a limited proportion of ticket sales in the UK enrich UK-owned companies. Further, listings magazines may indicate a surfeit of competing gigs (I once encountered 11 bands in three venues in one building on one night in Liverpool) but this does not mean that the earnings of musicians or the conditions of their existence have improved on a comparable scale in the period that 'live music' has become so popular; rather it is likely that the fortunes of musicians on the lowest, most fundamental, rungs of the UK live music sector have *worsened* over time.

As an economy of numbers, then, the UK music economy would appear to be in a mixed condition – much money changes hands for many music products, but not all of those products originate within the UK and neither does payment for them enrich UK investors, yet we are told continuously that music is one of the UK's most important *exports* and therefore, one of this country's principal industries – one of a comparatively recently designated set of *creative* industries. To explore this apparent anomaly we need to consider UK music in the context of another economy – as prominent within an economy of *signs*.

Music as an Economy of Signs

The now familiar concept of an economy of signs is one of several designed to describe the nature and consequences of the regeneration of advanced capitalism associated with, although not necessarily all traceable to, the implementation of Neoliberal economic policies in the 1980s (other descriptive terms would be the 'weightless economy', the 'information society' and the 'knowledge economy'). In brief, core Neoliberal policies, notably on the relaxation of controls on capital flows and company organization, became rapidly enmeshed with a profound transformation in communication technologies. Companies had already begun to recognize that brands helped differentiate equivalent products in the marketplace. Competitive advantage could be gained by encouraging the consumer's attribution of values to specific branded products. The onset of satellite television followed by the torrent of digitization then afforded opportunities to exploit brand recognition and value-attribution in ways that the marketing departments of major companies and the advertising agencies they hired could not have dreamed possible when the first US and UK Neoliberal governments were elected.

In exactly the period when major companies have merged and shed staff, the use-value of a commodity has come increasingly to take second place to what

Lash and Lury refer to as its 'sign value'.[3] Since the late 1970s, the definitive trend in advanced capitalism has been to relocate manufacturing to countries in which labour can be exploited to the hilt and to use the considerable cost savings so gained to concentrate expenditure on marketing and advertising. In turn this has encouraged a boom in an industrial sector rise whose only output is signs or their dissemination: media companies, graphic designers, web-designers, advertisers, marketing companies, PR firms, and so on. The proliferation of sign manipulators has then been facilitated by the onset of the digitization of communication. In an era in which processing power doubles every 18 months and mobile telephony becomes increasingly versatile, sign-manipulators prosper only to the extent that they can find ever-more inventive ways of maintaining and extending the brand penetration of their clients' products, with the result that lines that describe where marketing ends and where culture begins are increasingly erased.

Music is implicated deeply in all of this for three sets of reasons: firstly, the cultural place of music is a powerful and consistent one. Music creates meaning as language does, through the organization of symbols into codes, but it also works in ways that *exceed* language. As hymn singing, national anthems and marching tunes had already demonstrated, music can not only connote ideas far more rapidly and with far greater immediate 'reach' than a written or spoken text – of 'one true God', of 'nation', of 'one nation under god' – but it can also rapidly concentrate and consolidate those ideas as *feelings* (and so relocate and reinforce them as 'natural') through its dimensions of association and affect. Advertisers were quick to exploit the concentrated connotative capacity of music, quick to tap into its power to attach itself to concepts and remain in the memory, where both dimensions can be pertinent to the selling of the use-value of a particular product; 'you'll wonder where the yellow went when you brush your teeth with Pepsodent'.[4] Now, in these sign-intensified times, it is more the associative and affective dimensions of music (together with values attributed to music genres and to music makers) that are drawn on in marketing and advertising. The aim of, what are now permanent and cross-pollinating, marketing campaigns is to insinuate a brand as not just a complement to but an extension of feelings about the *self*, an extension of the values that individuals attribute to themselves or aspire to in groups they desire to be identified with. In this way, the lines that describe where identity ends and commodities begin are increasingly erased.

Music's second contribution to the economy of signs is the example offered by the music industry as a precursor or as a set of precedents for the stewardship of a brand. With the rise of rock music and its concentration on the record album rather than the song as the primary popular music commodity, record companies evolved marketing and promotional strategies that could be argued to prefigure the types of strategies now familiar in brand management, generally. While the Hollywood

---

[3]   Lash, S. and Lury, C., *Global Culture Industry* (Cambridge UK and Malden USA, 2007), p. 7.

[4]   http://video.google.com/videoplay?docid=-10090706806935780.

film industry had long used marketing and media promotion (as opposed to relying entirely on paid-for advertising) to sell films, the contribution of actors to marketing campaigns was to smile winningly, to stay out of trouble, and to give bland press interviews.[5] Rock musicians, on the other hand, were deemed to have 'something to say', so much so that they required sometimes years in a recording studio and a whole album to 'say it'. At its launch in 1967, what differentiated *Rolling Stone* magazine from the rest of the music press was that it carried 'in depth' articles, based on extended and extensive interviews, with the new rock stars. In the content and even more importantly the *framing* of *Rolling Stone* interviews (and in a style that came to define the rock press), readers were encouraged to admire, or disdain, the values expressed through albums of music under discussion or review as ones that reflected those evident in the lives and, more pertinently, the *lifestyles* of the musicians they discussed.

While record companies, as companies, found limited opportunity for brand identification (though Motown was successful with 'the sound of young America'), individual albums were subject to dedicated marketing campaigns that came to concentrate on selling to specific groups of buyers. This practice represented a profound break with aiming pop singles at the 'mass market' of implicitly undiscriminating consumers of popular music where this practice had characterized the record business almost from its inception, or at least from the rise of radio. The reconfigured logic was that rock music indicated a new level of discrimination *within* the mass market. The purchase of an album by an influential group of buyers could be contrived to act as a signal to a much wider swathe of potential customers that there was kudos to be gained not just by becoming associated with an artist and an album but by becoming associated with the people most likely to be first buyers of that album – 'hipsters' were 'cool' because they rejected materialism; 'hippies' were seduced rapidly into demonstrating cool through buying commodities.

The effectiveness of this 'targeted' marketing lived or died by the 'sensitivity' of the A&R department in signing new acts (or in sustaining existing ones) and of the marketing department in finding the correct channels and the correct cultural 'triggers' for stimulating and then generalizing sales. Record companies rarely succeeded in these aims but when they did, massive profits were the result. Ultimately this model has migrated to the making and selling of commodities by industries far removed from popular music – what worked for *Sgt Pepper's* now works for *Dr Pepper's*, where a further twist in irony is that music acts are now themselves more 'brand aware'. For example, I have no idea what U2 'stand for' as a pop act, but that they seem to stand for something substantial gives Bono the ear of Presidents, to the mutual benefit of both. Equally, I might not legally download Diddy's latest record but I might still wear his aftershave and one of his

---

5   Consider the fate of Frances Farmer in this light: Frances Farmer, *Will There Really Be a Morning?* (New York, 1973).

shirts. In these ways, music, and especially popular music, has become an integral and important component of the 'weightless economy'.

Music's third reason for prominence in the economy of signs is perhaps most pernicious of all – making music is the perfect Neoliberal paradigm for a form of *self*-employment that at once seems highly attractive to young, largely unemployable people yet one that allows no claim against the state for intervention when 'careers' go wrong. It appears perfectly reasonable to represent music as an individually-rooted, 'creative' occupation, so ideologically-imbued is it with romantic discourses of artistic, self-expression. Under these terms and conditions musicians become self-disciplining 'creative' workers who must work on their own creativity regardless of issues of health and safety, limitations on working hours and so on. They must also take full individual responsibility for all of their training and care needs. And if they should fail to make a living as a self-sufficient creative worker then the fault lies squarely with them – the 'invisible hand' of 'market forces' has indicated that they have not been 'creative' enough to succeed in the market place for symbolic goods and that, consequently, they are only fit for *un*creative jobs. This brutal equation takes no account of the organization of the conditions for market entry nor of the architecture of markets themselves, yet it is an equation that drives the enthusiastic embrace of creative industries by all tiers of government in the 'developed' world.

In *Popular Music and the State in the UK: Culture, Trade or Industry?*,[6] Martin Cloonan argues that, the contribution to the UK economy of what he, rightly, identifies as the music *industries* is often overstated, but so convinced is government that the services sector can continue to compensate for de-industrialization and the decline in manufacturing that economic strategy pivots on the creation of conditions believed appropriate to securing and facilitating the position of a range of services in 'global' markets. In its 2006 report, the Parliamentary Committee on Trade and Industry expressed such thinking and effort in these terms:

> five detailed sector strategies targeting financial services and the City, information and communication technologies (ICT), life sciences, creative industries, and energy [have been developed]. These strategies, will illustrate UK sectoral strengths, gaps, key messages, channels to market, activity plans, targets, and marketing and promotional initiatives ...[7]

Ultimately, though, what Government is willing to do (rather than *can* do) for music is restricted by its ideology.

---

[6]   Cloonan, ibid.

[7]   House of Commons Trade and Industry Committee, Marketing UK plc – UKTI's five-year strategy, sixth report of Session 2006-2007, Report together with formal minutes, p. 17 At http://www.publications.parliament.uk/pa/-cm200607/cmselect/cmtrdind/557/557. pdf.

The ideology of the 'new' Labour Government is that of the '3rd Way', one that describes a path between the completely unfettered markets of Neoliberalism and the direct economic intervention of Social Reformism. The problem with 3rd Way policies is, though, that very often economies *demand* intervention, although by methods and from perspectives that show greater respect to markets than in previous incarnations of intervention. Ultimately, in its current guise, government intervention in the economy is restricted to measures that support or enhance industrial infrastructure (for example, the legal framework for market activity and the regulation of competition) and that provide education for industrial activity or employment (for example support for emergent music businesses or the inculcation of skills thought appropriate to a career in the 'music industry'). However, in both its aspects, even this restricted intervention is susceptible to three key weaknesses:

1. A persistent flaw characterizes reports that identify the needs of the music industry as one of the creative industries – whether these are commissioned by government or submitted as contributions to policy formulation by external bodies. This flaw can be identified as a confusion between suppliers of music and producers of music. Put simply, musicians supply music, but companies who take music to market do so in the form of music *products*. A music product can be a recording, a live event, or a license to use a song or a recording; what counts is that an intermediary agency first decides what music is marketable and then decides on what terms that music should be taken to market. In this way, what is supplied is not what is *produced* and how production is organized *always* impacts on music, whether for good or ill. Where the infrastructural needs of commerce in music is concerned, policy is shaped by the perspectives and the perceived needs of producers and not suppliers – partly because (Bono aside) it is the former who have the ear of government and partly also because what the government understands is business, not music. In this way, music and musicians are left to be romanticized as a force of nature somehow above the mundaneity of support, or, if not above support, then likely to be offered it only on the terms and conditions of measures designed to favour *producers*.

2. In the course of his study, Cloonan details the inadequacy of the methodologies deployed in the formulation of reports into the needs of the UK music economy. In turn, these reports have contributed to the (restricted) interventions pursued by government under a succession of acts of Parliament and through complex reconfigurations of government departments and departmental responsibilities. The primary, if not sole, focus of all of this effort and upheaval has been to create a skills training infrastructure to support expansion in creative industries. But if neither government departments nor interested quangos nor indeed industry trade associations can agree what it is the music industry (rather than the more accurate 'industries') consists of and how its component parts inter-connect,

what confidence can any interested party have in the skill sets identified and in the skills training regimes so devised?

3. The most recent report on the creative industries, *Staying Ahead: The Economic Performance of the UK's Creative Industries* [April 2007][8] identifies eight 'drivers' of success for the creative economy future policy needs to note. In keeping with the Neoliberal conception of the restricted role of government, all of these drivers are identified as infrastructural; for example, the stimulation of 'cultural activities', enforcing 'intellectual property', and so on. The most notable driver for these purposes, though, is that government should ensure 'balance and the appropriate supply' of 'education and skills'. The issue here is that 'education' and 'skills' are not interchangeable with each other – at the very least, the former deals with 'know why' while the latter deals with 'know how'. Yet the collapsing of the two has been evident for some time, not least in the redesignation of the Department for Education and Science (1964) as the Department for Education and Employment (1995); the Department for Education and Skills (2001); and the Department for Innovation, Universities and Skills (2007). The point here is not just that skills can be obviated rapidly while understanding is tougher and less susceptible to short and medium term upheavals, but (although it is beyond the scope of this article to evidence the point) it is much more so that often what passes as 'knowledge' or 'know how' about the music industry in the realms of music industry training schemes does not bear scrutiny and this is especially the case when the testimony of 'guest speakers' is relied on uncritically. Music business intermediaries are notoriously un-self-reflexive. They continue to rely on a hotchpotch of deeply contradictory and discontinuous maxims and to speak in anecdotes rather than in concepts.[9] Yet time and again 'industry' figures are represented as people who have 'been there, seen it, done it',[10] as if experience is equivalent to understanding; as if knowledge can be developed in the absence of theory. Yet theory could indeed be the key to improved efficiency in an economy of signs, especially when the active work of an economy of *senses* is considered.

---

[8]   Hutton, W., O'Keefe, A., Schneider, P., Andari, R., Bakhshi, H., *Staying Ahead: The Economic Performance of the UK's Creative Industries* (London, 2007) Chapter 5, p. 2.

[9]   While this is difficult to evidence, here, a visit to www.hitquarters.com is illuminating in this regard. The interviews with music industry figures can yield considerable contradictions [thanks to Josie Robson for pointing this out].

[10]   This remark was made by the Chair of a public panel on band management organized by the Music Managers Forum at Doncaster Dome, June 2005.

(3) Music as an Economy of the Senses

Encountering music is never a 'pure' experience; it is always a mediated one. When we hear music that is new to us it is almost always in a context that establishes conditions of reception – a new record or act is introduced by a familiar radio DJ (or on a genre-based station); an artist new to us is urged on us by a friend in an affirmative way; a style we may be unfamiliar with is historicized for us, along with 'recommended' recordings and acts, by a professional media commentator or 'blog' we trust. The fact that music arrives at our senses in a mediated way suggests, firstly, that rather than music carrying its own values, it is the context of music use and the encounter with music that establishes the value of music for the receiver. Secondly, it indicates that sense experience, itself, is not a pure phenomenon but is historically and culturally specific. The distribution of the senses and their modes of production [of meaning] derive from our negotiation of how it is we are expected to 'sense' within the confines of our social position. Braverman[11] made this point some time ago with regard to the rise of 'scientifically'-managed workplaces and the ways in which visual acuity in workers (dealing with paper and numbers) came to be privileged over the tactility of craft working.

Music criticism, in the very broadest sense of establishing the cultural conditions for the reception of music, is never at rest: new music and new artists are given meaning by validating them (or otherwise) through a process of comparing their work against dominant accounts of who and what is valuable in the genre within which their work can be situated. The work of creating and maintaining 'canons' of music is integral to the formation of group identities and of individual membership of groups. The continuous need to process and locate new music means that there is much motion at the 'borders' of a canon in order that there is as little movement as possible at its centre or heart. If the centre shifts the entire edifice will require substantial reconstruction – where advantages of distinction and difference that accrue to group members wedded to the old order risk being lost in the reshuffle. It is clearly beyond these remarks to explore this phenomenon in any greater detail, but its relevance to the present argument is that so much effort goes into establishing why some music fits a canon, or why some music disrupts a canon in new and positive ways, that musicians are taken for granted while the possible emergence of new sensory economies are ignored. In this way, the 'supply' is taken for granted – and therefore that the conditions of the lives of music-makers are either neglected or 'supported' inappropriately. Further, the only creativity that is validated is the creativity that fits the existing models of profit making that underscore the mechanisms of the preparation of music reception. Take, for example, the recent emergence of 'Grime' music in the UK.

---

[11]   Braverman, H., Foster, J.B., *Labor and Monopoly Capitalism: The Degradation of Work in the Twentieth Century* (New York, 1999) cited in Koch, G in *Sexual Representation: Introduction*, *Jump Cut*, no. 35, April 1990, p. 16 at http://www.ejumpcut.org/archive/onlinessays/JC35folder/SexualRepnIntro.html.

Grime originated in London in the early 2000s as an 'underground' genre – underground in the sense that its mediation and consolidation as a genre pivoted primarily on pirate radio broadcasts. Characterized by very fast raps that explore contemporary urban experiences, Grime beats and basslines are generated entirely on digital audio workstations (DAW), with the release of 'Fruityloops' in 2000 a particular technological catalyst. The musical decisions in Grime were dictated by preceding practices in UK dance music, notably but not exhaustively, the very fast (DAW-generated) tempos of 'Jungle' together with that genre's looping of percussive effects; the tempo-alterations of 'speed garage'; the electronic syncopations of breakbeat music; and the foundational 'two step' drum pattern [the omission of the 2nd and 4th bass drum beats in a four beat bar] that evolved from modification of speed garage tracks by the desire of MCs or rappers to create space for their lyricism.

Taken together, while Grime's implication with technology is comparatively unremarkable, that its generic development afforded a 'voice' to formerly disenfranchised young people makes it significant. Further, that a social and cultural voice emerges through an intense immersion with DAW technology can be argued to have redistributed the senses in ways that echo Braverman – in a new configuration of seeing, hearing and touching required in the production of distinctive musical sounds through ICT applications. Change in the economy of the sense underscores a change in subjectivity; we practise ourselves differently because we process sensory information differently. New subjects are, then, new types of suppliers – they *create* in new ways, they contribute to an economy of signs *and* can contribute to an economy of numbers in new ways; but new subjects are also new sources of *demand*. If there is new supply and new demand then existing companies are given an opportunity to do new business in new ways yet the response of at least the *record* industry to Grime has been conservative and comparatively unproductive.

While a notable success has been Dizzee Rascal, his former associates, Roll Deep (a 14-strong 'crew' of MCs and producers) fared less well when signed to EMI. As one of their members, Target, told me in an interview:

> When we joined the label the MD just wasn't interested, he didn't get us. Then, as soon as the first single got to number 11 he was all over us, he kept saying 'the next one's top three, the next one's top three' but when it only got to 24 he lost interest and they dropped us.[12]

Instead of an alertness to, and a genuine desire to explore and nurture, a continuously changing sensual economy, EMI, as a far from atypical organizer of music reception, rehearsed their standard marketing and promotional routines with Roll Deep. When these failed to work they 'dropped' them as they have

---

[12]   In personal interview with Target and Flow Dan of Roll Deep, Liverpool, 19 April 2006.

dropped countless acts before them. Record companies 'drop' acts because they have, until now, worked in comparatively *fixed* ways. This is not to argue that, in contrast, the practice of musicians is unbounded (and so rehash a stale version of the 'Art versus Commerce' debate) – musicians want market success in order to create music *careers* – but the point remains that the perspectives of how 'success' is achieved have been EMI's and EMI's alone for a lengthy and unhealthy period of time. Equally, success more generally in the UK music economy is the product of parallel routines in parallel sectors. The economy of numbers, at least in recording, suffers because its main movers have been slow to respond to changes in the economy of signs and brutally indifferent to changes in the economy of the senses. What is of wider concern, though, is that as New Labour pushes forward a creative industries strategy for the music economy as a whole, lessons of this kind are likely to go unlearned, with repercussions for music businesses and musicians alike.

Conclusions

This argument begins with a paradox – that the UK music economy is both weak and strong and the case of Grime should exemplify why this is the case. Music in the UK remains 'strong' because there continues to be evidence of a huge urge to expression – Grime has already been replaced 'underground' by 'Dub Step'; but it remains 'weak' because waste is so prevalent. Not only do record companies go on signing and dropping acts and having 'hits' with a tiny percentage of all of the pop acts available to them but, such is the glut of sign manipulators and so amenable is music to cross-promotional strategies for the widest range of commodities, that an obsession with the 'unsigned' has been provoked. So desperate are companies for cultural currency, and for the competitive advantage this may bring, that there is almost more to be gained from being associated with the 'next big thing' than there is from being associated with existing stars. 'Reality' TV shows create 'overnight sensations' who disappear sometimes more rapidly than they are catapulted into visibility, while magazines and newspapers give away cover-mounted CDs in their millions – where the combined effect is to make disposable and to trivialize forms of music that have never truly escaped the idea that they are indeed inherently disposable and trivial. Considered in these ways, the main challenges to the UK music economy stem from its own practices rather than are forced on it from 'globalization' or 'digitization'.

Building a 'creative industries' strategy on these damaging practices would seem at the very least to require counter-strategies for damage limitation, but government goes on being heedless of this need. There is no room to expand on this point here; instead I would propose the following as measures to allow the UK music economy to meet its challenges.

Where the economy of numbers is concerned:

- Recognize that Neoliberal strategies for cost advantage are inapplicable to music (for example 'the 'offshoring' of services such as call centres; the 'outsourcing' of manufacture) and concentrate instead on identifying core competencies in music business. If Artist Management is a particular skill exhibited by UK music firms then why not create 'global' artist management agencies and earn 20 per cent (of the net rather than the gross) income of *international* artists?
- If the core competencies of a record company are actually the coordination of 'worldwide' marketing and promotional campaigns, then new *service-based* business models should be developed to replace the existing record company model of signing the rights to recordings and then, mostly, failing to sell them. Musicians should become businesses who hire in the specialist services they are unable to furnish for themselves. Record companies earn commission for their services and have a greater financial incentive to be 'efficient' as businesses.
- Restore the value of music by resisting 'deep discounts' on recordings sold to supermarket chains and by ending the practice of cover mounts.

Where the economy of signs is concerned:

- Creative industries strategies should be based on far clearer methodologies than are exhibited currently in the reports that inform policy.
- There should be an end to the confusion of 'suppliers' and 'producers' of music – the needs of businesses are not the needs of musicians; the business needs of musicians should not be restricted only to those that allow them to play on the currently steeply unlevel playing field of the 'music business'. Danish music policy could be a guide here.
- There is a pressing need for music and music business educators to determine the distinction between knowledge and skills with regard to the creation of music careers. The epistemological demands of specifying creative production, or of specifying creativity *within* a capitalist mode of production, are considerable. Better specification of creativity will invite a point of resistance to the strategic deployment of the term within the ideology of Neoliberalism.

Where the economy of the senses is concerned:

- New subjectivities are not self-evidently progressive *because* they are new. Even so, 'we' live in a new world, or, at least, the very richest and the very poorest UK citizens now live in worlds that have no point of connection between each other and that the vast bulk of the population find incomprehensible. It is not my ambition to find ways of monetizing new forms of demand that stem from new subjectivities – I would prefer that there were neither disgustingly rich city traders in Knightsbridge nor 'crackheads' in Sheffield. Even so, as young people find new ways of exploring these tensions, and arguably are changed themselves in the process through their relationships with technology, then the greatest single weakness of the creative industries is the tendency to subordinate the creative acts of suppliers to the routines of business and to justify this, complacently, through rehearsing a 'wisdom' that 'explains' the market success of the few and ignores the, business-derived, market failure of the many. The UK music economy, and with it the 'creative economy', will only fully prosper when 'spin' is eradicated and replaced with some form of mutuality between originators and disseminators of creative acts.

Postscript

In furnishing this account of the UK music economy I have not explored questions of intellectual property and contracts; I have not engaged with the online economy save to reference it in passing; I have not begun to examine the logics of market mechanisms; I have only made passing mention of creativity and have only with deep inference raised the fundamental question of what is 'industrial' about music. These absences, though, should indicate at least that we cannot discuss economies meaningfully if we restrict ourselves to discussing sets of figures. When vital sets of social relations are implicated so deeply in them, there is a pressing need to bring these larger concepts in to play, especially now that economic policy is being framed for areas of the general economy that have been ignored systematically for decades.

Chapter 7

The Economics of Music in France

Dominique Sagot-Duvauroux

Since the early 2000s, the economics of music has witnessed major upheaval.[1] CD sales are in freefall, concert revenues are once more becoming essential sources of income, money gained from legal licensing mechanisms (fair remuneration, private copying) is increasing whilst new business models are also appearing on the internet (free access to the back catalogue of large record labels in return for subscription to a service provider, customer involvement in production etc.). New key players emanating from the telecommunications or computing sectors are undermining the position of the major record labels. Although these developments have given rise to a number of economic research works, aside from these last few years, the economics of music has failed to lead to much academic work in France.

It is impossible to understand the structuring of academic research in French cultural economics without considering the central role played by the Ministry of Culture in instigating programmes of research linked to its own concerns regarding cultural policies, particularly from the 1980s at the behest of Augustin Girard, at the time Director of Research within this ministry.[2] The economics of music is no exception to this rule.

During the 1980s, the major preoccupation was to control the costs of cultural institutions. The condition set in return for the doubling of the budget of the Ministry of Culture in 1981 was to develop a regionalized network of training programmes for running cultural enterprises (the AGEC, cultural enterprise management associations) and to promote academic research into the economics and management of these enterprises. This policy encouraged the emergence of

---

[1]   This article offers a survey of research into the economics of music undertaken in France, chiefly in the academic field. Reference is only made to non-French research when dealing with articles or books which were fundamental and to which the research considered makes reference. This survey, which is by no means exhaustive, favours a thematic presentation of research, respecting as far as possible the chronology of publications. The many works undertaken into music by researchers from related disciplines (sociology, information and communication sciences) are not in principle discussed.

[2]   For an analysis of different research positions in the economics of culture in France, see Pierre-Jean Benghozi and Dominique Sagot-Duvauroux, 'Les économies de la culture', *Réseaux* (1994): pp. 107–30, discussed in *Problèmes économiques*, 3 May 1995, series title 'Science économique', 2422: pp. 19–29.

research teams focusing on the issues of public funding of culture, expanding on work undertaken by William Baumol in the United States and/or the economic analysis of bureaucracy. Classical music (concert and operatic), because it was a significant drain on subsidies, was thus a key focus for study, whereas contemporary musics drew relatively little attention due to a lack of sustained interest in them from public authorities (see part 1 below).

The reason behind this is that they held, at the time, a marginal place in cultural policy, being therefore considered more from the perspective of industrial policy. Confronted with the record crisis which struck at the beginning of the 1980s coupled with the industrial concentration which accompanied it, the 'musical system' was subject, often on the fringes of academia, to in-depth studies using the classical tools of industrial economics and leading to the establishment of prospective scenarios. Critical reflection into the 'commoditization' of culture was also stimulated, merging economics, sociology, and information and communication sciences, and which in the late 1990s resurfaced in debates regarding France's *exception culturelle* and, subsequently, the concept of cultural diversity (see part 2 below).

Although analyses of the music sector investigate consumer behaviour, notably regarding prices, it is clear that there have been few in-depth theoretical analyses into demand. The excess of supply over demand is considered as a structural given in the economics of culture. In France, it was not until the 1990s, in the wake of questions raised by studies into the cultural practices of French people which highlighted the relative failure of cultural democratization policies implemented since the 1960s, that attention focused more on the determinants of demand. The phenomena of addiction and imitation were thus studied in reference to founding research by the American economists Stigler and Becker on addiction or by Rosen[3] on the *star system*. This led to some consideration of the role played by uncertainty and risk in the economics of culture: the issues of artist remuneration and the French regime of 'intermittence' for workers in the arts have been analysed in this perspective (part 3).

Finally, from the late 1990s, faced with the record industry crisis instigated by new digital technologies of recording and its consequences – notably CD piracy – public authorities promoted research into the digital economy and royalties. This research brings together perspectives from industrial economics, the economic analysis of law and the public economics of culture. The musical field naturally became a privileged subject for such research, and the economics of music thus made a noted entry into academic research (see part 4 below).

---

[3]   Sherwin Rosen, 'The Economics of Superstar', *Journal of Political Economy*, 71 (1981): pp. 845–57.

1. An Economics of Musical Institutions

Leaving aside some precursors, the economics of culture developed properly following the innovative work into live performance undertaken by Baumol and Bowen[4] in the United States. Building on the observation that it is extremely difficult to make productivity gains in this sector, the researchers questioned the viability of this type of activity in a market economy. They demonstrated that, *ceteris paribus*, production costs of live performance increase relatively more rapidly than those in the rest of the economy, this creating the classic dilemma where performance organizers either pass on cost increases in ticket prices, thus fuelling the elitism of live performance, or they reduce the scale of the performance, or finally, seek indirect financing methods (sponsorship and primarily subsidies). Supervised by Henri Bartoli, Dominique Leroy was, at Paris I University, the first to undertake a PhD investigating the pertinence of the processes revealed by Baumol in live performance in France. Alain Hercovici,[5] with the same supervisor, undertook a PhD analysis inspired by Marxist analysis of the music system in which he qualified the importance of Baumol's law in favour of dynamics based on unequal power relationships within the music industries (see part 3 below).

The issue rapidly moved from the productivity of live performance towards that of the economic stakes of state intervention in culture. Three questions thus became subjects of research:[6] What are the economic bases of intervention? What are the results of such intervention? How can intervention be evaluated? At the initiative of Bartoli, a supporter of the systems approach to economics, and of Xavier Greffe, a specialist in public economics and particularly in what is termed the economic analysis of bureaucracy,[7] a generation of researchers at Paris I University investigated these questions for opera,[8] theatre,[9] literature,[10] cinema[11] or

---

[4]   William Baumol and William Bowen, *Performing Arts, the Economic Dilemma* (New York, 1966).

[5]   Alain Hercovici, *Essai sur l'économie de la musique moderne*, Doctoral thesis in economics, Paris 1 University (1983).

[6]   Joëlle Farchy and Dominique Sagot-Duvauroux, *Économie des politiques culturelles* (Paris, 1994).

[7]   Xavier Greffe, *Analyse économique de la bureaucratie* (Paris, 1981).

[8]   Xavier Dupuis, *Essai sur les pratiques culturelles de l'État: l'exemple de la musique*, Doctoral thesis in economics, Paris XIII University, 1981; Xavier Dupuis, 'La surqualité: le spectacle vivant malade de la bureaucratie?', *Revue Économique* (November 1983).

[9]   Dominique Sagot-Duvauroux, *Structure de financement et organisation d'un système, l'exemple du théâtre*, Doctoral thesis, Paris 1 University (1985).

[10]   Françoise Benhamou, *Essai d'analyse économique d'une pratique culturelle: l'achat et la lecture de livres*, Doctoral thesis, Paris 1 University (1985).

[11]   René Bonnell, *L'Initiative culturelle en économie de marché: l'exemple du cinéma français depuis 1945*, Doctoral thesis, Paris 1 University (1976); Joëlle Farchy, *Le Cinéma*

even television.[12] This public economics of culture, as well as revealing the bases of state intervention and regulation of culture, showed that such intervention was neutral neither in the choice of management structure, nor production costs, nor artistic choices made by cultural organizations. Xavier Dupuis thus criticized – for opera – the additional costs induced by the strategy of seeking excessively high quality productions requiring investment of all budgetary resources into a handful of prestigious productions (permanent opera) rather than an even distribution of funding across many productions of average quality (repertory opera).

The book entitled 'Les Malheurs d'Orphée' (*The Misfortunes of Orpheus*), edited by Robert Wangermee,[13] gives in its opening section a summary of these works up to the late 1980s.

Contemporary music, at the time still underdeveloped and being primarily the concern of industry, was subject to few studies in this strand of analysis, perhaps because current music had failed to forge a place within government cultural policies. It was only following the establishment of an institutional network of contemporary music scenes (Smac) in the 1990s that the economic stakes of such scenes gave rise to study. But, although research developed rapidly in professional networks, as highlighted by the publication of the proceedings from consultation exercises between 'public policies and amplified music',[14] few economists paid any attention to this sector which, in academia, was left to political science or sociology. Economic research at this stage focused mainly on gauging the economic importance of the sector so as to increase its visibility to government,[15] or of thinking about the importance of social and community economics in the sector.[16]

It was not until the 2000s that some tentative economic studies in the sector of contemporary music institutions could be observed. Two research areas were favoured, that of the position and viability of structures belonging to the social and community economy within the institutional framework overall, and secondly that of the role of performance venues in the music sector overall.

---

français sous influence: de la concurrence audiovisuelle à la différentiation des produits cinématographiques, Doctoral thesis, Paris 1 University (1989).

[12]   Pierre Kopp, *Télévisions en concurrence* (Paris, 1990).

[13]   Robert Wangermee (ed.), *Les Malheurs d'Orphée* (Brussels, 1990).

[14]   Adem-Florida, *Politiques publiques et musiques amplifiées, actes des premières rencontres nationales*, GEMA (Paris, 1997).

[15]   Gilles Castagnac, 'L'économie phonographique: de filières en filiales', in Jacques Perret and Guy Saez (eds), *Institutions et vie culturelle* (Paris, 1996), pp. 101–2; Pierre Mayol, 'Le poids économique du secteur des musiques amplifiées', in Adem-Florida, ibid., pp. 129–31.

[16]   Bruno Colin, *Vers une économie solidaire du spectacle vivant?* in Adem-Florida, ibid., pp. 150–54.

A study undertaken by the *Centre d'étude de l'emploi*[17] exemplifies the first research focus: it outlined a dynamic typology of current music organizations, in which organizations from the social and community economy, from the private profit-making economy and from the public-sector economy were found side by side.[18] Using this typology as a basis, Sagot-Duvauroux[19] located the development of structures of contemporary music within the economics of music as a whole. Benhamou[20] focused on the dual economics of contemporary music – industrial and public-funded – by looking at the way live concerts have become the central core of the economics of music. But at the beginning of this century, new technological developments fundamentally altered the whole architecture of the economics of music (see part 4 below).

2. An Industrial Economics of Music

The industrial aspects of the music sector have for a long time produced much research. In addition to essentially industry-led publications (such as reports by the Snep), contemporary developments in the music sector have seen the publication of important reports on this industry which have twin objectives; firstly that of analysing the economic significance of the music sector and its future economic developments, and secondly that of critically analysing the commoditization of culture, of which the music sector seems an exaggerated example.

2.1. Analysing the Music Sector

The research undertaken by the BIPE in the 1980s applies the concept of a 'branch' developed by this body to the music industry.[21] The approach – systematic in its objectives – identifies the dynamics at play during the various stages of adding value to musical products, in order to outline some predictive scenarios in a context of technological and regulatory change (transition from vinyl to CDs,

---

[17]   Marie-Christine Bureau, Bernard Gomel and Nicolas Schmidt, *Les associations de musiques actuelles, partenaires du programme Nouveaux services – emplois jeunes. Contribution à un état des lieux, CEE*, 04/02 (January 2004): p. 117.

[18]   See Gérôme Guibert, *Scènes Locales, Scène Globale. Contribution à une Sociologie Economique des Producteurs de Musiques Amplifiées en France* (Nantes, 2004) for a very detailed overview of the amplified music sector today and the problems in its economics.

[19]   Dominique Sagot-Duvauroux, 'Quel modèle économique pour les scènes de musiques actuelles', *Copyright Volume!* (2005): pp. 15–24.

[20]   Françoise Benhamou, 'Ce que révèle l'économie des musiques actuelles', in Lyliane Dos Santos (ed.), *Valoriser les musiques actuelles* (Charbonnières, 2003), pp. 37–50; Françoise Benhamou, 'L'analyse économique de la musique enregistrée. Qui connaît la chanson?', *Revue de la Bibliothèque nationale*, 16 (2004): pp. 54–6.

[21]   BIPE, *L'Économie du domaine musical en France* (Paris, 1984).

rising numbers of local radio stations etc.). These studies identified very early the structure of an oligopolistic core and competitive fringe, where a few major companies control the core of the industry, leaving many small independent firms on the periphery. The meta-economical analysis of the musical system was accompanied by micro-economic studies, notably on pricing in the record industry. Le Diberder[22] focused, for example, on low price elasticity in the demand for records making price an adjustment variable difficult to control. In a similar vein but rather more traditional in approach, the 1997 report by Mario D'Angelo analysed the particularities of supply, demand and the role of public authorities in the regulation of music markets.[23] This latter aspect introduced consideration of the effectiveness of support mechanisms for contemporary music, which had been subject to little research until that time. Research undertaken by André Lange[24] as early as the 1980s was informed by similar concerns. This highlighed the forms and stakes of industry concentration and the control of distribution on music markets, and work undertaken by the *Observatoire de la musique*, under the direction of André Nicolas, nowadays continues in this direction.[25]

Throughout all of this work, the industrial economics employed is relatively classical (analysis of market structures, product strategies) and draws little on the new industrial economics developing at the time around concepts of uncertainty, risk and asymmetrical information. Little reference is made to the nature of contracts between participants in production or the mechanisms for recovering royalties, and the theorization of two-sided markets remains embryonic. It was not until the 2000s that the industrial economics of music engaged with all contemporary tools of economic analysis in its investigation of changes imposed by the internet and developments in the economic study of networks (see part 4 below).

2.2. A Critical Reflection into the Commoditization of Music

Alongside these strategic analyses of the music sector, as early as the 1970s a strand of critical research into the commoditization of cultural goods began to develop in France, notably at Grenoble University. Bringing together ideas from the School

---

[22]   Alain Le Diberder, 'La formation du profit dans les industries culturelles', in François Rouet (ed.), *Economie et culture, tome III, Les industries culturelles* (Paris, 1990).

[23]   Mario D'Angelo, *Socio-économie de la musique en France, Diagnostic d'un système vulnérable* (Paris, 1997).

[24]   André Lange, *Stratégies de la musique* (Brussels, 1987); André Lange, 'Le nouveau tempo de l'industrie de la musique', in René Wangermee (ed.), *Les Malheurs d'Orphée* (Brussels, 1990), pp. 197–218.

[25]   André Nicolas, 'La diversité musicale dans le paysage radiophonique' (Paris, 2004); 'Baromètre de l'offre musicale dans les services fournis par voie électronique – 5e vague' (Paris, 2005); 'Les marchés de la musique enregistrée – rapport 2005' (Paris, 2006); 'Les marchés du support musical' (Paris, 2006).

of Frankfurt and Marxist analysis of capitalism, and marrying economics and information and communication sciences, this research considered the ways in which value could be produced in artistic markets and also the already present risks of globalization of culture. The general studies undertaken by Miège[26] and Flichy,[27] and that by Michel de Coster into music,[28] represent significant steps in thinking on multinationals and cultural diversity. Flichy introduced the subsequently classic distinction between the editorial logic and the logic of plenty, contrasting the economics of publishing with the economics of media, but also contrasted long-term strategies aimed at adding value to back catalogues with short-term strategies aimed at creating profit from culture considered as throwaway commerce.

In the 1990s the critical debate into cultural exception and then cultural diversity was underpinned by this research. If the domination of American cultural industries can be explained by the specific nature of artistic products which generate economies of scale and networks favouring early entrants to the market (see part 3 below) as much as by control of distribution channels, then cultural diversity may thus come about through implementation of mechanisms which guarantee – beyond mere diversity of supply – diversity of distribution. However, these studies are dominated by cinema and the audiovisual industries, music being rarely examined.[29]

3. From the Issue of Public Supply to that of Demand

Although the first study led by the Ministry of Culture into cultural practices of French people was undertaken in 1973, French economists were relatively late in focusing on issues relating to cultural demand. Culture was initially a question of supply. The article by Stigler and Becker[30] highlighted the addictive aspect of the consumption of culture, drawing a parallel with drugs and alcohol and drawing support from the example of music. These economists championed the hypothesis that future cultural consumption was inextricably linked to past consumption. Their work gave rise to much research focusing on detailed analysis of the dynamics of cultural consumption based on endogenous preferences for culture. In the early 1990s, at the behest of the Ministry of Culture, Louis Levy-Garboua and

---

26   Bernard Miège (ed.), *Capitalisme et industrie culturelle* (Grenoble, 1978).

27   Patrice Flichy, *Les Industries de l'imaginaire* (Grenoble, 1980).

28   Michel De Coster, *Le Disque, art ou affaires* (Grenoble, 1976).

29   Cf. Joëlle Farchy, *La Fin de l'exception culturelle* (Paris, 1999); Serge Regourd, *L'Exception culturelle* (Paris, 2002); Armand Mattelart, *Diversité culturelle et mondialisation* (Paris, 2005); Françoise Benhamou, *Les Dérèglements de l'exception culturelle, plaidoyer pour une perspective européenne* (Paris, 2007).

30   George Stigler and Gary Becker, 'De Gustibus Non Est Disputandum', *American Economic Review* (1977).

G. Montmarquette[31] began a large-scale research project building, notably, on the *Pratiques culturelles des Français* (Cultural Practices of French People) study.

Whilst their work confirmed the hypothesis of endogenous preferences, they complemented this by outlining a distinction between good or bad past experiences, thus outlining an economic analysis of the development of households' tastes for artistic cultural products, where taste gradually develops taste as cultural goods and services are tried out. The research undertaken by Champarnaud and Abbé-Decarroux represents important French-language references on this subject.

This research was complemented in the 1990s by further work on qualitative uncertainties in artistic markets. Based in part upon economic analyses of the star system and, additionally, on research dealing with imitative phenomena, this research attempted to explain how consumers decide whether to buy a product of whose quality they are not entirely sure. Personal experience, imitating people considered as understanding quality, artistic honours such as awards or simply success itself are amongst the resources available for consumers to help reduce this uncertainty. However, aside from personal experience, these indicators of quality may mislead if incorrect information is transmitted in a chain from the outset or is misinterpreted during transmission through such a chain when initiated by people with vested interests. In particular, control of distribution circuits for cultural works favours – beyond hypothetical differences in quality or talent – the circulation of information about some products and not others. Such selection procedures lead to concentration of demand on some creative works and artists linked to increasing returns to adoption caused by information savings made on star products.

Imitation reducing qualitative uncertainty may function in conjunction with more conformist imitation. The utility in consuming a particular cultural product is all the greater when other individuals have already consumed the same product ('bandwagon effect'). Inversely, increasing returns to adoption may be restricted by snob effects leading to the rejection of overly promoted products ('snob effect').

In France these mimetic models were first applied in the field of visual arts.[32] The economics of the *star system* was studied more systematically by Benhamou.[33] Adopting the main analyses explaining the strong segmentation of artistic markets and employment, she found many examples in the musical field explaining how natural hierarchies of talent are emphasized and distorted by market mechanisms.

This research naturally led to the question of markets' ability to ensure diversity in cultural productions and consumption, given that increasing returns to adoption

---

[31]   Louis Lévy-Garboua and Claude Montmarquette, 'A Microeconometric Study of Theatre Demand', *Journal of Cultural Economics,* 20/1 (1996): pp. 25–50; 'Demand', in Ruth Towse (ed.), *A Handbook of Cultural Economics* (London, 2003), pp. 201–13.

[32]   For an overview see Nathalie Moureau and Dominique Sagot-Duvauroux, *Le Marché de l'art contemporain*, (Paris, 2006).

[33]   Françoise Benhamou, *Économie du star system* (Paris, 2002).

leads to self-reinforcing phenomena of leading positions for products or countries (see part 2 above).

Mimetic behaviours concentrate demand on specific works, which in turn, leads to strong inequalities in income, since artists are paid more in reflection of the success of their creations than according to the time they spend working. In a project-based economy, such inequalities exist in conjunction with irregular periods of employment. Analysis of the cultural employment market has produced much research in France, notably due to the particular nature of the unemployment benefit system in place for people working in the arts, but such research avoids dealing specifically with musicians' income. The pioneering article by P.-M. Menger,[34] merging economics and sociology, conducted a detailed analysis of the particularities of the artistic employment market in a risk-based economy (*star system*, recruitment by peer recommendation, multiple employers). Star system economics has thus been the subject of much detailed research.[35] The crisis of the unemployment benefit system for occasional workers specific to France in the late 1990s gave impetus to research into such issues. The opportunistic behaviour of agents, the pernicious effects of government intervention which tend to increase the supply of employment without a parallel increases in markets and funding, were criticized at the same time as the artistic employment market and the social welfare systems associated with it, often presented as forerunners of 'flexicurity'.[36]

Very recently, the issue of conflicts between right to employment and right to intellectual property has captured the attention of researchers (primarily in the legal and economic spheres) who work on artistic employment markets. Insufficient harmonization between these two rights and ambiguity in the border area between royalties and salaries encourages opportunistic arbitration in the choice of method of remuneration, favouring royalties which involve little in terms of social charges but which allow fewer rights for artists (notably concerning unemployment) than salaries.[37]

4. The 2000s: What Business Models for the Music Sector?

Until the 2000s, the economics of culture and, more precisely, the economics of music attracted little interest in academia. However, as new concepts of knowledge-

---

[34]   Pierre-Michel Menger, 'Rationalité et incertitude de la vie d'artiste', *L'année sociologique*, 39 (1989).

[35]   Benhamou, *Économie*.

[36]   Pierre-Michel Menger, *Portrait de l'artiste en travailleur* (Paris, 2002).

[37]   Francine Labadie and François Rouet, 'Régulation du travail artistique', *Culture Prospective* (Paris, 2007): p. 20; Françoise Benhamou and Dominique Sagot–Duvauroux, *La Place du droit d'auteur dans la rémunération de la création artistique, une synthèse* (Paris, 2007), p. 16.

based economics, the digital economy or the information economy emerged, cultural activities became favoured areas in which research teams specializing in industrial economics, international economics and the economy of law began to operate. The publication of Varian and Shapiro's book[38] on the information economy as well as that by Caves[39] on the creative industries renovated the tools used by economists in analysing cultural markets. Similarly, research into the two-sided markets characteristic of the media industry where services are sold both to clients and from clients to advertisers, found new fields to investigate.[40] Concurrently, institutional royalty mechanisms appeared ill-adapted in this new economy, leading economists to focus on issues concerning the economic bases of royalties. In this perspective, music became a pertinent research field for studying industrial developments of an economics of digitalized knowledge.

4.1. A Digital Economics of Music

In the same way that the record crisis led to much research into the music sector in the 1980s, the digital revolution radically transformed methods of promoting music and stimulated research based upon the vast theoretical corpus on network economics. Whilst 'existing' economists actively participated in these debates, they faced new competition from network specialists. This was the case for the Cerna research team supervised by Olivier Bomsel[41] as well as the Cnam team led by Nicolas Curien, who from 2000 began work in the field of cultural industries; Curien and Moreau's book devoted to the recording industry[42] constitutes a perfect example of this. Market structure, dynamics of demand, and new business models all formed topics for analysis with contributions from the information and network economics. Difficulties in selling music in physical format favour experiments with new business models encouraged notably by the arrival of new stakeholders from the telecommunications and internet sectors. Bourreau et al.,[43] identified five scenarios ranging from the continued use of existing promotion models by the multiplication of technical protection measures, to models based on free content promoted by the sale of by-products and services, as well as models aimed at targeted clients enabling commercialization over a longer period of a diverse repertoire (long tail), or even by models in which online user communities play

[38]   Carl Shapiro, *Économie de l'information* (Brussels).

[39]   Richard Caves, *Creative Industries: Contracts Between Art and Commerce* (Harvard, 2000).

[40]   Jean Gabzewicz and Nathalie Sonnac, *L'Industrie des médias* (Paris, 2006).

[41]   See Olivier Bomsel, Anne-Gaëlle Geffroy and Gilles Le Blanc, *When Internet Meets Entertainement – the Economics of Digital Media Industries* (Paris, 2006).

[42]   Nicolas Curien and François Moreau, *L'Industrie du disque* (Paris, 2006).

[43]   Marc Bourreau, Michel Gensollen and François Moreau, 'Musique enregistrée et numérique: quels scénarios d'évolution de la filière?', *Culture Prospective*, 1 (2007): p. 16.

a structuring role in the supply of music and creation of fame by the propaganda effects of meta-information allowed by networks. The new role of consumers appears for Chantepie and Le Diberder[44] as the next significant trend affecting cultural sectors whose activities tend to become circular.

Brousseau and Feledziack[45] describe the radical changes created by new technologies in the music sector, analyse the development of contractual relationships between various agents in the sector and highlight changes in power relationships which now favour agents at the lower end of the chain following from the new roles of internet and telecommunications giants. Although the ability of music to generate added value continues to grow, it is in fact the position of producers and distributors which is increasingly undermined.

Further still, much research has developed into questions raised by free availability of music online. Bomsel[46] compared free music online to a Trojan Horse, whilst others consider free music as the emergence of a new largely un-commercial economy organized notably around creative common licences. These considerations bring us to the questions raised by digitization for royalty payment systems.

4.2. An Economic Analysis of Royalties and Copyrights

Following the pioneering experience of Napster, development of online 'Peer to Peer' networks has favoured large-scale piracy of musical works, destabilizing the music economy. This transformation led to much research in France into royalties in the digital age exploring the economic bases of royalties and copyrights. Two competing conceptions initially existed: that of royalties as a natural property right of authors over their creations – the basis of the French system – and, secondly, that of royalties as a social agreement guaranteeing simultaneously interests of both authors and society, on the basis of the Anglo-Saxon copyright system.[47] On this basis, Farchy[48] investigated the possibilities of adapting institutional royalties mechanisms in line with developments in the practices of cultural consumption online and respecting requirements to make culture available to the widest

---

[44] Philippe Chantepie and Alain Le Diberder, *Révolution numérique et industries culturelles* (Paris, 2005).

[45] Eric Brousseau and Barabara Feledziack, *Étude sur l'économie des droits d'auteurs dans le domaine de la musique* (Paris, 2007).

[46] Olivier Bomsel, *Gratuit, du déploiement de l'économie numérique* (Paris, 2007).

[47] Dominique Sagot-Duvauroux, *La propriété intellectuelle, c'est le vol! Les majorats littéraires de Proudhon et autres textes choisis et présentés by Dominique Sagot-Duvauroux* (Paris, 2002); 'La propriété intellectuelle, c'est le vol! le débat sur le droit d'auteur au milieu du xixe siècle', *L'économie politique*, 22 (April 2004): pp. 34–52; 'Quel modèle économique pour les scènes de musiques actuelles', *Copyright Volume!* (2005): pp. 15–24.

[48] Joëlle Farchy, *Internet et le droit d'auteur, la culture Napster* (Paris, 2003).

audiences. Rochelandet[49] studied the effectiveness of collective management methods for royalties given that technology makes individual management increasingly difficult. Benhamou and Farchy[50] summarize new developments in the economy of intellectual property rights applied to culture and conclude on the need to avoid exaggerated conflict between existing legal mechanisms and calls for their radical review, and suggest that current practices will gradually evolve.

These reflections naturally led to the issue of remuneration of artistic creativity. What is the relative importance of various methods of remunerating artists (salaries, royalties, commercial profit, non-commercial profit, etc.) in cultural sectors and how are emerging models challenging contractual relations between partners in various branches? Within a research programme initiated by the Ministry of Culture on the importance of royalties in remunerating artistic creation,[51] Brousseau and Feledziack[52] analysed the development of contractual relationships between various stakeholders in the sector and attempted to describe the sharing of added value in the music sector. Nevertheless, far too little is known about how the division of added value in the music sector is affected by changing models of remuneration.

Conclusion

This chapter has aimed to show how academic economists have analysed the economics of music. Focusing on academic studies, our survey arguably does not provide enough discussion of research undertaken by specialist bodies working on contemporary music such as *Irma* or the *Observatoire de la musique*.

The contemporary period has been characterized by the convergence of two major research traditions in the economic study of culture, these being firstly the analysis of the bases for state intervention, and secondly the industrial economics of culture, which intersect through the dematerialization of musical products and their consequent transformation into what economists call collective goods. At the end of its industrial revolution, since reproduction costs are zero, the economics of music represents an exciting field for research into what could be an economy in which products, once they exist, are available free of charge.

One of the major challenges for the future for stakeholders in the sector, and notably for creators and artists, will be to find ways of capturing value which is

---

[49]   Fabrice Rochelandet, *Propriété intellectuelle et changement technologique, la mise en œuvre du droit d'auteur dans les industries culturelles*, Doctoral thesis, Paris 1 University (2000).

[50]   Françoise Benhamou and Joëlle Farchy, *Droit d'auteur et copyright* (Paris, 2007).

[51]   See Françoise Benhamou and Dominique Sagot-Duvauroux, *La Place du droit d'auteur dans la rémunération de la création artistique, une synthèse* (Paris, 2007): p. 16.

[52]   Eric Brousseau and Barbara Feledziack, *Étude sur l'économie des droits d'auteurs dans le domaine de la musique* (Paris, 2007).

becoming, to paraphrase Yves Michaud, '*gaseous*'. The added value created by music largely overspills the traditional music sector, for example in the influence it has on the stock listing of companies whose success relies on the distribution of cultural content. Future research should be undertaken to measure the extent of the leaks in added value of this kind and to redefine the rules governing the way in which added value is divided.

Chapter 8

Mediation of Popular Music in the UK

J. Mark Percival

This chapter discusses mediation of popular music and presents a critical summary of academic approaches to the analysis of that process in the UK. I will be considering the three mass media most closely associated with the filtering, transmission and criticism of popular music, that is, print media, television and radio. All of these follow the traditional model of one-to-many dissemination of information which is fundamental to both their industrial structure and to the ways in which the production and consumption of popular music is constrained by the process of mediation.

Negus identifies three senses in which the term 'mediation' is used in cultural studies. These are:

1. the idea of coming in between, or of intermediary action;
2. a means of transmission, an agency that comes in between reality and social knowledge;
3. the idea that all objects, particularly works of art, are mediated by social relationships.[1]

Applying these definitions to popular music, Negus suggests that the first refers to the practices of all those individuals that work between the production and consumption of popular music and includes record industry employees (in various different departments, from talent-spotting in A&R, to marketing), DJs, journalists, television programme makers, copyright revenue collection agencies and retailers. Negus's second sense of 'mediation' refers to the use of various media technologies in the transmission of popular music, and of discourse around popular music. This includes print, broadcasting, the moving image, music carriers (records, CDs and so on) and networking technologies. His final definition draws on the Marxist tradition of cultural criticism, and is the mediation of social relationships – how power and influence in relationships affects the creation and interpretation of cultural objects. My approach in this chapter draws on all three of Negus's mediations and addresses print, television and radio as the prisms through which popular music is created, consumed and understood.

It is not yet clear how 'new' media have genuinely transformed the processes of mediation discussed in this chapter. Certainly digital file sharing is having some

---

[1] Keith Negus, *Popular Music in Theory: An Introduction* (Cambridge, 1996), p. 66.

impact on production and consumption of popular music but it is often difficult to see clearly through the arguments made by groups with vested interests, such as rights holders or those whose ideological position is that all culture should be free of charge.[2] In any case, digital file sharing is really just a more efficient way of doing something music fans, or those who intentionally breach copyright for profit (so-called 'pirates'), have been doing for years. Similarly, web-based fanzines, discussion groups, and social networking services are new ways of doing old things – sharing information and talking about music. Digital media impinge on existing mass media in the as-live distribution of content. This is often referred to as webcasting, and is distinct from downloading or sharing of media files like songs or music videos. Radio and television are available in the UK through digital terrestrial and satellite broadcasting, and through the internet (the last of which allows print media also to have a digital presence). For radio and television this introduces novel elements like viewing or listening on demand, and for print media an opportunity to update content in something approaching real time. As interesting as these developments are (and I do not underestimate their potential long-term cultural, social and economic impact), they do not change the fundamental relationship between mass media and popular music. Indeed, as potential musical choices proliferate, the processes and practices of mass mediation may become even more important to popular music culture.

As far as possible, I focus on studies that address mediation of popular music in the UK, but the influence of the United States on the production and mediation of popular music in Britain (and vice-versa) is inescapable. The most significant difference between the US and the UK in broadcasting is the presence of the publicly-funded BBC as a powerful, national cultural institution which has no real equivalent in the US and the significance of this will be addressed in more detail in the section on radio. The print media industry in Britain, on the other hand, is an overwhelmingly private sector enterprise and has more in common with the press in North America, particularly in terms of writing about popular music.[3] This has implications in any consideration of British rock criticism – Lindberg et al. suggest that in the period from the mid-1960s to the late 1970s there were successive waves of influence in writing about popular music moving both east and west across the Atlantic.[4] As the oldest technology addressed in this chapter (and one perhaps with a relatively late developing relationship with popular music discourse), I will begin my discussion of mediation and pop with the printed word.

---

[2]   See for a useful account of the issues Kembrew McLeod, 'MP3s are Killing Home Taping: The Rise of Internet Distribution and its Challenge to the Major Label Music Monopoly', *Popular Music and Society*, 28/4, (2005): pp. 521–31.

[3]   Jane Stokes and Anna Reading (eds), *The Media in Britain* (Basingstoke, 1999).

[4]   Ulf Lindberg, et al., *Rock Criticism from the Beginning* (Oxford, 2005).

Print Media

Shuker identifies a number of areas of the print media in which popular music is addressed, all of which are relevant to any discussion of the press and music in the UK.[5] These areas include music fan publications (fanzines), the specialist music press (weekly and monthly), and specialist coverage in generalist publications (newspapers and magazines).

Although these have many features in common, each serves a particular place in a segmented market, in which journalism becomes collapsed into, and often indistinguishable from, music industry publicity. Despite this symbiosis, popular music critics continue to function as significant gatekeepers and as arbiters of taste.[6]

Fanzines have largely (though not completely) been supplanted by web-based publishing, but the UK specialist music press appears to be relatively stable in a period of overall decline in the periodical market.[7] Popular music coverage in generalist sources (particularly 'quality' daily and weekly newspapers) has also steadily increased in the last decade. A useful example of this is the launch by the quality Sunday newspaper *The Observer* of a monthly music supplement in October 2003.[8] There is nevertheless remarkably little literature addressing popular music and the printed word. Notable exceptions include Jones's edited collection of papers[9] and Lindberg et al.'s thorough historical analysis of rock criticism.[10] One of the key recurrent themes of the latter is the work done by rock journalists and critics in helping to shape notions of taste and practices of consumption.

In seeking to understand how music journalism interacts with popular music culture, many academics choose to examine the texts and practices of music journalists. This approach reflects the first of Negus's three classes – to understand the processes of mediation, it is necessary to study the mediators. I have no serious methodological objections to this, indeed it is a strategy I use in my own work on music radio and much of the most instructive work in popular music studies as a field is in the close analysis of the working practices of musicians, or of musical texts themselves. Where it may become problematic is when the valorization of key music journalists may obscure the very processes the research seeks to investigate. My reservation is that in the decisions made about which journalists

[5]   Roy Shuker, *Understanding Popular Music* (London, 2nd edition 2001).

[6]   Ibid., p. 98.

[7]   MediaTel (2007), ABC (Audit Bureau of Circulation) consumer magazine round-up: music magazine circulation, January–June 2007. Online at http://www.mediatel.co.uk/abcroundup/2007/08/article08.cfm. Accessed 21 August 2007.

[8]   Caspar Llewellyn-Smith, Editor's letter *Observer Music Monthly*, 1 (September 2003).

[9]   Steve Jones (ed.), *Pop Music and the Press* (Philadelphia, 2002).

[10]   Lindberg, et al., *Rock Criticism from the Beginning*.

to study, critical academic work tends to re-enforce established, popular notions of the canonic.[11]

Jones cites Wyatt and Hull's survey, which confirms anecdotal notions about the middle-class, degree-educated, 30-something character of the majority of (American) music critics.[12] Jones notes also that until the growth of print media coverage of rap and hip hop, most musics originally associated with black musicians (jazz, blues, and so on) was by white critics. Similarly, there have been few women involved in mainstream popular music criticism, either as journalists or as the subjects of serious discussion.[13] According to Jones, Wyatt and Hull also found that there are relatively few negative reviews of records or performances, and they suggest that this probably reflects either a lack of a rigorous critical approach or the power of critics to choose what they review (implying that critics prefer to review music that they are already predisposed to like).

Lindberg et al., focus on rock criticism as a subset of all writing about popular music. In their work, rock criticism resides in reviews, long-form interviews, debates and essays, but not in news or purely descriptive writing. They also clearly differentiate between *criticism* in print, and *mediation* by radio and television, neither of which contains much in the way of explicit critical discourse.[14] Their work traces a narrative of rock criticism which sees the emergence of a serious critical attitude to rock in the UK in the mid-1960s, and through parallel but nationally specific processes in the US. They suggest that the US approach fed into a developing British rock critique, at least until punk arrived in early 1976 at which point rock criticism in the UK diverged from the 'ruling critical orthodoxy' of the US.[15] The historic relationships in the development of Anglo-US popular music and writing about pop are indeed as significant as Lindberg et al., suggest, but there is a relatively small body of work which focuses only on UK music writing. This may be in part due to greater numbers of scholars working in popular music studies in the US, but I suspect it is also related to some of the characteristics of US rock criticism identified by Lindberg – the formation of a canon of writers and an orthodoxy of seriousness which leads to a focus on journalist-as-artist, rather than journalism-as-field (the latter in the general sense of academic study, but also to a degree as a Bourdieu-informed field of cultural production).

Jones cites Shuker's argument that popular music critics exert less influence on consumption of music than do literary or drama critics, in their respective fields.

---

[11]   See, for example, Steve Jones and Kevin Featherly, 'Re-viewing Rock Writing: Narratives of Popular Music Criticism', in Steve Jones (ed.), *Pop Music and the Press* (Philadelphia, 2002), pp. 19–40.

[12]   Steve Jones, 'The Intro: Popular Music, Media and the Written Word', in Jones, ibid., pp. 1–15.

[13]   Holly Kruse, 'Abandoning the Absolute: Transcendence and Gender in Popular Music Discourse', in Jones, ibid., p. 135.

[14]   Lindberg et al., *Rock Criticism from the Beginning*, pp. 7–8.

[15]   Lindberg et al., ibid., p. 9.

Shuker suggests that this is because *hearing* a piece of music is more affecting than reading about it. Jones adds that the levels of commitment in terms of time or money associated with consuming literature and theatre tend to encourage use of the critical review as consumer guide (although it is also true that popular music album review pieces are very much part of a music fan's buying guide). Frith develops Shuker's argument and suggests that music journalism has shaped notions of, and discourse about genre in music, despite a readership representing a relatively small part of the music market.[16] So, if reading pop and rock criticism is an activity confined to a minority of the music market (a minority of which however includes, as Frith suggests, musicians and other journalists), that thus leaves the broadcast media as the channels through which the greater part of the music market sees, hears and judges popular music.

Television

Since MTV's 1981 launch in the United States[17] there has been a growing body of academic work on music video. A series of studies in the 1980s and early 1990s developed debates in music video in terms of industry and culture, with good examples from Abt on the growing significance of visuals in popular music,[18] Frith on video pop as a cultural phenomenon,[19] and Kaplan on the semiotics of music video.[20] Later authors address specific issues of music video form and content: Vernallis on Madonna,[21] Björnberg on the interaction of music and image in music video,[22] and Rodger on gender and music video.[23]

Popular music is frequently used in television as a soundtrack to material not directly related to the music itself. Useful studies in this area include the

---

[16]   Simon Frith, 'The Popular Music Industry', in Simon Frith, Will Straw and John Street (eds), *The Cambridge Companion to Pop and Rock* (Cambridge, 2001), p. 40.

[17]   Geoffrey P. Hull, *The Recording Industry* (London, 2nd edition 2004).

[18]   Dean Abt, 'Music Video: Impact of the Visual Dimension', in James Lull (ed.), *Popular Music and Communication* (London, 1987), pp. 96–111.

[19]   Simon Frith, 'Video Pop', in Simon Frith (ed.), *Facing the Music* (London, 1988), pp. 88–130.

[20]   E. Ann Kaplan, *Rocking Around the Clock: Music Television, Postmodernism and Consumer Culture* (London, 1987).

[21]   Carol Vernallis, 'The Aesthetics of Music Video: An Analysis of Madonna's "Cherish"', *Popular Music*, 17/2 (1998): pp. 153–85.

[22]   Alf Björnberg, 'Structural Relationships of Music and Images in Music Video', in Richard Middleton, *Reading Pop: Approaches to Textual Analysis in Popular Music* (Oxford, 2000), pp. 347–82.

[23]   Gillian Rodger, 'Drag, Camp and Gender Subversion in the Music Videos of Annie Lennox', *Popular Music*, 24/1 (2004): pp. 17–30.

investigation of music as documentary soundtrack,[24] music as television channel branding,[25] and the use of music in youth programming.[26]

Specialist popular music programming also features as part of generalist television broadcasting on most of the principal national British terrestrial analogue and digital television networks, the most important of which are the publicly-funded BBC1, BBC2 and BBC3, and the commercial sector networks ITV1 and Channel 4. There has been significant historical work in this area from Hawes on the seminal Manchester-based 1970s music show, *So It Goes*,[27] Hill on British television's coverage of, and use of popular music in the 1950s,[28] and Fryar on the period 1960–85, anchored around the BBC's long-running pop show, *Top of the Pops* (1964–2006).[29]

Shuker suggests that music video's emphasis of the visual in pop is merely a return to a norm of music consumption in which the audio and the visual are united, having spent most of the twentieth century separated by dissemination on disc and radio.[30] Negus agrees that 'for centuries music has been associated with performance and spectacle' and that the apparent separation of sound and image in the early years of the record industry was indeed temporary.[31] That separation was also to an extent illusory – music on vinyl records (later also audio cassette and CD) was usually accompanied by photographs or other images of the recording artists. There were moving images too: the jukebox-based antecedent of the music video, 'Soundies' were film clips of popular artists performing contemporary hits. Over 2000 such clips were produced and distributed between 1940 and 1947, and were significant in the dissemination of black music styles like jazz and R&B.[32]

Despite the long association between popular music and the visual, the relationship between pop and television has not been historically straightforward. Shuker identifies an early conflict between the values associated with popular music and television from the 1950s onwards. The former (as rock music in particular) connoting taste, difference and individuality; the latter (as family entertainment)

---

[24]   John Corner, 'Sounds Real: Music and Documentary', *Popular Music*, 21/3 (2002): pp. 357–66.

[25]   Mark Brownrigg and Peter Meech, 'From Fanfare to Funfair: The Changing Sound World of UK Television Idents', *Popular Music*, 21/3 (2002): pp. 345–55.

[26]   Karen Lury, *British Youth Television* (Oxford, 2001).

[27]   Steve Hawes, 'I Was There: Putting Punk on Television', in Andrew Blake (ed.), *Living through Pop* (London, 1999), pp. 51–62.

[28]   John Hill, 'Television and Pop: The Case of the 1950s', in John Corner (ed.), *Popular Television in Britain* (London, 1991), pp. 90–107.

[29]   Paul Fryer, '"Everybody's on Top of the Pops": Popular Music on British Television 1960–1985', *Popular Music and Society*, 21/3 (1997): pp. 153–71.

[30]   Shuker, *Understanding Popular Music*, p. 175.

[31]   Keith Negus, *Popular Music in Theory: An Introduction* (Cambridge, 1996), p. 87.

[32]   Amy Herzog, 'Discordant Visions: The Peculiar Musical Images of the Soundies Jukebox Film', *American Music*, 22/1 (2004): pp. 27–39.

predicated on a homogeneous audience in which differences of class, gender and ethnicity collapse.[33] Similarly, Frith characterizes the relationship between pop (and particularly rock) and television as uneasy. Television is perceived as central to promotional campaigns and the creation of stars, and it is implicated in shaping the social meaning of popular music. Yet music has never been a central strand of television programming because the television audience is not often understood to be a *music* audience.[34]

Frith notes the significance of television in the careers of the early rockers and the role that the medium played in breaking Elvis Presley (and others) in the 1950s as national stars in the US. It was not however until 1980s and MTV that television began to develop a relationship with the record industry that came close to that of its symbiosis with music radio. Frith builds on his argument with a number of examples, but the most convincing of these is the positioning of rock as *anti-television*. Rock and roll was widely associated with radio and with youth, just as television was replacing radio as mainstream domestic family entertainment – rock (and radio) represented rebellion and television represented conformity. Frith quotes a moment in American television history when Syd Barrett, the then leader of Pink Floyd, refused to lip synch with a recording of their then hit record during a television performance in 1967. It was a refusal to accept the conventions of the mainstream, which was also very much in keeping with the singer-guitarist's increasingly erratic behaviour. It nevertheless signified a moment of rock authenticity in opposition to the perceived fakeness of television. From a different perspective, television here works to reinforce rock's own construction of itself as oppositional, by giving it something (else) to oppose. Many years later Kurt Cobain of Nirvana, appearing in 1991 for the first time on the BBC's *Top Of The Pops*, not only insisted on singing live, but sang the verse in a gothically deep register and the chorus in a style similar to that of former Smiths vocalist Morrissey. The performance bore little resemblance to the polished studio recording of *Smells Like Teen Spirit*, but was nonetheless astonishing.[35] Not only does television here once again provide a context in which rock can demonstrate its 'authenticity', this example also supports Frith's concluding argument that 'to be *television*, music must not only be visualised but given a sense of occasion' (my emphasis).[36]

Radio

As in television, popular music is used in many ways on radio: as programme theme music, station branding, soundtracks to drama and documentaries, and most

---

[33]   Shuker, *Understanding Popular Music*, p. 181.

[34]   Simon Frith, 'Look! Hear! The Uneasy Relationship of Music and Television', *Popular Music*, 21/3 (2002): pp. 277–90.

[35]   A performance available at the time of writing on YouTube.com.

[36]   Frith, 'Look! Hear!', p. 288.

importantly as the primary content of music radio. The relationship between music radio and the record industry is often characterized as symbiotic, but as Frith points out, that notion conceals a more complex situation:

> ... radio needed music to attract its audiences, and the cheapest source of music supply was recordings; record companies needed radio play to reach its markets (and the rights income from radio play was itself substantial). But while the record and radio industries thus served each other's interests, it is not the case that their interests are identical.[37]

Frith argues that the *audiences* radio stations want are not always the same as the *market* that record companies want to reach, and that the record industry has tended to adapt its output to suit the needs of radio. The presence of the BBC has introduced the notion of popular music radio programming as public service, which has had some distinctive consequences for pop in Britain.[38]

Popular music on radio in the UK has a history which is dominated by the BBC as a cultural institution, but which is also constrained by government policy, regulation and the ideological constructs of 'public service' and 'free market'. Much recent public debate about radio in the UK, played out in the media pages of the quality daily newspapers and in reports generated by the UK communications sector regulator Ofcom, are most concerned with the apparent conflict evident in a radio market where a publicly-funded institution competes for audiences with commercial organizations whose interests are primarily those of their shareholders. British academics often therefore focus on policy studies, somewhat at the expense of radio-as-text, or as a cultural-economic force (for example Ofcom 2007a).[39] There has nevertheless been some excellent work in developing radio theory from a number of perspectives: journalism;[40] drama;[41] analogue and digital media.[42] There are also some significant studies of music radio, the most important of which include Barnard's history of UK music radio,[43] Chapman's account of the offshore 'pirate' radio stations of 1964–68,[44] and Hendy on the issues raised by

---

[37]   Frith, ibid., p. 40.

[38]   David Hendy, 'Pop Music Radio in the Public Service: BBC Radio 1 and New Music in the 1990s' *Media, Culture and Society*, 22/6 (2000): pp. 743–61.

[39]   Ofcom (Office of Communications) (2007), *Communications in the Next Decade.* http://www.ofcom.org.uk/-research/commsdecade (accessed 15 July 2007).

[40]   Tim Crook, *International Radio Journalism; History, Theory and Practice* (London, 1998).

[41]   Tim Crook, *Radio Drama: Theory and Practice* (London, 1999).

[42]   Jo Tacchi, 'The Need for Radio Theory in the Digital Age', *International Journal of Cultural Studies*, 3/2 (2000): pp. 289–98.

[43]   Stephen Barnard, *On the Radio: Music Radio in Britain* (Milton Keynes, 1989).

[44]   Robert Chapman, *Selling the Sixties: The Pirates and Pop Music Radio* (London, 1992).

the success of BBC Radio 1 and BBC Radio 2 as publicly-funded music radio stations.[45] The comparative lack of research on and around music radio seems all the more surprising when one considers the extent to which radio is a part of everyday life,[46] not just in the UK, but globally.

Music radio is important, because *radio* is important. Second quarter listening figures for radio in 2007 suggest that 91 per cent of the adult population of the UK regularly listens to radio – that is 45,621,000 individuals listening for an average of over 23 hours per week. The BBC's share of that is 54.3 per cent of all listening. More importantly for the discussion in this section, the Corporation's national popular music networks together have 25.9 per cent of all radio listening – Radio 1 with 10.3 per cent and Radio 2 with 15.6 per cent.[47] All UK commercial listening is 43.5 per cent, but this is shared between 332 stations, both analogue and digital. Of those stations the majority (324) are local or regional[48] and popular music or music-led formats overwhelmingly dominate, with 86 per cent of commercial listening.[49] The pervasiveness of radio has (and has had) far reaching implications for the production and consumption of popular music, and in particular, the *sounds* of popular music.

Negus considers the mediating role of radio to have emerged early in its history:

> ... as radio became a *mediator* between the worlds of the listener and the activity of the musicians, publishers and recording companies, so radio broadcasting began to have an important impact on the distribution of musical knowledge, styles and preferences.[50]

Music radio, argues Negus, worked to change the organization of the record industry – hit songs were UK *national* hit songs, in contrast to pre-radio *regional* sheet music hits, dependent on the ability of sheet music pluggers to move around the country, promoting those songs to local dance bands. There was an increased emphasis on the 'hook', the most catchy, memorable part of a song – normally, but not always, the song title in a vocal chorus. If listeners could remember the title of a song, they could buy it.[51]

---

[45]   Hendy, 'Popmusic Radio'.

[46]   Paddy Scannell, 'Public Service Broadcasting and Modern Life', *Media, Culture and Society*, 11/2 (1989): pp. 135–66.

[47]   RAJAR (Radio Joint Audience Research) (2007), http://www.rajar.co.uk/listening/quarterly_listening.php (accessed 15 August 2007).

[48]   Ofcom (Office of Communications) (2007), *The Communications Market 2007.* http://www.ofcom.org.uk/-research/cm/cmr07/cm07_print, p.193 (accessed 18 August 2007).

[49]   Ofcom (Office of Communications) (2007), ibid., p. 199.

[50]   Negus, *Popular Music in Theory*, p. 77.

[51]   Negus, ibid., p. 79.

There is, as with television and print media, an Anglo-US tension in academic studies of music radio. The genealogy of British music radio (and to a degree, of music radio elsewhere in Europe) means that much of its sound and style is derived from US hit radio formats of the 1950s and 1960s.[52] This might (erroneously) imply that the conclusions of American studies of music radio can be applied without reservation to UK music radio. 'The sounds', however, as Frith puts it, 'of the two countries' pop radio stations are quite different'.[53] There are a number of significant differences in the historical development of the industries on opposing sides of the Atlantic, not least of which is the role of public funding in broadcasting – the BBC had a monopoly on legal radio broadcasting in the UK from 1922–73,[54] whilst mainstream US radio was entirely commercial from the 1920s until the low-key, low-budget launch of part-federally-funded National Public Radio (NPR) in 1970.[55] Music radio in the UK is thus characterized by the apparently opposing poles of the BBC and commercial radio, with the BBC in 2007 holding the balance of the audience overall.

There are several important social histories addressing UK radio broadcasting (and so popular music on radio), the most comprehensive of which is Briggs's five volume history of UK broadcasting, up to 1975.[56] In addition to the previously noted works focused on music radio, the music radio historian should also read Crisell,[57] Scannell and Cardiff,[58] and Lewis and Booth.[59]

Barnard's work clearly shows that popular music was far from absent from the BBC's radio schedules in the decades since the organization's establishment as a public corporation in 1927 by Royal Charter (having spent its first five years as a private company joint venture between the General Post Office and a number of radio equipment manufacturers).[60] What *was* missing though was US-style presentation (a single, improvising DJ) and content (large numbers of commercial records). The absence of DJ-led formats on BBC radio networks, at least until the 1967 reorganization that launched Radio 1 as a national pop network, was partly a result of a conservative institutional culture. It was also partly due to historical

---

[52]   Stephen Barnard, *Studying Radio* (London, 2000), pp. 126–7.

[53]   Frith, 'The Popular Music Industry', p. 41.

[54]   Barnard, *Studying Radio*, p. 57.

[55]   David H. Ostroff et al., *Perspectives on Radio and Television: Telecommunication in the United States* (Mahwah, NJ, 4th edition 1998), p. 66; p. 594.

[56]   Asa Briggs, *The History of Broadcasting in the United Kingdom, Volumes 1–5* (Oxford, 1995).

[57]   Andrew Crisell, *An Introductory History of British Broadcasting* (Abingdon, 2nd edition 2002).

[58]   Paddy Scannell and David Cardiff, *A Social History of British Broadcasting, Vol. 1* (Oxford, 1991).

[59]   Peter M. Lewis and Jerry Booth, *The Invisible Medium: Public, Commercial and Community Radio* (Basingstoke, 1989).

[60]   Barnard, *Studying Radio.*

restrictions on the amount of airtime the BBC could devote to records, so-called 'needle-time'. The needle-time limits were part of an agreement involving the BBC, Phonographic Performance Limited and the Musician's Union, designed to protect the interests of music copyright holders and of working musicians.[61] In the late 1950s and early 1960s, around 14 hours per week of commercially recorded music was permitted on the BBC's Light Programme network,[62] one of three national stations, the others being the speech-led Home Service and the high-culture Third Programme.[63] BBC needle-time restrictions continued well into the 1970s which had unpredicted (and culturally valuable) consequences.

One of those consequences was directly related to the small amount of airtime Radio 1 was able devote to commercially released records. In order to make up the shortfall in available popular music, the BBC recorded bands and solo performers in live, or mostly-live 'sessions', for which the BBC did not have to pay performance revenues to the PPL.[64] This pragmatic solution to filling airtime has produced a huge and valuable archive of recordings, many of which closely reflect the contemporary live sound of artists in a way that commercial releases did not. With the beginning of legal commercial radio broadcasting in the UK in 1973, the presence of session tracks helped Radio 1 to sound distinct from its Independent Local Radio (ILR) competitors, and 'distinctiveness' remains a central tenet of the BBC's Royal Charter.[65] Many archive session tracks have had subsequent commercial release and remain part of the BBC's distinctiveness, as regular features on its digital radio station, 6Music.

There have been several periods of expansion of UK commercial radio, of which most stations are music-led formats (as noted earlier). In the 1980s the Conservative government of Margaret Thatcher passed a series of Acts opening up the communications market to competition, with a resulting proliferation of commercial stations, both FM and AM. For radio, the government expected (or at least, *claimed* that they expected) competition to force the market to adapt to the needs and desires of listeners, providing more diversity and thus more choice. However, as Berland[66] and others have shown, commercial radio is about delivering audiences to advertisers, and the oligopolist commercial radio industry in the UK segments audiences according to their potential to attract the interest of advertisers. Consequently, as Barnard observes:

---

[61]   Barnard, *Studying Radio*, p. 26.

[62]   Robert Chapman, *Selling the Sixties: The Pirates and Pop Music Radio* (London, 1992), p. 23.

[63]   Crisell, *An Introductory History*, p. 67.

[64]   Ken Garner, *In Session Tonight* (London, 1993).

[65]   BBC, *Annual Report and Accounts 2006/2007: The BBC Executive's Review and Assessment* (London, 2007), p. 2.

[66]   Jody Berland, 'Radio, Space and Industrial Time: The Case of Music Formats' in Tony Bennett et al. (eds), *Rock and Popular Music: Politics, Policies, Institutions* (London, 1993), pp. 105–18.

... there tend to be yawning gaps in the audience profiles targeted by commercial
radio as a whole, and an overwhelming bias towards the 'economically active'
(i.e. the employed) ... commercial radio ... is led by focus group research and the
input of high-salaried consultants whose prime motivation is minimise risk.[67]

A consequence of this avoidance of risk tends to be a conservative repertoire of
songs and sounds which audience research suggests will be least likely to cause
listeners to switch stations.[68] In the UK, the mainstream commercial FM market
is differentiated much more significantly by geographical distribution of stations,
rather than by genre (as in the US) – most stations are variations on Contemporary
Hits Radio (CHR) or the increasingly popular '80s, 90s and Now' format. Driving
through the UK, from the Scottish Central Belt to the south coast of England will
yield a selection of relatively undifferentiated commercial stations playing many
of the same records, at around the same time of day. What then is the alternative
offered by the BBC?

Negus suggests that the BBC (as a public service broadcaster) tends to
reproduce the sounds and structures of commercial music radio, as a consequence
of pressure from record companies and competition from commercial stations.[69]
Hendy however argues that this was not the case for BBC Radio 1 in the 1990s,
and that, on the contrary, commercial radio has actually tended to adapt to the
BBC. Radio 1, according to Hendy, played new, regional sounds in daytime
programming and commercial radio followed as those sounds became established
in the mainstream.[70] As Radio 1 Music Policy Executive, Sarita Jagpal told me in
2005, 'For us it's not as simple as what makes a good radio record, because our job
at Radio 1 is to challenge the audience, to take risks with music'.[71]

If, as Hendy suggests, the BBC has the power to break new records and new
sounds, how does this affect the relationship between the BBC's national music
radio stations and the record industry? My own research suggests that Radio 1 and
in particular, Radio 2, have become actively involved in the production practices
of the record industry. Colin Martin, Head of Music at BBC Radio 2 (2000–2007)
took a direct approach to encouraging the record industry's interest in particular
styles of music, and types of artist:

I wanted to persuade record companies to release tracks, music, artists and to
try and develop them, because I knew instantly that would create for me what
would be my gold music in 5 or 10 years time. And that is what has happened.
Record companies have all got behind artists, and Radio 2 got so big that it was

---

[67]   Barnard, *Studying Radio*, p. 65.
[68]   Jarl A. Ahlkvist and Robert Faulkner, 'Will This Record Work For Us? Managing
Music Formats in Commercial Radio, *Qualitative Sociology*, 25/2 (2002): pp. 189–215.
[69]   Negus, *Popular Music in Theory*, pp. 82–3.
[70]   Hendy, 'Popmusic Radio', p. 760.
[71]   Personal interview with the author, London, 30 November 2005.

hard to ignore [the station]. Now a lot of record companies look to A&R product knowing that Radio 2 has a massive influence.[72]

The power of radio, BBC or commercial sector, to influence the production of popular music is unlikely to wane in the immediate future, despite the growth of new media. Andrew Harrison, chief executive of the UK commercial radio industries trade body, the Radio Centre, is bullish about the future of radio in general, and of commercial radio in particular. 'Radio', he says, 'is the only medium that can be consumed at the same time as the internet ... it's perfect for the digital age.'[73] So, as radio critic Zoë Williams puts it in The Guardian newspaper:

> Radio's popularity does not simply climb – it dovetails with new technology, so that, unlike television ... it can see web developments as a boon rather than a threat ... it does not just dominate the mainstream, it picks up new listeners, from new generations, listening in new ways.[74]

Conclusion

In this chapter I have briefly considered three mass media and their interaction with popular music sounds and culture. Negus is correct that any notion of mediation of popular music is an overlapping complex of social relations, technology and individual agency within organizations. These processes are evident in print media, television and most importantly music radio. The small numbers of individuals writing for the specialist music press, and the relatively small readership of those publications together have a disproportionate effect on the ways that we think about and consume popular music. The printed word shapes the narrative of popular music, its values, the ways in which its history is understood.

Mainstream television has had values and associations which contrast with much popular music. Rock and roll in the 1950s may not have been able to break as a national phenomenon in the US without it, yet television as a medium is about creating a large, relatively undifferentiated *mainstream* audience. Rock (and, to a degree, various forms of dance music, jazz and hip hop) represents rebellion and opposition (to a supposed mainstream), despite an intrinsic conservatism of form, content and intentionality. It is the tension between television and rock that often makes for the most compelling (and influential) broadcast events.

Music radio in the UK is by far the most likely conduit through which audiences consume popular music, because of, rather than in spite of the internet and other digital media channels. The pervasiveness of music radio in the UK

---

[72] Personal interview with the author, London, 30 November 2005.

[73] Simon Marquis, 'Commercial Radio's Evangelist', *The Guardian*, 27 August 2007.

[74] Zoe Williams, 'The New Listeners', *The Guardian*, 24 August 2007.

gives it power to shape and influence the practices of the record industry. When the BBC's public service role is played out on its national pop networks, Radio 1 and Radio 2, the consequences tend to be an emphasis on new sounds or new artists – the BBC's substantial presence in the radio market balances the tendency towards conservative programming of most mainstream commercial music radio.

Finally, in thinking about the material in this chapter, I find myself once again considering the essential interconnectedness of popular music culture and the mediations that shape our every encounter with rock, pop and dance music. It is impossible, in the end, to imagine an industrialized popular music culture without the music press, television and music radio, and the richness these media contribute to that culture.

Chapter 9
Music and the Media in France:
The Sociological Viewpoint

Hervé Glevarec

Over the last two decades, French sociology seems to have held back from the cultural industries, unlike economics, for example.[1] Perhaps this is due to a certain disdain inherited from post-war sociologists towards cultural industries seen as competitors of literary culture. Another reason may perhaps be that cultural industries make relationships increasingly complicated between production and reception, through their expansion and the money incentives involved, which upset existing institutional patterns, and complexify links between production and consumption as well as creation and consumers. The two major issues which continue to fuel French sociology regarding this subject are, firstly, the socio-economic relationship between actors within a given cultural field and, secondly, the cultural values which underpin their creations/products and their reception; that is to say, a sociological and economic issue and a moral/aesthetic issue. The relationships between music(s) and media(s) illustrate the relationship between culture and cultural industries and, therefore, bring us to consider the core intellectual ground and objects of the sociology and ideology of culture in a society such as France. Moreover, music and media are two practices and two professional spheres which have undergone exponential growth since 1945.

By way of comparison, let us consider the domain of contemporary art as Natalie Heinich still found it in the 1990s. Whilst the 'triple game of contemporary art' is pyramidal (viewers, observers, creators) and sequential (transgression, reaction, integration),[2] it is difficult to envisage musical relationships following these same partitions and structurings, characterizable by the term – in the case of contemporary art – of 'legitimization' (making people accept something new and 'radical'). We can note in passing that music termed 'contemporary' nowadays has such a marginal and specialized status that it can no longer be uniquely representative of *avant-gardism*, any more than Björk, Dominique A or The Divine Comedy are typical examples of the operation of the musical domain. In music,

---

[1]   Nathalie Coutinet and Dominique Sagot-Duvauroux, *Économie des fusions et acquisitions* (Paris, 2003); Françoise Benhamou, *L'Économie de la culture* (Paris, 2004); Xavier Greffe (ed.), *Création et diversité au miroir des industries culturelles* (Paris, 2006), pp. 353–72.

[2]   Nathalie Heinich, *Le Triple jeu de l'art contemporain* (Paris, 1998).

we find a segmented organization with a core activity of 'promotion' (introducing and gaining a following), and music is thus an important sector for helping us to understand such transformations. The particularity of the musical domain is, also, that critical texts emanate almost exclusively from the media (journalism) and not from academia. This is a specificity which distinguishes it from the world of the visual arts, for example.

Cultural industries are particularly marked by a crucial concept which fuels all points of view, from the most ordinary to the most learned, namely the pernicious and harmful role of the media, and even producers, on artists and consumers. We can thus understand the three major terms of thought on this subject in the supposed clash between creation, broadcasting and promotion: the 'good' (artists), the 'bad' (media and producers), and, between the two, the consumers (fooled and manipulated). But let us note, to refute this last point, that qualified socio-professional groups currently consume more so-called popular than classical music.[3] Ironically put, if upper socio-professional groups, notably those who are intellectuals and young, wish to continue their populist lamenting of the alienation of the working classes listening to Justin Timberlake on NRJ and/or Christophe Willen on Star Academy, they should themselves stop listening to Katerine, the Arctic Monkeys or Carla Bruni, and the many other artists of genre of music termed 'popular' (at least in the terminology of an outdated state of sociology).

Finally, we can say that the current period is illogical in terms of musical tastes, since although the cultural industries are implementing close 'control' of taste, they are also increasing the supply of products/tastes, and are thus favouring freedom of choice amidst increased abundance. Here we find the sociological issue raised by the 'musicalization' of daily life, notably the considerable place taken by music in current cultural practices.[4] The greater the diversity, the more difficult it will be to raise the question of who dictates taste ('radio stations do not set tastes because there are different tastes', I was told by a marketing manager from an independent label in 2007); and this begs the question regarding the recipient population. About whom are we talking, precisely? Young people who listen to radio and music channels or watch musical reality television? All the 20- and 30-year-olds who go to the hundreds of summer music festivals to listen to Sanseverino, Bénébar, Justice, Kaiser Chiefs, Rita Mitsouko, Kasabian, The Infadels, etc? Do they go because their tastes are prescribed? If so, through which mediators?

Of the actors in the musical domain, here we will only concern ourselves with those called 'mediators' (and demonstrate that such a term is problematic for

---

[3]   Hervé Glevarec, 'La fin du modèle classique de la légitimité culturelle. Hétérogénéisation des ordres de légitimité et régime contemporain de justice culturelle. L'exemple du champ musical', in Eric Maigret and Eric Macé (eds), *Penser les médiacultures. Nouvelles pratiques et nouvelles approches de la représentation du monde* (Paris, 2005), pp. 69–102.

[4]   BIPE/Deps, *Approche générationnelle des pratiques culturelles et médiatiques* (Paris, 2007).

sociology even slightly ethnographic in intent) and we shall limit ourselves to the period since the end of the 1980s. Moreover, our main focus is radio, which may be justified to some degree by its favoured position in relation to music, compared to the written press and television. To understand such a subject we shall use three approaches:

1. An historical and organizational approach since the 1980s – a period which marked the 'large shift' in tastes (when popular music became socially legitimate and, furthermore, dominant in portfolios of musical tastes).[5] This shift is in fact one that, since 1945, reflects change from an institutional system to a pluralist structure of music.
2. An analytical perspective: what model emerges from comparing the past and the present to characterize the current situation?
3. A theoretical perspective: what sociological models exist to explain relations between 'music and media'?

The Sociological Description of Agent Interplay in the Musical Field

The principal feature of the sociology of music, when it is not focusing on explaining musical tastes, or musical creativity, is that it considers the musical sphere as a multi-level and complex system of agents. The musical domain is neither an organization nor a profession; it is a group of actors, more or less divided into sectors or integrated in their roles. The most clearly comprehensible linear model of communication places artists and listeners at either ends of the chain, and in the centre – around the three primary roles of production, adding value and consumption – producers, editors and broadcasters. The linear model takes strength from the functional clarity of a system based on a hierarchy of agents[6] but does not consider properly processes of rationalization and control which may be retroactive and opportunistic. For instance, production companies and the media actively prospect, as much as they wait to receive, songs, album demos and artists. Furthermore, production companies adapt (because they cannot have in-house broadcasters) to their clients, for example releasing tracks in radio 'format'.[7]

As happened in the United States and England,[8] serious rock reviews developed in France from the mid-1960s. *Rock & Folk* was established in 1966, *Best* in 1968

---

[5] Olivier Donnat, *Les Français face à la culture: de l'exclusion à l'éclectisme* (Paris, 1994).

[6] Philippe Hirsch, 'Processing Fads and Fashions: An Organization-Set Analysis of Cultural Industry Systems', *American Journal of Sociology*, 77/4 (1972): pp. 639–59.

[7] Keith Negus, 'Plugging and Programming: Pop Radio and Record Promotion in Britain and the United States', *Popular Music*, 12/1 (1993): pp. 57–68.

[8] Ulf Lindberg et al. (eds), *Rock Criticism from the Beginning* (Oxford, 2005), and Mark Percival in this current volume.

with, as can be seen from their names, a strong Anglo-Saxon influence. Radio programming contributing to the spread of rock (*Salut les Copains*, *Le Pop Club*, *Dans le vent*, *Campus*) existed as early as the 1950s.[9] The 1980s saw significant modification of the impact of media in the musical field in the liberalization of a key audiovisual sector, FM music radio stations. Television (with shows such as *Les enfants du rock, H.I.P. H.O.P.*), the written press and radio swung towards increased promotion – central or peripheral to their programming – of primarily 'popular' music (*chanson*, rock, hip-hop).

Note about the Notion of 'Mediation' and 'Mediator'

The notion of mediation as understood in ordinary language meaning transmission and facilitation is problematic for sociology, as it is more an *a priori* theoretical concept than an ethnographically appropriate sociological term. Its recent re-elaboration by French sociology focuses on the 'networking' aspects rather than simple transmission of mediator activities.[10] It seems that Keith Negus, when writing about 'intermediaries' and 'mediators' in music, is not talking about mediation in its precise meaning as a passage between two terms (here production and consumption) but, on the contrary, rather discussing 'constructor' and 'construction'.[11] Whilst his analysis is ethnographically appropriate, the term 'mediation' is, paradoxically, poorly chosen to discuss this phenomenon.

The common approach to intermediation is usually formalistic and literally ignores the work dimensions and – particularly, let us insist – the professional ideologies of mediators.[12] Intermediaries are never just intermediate. Every intermediary wants, thinks and adds something more of and to what might be only mere mediation of a product/work already produced: the tv listings magazine *Télérama* aims at constructing a critical discourse, the trendy intellectual magazine *Les Inrockuptibles* a political and avant-garde discourse, Skyrock radio wants to *defend* a musical genre and its artists, TV channels TF1 and France 2 create musical reality television shows which are of their own making and not simply

[9]   Anne-Marie Gourdon (ed.), *Le Rock. Aspects esthétiques, culturels et sociaux* (Paris, 1994).

[10]   Antoine Hennion, *La Passion musicale. Une sociologie de la médiation* (Paris, 1993).

[11]   Keith Negus, 'Music Divisions: The Recording Industry and the Social Mediation of Popular Music', in James Curran (ed.), *Media Organisations in Society* (London, 2000), pp. 240–54.

[12]   Hervé Glevarec, 'Les producteurs de radio à France Culture, Journalistes', 'Intellectuels' ou 'Créateurs'?: de la définition de soi à l'interaction radiophonique', *Réseaux*, 86 (1997): pp. 13–38.

broadcasts of music videos etc. Intermediaries never describe their role as simple mediation or would accept such restriction.

The Impact of 'Mediators' on the Structure of the Musical Field

The major, recurring, issue in the musical domain is that of the 'harmful relationship' between content producers and broadcasters. The *Baptiste* report shows this regarding Radio.[13] This report shows the principal features of relations between partners operating in what is described as a 'struggle for power'. Simultaneous attempts made by both actors to control each other are evident, as record companies want broadcasters to be better matched to their timescales and products and radio stations want programming autonomy. 'Power travels', I was told by a marketing manager at an independent label on the issue of distribution seen from his point of view. It 'travels' because there is mutual dependence between two actors, one a producer of content dependent upon a radio station for its promotion, and the other a radio dependent upon the content producer for supplying quality programming. A radio playing a particular format depends on the popularity of the musical styles on which it focuses (for example, *dance* in the 2000s) in terms of numbers of records produced.

Record companies have marketing and promotion departments which construct strategies, in an environment where they are powerless, for managing the media. They may, for example, on the basis of a particular new album, prefer to send out different tracks to different media, depending on their type and musical sensitivity/ preference: a hip-hop track for one radio station, a *slam* track for another. Each medium is 'worked' depending upon the artist's 'position'. There are, therefore, privileged relationships between labels and certain media resulting from past partnerships and notably on past successes. For example, independent labels such as Tôt ou tard or Atmosphériques have privileged links with the generalist public radio station France Inter.[14] It must be understood that, repeatedly, radio producers and programmers do not – paradoxically, and contrary to commonsense – come across as great strategists. Their discourse inevitably centres on 'discovery', 'falling in love', 'artists': 'I have to like [an artist] before signing, if I don't then I just can't, even if I think it might work. But I have to have respect and esteem for what the guy does', states the managing director of a major label. Similarly, every artistic director for major or independent labels explains that labels have 'cultures'. This claimed 'culture of labels' may co-exist alongside opportunistic strategies, such as momentarily joining forces with reality TV. Indeed, the musical expertise of artistic directors could in future coexist alongside a 'test culture'

---

[13]   Eric Baptiste, *Rapport du groupe de travail sur les relations entre les radios et la filière musicale* (Paris, 2002).

[14]   For an overview, see annex 1, *Distribution of audience by type of label, quarterly average in 2006* in André Nicolas, *Indicateurs de la diversité musicale dans le paysage radiophonique* (Paris, 2007).

(testing new artists with a focus panel of listeners) as was implied by the director of EMI in 2008.

What is the share of the various actors, producers and broadcasters in the construction of discourses on musical aesthetics? The task of analysing the elaboration of musical genres, and the aesthetic and industrial strategies which underpin them is undoubtedly huge,[15] but this issue, like Poe's Purloined Letter before our unknowing eyes, is one of the most crucial features of the structuring of the musical world. Genres serve as musical and social reference points just as much for producers as for listeners. To do this, they need to crystallize an aesthetic and for musical agents to adopt them.

Limiting Uncertainty: Radio Formats

FM radio stations resulting from the freeing of the airwaves relatively quickly adopted the American model of rotating and structured playlists, the 'format', supposedly pleasing to listeners, more repetitive than vagabond in their fleeting pleasures and more coherent than eclectic in musical taste.[16] The implementation of the 'format' – one of the clearest manifestations of rationalization of musical programming on radio – led to standardization of running times for tracks broadcast (and anticipation of this in production) and to a stylistic tropism constantly in operation around passingly successful genres (rap, R&B, techno, boy bands, dance, groove, metal, tecktonik etc.). But 'format' has the collateral effect of generating differentiation; its initial movement of defining the parameters of a style is accompanied by promotion of competing 'formats' (as shown in the 2000s with the competition between electro, rap and rock formats).

The 'format' is a perfect example for discussing recent production forms in cultural industries and their nature as prototypes in a world of risk.[17] The 'format' is an industrial and professional invention by a cultural industry – radio – attempting to somehow control its reception. To do this, radio constructs a cultural object called a musical style and a representation of itself (NRJ as a radio evoking 'youth' and 'feeling good', Skyrock evoking feelings of 'being young', etc.). The error consists in believing that audiences are determined by formats, whereas these two objects and professional issues are autonomous.[18] Contrary to popular belief, radio stations do not construct their 'format' from an advertising objective; it constructs it from a 'format target'. As such, a radio station has a share of listeners which it

---

[15] David Hesmondhalgh, 'Indie: the aesthetics and institutional politics of a popular music genre', *Cultural Studies*, 13/1 (1999): pp. 34–61.

[16] Pete Fornatale and Josh Mills, *Radio in the Television Age* (New York, 1980).

[17] Marc Ménard, *Éléments pour une économie des industries culturelles* (Montréal, 2004).

[18] Antoine Hennion and Cécile Méadel, 'Programming Music: Radio as a Mediator', *Media, Culture and Society*, 8/3 (1986): pp. 281–303.

sells but which it does not consider when establishing its musical radio 'format' (see Figure 9.1).

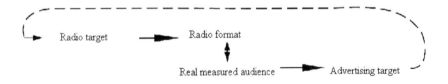

Figure 9.1 The disjunction of the radio target and format

Similarly, there is a disjunction, no doubt contrary to what one might initially suppose, between the station and its advertising department, the best example of this being the frequent heterogeneity of advertising broadcast in youth formats.[19]

The Structuring of the French Musical Radio Scene

The field of radio media in France has been regulated by a public policy of quotas for French-language songs since 1994. This required the vast majority of radio stations to broadcast, at peak listening times, a minimum of 40 per cent French-language songs, with at least half representing 'new talent' or 'new productions'. Promoted as defending the French musical production sector from Anglo-Saxon programming, its effects have been clear for the promotion of French artists but with side effects, not anticipated by the legislator, such as the promotion of new sectors such as rap and electronica.[20] As for the policy's impact on French artists' sales, this seems less convincing, results being similar to other European countries without quotas.

From the 1980s, a second group of stations, including radios created by the liberalization of the airwaves or what it permitted (retroactive legalisation of publicity on private local radio stations in 1982, constitution of national networks by taking over smaller stations in 1986), added itself to the radio stations previously termed 'peripheral' and the public service stations; these were the musical radio networks for young people which became NRJ, RFM, Fun Radio, Skyrock and Nostalgie.[21] 'As of 1984 there was a clear change of era', writes Jean-Jacques

---

[19] As exemplified by the Carglass advert for car windscreens broadcast on youth radio stations in 2006.

[20] Marcel Machill, 'Musique as Opposed to Music: Background and Impact of Quotas for French Songs on French Radio', *The Journal of Media Economics*, 9/3 (1996): pp. 21–36.

[21] Jean-Jacques Cheval, *Les Radios en France. Histoire, état et enjeux* (Rennes, 1997), p. 82.

Cheval. 'Throughout France, the question "who speaks on free radio stations" (with political and social undertones), was replaced by "who listens to private local stations" with a clearly self-interested signification. Early on, the rapprochements initiated between these stations heralded the creation of national networks which appeared, moreover, with the first of them in that same year: NRJ. ... NRJ quickly became the most famous and representative of new FM radio stations. The success of this Parisian radio station is well known: by creating a network of franchised stations then subsidiaries, it succeeded in broadcasting its Parisian programme throughout France, matching "peripheral" and national public radio stations.'[22]

From the 1990s, other national stations were established on the basis of generational/musical formats, such as RTL 2 or Le Mouv. These are 'intermediary' or 'interstitial' radio stations which react to and target audience fragmentation, primarily in terms of age group and musical tastes.[23] A recent change in quotas of French songs has ratified this new structuring by format: in 2000, the French Broadcasting Authority (CSA) allowed stations to adopt one of two exceptions to the quotas.[24] These alternatives to the 40 per cent correspond to the target audiences of these stations: young people for some, adults for others. The change of 'CSA formats' confirms the current development of music radio stations whose programming, established in the early 1990s as generalist to reach a wider target, is now leaning towards growing fragmentation in terms of target audience and musical genre (sic).[25]

Musical Formatting ...

French radio has moved towards musical formatting, in other words, towards the specialization of radio stations in particular genres, this resulting in the current

---

[22]   Jean-Jacques Cheval, 'Le public des radios locales privées: évolution nationale et exemples aquitains', in Michèle de Bussière et al. (eds), *Histoire des publics à la radio et à la télévision* (Paris, 1994), pp. 148–9.

[23]   Hervé Glevarec and Michel Pinet, 'De la radio en France. Hétérogénéité des pratiques et spécialisation des auditoires', *Questions de communication*, 12 (2007).

[24]   These are either 60 per cent French-language songs and 10 per cent 'new productions' for radio stations specializing in promoting musical heritage, or 35 per cent French-language songs and 25 per cent at least of the total coming from 'new talent', for radio stations specializing in promoting 'young talent'. The first option places greater emphasis on French-language content than on 'new talent', whereas the second emphasizes 'new talent' more than French-language content. The term 'new production' means any record produced within a six month period from the date of first broadcast on any Ipsos Music Panel radio station. The notion of 'new talent' refers to any artist or group having not already received, prior to the new recording, two gold album records (100,000 albums sold), and having produced a first album after 1974 (year of creation of the certifications gold, double gold, platinum and diamond).

[25]   *La Lettre du CSA,* 139 (April 2001).

range of major musical genres (and it is necessary to consider the development of major genres). In 1996, musical formats were still relatively eclectic (probably with a large proportion of *me too* radio stations, for example around NRJ), whereas generalist formats remained French-language dominated.

The annual broadcasting data for songs in 2005 is not without surprises, despite the relativity of musical categories used (the musical or social value – or distance – of one genre compared with another).[26] An initial reading of Graph 2 (from left to right) suggests that amongst the stations included in the Yacast Panel (31 radio stations selected by professionals representing 92.5 per cent of the national audience), three major groupings appear: radios with a 'variety' profile where the primary station is French-language; stations with a 'pop-rock' profile where the primary station is international; and, finally, stations with an 'R&B' profile (a genre which does not appear here, but which aids in grouping the genres 'groove, dance and rap'). Fun Radio has since increased its share allocated to the dance format. In terms of these sub-genres, the three youth radio stations, NRJ, Fun Radio and Skyrock, have a less 'monolithic' profile than appears at first glance. In terms of diversity of programming, France Inter is the most eclectic generalist station.[27] Jazz and classical music represent minor genres on the contemporary French radio scene.[28]

The setting up of private music radio stations caused a change in the radio audience which moved from the previous duopolistic public/private model, to the 'dominant profile' of the young listener of music radio stations.[29] Henceforth, the majority of people listening to radio in France were young people listening to private music radio stations. A series of modifications to the social distribution of musical preferences followed, largely favouring 'popular' music.

... and Structural Un-formatting (or the Loss of the Monopoly Held by Cultural Intermediaries in their Role as Prescribers)

> The physical market henceforth is greater than radio broadcasting. ... In the space of two years, we have seen that 95 per cent of playlists are no longer

---

[26] Seen from this perspective, comparison of the musical and/or social 'distance' potentially separating (or not) classical music/jazz for example, and 'international pop-rock'/'French-language pop-rock' could lead to certain genres being incorporated into shared classifications or to questioning their internal homogeneity. There is a 'black box' effect.

[27] In fact, the most eclectic FM programming analysed by Yacast was that of Fip, which is a station broadcast, not including satellite, cable or internet listening, solely in Paris, Bordeaux, Nantes and Strasbourg.

[28] André Nicolas, *Le Jazz dans le paysage radiophonique* (Paris, 2004).

[29] Hervé Glevarec and Michel Pinet, 'From Liberalization to Fragmentation: A Sociology of French Radio Audiences since the 1990s and the Consequences for Cultural Industries Theory', *Media, Culture and Society*, 30/2 (2008): pp. 215–38.

new, lasting for barely two months. ... Songs which have never before been
scheduled on NRJ are successfully tested. Depuis Louise Attaque.

In December 2006 a music programmer at a large music station, NRJ, made this
statement – we shall leave the verification and exact meaning to one side to focus
solely on the 'experiential' value – which roughly summates to the following:
since the beginning of the 2000s and the rise of internet and digital music files,
a large-scale transformation has taken place. Radio has lost its power of control
(the market surpasses programming), of coercion (new material comes from
elsewhere) and of market composition (success is achieved elsewhere). 'Depuis
Louise Attaque': the first album by the French group Louise Attaque was released
in 1997 and sold 2.5 million copies. The group is famed for having 'emerged'
from outside of radio programming, *via* the music scene. Furthermore, for several
years, declining numbers of young radio listeners have been observed.[30] Internet
and digital audio files allow access to music, without much restriction. Music
radio stations are thus confronted with competition in their three primary roles of
identification ('we the listeners'), of discovery, and of programming.

Should the sharp decrease in the average song rotation rate on key music radio
stations over recent years be seen, therefore, as a response to the new sociological
and musical situation of accessing music which – a hypothesis we suggest –
requires a wider playlist? Let us use the radio station NRJ as a guide, a random
choice admittedly but one which seems to be coherent since it embodies so-called
prescriptive commercial radio (it is accused of setting trends). What happens for
NRJ? Its average rotation rate fell sharply between 2003 and 2006, going from 8.4
to 5.9 rotations on average per song per week, whereas its playlist increased by
16.7 per cent.[31] Consider further the various criteria of newly-launched material
by a radio station as the expression of desire/power of recommendation held by
radio stations. First time broadcasts on NRJ increased by 66.2 per cent, whereas its
first new material and first high rotation material decreased (17.9 per cent and 16.9
per cent). This seems to show, for this 'monopolistic' station, a clear opening and
loosening of its playlist. In other words, everything shows that a station like NRJ
has become more open and/or less 'certain' of its programming in recent years.

This seems to be counterbalanced by an increase in the share of the Top 40 held
by playlists. In fact, everything suggests a puzzling configuration where the 'peak'
in the programming of major radio stations is narrowing (greater focus) whereas
the base is widening (greater diversity of songs). 'Structural un-formatting' seems
to respond to the necessity to open up playlists faced with listeners more competent
and diverse in their tastes, thus, paradoxically, seems to react to formatting.

---

[30]   *Le temps des médias. L'essentiel* (Paris, 2005).
[31]   Nicolas, *Indicateurs de la diversité musicale dans le paysage radiophonique.*
This report, and others like it, provide a wealth of statistical detail on trends in music
broadcasting.

The Power of Broadcasters over Producers and its Development towards a Model of Diversification

For a long time producers have lamented their decreasing power over broadcasters, notably television and radio.[32] Henceforth, intermediaries themselves seem to be losing power over the public as shown by 'structural un-formatting'. Mobile telephony is of increasing importance alongside radio in terms of music broadcasting: Orange, instead of radio, was the medium on which Madonna's new productions were released, SFR was the first to broadcast Michel Polnareff's first French concert and Orange partnered the latest French music awards (*Victoires de la musique*). In 2007, Prince interacted with the public without using the traditional sales method in record shops. No doubt, these promotion methods are residual in scale compared to total numbers of songs broadcast annually, as shown by the renegotiation, in 2006, of the 'legal licence' scale regulating the share of 'neighbouring rights'[33] paid by music 'users', such as radio stations and television channels, to the SPRE (Equitable Remuneration Collection Company) royalties organization. The renegotiation aimed at a 'gradual' scale (between 4 per cent and 7 per cent on the basis of operators' advertising revenues). This modification highlights producers' desires to increase resources gained from 'uses' termed 'secondary' (compared to sales) and moreover greater involvement of radio stations in the economy of music. The legal licence is indeed a system which grants autonomy to radio stations in relation to musical producers, enabling them to freely use music produced. They do not have to negotiate broadcasting nor rely upon any authorizations or bans issued by producers.

However, major radio stations are never the first to reveal new artists, they often, strictly speaking, relay previous programming undertaken, for instance, by associative radio stations which are able to programme many new songs. Subsequently, radio station programmers select from baskets of songs already produced by record companies. Private music radio station programmers cannot, therefore, be considered as 'revealers' in the strict sense of the term. They are merely promoters of songs already programmed elsewhere (France or abroad) or already selected (by record companies). However, they do intervene on the broadcasting duration, sound tone, and even the promotion of mash-ups (mixing of two songs) and, notably, they *choose* from what is on offer. What is new, in terms of producers, are initiatives reflecting the desire or aim to forego media and traditional mediators in favour of mechanisms providing more 'direct' contact between record companies or labels and audiences. Two examples demonstrate this: the first, more modest, of Valéry Zeitoun, managing director of the AZ label at Universal, who creates and uploads his podcasts, both musical and professional

---

[32]   Véronique Cayla and Anne Durupty, *Relations entre télédiffuseurs et filière musicale* (Paris, 2005).

[33]   Resulting from the Lang Act 1987 concerning performing artists and producers; singer-songwriters and publishers were paid for a long time by the SACEM.

(which is similar to a record company proto-radio station).[34] Secondly, more ambitious it would seem, is the Because Music label, established in 2004 by Emmanuel de Buretel, former chairperson of EMI France. The project is described by Because Music on its website:

> It is no longer a question of listening over and over again to the fatalistic and undermining speeches from major recording companies. Artists have never had so many tools at their disposal to broadcast and distribute their music and songs. With an unashamed diversity and an amazing vitality, music has never been in such great shape as in 2006. Now that artists are used to the freedom and possibilities that new communication tools offer them, they reject standard industrial formulas: networks like myspace.com have created an ideal reference library in the global village, and a wonderful link between musicians and fans. In this context, why would they remain within Franco-French borders? More than a record company, Because is a platform where artists can meet, exchange ideas and express themselves. No more compartmentalizing: as an international and open-minded label, Because will stand alongside artists, helping them to spread their message, their image and their ideas in the best manner possible. ... We'll offer the care and attention of craftsmen, coupled with the vision, means and modernity of a multi-cultural firm: this is the strength of Because, facing the future challenges of musical broadcasting, from Internet to wireless telephony.[35]

This label claims to be a medium, a distributer and a tour manager and calls for 'un-formatting'. It pits liberty against restriction: 'The label will also be reiterating that the era of exclusive interests is over: since, in 2006, it is normal to listen to sounds from across the world in shuffle mode on an iPod, therefore, the label opens its arms to Justice's electro-shock or Asyl's biting rock, and even Tandem's rough rap ...'

This development of the three-way relationship between producers-broadcasters-public must be contextualized in a new sociological model moving producers of content and broadcasters from the monopoly of functions to the diversification of contacts.[36] Figure 9.2 represents the changeover from a traditional and old-style method of introducing consumers to music/artists *via* producers-reviewers-broadcasters towards a model which opens up sideways favouring different introduction methods, more or less bypassing the traditional dominant method, for example introduction via websites, illegal downloads and digital audio files. Two new methods may be mentioned which have gained in importance in

---

[34]   http://rss.universalmusic.fr/podcast/AZ/.

[35]   http://www.because.tv/en/editorial/index.html.

[36]   Jean-Samuel Beuscart, 'Les transformations de l'intermédiation musicale. La construction de l'offre commerciale de musique en ligne en France', *Réseaux*, 25/141–2 (2007): pp. 143–76.

recent years: 'MP3-internet-downloads' and 'concerts-festivals'. We can add two further methods to these: online radio (understood in the widest sense of possible formats, from web-radio to podcasts) and digital music players making people more independent of traditional broadcasting methods.

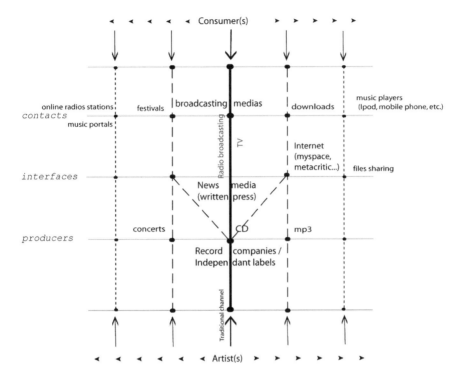

Figure 9.2   From the monopoly of functions to the diversity of contacts

Ideological and Aesthetic Issues: Canonization of Popular Genres

The general trend which has characterized the musical domain since the birth of rock is the growth in musical genres and the 'musicalization' of daily life.[37] While the idea of an old-style legitimization process of rock music as art may be defended,[38] a 'canonization' process seems just as relevant. Thus the 'disqualifying

---

[37]   Tia Denora, *Music in Everyday Life* (Cambridge, 2000).

[38]   Motti Regev, 'Producing artistic value. The case of rock music', *Sociological Quaterly*, 35/1 (1994): pp. 85–102.

celebration' characteristic of *Rock & Folk* described by Philippe Teillet[39] does not claim legitimacy, but rather establishes rock as a distanced cult. The 'logic of rock' is just as much opposed to that of 'learned music where admiration goes to works of art and genius' as to that of 'variety (*Le Temps des copains*, for example) where it is considered that admiration is more blind or naive'.[40] The *magazine Les Inrockuptibles* has developed, without mentioning it – and paradoxically referring to intellectual authorities such as P. Bourdieu – amidst the social and ideological context of the 'end of the cultural legitimacy model'.[41] The illegitimacy of 'popular' (non-classical) music and artists as chronicled and discussed in this magazine is inappropriate for a readership of intellectuals, and moreover, the magazine's mandate is more political than aesthetic. Nothing is less evident than the fact that rock music and its followers needed legitimization (since some people classify these as 'genres with low or average legitimacy') to reach the position which is henceforth its own. Practices seem, here, to have been more legitimizing than discourse.

Pluralization of the musical field and segmentation of listeners has literally turned the *distinction* analysis model into a *differentiation* model. This should be made clear and clearly understood. This is what we earlier called the 'end of the classic legitimacy model' on the basis of the statistical and empirical observation that young upper socio-professional groups first and foremost listen to genres termed 'popular' produced by cultural industries. The end of this model means that thinking about the current structuring of musical preferences in terms of hierarchical social position is inadequate. On the contrary, we must work towards a 'tabling' of musical tastes and new social judgements between musical genres and individuals based upon tolerance, and openness/neutrality.

Former Terms of Critique

The major issue – legitimization/canonization – of the musical field is accompanied on the ideological level by a theme symmetrical to the 'harmful relationship': commoditization, instrumentation or influence on the public ('not being influenced by a communication campaign', said Thom Yorke, Radiohead singer, regarding their free online download strategy in 2007 for the *In Rainbows* album).[42] 'Target', 'format', 'broadcasting', 'advertising' in this perspective seem to be just so many denials of humanity. Work led by the *Observatoire de la musique* has shown that the

---

[39]   Philippe Teillet, 'Les cultes musicaux. La contribution de l'appareil de commentaires à la construction de cultes; l'exemple de la presse rock', in Philippe Le Guern (ed.), *Les Cultes médiatiques. Culture fan et œuvres cultes* (Rennes, 2002), pp. 309–41.

[40]   Philippe Teillet, 'Les cultes musicaux. La contribution de l'appareil de commentaires à la construction de cultes; l'exemple de la presse rock', in Le Guern, ibid., p. 324.

[41]   Glevarec, 'La fin du modèle classique de la légitimité culturelle'.

[42]   *Télérama*, n° 3026, 9 January 2008.

'low-level of advertising investments from the musical edition sector (representing 3.6 per cent of total revenue of radio stations in the Yacast Panel and 5.6 per cent for music radio stations) seems to indicate that there is no real community of economic interest between the production and broadcasting sectors, particularly for music radio stations'.[43] Radios gain their advertising revenues primarily from major retailing, telephone service providers and gaming. The interest of producers is thus indirect, *via* exposure.

Some people criticize the funnel effect of the media and their gatekeeping role over supply. But they also expect value criticism from them. Others simply want something for every taste. But who knows what the tastes (of French people) are? Others look at sales after production and presume there to be a link between media exposure and physical sales (or downloads). Some ask what has been said about artistic legitimacy? Nothing. We have merely analysed the effect of exposure on sales, with no comment about artistic value. The concentration of supply is criticized, but recent research into cultural diversity in general, and musical diversity in particular, is well-balanced in its findings.[44] Its conclusions, irrespective of genres, can be succinctly summarized: diversity has increased, but with a top-down structuring of cultural products (books, records, cinema).

'Diversity' as New Legitimacy and Public Ideology in France

Is 'cultural diversity' the remains of French-style cultural policy abandoned for almost 20 years, as suggested by Philippe Urfalino?[45] Should it, therefore, be considered as the last spark of the philosophy of the Jack Lang period, which Urfalino describes as being spurred by 'cultural vitalism', as an extension of 'cultural democracy' ('every culture has the right to exist, and even be visible' we could summarize)? Formulated in 2001 internationally, by UNESCO, the notion of cultural diversity responded to the end of classic legitimacy. It is well known that cultural industries led to the rise of a rival legitimacy to classic legitimacy,[46] but not as widely known is the State and state institutions' resort to a new ideological

---

[43]   André Nicolas, *Baromètre des investissements publicitaires du secteur des éditions musicales en radio et télévision. Année 2005* (Paris, 2006): p. 17.

[44]   Françoise Benhamou and Stéphanie Peltier, 'Une méthode multicritère d'évaluation de la diversité culturelle: application à l'édition de livres en France', in Greffe, *Création et diversité*, pp. 313–44; Nicolas Curien and François Moreau, 'L'industrie du disque à l'heure de la convergence télécoms/médias/Internet', in Greffe, ibid,, pp. 73–104; Jean Gabszewicz and Nathalie Sonnac, 'Concentration des industries de contenu et diversité des préférences', in Greffe, ibid., pp. 353–72; Nicolas, *Indicateurs de la diversité musicale dans le paysage radiophonique*.

[45]   Philippe Urfalino, *L'Invention de la politique culturelle* (Paris, 2004), p. 385.

[46]   Donnat, *Les Français face à la culture*.

discourse, that of 'diversity'. Let us look back on the two legitimacies which governed, until recently, sociological thinking and theory on cultural affairs.

1. Artistic legitimacy: 'the best are those selected by experts'
2. Commercial legitimacy: 'the best are those who are successful'

A third has, therefore, been added (new in the field of cultural policies):

3.   Democratic legitimacy: 'everyone has the right to exist and to be seen'.

Public actors were forced to change discourse on culture and move from 'grandeur' to 'diversity', from supporting 'legitimate works' (a register which failed faced with tastes for 'common' genres), to supporting all works (against monopoly and in favour of pluralism). But these public agents are not (yet) proclaiming this high and loud. And the ideology of 'diversity' is not, however, quite the same as the ideology of 'cultural democracy'.

In sociological terms, 'musical diversity' is probably a bad sociological expression as it is too fluid. The play on the double meaning of the term 'diversity' is, indeed, allowed: 'plurality' of genres and 'pluralism' of genres. 'Plurality' refers to things, 'pluralism' to ideas: it is also said that there is a plurality of political parties and a pluralism of political ideas. In one case monopoly is criticized, in the other uniformism is criticized. There may of course be plurality without pluralism and pluralism without plurality, diversity of actors and little musical diversity,[47] a monopoly of actors and musical diversity.[48] The role of the *Observatoire de la musique*, established in France in 2000, is based upon this double meaning never entirely resolved, no doubt because it leads to a conceptual *cul-de-sac*. Reflection on so-called 'diversity' must in effect include a *democratic* term ('diversity for diversity') which cannot be fully achieved ('one radio station for each genre', 'one broadcast for each song' are imaginable situations but not very desirable) and by a *uniformist* term, whether aristocratic or populist, which is not desirable for artistic reasons, as its establishment would deny the idea of a hierarchy between songs, an attitude rejected by champions of diversity. The difficulty is therefore that of defining the ideal, the optimum of diversity in this spectrum. Where is it? Can it really be conceived?

Behind the debate regarding diversity lies an accusation levelled at the media of controlling record companies, rather than merely being an extension of them, but the problem remains, merely moved a link up in the chain, since one could, in such a system, similarly accuse production companies (also a highly concentrated sector) of not correctly doing their artistic job of separating the wheat from the

---

[47]   Richard Peterson and David Berger, 'Cycles in Symbol Production: The Case of Popular Music', *American Sociological Review*, 40/2 (1975): pp. 158–73.

[48]   Peter Steiner, 'Program Patterns and Preferences, and the Workability of Competition in Radio Broadcasting', *The Quarterly Journal of Economics*, 66 (1952): pp. 194–223.

chaff (for easily influenced consumers with little knowledge) and, on the contrary, selecting, most of the time, the chaff.

Conclusion: The Chicken and the Egg

A recurring question posed by the very functioning of the musical world is that of the origin of success. Does it originate from adoring consumers or from supporting producers? Who is the chicken and who is the egg? To try to answer this we must leave behind both industrial populism ('listeners' preferences determine the programming') and intellectual miserabilism ('the interest shown by the public for new songs is created by radio broadcasting and other forms of media exposure'). The sociology of fans has provided, in recent years, tools to think through active relationships to music, with taste being constructed, and the relationship of the media with their receivers moving towards a more balanced rapport.[49]

Everything we have hitherto discussed indicates a move in sociological models of description and explanation towards the study of new structurings of actors and objects which appear, paradoxically (in other words despite rationalization and concentration), denser than in the past. Confronted with the development, diversification and segmentation of the musical field and under the dual stimulus of 'popular' music and electronic communications, actors and ideologies have been undergoing reconfiguration. Actors are more subtly weaving their links with music, and are changing, without explicitly accepting this change, from the legitimist model to the pluralist model, as is shown by the ideology of 'cultural diversity', the new fulcrum of pluralist societies. This is why we mentioned in the introduction that the idea of the 'mediator' – when talking about disseminators in the musical field (journalists notably) – simplifies a professional reality involving actors who are far from thinking themselves as such (aside perhaps in the specific field of socio-cultural mediation). This notion is ambiguous in its implication – according to the recognized meaning of mediation – of production working towards reception, whereas sociological studies demonstrate its palindromic movements, the importance of professional ideologies and the uncertainties and breakdowns in links between production and reception.

The new industrial model brought about by the internet and electronic media since the 2000s has, no doubt, not yet stabilized. Music industry sales in France continue to fall, whilst legal download sales are not compensating for this deficit. Publishing as the economic cluster potentially replacing production is proposed by some. This being the case, as we have set out to show, many transformations

---

[49]   Henry Jenkins, *Textual Poachers: Television Fans and Participatory Culture* (New York, 1992); Jean-Charles Ambroise and Christian Le Bart, *Les Fans des Beatles. Sociologie d'une passion* (Rennes, 2000); Le Guern, *Les Cultes médiatiques*; Antoine Hennion, 'Affaires de goût. Se rendre sensible aux choses', in Michel Peroni and Jacques Roux (eds), *Sensibiliser. La sociologie dans le vif du monde* (Paris, 2006), pp. 161–74.

cannot be attributed to economic causes but are the effect of aesthetic criteria (the long-term rise of popular music), technical criteria (diversification of access to music) and ideological criteria (new system of cultural fairness or justice).

Chapter 10
Genres and the Aesthetics of Popular Music in the UK

Simon Warner

At the heart of the British discourse on genre in popular music lies a key debate about the distinctions between the terms 'pop' and 'rock' and, within that debate, rest a number of contentious issues linked to notions of aesthetics and ideology, authenticity and manufacture, production and consumption. While popular music in the UK, over the last 40 or so years, particularly – once the Beatles and their fellow travellers had challenged the American hegemony in such matters after the so-called British Invasion from 1964 – has become a fertile breeding ground for many different kinds of expression and practice, if we are to stand back from the multitude of genres and sub-genres – and even smaller sub-sets – that exist, the tendency to identify particular kinds of music in relation to those larger umbrella descriptions of pop or rock is evident both in the analysis undertaken by musicologists and social theorists and the criticism of journalists. In Popular Music Studies, a field of scholarly enquiry barely 20 years old at university level in the UK, most of the key British thinkers have drawn attention to a binary distinction, a kind of opposition or tension, at least, between pop and rock.[1] In the field of printed media, quality newspapers like *The Guardian* and *The Times* distinguish between pop and rock reviews in their sub-headings and there are magazines that pursue specific agendas – *Kerrang!* and *NME* are concerned primarily with rock, while *Top of the Pops* magazine, originally linked to a long-running BBC television

---

[1]   See, for example, Roy Shuker, *Key Concepts in Popular Music* (London, 1998); Simon Frith, *Performing Rites: On the Value of Popular Music* (Oxford, 1996) and (with co-eds. John Street and Will Straw), *The Cambridge Guide to Pop and Rock* (Cambridge, 2003); Jason Toynbee, *Making Popular Music: Musicians, Creativity and Institutions* (London, 2000); Allan Moore, *Rock: The Primary Text – Developing a Musicology of Rock* (Aldershot, 2001); Stan Hawkins, *Settling the Pop Score: Pop Texts and Identity Politics* (Aldershot, 2002). Non-UK commentators Franco Fabbri, 'A Theory of Musical Genre: Two Applications' in D. Horn and P. Tagg (eds), *Popular Music Perspectives* (Göteborg and Exeter, 1982), K. Keightley, 'Reconsidering Rock' in *The Cambridge Companion to Pop and Rock* (Cambridge, 2001) and F. Holt, *Genre in Popular Music* (Chicago, 2007) have also formed part of this ongoing debate but I am keen within this chapter to ascertain British positions on the idea of genre.

series, and the late *Smash Hits*,[2] which enjoyed a flourishing history for much of its life, have been strongly inclined to report the world of pop.

This widespread reliance on such a code begs a number of questions. How far are these terms useful or accurate in actually defining musical types? How far can we consider pop and rock to be generic descriptions? How far is this system of categorization linked to market forces and the way the industry wants to present its products to its customers? And how helpful is the system to the record buyer? We might even contemplate how far are these central reference points are tied to white, Anglo-Saxon notions of musical practice as they may be less useful in considering the large range of imported styles and sounds – from the Caribbean and the Indian sub-continent, for instance – that have been introduced to indigenous British ears since the mid-1960s. In this chapter I hope to touch upon a number of these issues but with the principal focus on British understandings of these two terms, their relationship to each other and wider notions of popular music as an over-riding category. I will attempt a concise overview of the larger descriptor – popular music itself – in order to better understand where pop and rock may fit into the hierarchy of generic and sub-generic forms that exists. I will then present some definitions of pop and rock, comparing a number of academic interpretations, and then aim to compile some common understandings of the two musical forms. I will begin, however, with some thoughts about the ways in which genre analysis has been applied as a general theoretical framework and how such a methodology might be employed in relation to popular music.

In the latter half of the twentieth century, genre analysis has emerged as a crucial tool in the process of textual interrogation – whether we are considering film or television, novels or plays, and certainly popular music. Genre, says popular music scholar Shuker, is 'a key component of textual analysis'.[3] In similar, general terms, McLeish states that: 'Genre analysis emphasises the ways in which certain patterns, themes and structures may be identified ... The key elements of a genre text, therefore, are repetition, recognition and familiarity. Given these factors, the part played by the audience ... in recognising and responding to generically identifiable texts is seen as crucial.'[4] Film analyst Neale outlines the central importance of the producer/consumer intersection when he refers to genre as 'a system of orientations, expectations and conventions that circulate between industry, text and subject'.[5]

So we must also stress that the use of genre and generic identification has become much more than a means for academics to make critical sense of an artistic

---

[2]   *Top of the Pops* was axed by BBC TV in 2006 after a 22 year, continuous run. The show's associated magazine, founded in 1995, is still published monthly. *Smash Hits*, a fortnightly founded in 1978, closed in 2006.

[3]   Shuker, *Key Concepts in Popular Music*, p. 145.

[4]   Kenneth McLeish (ed.), *Guide to Human Thought: Ideas that Shaped the World* (London, 1993), p. 312.

[5]   S. Neale cited in Toynbee, *Making Popular Music*, p. 103.

scene or set of creative practices; this system of understanding is just as important to journalists and their consumers, film-makers and their viewers, producers of literature and their readers. For the intermediaries – the publishers and producers, the publicists and the promoters – the system is vital, too. By generic classification of their artists' output they are able to make sense of their products for their reviewers and their customers. Without clear notions of what a sci-fi novel is, what we can expect of a piece of musical theatre, what ingredients make up a soap opera or what components comprise a work of reality television, it is hard to know how a network of common understanding and appreciation, a means of stylistic recognition, a process of critical exchange, between creator and consumer, could be established. Frith refers to 'the seemingly inescapable use of generic categories in the organisation of popular culture'.[6]

Yet we should also add that Adorno, who both identified and described then vilified the culture industry, saw genre as one of the creeping menaces of a commodified arts world. That ability to codify, to digest, the artwork within the parameters of a generic template was symptomatic for the Frankfurt School-honed, German émigré, of a weakening and diluting in the realms of true creativity and worthwhile art. Genre made understanding too simple; the boxes into which styles could be placed both constrained the artist, compromised the art and asked too little of the receiver. As Bannister states, with reference to the philosopher's position:

> A classic aesthetic approach (such as high modernism), which assumes aesthetic values as autonomous and uniquely expressive, would regard the extent to which a text can be constructed as generic as proof of its lack of aesthetic value, for example soap operas and reality TV, or in music, disco and teenybopper bop. Adorno's classification of popular music as standardised and repetitive uses generic similarity and social function to qualify aesthetic value.[7]

However, despite Adorno's reservations, a system of genres and a connected method of analysis have proved an effective means of making sense of a kaleidoscope of texts – burgeoning in the age of the electronic and digital media, and specifically in the field of popular music where the new applications have been particularly prevalent as they challenge a century of rampant phonography – even if it has constructed a somewhat restricted or claustrophobic environment: a requirement to follow the existing rules. But, as Borthwick and Moy argue:

> Genre-based analysis ... allows for both textual and contextual characteristics to be considered when analysing a musical example. Associated terms such as metagenre or subgenre can be used to broaden the critical frame or to narrow it

---

[6]   Frith, *Performing Rites*, p. 75.

[7]   Matthew Bannister, *White Boys, White Noise: Masculinities and 1980s Indie Guitar Rock* (Aldershot, 2006), p. 65.

> ... Of course, the use of such terms is contestable, subjective and not without controversy. Nevertheless, put simply, genre analysis allows texts to be interpreted and demythologised in the light of a broad range of critical criteria.[8]

Toynbee stresses the role of genre still further, emphasizing the industrial context in which such a system of recognition is sustained, arguing that 'genre is central to the music apparatus'. He comments: 'It is true that well established stars sell records on the basis of supra-generic aura. But for the most of the popular music market, genre provides a vital form of packaging and a means of organizing audience expectation about the sound of music ... the industry needs to make music knowable, to place that which cannot be seen and which has not yet been heard in the realm of the familiar.'[9] He adds:

> Above all identification depends on being able to read a generic signature right through the fabric of the music; indeed a style will usually 'introduce itself' in the first few bars of a song. But genre is also constructed through the structure of record labels, the layout of bins in a record shop, in the constitution of music magazines or radio station formatting.[10]

If we are to regard pop and rock as genres, we might see them as the equivalent of a *genus*, or *genera*, in the family tree that describes and defines the natural world. Popular music, I would propose, is a metagenre (*meta*,[11] Greek, over or above) an over-arching umbrella that contains a number of genres. This we may possibly identify as the equivalent of the family in taxonomic models; sub-genres (*sub*,[12] Greek, below or under) we might interpret as the equivalent of species.[13] The descriptive phrase popular music is, however, also charged with those testing distinctions, qualifications and disputes that characterize the use of the adjective popular on its own. As Williams[14] has suggested (and Bennett et al.,[15] have broadly

---

[8]   Stuart Borthwick and Ron Moy, *Popular Music Genres* (Edinburgh, 2004), p. 224.

[9]   Toynbee, *Making Popular Music*, p. 115.

[10]   J. Toynbee, ibid.

[11]   'Sub-', Latin, under, below (*Chambers English Dictionary*, 1988).

[12]   'Meta-', Greek, over, beyond (*Chambers English Dictionary*, 1988).

[13]   If we were to extend the taxonomic model followed within the field of natural history to music, we might propose the following comparable categories: *Kingdom* – The Arts; *Phyla* – Performing Arts; *Class* – Music; *Order* – Art/Vernacular; *Family* – Dance/Popular/World/Traditional; *Genera* – Rock, soul, reggae, disco, jazz, etc; *Species* – Punk, metal, urban, dancehall, house, fusion, etc.

[14]   'Popular' in Raymond Williams, *Keywords: A Vocabulary of Culture and Society* (London,1988), pp. 236–8.

[15]   'Popular' by John Storey in Tony Bennett, Lawrence Grossberg and Meaghan Morris (eds), *New Keywords: A Revised Vocabulary of Culture and Society* (Oxford, 2005), pp. 262–4.

updated) popular is one of the most fluid and contentious terms that students of cultural studies and sociology, media and communications, have to handle. In British English, terms like the popular press, popular television and popular music have very clear connotations linked, not just to the means of production and consumption associated with theories of mass culture but also attached to notions of class and status. Historically, too, the term popular has been saturated in ambivalence: a progressive and positive adjective to the liberal advocates of rights of the general populace but a term tinged with potential menace for the ruling classes, with its negative implications of rebellious, even revolutionary, activity. As Storey observes: 'The popular culture of the majority has always been a concern of powerful minorities. Those with political power have always thought it necessary to police the culture of those without political power.'[16]

Thus, when we turn to a descriptive phrase like popular music we really need to unpack, maybe offload, some of the historical baggage the term has taken on board over a number of centuries and re-locate it in a contemporary setting. For, while Shuker identifies the first published use of the phrase 'popular music'[17] in 1855 in William Chapple's published series of *Popular Music of Olden Times*, a title that plainly contains echoes of a reconstituted folk past, a hundred years later, in the mid-twentieth century, it seemed that the application of popular had everything to do with the immediate present rather than any notion of the historical or the traditional. Williams points out that it was at this point that popular, in relation to music certainly, was 'characteristically shortened to pop, and the familiar range of senses, from unfavourable to favourable, gathered around this'.[18] He adds that 'the shortening gave the word a lively informality but opened it, more easily, to a sense of the trivial'.[19] Williams appears to propose that there is something quite straightforwardly inter-changeable between popular and pop in this usage, something close to synonymity even. However, I would challenge that and assert instead that, for scholars of popular music not to mention critics and fans, pop has come to stand for something rather more than a mere abbreviation of popular. It has, on the contrary, emerged, in time, as a distinctive musical form, a genre in its own right, one which shelters under the larger, metageneric umbrella of popular music.

So, part of my argument in this account will rest on the case that while popular music and pop music are patently related they actually mean *different* things, and that while pop is clearly, *per se*, a truncation of popular, the abbreviation shifted

[16]   John Storey, *An Introduction to Cultural Theory & Popular Culture* (Hemel Hempstead, 1993).

[17]   Roy Shuker, *Understanding Popular Music* (London, 2001), p. 5.

[18]   Williams, *Keywords*, p. 238.

[19]   Williams, ibid. It is perhaps interesting to note that Storey, on re-visiting the definition of 'Popular' in *New Keywords* (Bennett et al., 2005), does not make reference to pop at all, hinting that Williams' earlier conflation of the full and brief form no longer applies.

meaning from its source word. Nor has the term pop itself enjoyed a fixed status. In the decades since Elvis Presley and the sounds of rock'n'roll first erupted, the notion of pop and its value have been regarded rather inconsistently. As Warner describes: 'Pop has sometimes been seen as a derogatory description, at other times a golden seal of approval, depending on the moment. If, in the 1950s, rock'n'roll was seen as a vigorous antidote to pop ballads, by the 1960s the Beatles were being acclaimed as a pop group. By the latter half of that decade, however, rock bands were distinguished from pop groups: the former were serious, thinking music-makers; the latter, bubblegum trivialists.'[20] We will return to the identifying musical traits of pop in due course.

If pop appears to possess something of a multivalent quantity, later in this piece I will claim that rock, as well, has tended to represent a sliding signifier, initially itself an abbreviation for rock'n'roll from the mid-1950s to the early 1960s, then a stand-alone term describing the new brand of popular music that emerged in the mid-1960s in the wake of the new experimentation of first Bob Dylan and the Beatles then a transatlantic wave of white blues bands and psychedelic and progressive innovators – from Cream to the Doors, Jefferson Airplane to Pink Floyd – in the later years of the decade, a little later still a tag attached to styles as ideologically disparate as heavy metal and punk, and then, by the closing stages of the 1980s, seen, in some quarters, as a description of a regressive rump, what *New Musical Express* dubbed 'rockism', an almost Luddite dedication to amplified power and noise, exuded via the phallic metaphor of the electric guitar, a brand of music which Frith & McRobbie would typify as 'cock rock'[21] and running counter to more introspective sensibilities of the predominant indie sound, well summed up in Bannister's *White Boys, White Noise*.[22]

How though might we locate rock and pop within a broader orbit? Although there is no definitive framework to which we can defer,[23] we might propose a number of significant genres framed under that wide-ranging metagenre of popular music – country, soul, blues, jazz, folk, reggae, dance and world, come to mind, and, under this over-arching scheme, I would add pop and rock to that list of important generic forms. Yet there are possible weaknesses or paradoxes in this model to which we might sensibly draw attention. For instance, can a ubiquitous

[20]   'Pop' in Simon Warner, *Rockspeak: The Language of Rock and Pop* (London, 1996), p. 262.

[21]   Simon Frith and A. McRobbie in 'Rock and sexuality' in Simon Frith and A. Goodwin (eds), *On Record: Pop, Rock and the Written Word* (London, 1990).

[22]   Bannister, *White Boys, White Noise*.

[23]   'All too often, the kind of thinking I am referring to encircles the intricate problematics of definition, Like the overarching categories of world music, pop-rock, folk, funk and jazz, pop, as a term in itself, is often applied to that broad expanse of music that has undergone industrialisation and commercialisation. Alone the interchangeability of the terms "rock" and "pop" highlights the constraints of narratives that embrace countless definitions of popular music.' Hawkins, *Settling the Pop Score*, p. 2.

and arguably distinctive style such as hip hop be merely a sub-genre of soul or has become a genre in its own right? Is reggae a branch of world music or that one form outside the Anglo-American nexus that has truly established a place on its own terms? Are jazz and blues too closely linked to be truly autonomous? Are jazz or folk metagenres themselves, evidenced in cultures in all corners of the globe? And is dance as a descriptor far too widely stretched? Perhaps the music known as dance within its post-1980s, popular music context, arising in Chicago, Detroit and New York, spreading to London, Manchester and the Balearics, should be called something else – club culture? electronica? – because plainly the term excludes older practices such as ballet, the foxtrot and the waltz but, then again, might have more than passing associations with, for example, more recent styles like the tango or bossa nova and those other Latin rhythms that complement, from time to time, the principal US black-derived styles such as house, techno and R&B and other UK hybrids like jungle, drum'n'bass and garage. Such a remark also draws attention to the fact that this economic overview may offer a basic generic map to the reader but cannot begin to offer a full account of the multifarious subgenres that have made their presence felt, to a greater or lesser degree, over the last half century of British popular music-making: styles such as skiffle, Merseybeat, R&B, glam, punk, ska, disco, goth, Northern soul, C86,[24] handbag, Britpop and new rave provide only a taste of the numerous off-shoots that have left a mark in recent decades. It is also interesting to note that many of these subordinate musical forms have been closely connected to distinctive subcultural communities, with strong UK roots – for example, Teddy Boys and rockers, mods and skinheads, punks and goths – who have employed their musical choices as a significant badge of identity to the extent that theories of homology, advanced by Hebdige[25] among others, have identified close relationships between the ideological attitudes and behaviour of particular subcultures and the sonic characteristics of the music its members are drawn to.

But these wider questions – relating to generic definition, regarding the numerous and diverse offspring these genres have spawned and their frequent links with British subcultural activity – we must set to one side in the context of this shorter, more focused investigation. It is pop and rock that are of most concern here and what those adjectives have come to mean within the specific setting of British popular music-making, selling and listening. That said, I do think it is instructive to make one qualification in relation to the US and its approaches to this debate. The way meanings differ in respect of American interpretation of these concepts may be subtle and this is not the place to thoroughly deconstruct

---

[24]   In 1986, *New Musical Express* produced a compilation cassette entitled *C86*, featuring a number of bands of the time – the Wedding Present and the Bodines among them. The particular brand of indie rock featured on the tape became influential in its own right, shaping many new groups' approach to their music-making in the latter years of that decade.

[25]   See Dick Hebdige, *Subculture: The Meaning of Style* (London, 1979).

the US position but, suffice to say that the term rock'n'roll has been used much longer and quite all-embracingly on the other side of the Atlantic to mean music made by performers as varied as Elvis Presley, the Rolling Stones and Bruce Springsteen. In the UK rock'n'roll has enjoyed a more restricted usage: that music made between c.1954 and 1959 in the US (and, of course, copied by UK bands of a similar period) and usefully summed up in the five different brands of rock'n'roll that Gillett, an Englishman, outlines in his well-regarded history *The Sound of the City*.[26] Once the rising generation of American, then British, popular music writers, from around 1966, began to use the shortened form rock to stand for something ideological – linked to the social, political, cultural and narcotic transformations of that subsequent era – rather than merely an abbreviating of rock'n'roll, British commentators tended to see rock as something quite distinct from rock'n'roll. American critics meanwhile have been less assiduous in separating the two, as they perhaps attempt to sustain a seamless metanarrative from the mid-1950s to the present day, one that attempts to join Chuck Berry and Jerry Lee Lewis to Jefferson Airplane and Prince, Jeff Buckley and Green Day. It is useful, in this context, to note the titles of widely-read US histories of post-Presley popular music – DeCurtis and Henke's *The Rolling Stone Illustrated History of Rock & Roll* (1992) and Palmer's *Dancing in the Street: A Rock and Roll History* (1996) serve as helpful examples – titles which cover considerably more, at least in UK terms, than the story of rock'n'roll.

To return though to the specific matter of British takes on the areas of pop and rock, what do leading scholars tell us about this relationship of this debate? Let us reflect on some definitions from various places of pop and rock to illustrate the common areas of agreement and those places in the conversation where there remains a lack of clear concord. Borthwick and Moy state that '[w]hereas "overarching" metagenres such as rock and pop transcend historical epochs, others, such as progressive rock or Britpop do not'.[27] Shuker regards the notion of the metagenre rather differently (for him, alternative rock and world music represent that concept more closely)[28] and he is more inclined to see pop and rock as part of a range of genres. Frith remarks that 'pop music is a slippery concept, perhaps because it is so familiar, so easily used'. He says that '[i]t is music produced commercially, for profit, as a matter of enterprise not art'. He suggests that we might work on the basis that '"pop music" (*sic*) includes all contemporary popular forms – rock, country, reggae, rap, and so on'.[29] But he speedily challenges such a definition and points out that rock ideologues, for instance, 'want to distance their music from pop, for them a term of contempt'.[30] Shuker concurs with the latter position. He, too, is keen to regard pop and rock quite distinctly. 'Pop', he asserts,

[26]   Charlie Gillett in *The Sound of the City* (London, 1983).
[27]   Borthwick and Moy, *Popular Music Genres,* p. 3.
[28]   Shuker, *Key Concepts in Popular Music*, p. 147.
[29]   Frith, 'Pop Music', p. 94.
[30]   Frith, ibid., p. 95.

'is often used in an oppositional sense to rock music'.[31] He goes on to talk about pop's 'disposability; general accessibility; memorable hooks; preoccupation with romantic love'.[32]

If we acknowledge Shuker's description of pop as a useful starting point, there are, I would suggest, other characteristics we can add to this list. Pop has been a musical form most associated with the recording and marketing format known as the single, predominantly conveyed via the 45 rpm, 7", vinyl record, which held court between the mid-1950s to the start of the 1990s. If the format has largely been superseded by technological advances,[33] the idea of showcasing a stand-alone pop composition has nonetheless survived into the CD and MP3 era, even if the modes of delivery have been significantly transformed. Usually framing a featured song of approximately three to four minutes, this one-track vehicle[34] has been aimed at the Top 40 singles chart listing and shaped in such a way that would encourage daytime radio airplay[35] and reach the mass market that would purchase the record and propel it to hit status. As for musical and lyrical signs, we might typify pop as melodically and harmonically appealing, lyrically simple and unsophisticated, possessing an easily assimilated tune supported by a consistent beat, with songs generally centred on a regular verse-chorus pattern linked by a middle eight or a short instrumental bridge, with the lead vocal – supported usually by complementary backing vocals – privileged in both the arrangement and the mix. However, if pop is most likely to feature relatively simple progressions, coupled to words that are easily remembered by the listener, and avoid extended, virtuosic solos or lengthy instrument-centred sections, an aesthetic paradox is still frequently evident: this musical form often utilizes state-of-the-art technology and cutting-edge production techniques to deliver a sound that is compellingly crisp, sharp and clean. Pop's relatively unchallenging lyrical narratives stand in contrast to the high-powered production values that often accompany the musical

---

[31]   Shuker, *Key Concepts in Popular Music*, p. 226.

[32]   Shuker, ibid.

[33]   The vinyl 45 retains a lasting kudos among UK indie bands and their fans and the format survives, if on a tiny scale, as a result of such groups continuing to issue 7" singles, often courtesy of the few remaining pressing plants in middle Europe, as limited edition issues, complements rather than substitutions for the other formats that have now superseded such releases.

[34]   While single records – whether vinyl or CD – have always included other tracks – B–sides, re-mixed versions and so on – the main focus has been on a titular song, the item actually featured in the chart listing. The only exception to this has been the occasional double A-sided single best exemplified, perhaps, by the Beatles' 1967 release 'Penny Lane'/ 'Strawberry Fields Forever'.

[35]   In the UK this process was given particular impetus after Radio One a national publicly-owned station, focusing essentially on post-1956 popular music, was launched by the BBC in 1967, though a chart had existed in Britain since 1952 when *New Musical Express* unveiled a Top 12 based on record, rather than sheet-music, sales.

style. Journalist and cultural critic Jon Savage provides a personal, yet perceptive, consideration of the power of pop music in his sleeve notes to the 2006 compilation album *Pop Justice*, a collection linked to the website of the same name[36] which unreservedly espouses the pop ethic. Savage, suggesting that pop music can possess elements that actually endure rather than instantly evaporate, proposes that this CD 'enshrines the central pop paradox'. He continues:

> Although designed as ephemeral the best pop songs transcend their transience to become perennial. This cannot be planned but is the result of a curious alchemy that fuses sound and emotion, performer and audience, mass production with individual desire. In their total concentration on the moment, these songs make it clear that the perfect pop time is, and always has been, forever NOW.[37]

It is also worth remarking, too, that if we do accord pop the status of a genre, we should, in addition, identify some of the sub-genres that arise from it: older terms like chart and Top 20/40, bubblegum and teenybop have been joined in more recent times by descriptive terms such as 'boy band' and 'girl group', a useful shorthand for material performed by single sex acts, and framing a style that has all of those marks of pop we have touched upon above. It is worth adding, too, that the groups who represent this subgenre are frequently associated with another adjective that has long been linked, and generally pejoratively, to pop: manufactured.

To move beyond generic classification, however, we can provide some illustrations of producers, composers and practitioners who seem to well exemplify notions of what pop represents. The mode in which much of their music is created underpins the style's association with notions of manufacture – a factory line dispensing consistent, easily-coded products with mass appeal, conveyor-belt items which are approachable, affordable and lacking any claims to durability or longevity. Phil Spector was the svengali behind the Wall of Sound and a string of artists – the Teddy Bears, the Ronettes – he sourced and groomed for stardom in the 1960s; Nicki Chinn and Mike Chapman were English songwriters who delivered a sequence of major chart entries to groups like Mud, Sweet and Blondie in the 1970s; Mike Stock, Matt Aitken and Pete Waterman penned dozens of successful records for Dead or Alive, Rick Astley, Bananarama and Kylie Minogue in the 1980s; while Max Martin and Xenon have been the independent writer/producers behind acts such as Britney Spears and Girls Aloud in the late 1990s and early 2000s. In a number of these cases, the creative masters behind the composition and its actual recording have, in addition, also discovered, then moulded, the singer or group in a manner they see as best suited to the song's projection, presentation and ultimate commercial progress. It is that marriage of manufacture and commerce that is generally at the foundation of high-selling and thus profit-generating pop

---

[36]   See http://www.popjustice.com.

[37]   Jon Savage in sleeve notes accompanying the 2006 CD release *Pop Justice: 100% Solid Pop Music* (Fascination B000JCESCU).

music. From the early 1990s, the emergence of the so-called boy band – best represented in Britain by Take That and the Irish acts Boyzone and Westlife – and the girl group – the Spice Girls and Girls Aloud offer typical examples – has, if anything, emphasized the notion of pop act as a constructed platform devised to realize the money-making intentions of an astute management or production team. The rise of the reality TV talent show, particularly at the beginning of the new century, has further refined the concept of the star act who emerges from nowhere and, through the deft talents of a puppet-master and the plain advantages of prime-time exposure, attains national fame.[38]

But what of rock? How have scholars attempted to define this particular musical form? Moore draws attention to the problems associated with defining what we might mean by rock as he outlines the dizzying number of categories that have attached themselves to the form. He comments:

> Rock supports a vast range of labels: progressive rock, stadium rock, classic rock, folk rock, gospel rock, country rock, swamp rock, glam and glitter rock, psychedelic rock, cock rock, rock'n'roll, rockabilly, ballad rock, melodic rock, synthesiser rock, pomp rock, acid rock, punk rock, art rock, soft, heavy, thrash, hardcore and death metal, soft and hard rock, goth rock, adult-oriented rock, pub rock, indie rock, authentic rock … . The list is as long as a publicist's thesaurus. Fortunately, many of these descriptions are not of styles themselves but of institutions (melodies can be found in both stadia and pubs), ideologies (the aestheticism of art rock, or the macho pose of cock rock), critical appraisal (pomp rock is by definition pretentious) and even forms (the ballad), as derived from Tin Pan Alley.[39]

In the midst of this plethora of adjectives, how might we effectively segregate rock from pop? The contrasting place of the single and the status of the album[40] may provide useful touchstones as we contemplate this generally, though not exclusively, oppositional relationship. It is instructive to note that Led Zeppelin, the band who, arguably, most came to personify our understanding of rock music, certainly that brand of high volume, high octane electric blues at the end of the 1960s and the start of the 1970s, released no singles – at least not in their British homeland – deciding to deliberately ignore that particular marketplace and release

---

[38]   *Pop Idol*, *Pop Stars: The Rivals* and *X-Factor* are examples of British TV talent search shows that have proved to be both audience ratings-winners and contributors to the hit-making conveyor belt in the early 2000s.

[39]   Moore, *Rock: The Primary Text*, p. 66.

[40]   An industry-devised format division, prompted by the US Federal Communications Commission, was formed in the early 1950s when the long-playing, 12", 33.3 rpm record was dedicated to classical music while the 7", 45 rpm disc was regarded as a suitable outlet for pop songs. By the mid-1960s, the commercial supremacy of the single in popular music was being challenged, and eventually overtaken, by the rock album.

only LPs. It was a gesture of resistance which snubbed the whole concept of the Top 40. For their record label Atlantic, it may have been regarded, at least initially, as an act of commercial foolhardiness. After all, whether the singles market was merely an ephemeral, teen-oriented playground or not, the ongoing value of the 45 was widely recognized in that it provided an instant calling card for acts of all kind – whether rock or pop, soul or blues – in a way an album could not. Radio airplay of a single, even if such a release proved to be no more than a loss leader, would ensure an act's work appeared in the biggest of shop windows. Bands like Cream, Black Sabbath and Deep Purple – groups who shared an aesthetic with the hard and heavy rock of Led Zeppelin – did not side-step the opportunity to enjoy the benefits of national air-time and a presence in the chart that a single release at least promised. But Led Zeppelin, by eschewing the hit-making machinery and the temporary limelight linked to it and, it has to be said, resisting the relatively modest financial returns of Top 40 success, retained an unblemished credibility. Nor did their strategy backfire – by the early 1970s, their album sales and global tours had placed them at the very pinnacle of the rock pyramid. However we view Led Zeppelin's act of defiance – an artistic statement underpinned by a certain ethical purity or a carefully planned PR stunt, a rejection of popular music's commercial character or a disingenuous acceptance that massive album sales would always be the more lucrative option in the long run – it stands as an engaging allegory of rock's deep suspicion of pop's assumed shallow values.

At the core of this tension is rock's claim to espouse a cause that represents the antithesis of pop and its manufactured[41] and all too manicured character: authenticity.[42] Within that term – drawn from *authenticus*, a word of Latin origins that has given us the related author and authority – is distilled a series of notions that underpin the rock ethos: originality, independence and autonomy. Although we can challenge most rock music – essentially a white, amplified form built on powerful yet relatively unsophisticated, 4/4 drum and bass rhythms, overlain by guitar power chords and lengthy solos premised on pentatonic patterns and the full armoury of axe warfare (for example, distortion, sustain and feedback) and vocals with a rugged edge and a brooding machismo – on each of those grounds, it is the *myth* of rock that persists: relentlessly enduring despite the vagaries of fashion, physically menacing, deeply patriarchal and sometimes misogynistic, the music has a compelling, cacophonous energy that brooks resistance. Thus, while

---

[41]   'Manufacture(d), "To make, originally by hand, now usually by machinery and on a large scale; to fabricate, concoct; to produce unintelligently in quantity" (*Collins English Dictionary*, 1988); "To produce, or make, (a product) from a raw material especially a large-scale operation using machinery; the production of goods especially by industrial processes" (*Collins English Dictionary*, 1998).

[42]   'Authentic/authenticity', "Of undisputed origin or authorship; genuine; accurate in representation of the facts; trustworthy; reliable"; from the Latin, *authenticus*, "coming from the author"; from the Greek, *authentes*, "one who acts independently" (*Collins English Dictionary*, 1998).

rock may owe almost everything to black blues traditions and be enveloped, in most instances, by a global industry concerned primarily with profit, the bands who make the music – whether attached to subgenres such as prog, hard rock or heavy metal, thrash, speed or death metal – have persisted in believing they fly a flag for the individual, the rebel, the outsider, and thus stand against incorporation in all senses.

Yet this is almost a caricature of rock and rock at a quite precise historical moment, perhaps. The fact that the term has been used to describe a particular kind of music made by a specific brand of long-haired and be-denimed outlaw, tends to ignore the case that it was Dylan and the Beatles as they moved, respectively, from folk and pop after 1965 who virtually consummated the new vision of rock, a sound riddled with smart social critique and muso-lyrical sophistication; that rock also then enjoyed conjugal relations with jazz and funk, folk and country to produce a string of new and enriching subgenres; and by the mid-1970s had spawned so many extra offshoots – glam, punk, new wave, indie, grunge and more – that the turned-up, tough-edged, 12-bar version of the end of the 1960s and the beginning of the 1970s was merely one variation of what rock actually stood for. Rock, as Moore has already confirmed, is a creature with multiple personalities, capable of embracing Yes and the Eagles, Television and Aerosmith, Guns N' Roses and REM, Iron Maiden and the Smiths, Radiohead and Razorlight, groups sharing few sonic or ideological standpoints. As Shuker remarks on the style's wide span and its assumed substance: 'Rock is the broad label for the huge range of styles that have evolved out of rock'n'roll. Rock is often considered to carry more weight than pop, with connotations of greater integrity, sincerity and authenticity.'[43]

It is interesting to note, too, that in Borthwick and Moy's volume *Popular Music Genres* neither pop nor rock are among those genres even under the microscope. As these two commentators regard pop and rock as metagenres, it is perhaps not surprising that their generic survey does contain a number of kinds of rock – progressive, punk, heavy metal and indie – but, maybe significantly, only one kind of pop, synthpop, hinting that they, rather like their colleagues and counterparts – scholars and critics – have a tendency to under-rate the value of pop and see it as a less worthy, less serious, form of consideration than rock. Rock's realism and encoded authenticity seems to generally appeal to both the serious critic and the enquiring scholar, possibly because its intentions – whether, musical or lyrical, subcultural or gestural, performative or technological – appear to be charged with more substantial ideas and messages than pop which, almost of itself, tends to dilute, even expunge, its cerebral components and focus on the more ephemeral intensities of adolescent romance. Rock speaks of the political in the personal and, on occasions, communicates in the social or communal sense: if the songs rarely express protest ideas or radical messages in a direct manner (The Mothers of Invention, Gang of Four and Rage Against the Machine have, for instance, used their music as a platform to relay specific manifestos), they often

---

43   Shuker, *Key Concepts in Popular Music*, p. 263.

frame notions of the individual against the world in a classic romantic style[44] (Jimi Hendrix's 'Ezy Ryder', Cream's 'I Feel Free', the Doors' 'Riders On the Storm' and Oasis' 'Rock'n'Roll Star' are just four of many available examples). Also, as most material in this field is original and penned by the singer/musicians who perform it, there is an assumption, at least, that something genuine, something sincere, is being expressed within the framework of the piece; pop almost invariably addresses the romantic condition of the individual – found love, lost love, love desired – and then, generally, only in a vicarious fashion, as the songs performed tend to be the product of someone else's pen rather than the creation of the artists themselves.

Yet there are contradictions even within this account. In the UK in the middle of the first decade of the new century, recent hit-makers like McFly and Busted have been presented and promoted as pop artists, even boy bands, even though they write their own songs and plainly draw on the guitar, bass and drums traditions we generally link to rock; the Magic Numbers, meanwhile, make a melodious music based on appealing harmonies and marked by few of the expected signs of rock yet are sold to audiences as a act with a quirky, indie quality. Thus, it appears that the differentiations between the two central terms in this survey are not always clear-cut, often based less on the sounds that are recorded and performed and more on ideological perceptions, constructed on image, accompanying advertising campaigns and the media outlets where artists enjoy high-profile representation, for example, and imposed and projected by the label publicists and absorbed and accepted by the record buyers. Consequently, McFly are likely to make frequent appearances in the teen glossies like *TOTP* magazine while the Magic Numbers are generating the critical interest of a more serious rock publication like *Mojo*, for example. This relationship between artists, their record releases or live tours and target readerships is almost indivisible from the industrial forces which drive the promotional vehicle. As Frith comments:

> Genre distinctions are central to how record company A&R[45] departments work. The first thing they ask about any demo tape or potential signing is what *sort* of music is it, and the importance of this question is that it integrates an inquiry about the music (what does it sound like) with an inquiry about the market (who will buy it).[46]

---

[44]   These ideas are further explored in Robert Pattison, *The Triumph of Vulgarity: Rock Music in the Mirror of Romanticism* (Oxford, 1987) and Simon Reynolds and Joy Press, *The Sex Revolts: Gender, Rebellion and Rock'n'Roll* (New York, 1995).

[45]   Artists & Repertoire. A&R departments are at the heart of the search for new talent. Staff members will listen to demo submissions by unsigned bands or trawl the clubs and bars to hear new acts play live.

[46]   Frith, *Performing Rites*, pp. 75–6.

So, against this broader canvas of generic pigeon-holing, the contrasts and oppositions between rock and pop continue to provide a lively forum of discussion, perhaps *the* cornerstone of popular music debate in the UK. Within academic, journalistic, industrial and fan circles, these binary positions set out much of the contested ground within the field of intellectual, cultural and commercial exchange, even if the boundaries are not always clearly drawn and the walls are breached with fair regularity. Nevertheless, while the signs that connote these generic categories – whether sonic or visual, sociological or ideological – are occasionally hazy and the subject of ongoing disagreement and argument, those indicators and their generally understood meanings remain a crucial tool in identifying and categorizing new sounds and styles. In a dynamic and voracious marketplace like Britain, where popular music has been a particularly vivacious, capable of regular cross-fertilization and frequent re-invention, the need for genre analysis becomes more than just an academic exercise. It is rather, for scholars and students, reviewers and talent-spotters, a means of making sense of an ever-changing landscape.

Chapter 11
The Issue of Musical Genres in France

Fabien Hein

This chapter aims to summarize French academic knowledge dealing with musical genres falling under the category of 'amplified music'. Although in the academic community, it is common to hear or read that such knowledge is scarce, upon examination, it appears that the collection of research is vast; I have personally listed almost 550 articles, books and other works.

The Problem of Categorization

The categories 'amplified music', 'contemporary music' or 'popular music' raise questions. Their advantages and disadvantages have been largely demonstrated,[1] even if we don't know exactly their scope, except that they cover an extremely composite and continuously proliferating range of musical genres. These categories have qualities in their flaws, and *vice versa*. They are imprecise, permeable and dynamic. To some extent, amplified/contemporary music 'is' the musical genres scheduled in the performance venues specifically provided for them, and popular music covers the musical genres discussed in academic journals dedicated to such music. On this basis, their musical spectrum thus ranges from blues to electronic music, including rock, rap, techno and so-on.[2] This in itself causes further problems. What do these denominations include? Exactly what is meant when we use the term rock? Is it punk, metal or even hardcore? If we accept that it is metal, it remains to be determined what genre of metal. Black metal? Grindcore? Power metal? And if so, American or European? These are different genres just as much as they different kinds of work. The Russian-doll nature of musical categorization raises dramatic questions, and although not insurmountable, this lack of differentiation can nonetheless lead to misleading generalizations, as categories themselves are never probed – as if they were self-explanatory, which is often far from the case.

---

[1] Philippe Teillet, 'Éléments pour une histoire des politiques publiques en faveur des "musiques amplifiées"', in Philippe Poirrier (ed.), *Les collectivités locales et la culture. Les formes de l'institutionnalisation, 19ème–20ème siècles* (Paris, 2002), pp. 361–93.

[2] I have also included in this vast spectrum three cultural phenomena inseparable from musical genres: hippies inseparable from psychedelic rock; skinheads, inseparable from Oi! music, and zulus and B-Boys inseparable from rap.

It is important to remember that as early as 1987, Patrick Mignon[3] underlined how rock was an undifferentiated category, but this failed to have real effect upon French researchers. In light of this situation, I shall therefore strictly confine myself to categories used by researchers themselves.

To my knowledge, we have a corpus of some 550 academic documents produced throughout France. Before dealing with their epistemological frameworks, in other words the question of 'how', it seems important to investigate 'when' (year of publication), 'where' (publication medium), 'what' (musical genre) and 'who' (researcher discipline).

The corpus spans the 1960s to the present day. In 1964, Yvonne Bernard[4] published the first of – currently – 300 articles on music which have appeared in general or specialist journals. In 1973, Bernard Gensane[5] defended the first of 75 doctoral theses dealing with amplified music genres.[6] In 1981, Gérard Herzhaft[7] published the first of a hundred or so books dealing with a musical subject area. In 1983, Marie-Christine Pouchelle[8] published the first of 70 edited book chapters.

Journals unquestionably represent the primary publication medium for studies of amplified music. Amongst these, only two titles are exclusively devoted to popular music (*Vibrations*,[9] and *Copyright Volume!*[10]). Other journals occasionally devote a study, or a special edition to amplified music (*Sociétés*, *L'Homme*, *Mouvements*, *Autrement*, *Musurgia*, *Cercles*, *Réseaux*). Yet, in the vast majority of cases, articles dealing with a musical subject area are published in journals without a primary, or even one-off, focus on amplified music.

The corpus covers 38 musical categories. To restrict this, I shall group these by musical family. On this basis, the family of rock (38.5 per cent), techno (20.4 per cent) and rap (15.7 per cent) represent two thirds of research undertaken. The remaining third covers eight families, amongst which jazz (11.8 per cent) and *chanson* (4.2 per cent) are the most significant. Pop, blues, soul, world music, reggae and country/folk occupy relatively marginal positions (below 2 per cent).

---

[3]   Patrick Mignon, 'Les jeunesses du rock', Actes de l'Université d'été, *Les Musiques des Jeunes*, Rennes, 7–11 July 1986 (Paris, 1987): pp. 27–33.

[4]   Yvonne Bernard, 'La chanson, phénomène social', *Revue Française de Sociologie*, 5/2 (1964): pp. 166–74.

[5]   Bernard Gensane, *La pop music 1955–1970: existence, essence et fonction*, Université de Paris 8, Doctoral thesis (1973).

[6]   These doctoral theses in the subject area of music are constantly increasing. In the 1970s there were five theses, in the 1980s 12, in the 1990s 25 and 31 in the 2000s.

[7]   Gerard Herzhaft, *Le blues* (Paris, 1981).

[8]   Marie-Christine Pouchelle, 'Sentiments religieux et show-business: Claude François, objet de dévotion populaire', in Jean-Claude Schmitt (ed.), *Les saints et les stars. Le texte hagiographique dans la culture populaire* (Paris, 1983), pp. 277–99.

[9]   Six editions appearing between 1985 and 1988.

[10]   Twelve editions appearing between 2002 and 2007. The adventure was to finish following the publication of the 12th edition.

It is obviously impossible to exhaustively analyse herein each of these families, so this chapter shall, therefore, discuss only the three dominant components of amplified music: rock, techno and rap.

The discipline which strongly dominates (44.1 per cent) French research into amplified music is sociology. Sociology is strongly represented in research into rock (20.6 per cent), techno (11.6 per cent) and rap (7.2 per cent), but political science, history, philosophy and musicology also heavily focus on these musical families. With these preliminaries established, it now remains to consider how such musical genres are problematized, with the general aim of seeing just how knowledge about these different musical genres is developed.

Studying Amplified Music

The expression 'amplified music' refers to an administrative definition or category[11] indicating the involvement of the French State in this domain. It designates a vast range of music which, in broad terms, incorporates rock, rap, techno and many other genres. This category was advocated by the sociologist Marc Touché in 1994, for whom this term 'represents a unifying instrument combining widely contrasting musical worlds: some forms of *chanson* called variety, some forms of jazz and music called world, fusion; jazz rock, rock'n'roll, hard-rock, reggae, rap, techno, house-music, industrial music, funk, dance-music and all 'DIY' musical genres not yet identified'.[12]

The category 'amplified music' has given rise – under this or neighbouring names – to more than 25 research works, including three doctoral theses, five books and almost 20 chapters and articles published in edited books or journals. The 'amplified music' classification is as ambiguous as it aims to be all-encompassing, and it introduces a macro-sociological approach. In practical terms, it seeks to cover several large musical families, without necessarily establishing links between them, and with the objective of excluding none. This happens to be the precise ambition of French cultural policies. However, this game of all-encompassing categorization is misleading, as it occults more clearly-targeted approaches. Indeed, upon observation, analyses led by the four French researchers who most concentrate their efforts on amplified music are seen to most frequently draw on the world of rock: Touché is an astute sociographer of rock musical practices; Philippe Teillet, an eminent specialist of cultural policies in the 'amplified music' sector, draws his references from the world of rock; Gérôme Guibert and Emmanuel Brandl are also well anchored in rock music. However, their research additionally looks, albeit to a lesser extent, into other musical families such as rap, techno or even

---

[11] Teillet, *Élements*, pp. 361–93.

[12] Marc Touché, 'Musique, vous avez dit musiques ?', in Pierre Quay-Thévenon (ed.), *Les Rencontres du Grand Zebrock. A propos des musiques actuelles* (Noisy-le-Sec, 1998), pp. 13–15.

jazz[13] which they compare and attempt to interlink, and by so doing, their work is effectively that which best fits the expression 'amplified music'. But aside from these exceptions allowing researchers to accumulate general observations, studies into 'amplified music' devote very little space to techno, for example, which is overshadowed by rock. This is doubtless the result of the historical importance of rock in France[14] as well as of the emotional closeness of many researchers to this musical genre. Furthermore, given researchers' socio-historical approach, the category of rock appears unavoidable, since it is the original subject for all writing on amplified music. It is difficult to clarify the ambiguity inherent in the expression 'amplified music', but in attempting to do so, we shall now examine the ways rock, techno and rap, specifically, are studied.

Studying Rock

Quantitatively, rock is by far the most widely studied musical family in France, covered by some 180 research works including 20 doctoral theses, 30 books and almost 140 articles and chapters in numerous journals and edited books. We have just seen that rock can be studied, in veiled terms, as a genre of amplified music, but more generally, researchers view it in two ways: firstly, as a generic category, and secondly, as a specific sub-genre. These two levels of reading present somewhat different visions of rock. On the one hand, rock is understood as a portmanteau concept, and as the originator of a prolific and undifferentiated family of descendants, thus introducing a meso-sociological level of analysis. On the other hand, it is viewed more discretely as a segment of a wider musical family, in other words as the sub-genre 'rock', and this implies a micro-sociological analysis.

Meso-level analysis is currently the approach most frequently undertaken by French researchers. It considers rock as a generic category of the musical world. The first books dealing with rock in this manner – *Rock. De l'histoire au mythe* edited by Patrick Mignon and Antoine Hennion;[15] *Le rock. Aspects esthétiques,*

---

[13]   See for example Gérome Guibert, *La production de la culture. Le cas des musiques amplifiées en France. Genèses, structurations, industries, alternatives* (Paris, 2006). The author deals with the eleven major musical families looked at in this article. However, when undertaking a count of sections attributed to each family, the following number is obtained: rock (23), jazz (8), *chanson* (5), techno and hip-hop (respectively 3), pop, blues, folk, reggae (respectively 2), world, soul (respectively 1). The rock family itself represents half of all sections, which is all told quite representative of the imbalance which affects the term 'amplified music'.

[14]   Philippe Le Guern, 'En arrière la musique! Sociologies des musiques populaires en France. La genèse d'un champ', *Réseaux*, 'Sociologies des musiques populaires', 141/2 (2007): pp. 15–45.

[15]   Patrick Mignon and Antoine Hennion (eds), *Rock. De l'histoire au mythe* (Paris, 1991).

culturels et sociaux edited by Anne-Marie Gourdon[16] – contain two focuses which have influenced paths taken by subsequent research. The first focus relates to 'localized' research, the second relates to thematic research.

Localized studies are those undertaken within a specific geographical area used by the researcher as a defined area for analysis. Such research usually reflects four types of administrative/government levels in France: municipal, *départemental*, regional and national. Analysis at the national level tends to concentrate on political issues, and studies at the lower levels generally focus on musical practice.

Localized research is typically combined with particular themes, although thematic research is not necessarily localized, and is therefore derived from undefined geographical spaces, whose contours may or may not be discernable. Six recurring large-scale themes can be identified, focusing on history, politics, production, fans, objects, and media.

Much work on rock contains introductory syntheses providing an international historical perspective (United Kingdom/United States). In the best of cases,[17] the French historical context is meagre, but more often than not is absent. In a recent article, Philippe Le Guern has underlined that it is 'striking to observe that some of the little research devoted to the history of rock in France is undertaken by learned enthusiasts – who often undertake remarkably well-documented work – and not by academics'[18]. And when a few rare academics do produce historical data, it often comes from sociologists, never historians. It is clear that the history of rock in France remains largely unwritten.

The history of French cultural policies relating to rock has been studied in greater depth, synchronically by Anne-Marie Gourdon,[19] and diachronically by Philippe Teillet.[20] Teillet's long-term study covers a period during which it is interesting to observe the terminological shift in research, moving progressively from 'rock' to 'amplified/contemporary' music. Nevertheless, the work of Teillet constitutes, in France, a background structuring much other research. Conversely, the issue of politics may additionally be envisaged from the viewpoint of the political commitment of artists; a perspective initiated by Anne Benetollo[21] and

[16]   Anne-Marie Gourdon (ed.), *Le rock. Aspects esthétiques, culturels et sociaux* (Paris, 1994).

[17]   Anne Benetollo and Yves Le Goff, 'Historique du rock', in Gourdon, ibid., pp. 11–53.

[18]   Le Guern, *En arrière*, pp. 19.

[19]   Gourdon, *Le Rock*, pp. 141–50.

[20]   Philippe Teillet, 'Une politique culturelle du rock ?', in Mignon and Hennion, *Rock*, pp. 217–46.

[21]   Anne Benetollo, *Rock et politique: Censure, Opposition, Intégration* (Paris, 1999).

recently continued by Jean-Marie Seca.[22] Here, however, researchers tend to focus on countries other than France.

The producers of rock are primarily considered in their most common form, that of rock groups and their component musicians. The first to take an interest therein were Jean-Marie Seca[23] and Catherine Dutheil,[24] followed more recently by Damien Tassin.[25] Their work, generally based on empirical sociology, aims at presenting the social and experiential dimensions of rock.

Strongly influenced by Howard Becker, Mignon[26] took a broader perspective in examining the network of cooperation necessary for producing rock. In his view, rock is the product of collective activity by an ensemble of actors. This perspective has guided much research, that of Gérôme Guibert[27] especially. Guibert's study aims at an account of the cultural production network of the French music industry, requiring him to provide a wide sociological, economic, and historical overview. This research highlights a clear division between on the one hand, a dominant cultural industry, professional, centralized and integrated, and local, amateur, decentralized and often invisible cultural production. But it additionally underlines the close interdependence of these spheres, and this double system of cultural production is inseparable from a consumption system, which thus leads us to consider the reception of rock cultural products and, notably, their fans.

Within French research, the dominant representation of the rock fan is that of a cultural consumer. This representation is not, however, homogenous and may adopt several forms of which it is possible to establish a chronology.

Initially, the rock fan was seen as a cultural consumer alienated by capitalist consumer society. In the early 1980s, Jean-Charles Lagrée[28] and David Buxton[29] published studies with Marxist overtones, strongly marked by Adorno, aiming to denounce mass consumption. They saw rock as a dominated class identity of which youngsters were the unknowing victims. Subsequently, the rock fan was seen as a 'young' cultural consumer. In this framework, links between rock and youth was established in the later 1980s through a series of seminal edited volumes with

---

[22] Jean-Marie Seca (ed.), *Musiques populaires underground et représentations du politique* (Paris, 2007).

[23] Jean-Marie Seca, *Vocations rock* (Paris, 1988).

[24] Caroline Doublé-Dutheil, 'Les groupes de rock nantais', in Mignon and Hennion, *Rock*, pp. 147–58.

[25] Damien Tassin, *Rock et production de soi. Une sociologie de l'ordinaire des groupes et des musiciens* (Paris, 2004).

[26] Patrick Mignon, 'Paris/Givors: le rock local', in Mignon and Hennion *Rock*, p. 197.

[27] Guibert, *La Production*.

[28] Jean-Charles Lagrée, *Les jeunes chantent leurs cultures, coll Changements* (Paris, 1982).

[29] David Buxton, *Le rock, star-système et société de consommation* (Grenoble, 1985).

evocative titles such as 'Les musiques des jeunes'[30] and 'Jeunes et musique'[31]. While nowadays we may question such a direct link, this research aimed nonetheless to demonstrate the socializing character of rock and people's new relationships to leisure time. Next, the rock fan was seen as a consumer of psychoactive products. From the 1990s a series of studies presented the consumption of alcohol or drugs as an inseparable element of rock culture. The festive nature of rock combined with alcohol as a stimulus to sociability was underlined by Patrick Mignon.[32] Sylvain Aquatias[33] refined these observations, allowing him to contrast routine drug use (making daily life more bearable) and excessive use (breaking free from daily life). Most recently, the fan has been seen as a passionate cultural consumer. In a break from the three previous analyses, studies in the 2000s re-envisage the fan. In a book about Beatles fans, Christian Le Bart[34] investigates the fan's identity processes, and Gabriel Segré[35] unpacks the cult of Elvis using insights from the sociology of religion.

On the whole, these studies remain focused on human interactions. They are deeply marked by the American interactionist school and notably the work of Howard Becker.[36] The sociology of mediation as developed by Antoine Hennion[37] pushed the interactionist logic to its limit by underlining the irreversible mixity between humans and objects. Otherwise put, if rock is the product of a network of collective activities, it is important to repopulate this network with all of its mediators, both human and non-human; and thus, to recognize the equal powers of people and of things, as they are both components of and participants in this network. On this basis, records become mediators in the same way as fans. It is in this widened perspective that I personally[38] have attempted to explain the functioning of the world of rock. Not only by focusing on the actors of the rock world, but additionally on items produced, on what items may do, or on their cost; this has allowed me on the one hand, to establish socioeconomic data, and also to

---

[30]   *Actes de l'Université d'été*, 'Les Musiques des Jeunes', Rennes, 7–11 July 1986 (Paris, 1987).

[31]   *Cahiers Jeunesses et Sociétés*, 'Jeunes et musique', n° 10 (1988).

[32]   Patrick Mignon, 'Rock et alcool', *Sociétés & Représentations*, Les Cahiers du CREDHESS, 1 (1995): pp. 103–10.

[33]   Sylvain Aquatias, 'Les consommations de produits psychoactifs dans les milieux festifs de la culture rock', *Observatoire français des drogues et des toxicomanies*, 27 (2002). Available at: http://www.drogues.gouv.fr.

[34]   Christian Le Bart, with the collaboration of Jean-Charles Ambroise, *Les fans des Beatles. Sociologie d'une passion* (Rennes, 2000).

[35]   Gabriel Segré, *Le culte Presley* (Paris, 2003).

[36]   Howard Saul Becker, *Les mondes de l'art* (Paris, 1988).

[37]   Antoine Hennion, *La passion musicale. Une sociologie de la médiation* (Paris, 1993).

[38]   Fabien Hein, *Le monde du rock. Ethnographie du réel* (Paris, 2006). Preface by Antoine Hennion.

describe a dynamic and balanced world of rock where actions are shared between bodies, items and judgements and are held together by attachment, pleasure and participation. This epistemological choice was subsequently adopted by François Ribac[39] who paid particular consideration to records as objects, thereby reconstituting the socio-technical networks leading to fans.

While the mediation model is still relatively rarely used in studies of rock, the interest in objects and mechanisms is evident. The importance of the electro-amplifier was highlighted as early as 1985 by David Buxton.[40] This issue would be specifically developed by Touché[41] who as well as establishing its sociology was also its museographer.[42] Beyond this material aspect, a further contribution of Touche's work has been his widened reflection on the sound environments of musicians, notably in terms of rehearsals.[43] A handful of researchers have occasionally focused on the objects/mechanisms of rock performance venues (bars,[44] concerts,[45] festivals[46]) and these studies are all the more significant because, generally speaking, the entertainment aspect of rock is less frequently dealt with from a socio-technical perspective than in terms of emotions.

The mass media are the mediators of choice for rock, but in France, radio and television remain poor relations in terms of studies focusing on the relations between rock and the media, since the written press receives much greater coverage of its three primary elements: the general or specialist musical press (magazines), the daily news press (newspapers) and alternative musical press[47] (fanzines). Such

---

[39]   François Ribac, *L'Avaleur de rock* (Paris, 2004).

[40]   Buxton, *Le Rock*.

[41]   Marc Touché, *Ethno-sociologie des musiciens utilisant des instruments électroamplifiés* (Montluçon, 1998).

[42]   On behalf of the Musée National des Arts et Traditions Populaires (MNATP). See Marc Touché, 'Muséographier les "musiques électro-amplifiées" '. Pour une socio-histoire du sonore, 'Sociologies des musiques populaires', *Réseaux*, 141/2 (2007): pp. 97–141.

[43]   Marc Touché, 'Les lieux de répétition de musiques amplifiées. Défaut d'équipement et malentendus sociaux', *Les Annales de la Recherche Urbaine*, 70 (1996), pp. 58–67.

[44]   Julie Cavignac, 'Nécrologie d'un bar rock. In memoriam luxoris. Ou du vécu comme source du travail ethnologique', *Cahiers ethnologiques*, 'A nos sources', 9 (1988): pp. 49–65.

[45]   Anne-Marie Gourdon, 'Le spectaculaire dans les concerts de rock et de variétés: les éclairages', in Anne-Marie Gourdon (ed.), *Le spectaculaire dans les concerts de rock et de variétés: les éclairages*, pp. 68–72.

[46]   Vanessa Valero, 'Le festival de rock, entre passion et désenchantement', *Copyright Volume!*, 1/1 (2002): pp. 113–23.

[47]   'La presse musicale alternative au 21ème siècle' *Copyright Volume!*, 5/1 (2006).

research generally investigates three aspects: the reception of rock as cultural production;[48] rock criticism as discourse;[49] and finally, rock criticism as work.[50]

We have seen that rock is saturated by contradictory logics, and that it is an umbrella category so vast that it is impossible to have an overall view of it. It may be that a clearer and more precise idea of rock can be obtained through more detailed studies. Such a 'micro' approach involves three levels of analysis: firstly, rock sub-genres; secondly, rock movements/milieus; and, thirdly rock musicians themselves.

Punk and metal are the two musical genres most widely covered by French researchers. Studies into punk, which has the longest history, are both rare and relatively caricatured, and often without real empirical bases, tend to be unconvincing. More recently, the metal genre has been studied in a series of works. I personally undertook a socio-historical ethnographic study on the subject;[51] this book was followed by two 'metal' thematic research dossiers in *Sociétés*[52] and *Copyright Volume!*[53] This research demonstrates that it is ultimately just as difficult to discuss certain musical genres in general terms. For instance, my book considered over 70 musical genres and sub-genres belonging to the metal family; it is somewhat difficult to observe any unity in this family.

After genres, it was movements/milieus strongly linked to rock which were studied. Three principal focuses can be observed; firstly, the hippy movement; secondly, the skinhead phenomenon; and finally the Goth milieu. The hippy movement is typically approached from the perspective of research on gangs or counter-cultural groups.[54] The skinhead phenomenon is profusely examined from the political viewpoint.[55] As for the Goth milieu, this is above all studied in its

---

[48] Mireille Willey, 'Le rock à travers la presse spécialisée', in Gourdon, *Le spectaculaire*, pp. 181–212.

[49] Thomas Mansier, *Identité du rock et presse spécialisée. Évolution d'une culture et de son discours critique dans les magazines français des années 90*, Lyon 2 University, Thesis (2004).

[50] Fabien Hein, 'Le critique rock, le fanzine et le magazine: "Ça s'en va et ça revient"', *Copyright Volume!* special number on 'La presse musicale alternative au 21ème siècle', 5/1 (2006): pp. 83–105.

[51] Fabien Hein, *Hard Rock, Heavy Metal, Metal. Histoire, cultures et pratiquants* (Paris, 2003).

[52] *Sociétés*, 88, special number on 'La religion metal' (2005).

[53] *Copyright Volume!* 5/2 (2007), special number on 'Les musiques metal. Sciences sociales et pratiques culturelles radicales'.

[54] Gérard Mauger, *Hippies, zoulous, loubards: jeunes marginaux de 1968 à aujourd'hui* (Paris, 1998).

[55] Angelina Péralva, 'Skinhead: une identité politique ?', in CERI/CURAPP, *L'identité politique* (Paris, 1994): pp. 94–110.

aesthetic aspects.[56] Curiously, this research deals very little with music itself, which is treated as a given. Only Gildas Lescop[57] truly touches on the matter by retracing the socio-history of Oi! music, favoured genre of skinheads.

A handful of researchers have studied the careers or music of rock artists: Noir Désir, the Pretenders, Frank Zappa, Marilyn Manson or even Living Colour have been the subject of articles. The most significant research here is that on Elvis Presley by Sébastian Danchin,[58] on Bob Dylan by Thomas Karsenty-Ricard[59] or on Jim Morrison by Jacob Thomas Matthews.[60]

Ultimately, it is particularly difficult to draw broad epistemological outlines because of the extent to which studies into rock reflect differing thematic choices, theoretical options and varied disciplines. We will now consider whether this is also the case for other musical families.

Studying Techno

Techno is the second most widely studied musical genre in France in terms of the quantity of publications, with almost 90 research works including half a dozen doctoral theses, almost a dozen books and nearly 70 articles found in a range of edited books and journals.

Techno is very rarely studied as a category of amplified music. It is more readily viewed as a generic category; that is on a meso-level of reading which offers a relatively general view of techno since it is considered in an undifferentiated manner as one genre amongst others of electronic music.

Considering techno as a generic category allows investigation to focus in more detail, referring to it as a genre of electronic music, and subsequently as a genre of dance music. Although these nesting categories may temporarily mislead, it is important to remember that the word techno, as the word rock, is a vast umbrella-category covering multitudinous specific sub-genres (house, jungle, drum'n'bass, etc.). But these sub-genres are largely ignored in French studies of techno which prefer an analytic perspective based on four themes: parties, drug use, artistic practices, and tools and techniques.

Techno as a festive phenomenon is a fundamental aspect of research into this music. Its treatment is generally divided between the two key themes of raves and free parties.

---

[56]   Antoine Durafour, *Le milieu gothique. Sa construction sociale à travers la dimension esthétique* (Paris, 2005).

[57]   Gildas Lescop, '"Honnie soit la Oi !": naissance, émergence et déliquescence d'une forme de protestation sociale et musicale', *Copyright Volume!* 2/1 (2003): pp. 109–28.

[58]   Sebastian Danchin, *Elvis Presley ou la revanche du Sud* (Paris, 2004).

[59]   Thomas Karsenty-Ricard, *Dylan, l'authenticité et l'imprévu* (Paris, 2005).

[60]   Jacob-Thomas Matthews, *Communication d'une star: Jim Morrison* (Paris, 2003).

Partying is a shared and unifying element for both thematic approaches. Generally speaking, researchers view it as an intense moment stimulating and encouraging group cohesion. They view parties as individual and group experience; and notably, as ephemeral experiences of converging emotions;[61] events strengthening social bonds and allowing psychological release, or what is termed 'effervescence'.[62] In this sense, the techno phenomenon highlights the functional dimension of its music as well as the participative and hedonistic dimensions of all musical practice. Stéphane Hampartzoumian[63] and Jean-Christophe Sevin[64] have traced the history of raves, the conditions of their development into free parties and the forms of sociability they generate. These researchers are additionally, two of the few who consider the body and dance.

Despite much research on techno parties in general, and free parties in particular, there is relatively little information concerning the actors of these mechanisms of festivity. Loïc Lafargue de Grangeneuve has pointed out recently that in France, 'academic research into techno often resembles more magic tales of festive experiences than true analysis'.[65] There is indeed a vast array of research generally not tied to the body and in which ethnographic approaches are underused. The study by Sandy Queudrus[66] is one of the few research works which breaks this trend,[67] providing keys for the concrete understanding of the functioning of free parties, in terms of both participants and organizers.

The consideration of the consumption of psychotropic substances is a constant in studies dealing with techno. Much research reinforces the mythicization of techno. It can, for instance, be read that 'technoid subculture is a culture of escapism, where, furthermore, drug taking has a place. Yet it is much more than drug taking in the sense that it is more all-embracing and more diversified in terms of stimuli'.[68] Conversely, authors in the journal *Psychotropes* (an international journal on drug addiction) seem less indulgent and more objective.[69]

---

[61]   *Autrement*, 231, 'La fête techno. Tout seul et tous ensemble' (2004).

[62]   *Sociétés*, 65, 'Effervescence techno' (1999).

[63]   Stéphanie Hampartzoumian, *Effervescence techno ou la communauté trans(e)cendantale* (Paris, 2004).

[64]   Jean-Christophe Sevin, 'Hétérotopie techno', *Ethnographiques.org*, 3, 2003, available at: http://www.ethno-graphiques.org/2003/Sevin.html.

[65]   Loic Lafargue de Grangeneuve, 'Une sociologie des fêtes techno clandestines', *Mouvements*, 42 (2005), special issue on 'Techno. Des corps et des machines': p. 143.

[66]   Sandy Queudrus, *Un maquis techno. Modes d'engagement et pratiques sociales de la free-party* (Nantes, 2000).

[67]   Admittedly, the study's results can be criticized for using a small sample (65 people). Yet, given that the majority of studies into techno used no sample, it should be admitted that any sample is better than none at all.

[68]   Lionel Pourtau, 'La subculture technoïde, entre déviance et rupture du pacte hobbesien', *Sociétés*, 'Des technoïstes aux technoïdes', 90 (2005): p. 78.

[69]   *Psychotropes*, 9/3–4, 'Fêtes sous influences' (2003).

The links between techno and drugs were underlined in the very first studies into techno.[70] But studies specifically focusing on the subject only appeared in the early 2000s. A team of economists[71] retraced the various branches of the drugs market to which techno parties have offered new openings, and in the third section of her book, Queudrus[72] also discusses the economy of drugs within free parties (also becoming a close observer of drug users). She insists on two points: the first, widely shared, underlines drug use as both a socialization factor and a component of a party; the second, less frequently heard, emphasizes how excessive drug use poses serious health risks, particularly to mental health.

Beyond the event of the 'party', studies into artistic practices of techno place a clear emphasis on DJs as cultural producers, or more precisely as creators and performers. Researchers who devote a central place to this typically follow three levels of analysis. The sociologist Anne Petiau[73] focuses on electronic musicians. Lionel Pourtau[74] considers the DJ as an element of the Sound System. And Morgan Jouvenet[75] tries to widen the perspective to place DJs at the heart of the music industry through a theoretical framework using the sociology of artistic work. The figure of the artist is relatively rarely researched, however, and techno music even less so. Only a handful of musicologists have taken an interest in this issue; Emmanuel Grynszpan[76] under the overall perspective of sound, for example and Guillaume Kosmicki[77] with a more direct focus on techno hits.

Beyond actors, practices and music, techno is inseparable from a host of technological innovations. The tools of techno are the equipment of electronic musicians, from the record to the turntable, via the synthesizer and sampler etc. But these tools also involve use and their technical aspects (mixing, remix, sampling). In reality, existing research suggests that the tools and techniques making partying possible are markedly less important than the parties themselves. This is a strange imbalance. A handful of researchers have nonetheless focused on these objects and techniques which are just as fundamental as they are ordinary. The journal

---

[70]   Astrid Fontaine and Caroline Fontana, *Raver* (Paris, 1996).

[71]   Thierry Colombié, Nasser Lalam and Michel Schiray, *Drogue et techno. Les trafiquants de rave* (Paris, 2000).

[72]   Queudrus, *Un maquis*.

[73]   Anne Petiau, *Musiques et musiciens électroniques. Contribution à une sociologie des musiques populaires*, Paris 5 University, Doctoral thesis (2006).

[74]   Lionel Pourtau, *Frères de son. Les socialités et les sociabilités des Sound System technoïdes*, Paris 5 University, Doctoral thesis (2005).

[75]   Morgan Jouvenet, *Rap, techno, electro ... Le musicien entre travail artistique et critique sociale* (Paris, 2006).

[76]   Emmanuel Grynszpan, *Bruyante techno. Réflexion sur le son de la free party* (Nantes, 1999).

[77]   Guillaume Kosmicki, 'Analyse de "Let's Play" de Crystal Distortion: les paradoxes d'un "tube" de la Free Party', *Musurgia*, 9/2 (2002): pp. 85–101. Special number on 'Musiques populaires modernes'.

Mouvements devoted a special study to the subject.[78] The first person to consider the crucial relationship between techno music and its technological tools was Joseph Ghosn. However, his perceptive identification of the need for a programme of research has apparently not yet received the resonance it deserves. He writes:

> It is necessary to undertake extensive studies into raves so as to outline a statistical analysis of those taking part … studies should be made in various locations where instruments required for making techno music are sold and we must try to understand the very practice of this genre by living in the world of techno musicians and in so doing, understand that techno does not correspond to any single musical genre but to a variety of sub-genres, themselves often distributed corresponding to geographically specific areas.[79]

Much of the research into techno parties has appeared in the journal *Sociétés,* edited by Michel Maffesoli. Researchers publishing in this journal are primarily students inspired by his thinking and it is unsurprising that they abundantly use his paradigms and concepts, with evident consequences on their work. In their view, techno should be envisaged as a symptom of contemporary society. In this way, Maffesolian researchers (dominant in this field) aim to produce explanatory research, whereas a handful of other researchers (closer to *Mouvements*) attempt to produce exhaustively descriptive research in the sense of a Beckerian 'world'. The desire to 'mythicize' on the one hand and to 'demystify' on the other constitutes a major epistemological division. It now remains to be seen whether this obtains equally clearly for studies into rap.

Studying Rap

In terms of numbers of publications, rap is the third most widely studied musical genre by French researchers. It represents around 60 research works including eight doctoral theses, ten books and 40 or so articles or chapters in edited books and journals.

Rap music is typically studied in three manners in France. Firstly, in the same way as rock and techno, it may be studied more or less explicitly as a genre of amplified music. Similarly, it may be studied from the viewpoint of 'urban cultures' or as an element of hip-hop culture. These perspectives position observation on a macro level. Secondly, it can be studied on a meso-level, that is, as a genre which is the originator of a prolific and undifferentiated offspring. Thirdly, it may be studied in a much more detailed manner as a segment of an extended musical family and therefore be viewed on a micro level, from the viewpoint of artists

---

[78]   *Mouvements*, 42, 'Techno. Des corps et des machines' (2005).

[79]   Joseph Ghosn, 'Du "Raver" au "Sampler": vers une sociologie de la techno', *L'Homme et la Société*, 126 (1997): p. 89.

or as a sub-genre of rap (new school, gangsta-rap), with the effect of presenting relatively nuanced visions of rap.

Rap forms one of the four disciplines in hip-hop alongside DJing, dance and graf. But these disciplines coexist without necessarily sharing the same values, or sharing the same social networks. Hip-hop can no longer therefore be viewed as a 'common culture', as was envisaged in the 1980s. Despite this, some pioneering research has been important in the development of work on rap music. Although Christian Bachmann[80] established a link between smurf and rap very quickly, the most significant research is doubtless that of Hugues Bazin[81] and Virginie Milliot-Belmadani.[82] This adopted a macro view of hip-hop culture as street culture but understandably their research only devoted a few paragraphs to rap. This is why it is important to examine research which has progressively focused more specifically on rap as a generic category.

The meso level is that most frequently adopted by French researchers. It presents research dealing with the musical dimension of hip-hop, namely rap and, to a lesser extent, DJing. It adopts two primary focuses: that of localized research, and that of thematic research. These studies generally include introductions giving historical presentations of rap. This amounts to a common thematic section in these studies, which can however be criticized for not being the result of exclusive and thorough historical research.

Social and geographic identifications defining a sense of local belonging are of great importance for many rappers. They are of equal importance for researchers. Localized research into rap involves levels of spatial differentiation slightly less elaborate than those to be found in research into rock.[83] National, local and urban-peripheral *(banlieue)* territories constitute the three major scales of focus. Given that rap is considered as representative of urban culture, the 'national' territory is to be generally understood as a territory located on the outskirts of major cities. Some researchers explicitly use the terms '*banlieues*', 'projects' or even 'areas of relegation'.[84] But the majority of these studies locate themselves 'nationally' in general terms. The only exception to this is the particularly wide-ranging study

---

[80]   Christian Bachmann and Luc Basier, 'Junior s'entraîne très fort ou le smurf comme mobilisation symbolique', *Langage et Société*, 34 (1985): pp. 58–68.

[81]   Hugues Bazin, *La culture hip-hop* (Paris, 1995).

[82]   Virginie Milliot-Belmadani, *Les Fleurs sauvages de la ville et de l'art. Analyse anthropologique de l'émergence et de la sédimentation du mouvement hip-hop lyonnais*, Lyon II University, Doctoral thesis (1997).

[83]   *Copyright Volume!* 3/2, 'Sonorités du hip-hop. Logiques globales et hexagonales' (2004).

[84]   Laurent Mucchielli, 'Le rap de la jeunesse des quartiers relégués. Un univers de représentations structuré par des sentiments d'injustice et de victimation collectives', in Manuel Boucher and Alain Vulbeau (eds), *Émergences culturelles et jeunesse populaire. Turbulences ou médiations?* (Paris, 2003), pp. 325–55.

undertaken by Manuel Boucher[85] which successfully alternates analysis between national, regional and local levels. A further assumption to be decoded is that this territory of 'urban-peripheral', both national and outlying, is generally understood essentially in relation to areas around central Paris. But the capital is however rarely mentioned, in contrast to Marseille, France's second city, which alongside Paris is a hub of hip-hop culture in France. Marseille has been much studied by a handful of researchers, notably Béatrice Sberna.[86] Such an intensive emphasis on the urban nature of rap hides its development in rural areas, which to date have been rarely studied, but whose analysis offers the advantage of counterbalancing the aspect of 'unrest in the *banlieues*' traditionally attached to rap. Moreover research remains largely centred only on rap in France.

Localized research is typically combined with particular themes of investigation. Inversely, thematic research is not necessarily localized, being therefore situated in an undefined geographical space, whose real boundaries may or may not be discernable. Recurring themes of investigation are forms of expression, politics, youth, and musical practice.

Rap is very commonly seen as a form of expression. Through their founding work, *Le rap ou la fureur de dire*, Georges Lapassade and Philippe Rousselot[87] set the tone. The general idea is that of voice articulated with sound; expression both spoken and musical relying on a message and a mediator; this message being acknowledged to potentially produce an identity, sociability, meaning. Beyond this, it is further acknowledged that this message carries a socio-political discourse marked by protest and violence.

This discourse relies on an aesthetic dimension including lyrics and music. Christian Béthune[88] defined the contours of this, attributing rap with an autonomous aesthetic value. More generally, inter-textual interpretation has interested many French researchers. A handful amongst them study rap as a form of oral poetry.[89] Others, more numerous, view lyrics in their political dimensions. However, whatever the approach, these studies do not so much aim at establishing pure textual analysis as at revealing a specific relationship to the world, notably political, with, in relation to this, the idea that the violence of lyrics is a sustitute for actual violence. Otherwise put, the notion that 'the word replaces the knife', of which the book title *Je texte termine*[90] is apt illustration.

---

[85]   Manuel Boucher, *Rap. Expression des lascars. Significations et enjeux du rap dans la société française* (Paris, 1998).

[86]   Béatrice Sberna, *Le rap, à Marseille*, EHESS, Paris, PhD thesis (2005).

[87]   George Lapassade and Philippe Rousselot, *Le rap ou la fureur de dire* (Paris, 1990).

[88]   Christian Béthune, *Le rap. Une esthétique hors la loi* (Paris, 2003).

[89]   Mathias Vicherat, *Pour une analyse textuelle du rap français* (Paris, 2003).

[90]   Augustin Aubert, Marc Casimiro de San Leandro and Virginie Milliot, *Je texte termine. Anthologie de textes rap* (Vénissieux, 1998).

Using the idea of katharsis, Anthony Pecqueux[91] demonstrates that although such verbal violence is effectively a psychological response to social problems experienced by peripheral groups of socially excluded individuals, he also underlines its intensely political implications, which, in this sense, more generally concerns all citizens, and enables one to better understand how the popularity of rap in France is not restricted to immigrant communities in underprivileged areas. In counterpoint, the research of Nathalie Karanfilovic[92] into American rap continues such thinking: by contrasting 'conscious' (protest and politicized) rap with 'gangsta' (violent and nihilistic), understanding of the rap scene indisputably increases in complexity and in clarity. Merely comparing genres of rap can increase the clarity of research and allows useful results to be produced.

Political issues are inseparable from rap. Despite its nature as protest, rap benefits from state support through cultural policies for amplified music, in the same way as rock or techno. More widely, it is commonly acknowledged in France that bridges must be built between cultural practices and social intervention. Rap music, like sport, is viewed as allowing the creation or continuation of links with certain marginalized groups of young people. In this sense, integrative virtues are attributed to it and a capacity to maintain social harmony. In addition, such state support encourages production of artistic and economic wealth,[93] with the prospect of social and professional integration for those involved. This does not go without causing problems born from tensions between institutional issues (social control and image strategies for politicians for example) and ethical issues (rappers torn between authenticity and commercial/cultural recognition). Such logics of the positioning of hip-hop culture within the social and economic environments were subtly studied by Loïc Lafargue de Grangeneuve,[94] and also by various researchers as part of a special 'hip-hop' edition of *Mouvements*.[95]

Rap became a political issue via state intervention during the 1980s. Concurrently, 'youth', notably groups of young people born of immigrant descent and living in areas of deprivation, also became a political concern. For this working-class younger generation, unruly and frightening to some, rap can also constitute the mainspring of upwards social mobility.[96] Through its capacity to favour expression, creativity and experimentation, rap allows young people to denounce

---

[91]   Anthony Pecqueux, *La politique incarnée du rap, socio-anthropologie de la communication et de l'appropriation chansonnières*, EHESS, Marseille, Doctoral Thesis (2003).

[92]   Nathalie Karanfilovic, *Les implications sociopolitiques du rap afro-américain: de l'engagement* new school *au nihilisme* gangsta, Metz University (2004).

[93]   André Prévos, 'Le business du rap en France', *The French Review*, 74/5 (2001): pp. 900–921.

[94]   Loic Lafargue de Grangeneuve, *Fonctionnaliser la culture? Action publique et culture hip-hop*, École Normale Supérieure, Cachan, Doctoral Thesis in Sociology (2004).

[95]   *Mouvements*, 11 (2000), 'Hip-hop. Les pratiques, le marché, la politique' (2000).

[96]   Boucher and Vulbeau (eds), *Émergences culturelles*.

their living conditions but also to become involved in society. Following the study by Véronique Bordes,[97] most French researchers underline the socializing effects of rap and how it benefits the construction and even the conversion of young rappers' identities, notably through interactions with local institutions (such as municipal young people's services responsible for communicating political decisions about socio-cultural issues). But – and this is the primary value of Bordes' study – this socialization is not unilateral, but mutual: disputes and negotiations between the two sides also have socializing effects on institutions. All things considered, the interactions resulting from investment in rap enable social participation, along with a range of necessary adaptations. Otherwise put, rap is a resource favouring socio-cultural action which itself is a resource for rappers. But this vision of the world is nonetheless relatively idealized, and furthermore, the 'youth' perspective presents a double disadvantage: firstly, that of not undertaking investigation into different genres of rap; secondly, that of overlooking what happens to rappers when they are no longer young.

The musical practice of rap is relatively little studied by French researchers. The research of Morgan Jouvenet,[98] previously mentioned under the section dealing with techno, figures amongst the most substantial in the domain to date. He insists upon the *continuum* between amateur practice and professional practice. But, he additionally deals with the MC and DJ not just from the viewpoint of their sources of creation, but also from the viewpoint of technology (home studio, laptop) and techniques (sampling). Jouvenet raises the idea that social critique is not a domain reserved solely for MCs and their 'killer' lyrics, but that it is also a constitutive element of djing. The practice of sampling may thus be a criticism of private ownership or a criticism of dominant consumerism, and thus constitute a sort of creative poaching. This is a viewpoint which contradicts an erroneous idea, widespread in France, according to which it is lyrics are central to rap music.

With the exception of a few studies, rap is not dealt with from the viewpoint of its sub-genres, which constitutes a significant epistemological problem. Just like rock, or techno, it is an umbrella category which confuses, rather than clarifies. Nevertheless, rap is occasionally viewed from the micro-sociological viewpoint of the figure of the artist. In this perspective, no other artist has received as much attention from French academics, notably from musicologists,[99] as the Marseilles group IAM. This is odd given the number of rappers in France who figure in much research, but are never the sole subject of chapters or articles (aside from NTM on

---

[97]   Véronique Bordes, *Le rap est dans la place ou du bon usage du rap par les institutions locales et les jeunes. Étude des relations entre des sociabilités juvéniles et des politiques locales de la jeunesse*, Paris 10 University, PhD thesis unpublished (2005).

[98]   Jouvenet, *Rap, techno, électro*.

[99]   Médéric Gasquet-Cyrus, Guillaume Kosmicki and Cécile Van Den den Avenne (eds), *Paroles et musiques à Marseille. Les voix d'une ville* (Paris, 1999).

whom Manuel Boucher[100] focused a short chapter discussing their conviction for insulting a police officer).

Conclusion

Comparison of the three musical families dealt with in this article demonstrates both similarities and differences in their treatment by academic research in France. The first striking similarity is that French cultural *history* of these musical genres is almost non-existent.[101] The second commonality is the lack of differentiation of musical genres within their original families. This lack of differentiation has repercussions in terms of the study of age-groups, ethnicity or even sexual identity; almost as if everything was equal. As if there was no difference in the composition of the audience for Diam's (27-year-old female rapper) and that of Joey Starr (40-year-old male rapper, formerly with NTM). Nor any difference between their careers, their discographic production and their influence on the world of rap. Although these first two similarities underline a certain number of weaknesses inherent in French research, a third seems, on the contrary, rather encouraging. It would seem indeed that research undertaken on all musical families increasingly favours *empirical* studies to the detriment of philosophical speculation, notably through renewed importance given to ethnographic studies.[102] Such an approach leads not only to taking an interest in human interactions, but also aims at retracing the socio-technical networks thereof. However, in such a framework, it is regrettable that research into fans and 'minor' cultural producers (often invisible) are only particularly developed in rock.

In terms of differing treatments, it appears that techno, contrary to rock and rap, is rarely the subject of geographically-situated research. It can thus be further underlined, that on the whole, the distinction between rural and urban society is not truly considered in studies of these three musical families, which is all the more strange since free parties often take place in rural areas, for instance. Evidently, rock is the subject of the largest amount of thematic research, presenting situations and raising problems which studies into rap and techno have yet to address. Little socio-economic information into specialist media or fans, for example, exists for

---

[100]   Boucher, *Rap. Expression des lascars.*

[101]   A situation which will hopefully improve thanks to studies into other musical genres, such as those by Ludovic Tournès, *New Orleans sur Seine. Histoire de Jazz en France, 1917–1992* (Paris, 1999), and more recently Vincent Sermet, *Musiques soul et funk en France: histoires et cultures des années 60 à nos jours*, Marne-la-Vallée University, Doctoral thesis (2006).

[102]   The symposium entitled 'Ethnographies du travail artistique' (organized by Marie Buscatto and Philippe Le Guern) held at the Sorbonne on 21–22 September 2006, is a good indicator thereof.

rap and techno. Where comparisons are possible on the basis of common themes, they remain to be undertaken.

It would clearly be pertinent to link the different approaches: macro, meso and micro, but starting modestly from micro. Within academic research, it seems increasingly difficult to perpetuate a macro category such as 'amplified music'. There are at least three reasons for this. Firstly, due to the contradictory logics it contains; secondly, given the resulting confusion; and thirdly, given that we have other much more effective categories, such as music *scenes*. The concept of music scenes enables both local and global analysis, whilst also interlinking micro, macro and meso approaches, in the manner of ethnography, ethnology and anthropology. There can be no anthropological discourse without ethnographic data or ethnological analysis, in the same way that it is impossible to have amplified music without music scenes or musical genres. Given the international context, it is probably on the basis of this particular epistemological orientation that future research in France will develop.

Chapter 12
Mapping British Music Audiences: Subcultural, Everyday and Mediated Approaches

Dan Laughey

Three main approaches to the analysis of popular music audiences – or consumers – have emerged since the post-1950s expansion of the music industry in Britain. First, there is an approach that understands music audiences as subcultures or club cultures that oppose a dominant, mainstream culture. A second approach has taken a different view of popular music consumption as a feature of everyday practices and localized experiences. Third and more recently, a media studies approach has emerged in the light of technological developments in popular music production, distribution and consumption. The three approaches are distinct but share some common concerns, so they should not be regarded as entirely separate fields of inquiry. I will compare and contrast these three approaches, and consider how they map on to contemporary cultural trends in British popular music.

The Subcultures/Club Cultures Approach

The work of the Centre for Contemporary Cultural Studies (CCCS) at the University of Birmingham in the 1960s and 1970s became internationally recognized as the face of 'British Cultural Studies'. The CCCS approach to popular music as a cultural form was to associate it with the popular arts[1] and with youth subcultures.[2] Popular music was considered to be subversive precisely because it was 'popular' across all social classes and particularly among young people, and therefore not the reserve of highbrow culture in its appreciation of the established arts (theatre, classical music, opera and so on). A succession of youth subcultures that appeared in Britain from the end of the Second World War – teds, hippies, mods, rockers and punks – were considered by 'right-thinking people' such as politicians and

---

[1]   Stuart Hall and Paddy Whannel, *The Popular Arts* (London, 1964).
[2]   Stuart Hall and Tony Jefferson (eds), *Resistance Through Rituals: Youth Subcultures in Post-war Britain* (London, 1975); David Hebdige, *Subculture: The Meaning of Style* (London, 1979).

newspaper editors to be a threat to established social norms.[3] Moreover, these youth subcultures were distinguished – in addition to stylistic features such as their fashion for clothes – by their music tastes. The teds were fans of rock'n'roll, the hippies listened to folk rock, the mods liked ska and reggae, and so on. Subcultural were succeeded by club cultural audiences in the 1980s and 1990s, but analyses of the latter owe much to the former, as I will discuss later.

Although framed in a distinctly British context, the subcultures approach to popular music audiences built its theoretical foundations on French structuralism. The ideas of Claude Levi-Strauss and Roland Barthes were especially influential to the CCCS. As is well known, Barthes applied the structuralist method known as semiotics to a range of everyday phenomena, such as wine and cars, so as to decode cultural myths peculiar to 1950s France.[4] Semiotics as a method and structuralism as a theoretical framework were used to great effect by Barthes in his deconstruction of French culture. It was this blend of method and theory that inspired David Hebdige's *Subculture* (1979) and Paul Willis's *Profane Culture* (1978).[5] Both of these works embrace the concept of 'homology'. Homology was first theorized by Willis as the (sub)cultural relation between a lifestyle and an artefact, such as a popular song,[6] and was later defined by Hebdige as 'the symbolic fit between the values and lifestyles of a group, its subjective experience and the musical forms it uses to express or reinforce its focal concerns'.[7] For example, the teds were only rock'n'roll lovers to the extent that rock'n'roll music corresponded to the values they attached to their other cultural forms and artefacts, such as Edwardian-style suits and cigars.

The subcultural approach, therefore, situated popular music audiences in homologous relation to other cultural forms. In order for this formula to work, however, the youth subcultures themselves had to be decoded – in accordance with an *a priori* structuralist framework – as homologous. Members of subcultures had to share common identities and demographic characteristics, including a unified politics of resistance to government policies and dominant cultural agendas. Music became a political expression of subcultural resistance. For instance, Hebdige decodes the use of ska and reggae – musics of black origin – by white, working-class mods as an expression of their opposition to the conservative values of a dominant British culture in which they had been nurtured.[8] This notion of 'shock value' was similarly evident in punks' use of Nazi motifs such as the swastika, which accorded to their tastes for anarchistic punk rock. According to Hebdige's

---

[3]   Stanley Cohen, *Folk Devils and Moral Panics: The Creation of the Mods and Rockers* (Oxford, 1980).

[4]   Roland Barthes, *Mythologies* (London, 1993).

[5]   Hebdige, *Subculture*; Paul E. Willis, *Profane Culture* (London, 1978).

[6]   Paul E. Willis, 'Symbolism and Practice: the Social Meaning of Pop Music', *CCCS Stencilled Paper No. 13* (Birmingham, 1972).

[7]   Hebdige, *Subculture*, p. 113.

[8]   Hebdige, *Subculture*.

semiotic analysis, the punk subculture did not espouse fascist politics, but it used the shock value of fascist symbols as a means of articulating resistance to dominant political and social structures.

While the notion of homologous subcultural resistance assumed a mutual relationship between youth music audiences and subversive politics, the method of semiotics favoured by the subcultures approach presents several problems in attempting to prove such a notion. Semiotics is best applied to 'the general' rather than 'the particular', as Barthes demonstrated in his analysis of French cultural forms. By contrast, when semiotics was applied to specific forms of resistant subcultural style, any potential anomalies had to be dismissed from analysis. As Stan Cohen points out, 'This means that instances are sometimes missed when the style is conservative or supportive: in other words, not reworked or reassembled but taken over intact from dominant commercial culture'.[9] Moreover, the subcultural approach's emphasis on 'youth' and 'working class' demographics meant that older and more affluent individuals were excluded from analysis. As Phil Cohen claims, 'I do not think the middle class produces subcultures, for subcultures are produced by a dominated culture, not a dominant culture'.[10] The subcultural approach is at times guilty of such inverted snobbery which demands that popular music audiences must always be subordinate, radical and nonconformist. Gary Clarke's critique of subcultural theory rightly suggests that 'any empirical analysis would reveal that subcultures are diffuse, diluted, and mongrelized in form'.[11]

Despite a sustained sociological critique of the subcultures approach[12] it has lived on – in a slightly different guise – within the study of club cultures. The club cultures approach to popular music audiences, like the subcultures approach, is premised on exclusiveness rather than inclusiveness. Clubbing audiences are portrayed as radically alternative, in keeping with their hardcore dance music tastes. Accounts of club cultures are often strikingly similar to accounts of subcultures, and have been conceptualized according to familiar structuralist notions of

---

[9]   Stanley Cohen, *Folk Devils and Moral Panics: The Creation of the Mods and Rockers* (Oxford, 1980), p. xi.

[10]   Phil Cohen, 'Subcultural Conflict and Working-class Community', in Stuart Hall et al. (eds), *Culture, Media, Language: Working Papers in Cultural Studies 1972–79* (London, 1992), p. 85.

[11]   Gary Clarke, 'Defending Ski-jumpers: A Critique of Theories of Youth Subcultures', in Simon Frith and Andrew Goodwin (eds), *On Record: Rock, Pop, and the Written Word* (London, 1990), p. 83.

[12]   Gary Alan Fine and Sheryl Kleinman, 'Rethinking Subculture: an Interactionist Analysis', *American Journal of Sociology* 85/1 (1979): pp. 1–20; Sue Widdicombe and Robin Wofitt, *The Language of Youth Subcultures: Social Identity in Action* (Hemel Hempstead, 1995); David Muggleton, *Inside Subculture: The Postmodern Meaning of Style* (Oxford, 2000).

homology[13] and (sub)cultural capital.[14] Sarah Thornton's *Club Cultures* (1995) draws on the work of sociologist Pierre Bourdieu rather than Barthes, but it is far from a rigorous sociological analysis of clubbing and music practices. Semiotics is no longer the central method, but Thornton's brief participant observation account of dancing and drug-taking is overshadowed by her textual analyses of cultural artefacts such as fly posters. Like most subcultural studies of popular music audiences, Thornton's club cultural thesis fails to analyse the words and actions of music consumers themselves. Instead, the avid pursuit of subcultural distinctions means that instead of examining what happens 'inside' clubbing contexts and how clubbers use music to form identities, Thornton focuses too narrowly on the exclusionary boundaries that distinguish alternative from mainstream clubbing.

On a more positive note, however, the club cultures approach has been diverted from the same dead-end reached by the CCCS's subcultural theory thanks to the work of Ben Malbon.[15] Drawing on the work of sociologist Erving Goffman and gender theorist Judith Butler, Malbon's ethnographic work conceptualizes the clubbing crowd as a dynamic congregation wherein 'there is a collusion between the clubbers as audience and the clubbers as performers'.[16] Clubbing enables individuals within crowd contexts to lose their inhibitions and perform different identities. Moreover, the clubbers studied by Malbon 'often define themselves in terms of their preferred music(s) and the associated crowds thereof'.[17] Music and clubbing practices create a sense of belonging – rather than subcultural distinction – wherein emotional experiences and lasting memories are collectively consumed and produced. Club cultures as popular music audiences are therefore active agents of their own life choices and experiences, using music – as well as other stimulants – to take off and put on presentations of themselves to like-minded others. In addition to Malbon's useful approach to club cultures, a post-subcultures approach has made some contributions to an understanding of contemporary British music audiences,[18] but the extent to which it sufficiently departs from the

---

[13]   Hillegonda Rietveld, 'Living the Dream', in Steve Redhead (ed.), *Rave Off: Politics and Deviance in Contemporary Youth Culture* (Aldershot, 1993).

[14]   Sarah Thornton, *Club Cultures: Music, Media and Subcultural Capital* (Cambridge, 1995).

[15]   Ben Malbon, 'Clubbing: Consumption, Identity and the Spatial Practices of Every-night Life', in Tracey Skelton and Gill Valentine (eds), *Cool Places: Geographies of Youth Cultures* (London, 1998); Ben Malbon, *Clubbing: Dancing, Ecstacy and Vitality* (London, 1999).

[16]   Malbon, 'Clubbing, Consumption, Identity', p. 83.

[17]   Malbon, *Clubbing: Dancing, Ecstacy and Vitality*, p. 80.

[18]   Muggleton, *Inside Subculture*; Paul Hodkinson, *Goth: Identity, Style and Subculture* (Oxford, 2002); Andy Bennett and Keith Kahn-Harris (eds), *After Subculture: Critical Studies in Contemporary Youth Culture* (Basingstoke, 2004).

flawed subcultures approach has been questioned.[19] David Hesmondhalgh goes so far as to suggest that the sociology of youth (and youth subcultures) has offered little insight into – and has nothing left to contribute to – the study of popular music.[20]

The Everyday and Local Approach

A further problem with both the subcultures and club cultures approaches is their tendency to focus on spectacular, deviant or extraordinarily committed music consumers to the neglect of more ordinary, mundane music audiences. Several British sociologists and social psychologists have attempted to redress this problem by rejecting 'the fallacy of meaningfulness' associated with semiotics and participant observation techniques.[21] An example of this fallacy is Paul Willis's participant observation of motorbike boys and hippies.[22] Willis's study reveals in ethnographic detail how popular music fits into the leisure-time pursuits of these youth subcultures, but lacks a longitudinal dimension for analysing how members of these subcultures are situated as less meaningful music audiences in other everyday contexts – for example, in the workplace.

The everyday and local approach has tended to draw on other social research techniques such as focus-group interviewing[23] and the 'life narrative' method[24] in order to capture the habitual experiences and perceptions – what Joke Hermes calls the 'cultural repertoires' – of popular music audiences.[25] In turn, focus has changed from the notion of countrywide, *national* 'British' music subcultures to *localized* music communities, scenes or neo-tribes[26] – although, in practice, even youth subcultures such as teds and mods were mostly located in specific urban areas, especially in London and south-east England. Simon Frith was the

---

[19]   See David Hesmondhalgh, 'Subcultures, Scenes or Tribes? None of the Above', *Journal of Youth Studies*, 8/1 (2005): pp. 21–40; and Dan Laughey, *Music and Youth Culture* (Edinburgh, 2006).

[20]   Hesmondhalgh, 'Subcultures, Scenes or Tribes?'.

[21]   See for example Joke Hermes, *Reading Women's Magazines: An Analysis of Everyday Media Use* (Cambridge, 1995).

[22]   Willis, *Profane Culture*.

[23]   For example in Simon Frith, *The Sociology of Rock* (London, 1978) and Simon Frith, *Sound Effects: Youth, Leisure, and the Politics of Rock 'n' Roll* (London, 1983).

[24]   Ruth Finnegan, *The Hidden Musicians: Music-making in an English Town* (Cambridge, 1989); Chris Richards, *Teen Spirits: Music and Identity in Media Education* (London, 1998); Tia DeNora, 'Music as a Technology of the Self', *Poetics*, 24 (2000): pp. 31–56.

[25]   Hermes, *Reading Womens' Magazines*.

[26]   For example, Andy Bennett, *Popular Music and Youth Culture: Music, Identity and Place* (Basingstoke, 2000).

first British sociologist to adopt an everyday and local approach to popular music audiences. Frith interviewed groups of young people who lived in a small town in Northern England (Keighley) about their music tastes and practices. Contrary to the subcultural approach, he explains how the different youth groups' uses of music were different, not because some groups were more resistant to commercial pressures than others, not even because some groups were more organized in subcultural terms than others, but because the groups each had their own leisure needs and interests.[27] The vocabulary has changed, therefore, from subcultural 'values' and 'lifestyles' to locally specific 'needs' and 'interests'. Moreover, Frith has also observed how music is the soundtrack to – rather than the focus of – young people's everyday leisure practices: 'Music is the accompaniment of an activity, not its expression.'[28]

Rather than overt political resistance, the politics of popular music for Frith's young respondents is a politics of fun and playfulness. Music is used in everyday contexts as a means for youth groups to articulate and change their identities in relations with others – relations that are not always hostile. As Frith perceptively points out, 'in interpreting music as a *symbol* of leisure values, sub-culturalists fail to make sense of it as an *activity*, one enjoyed by the vast number of non-deviant kids'.[29] The young people studied by Frith considered music to be a pleasurable activity in the context of their everyday school and work routines, but at the same time these pleasures were inseparable from wider everyday and local concerns. More recently, Frith has reflected back on his early studies of music and everyday life, which have inspired remarkably little in the way of follow-up studies.[30] This is particularly remarkable when we consider the proliferation of new music technologies that have become such an everyday feature of contemporary life since the 1970s, although a third approach to popular music audiences as *media* audiences (discussed later) has begun to redress this absence. For Frith, music is the mass medium that matters most because it infiltrates into our daily lives (public and private) with an omnipotence and omnipresence like no other medium. Frith's everyday approach does not, however, assume a passive audience: 'people nowadays routinely use music to manipulate their moods and organize their activities *for themselves*'.[31]

In addition to Frith, important contributions to the everyday and local approach have been made by Ruth Finnegan and Tia DeNora. Finnegan's 1989 ethnographic study of music-making in the large English town of Milton Keynes considers how live music audiences play an important participatory role in local practices and

---

[27]   Frith, *Sound Effects*, p. 212.

[28]   Frith *The Sociology of Rock*, p. 48.

[29]   Frith, *ibid.*, pp. 52–3.

[30]   Simon Frith, 'Music and Everyday Life', in Martin Clayton et al. (eds), *The Cultural Study of Music: A Critical Introduction* (London, 2003).

[31]   Frith, 'Music and Everyday Life', p. 98.

traditions.[32] She notes that the audience in a live musical event are themselves part of the performance, playing the role (or range of roles) expected of audience participants in the appropriate music world – or, perhaps, disrupting the event by refusing to follow the conventions.[33]

However, the conventions of these music worlds are rarely disrupted by subcultural audience or performer roles. On the contrary, they are learnt and enacted with enthusiasm, which accounts for the maintenance of local music traditions. Moreover, Finnegan observes how audiences at live music events – far from being youthful or subcultural – span all age groups. Even audiences for rock bands in pubs (licensed public houses) exhibit mixed demographics, not least because audience members are often friends or relatives of the musicians who perform: 'family audiences were nothing unusual'.[34] Finnegan's more recent work has explored the anthropology of emotion in relation to music audiences, and in particular, 'the contextualized manner of people's musical engagements' that reveals how 'music provides a human resource through which people can enact their lives with inextricably entwined feeling, thought and emotion'.[35] The everyday power of music to touch – and intensify – our innermost memories and emotions, Finnegan suggests, should not be underestimated, particularly by musicologists with little interest in the musical experiences of audiences.

Finnegan's 'anthropology of emotion' perspective draws parallels with DeNora's work on music as a technology of the self in local, everyday contexts. Informed by empirical investigations of music in everyday life, DeNora suggests that individuals use music to express their moods – they work 'like disk jockeys to themselves'.[36] For DeNora, music functions as 'an accomplice in attaining, enhancing and maintaining desired states of feeling and bodily energy (e.g. relaxation)'.[37] She also refers to the importance of personal music maps as resources for identity formation. The everydayness of music enables individuals – whether young or old – to build up a collection of memories that can be stored away but easily retrieved when the sounds of the past return, often unexpectedly. Moreover, music is associated most frequently with romantic and intimate life experiences.[38] As such, technologies of the self ensure that popular music has the capacity to bring extraordinary moments of emotion and feeling into ordinary audience contexts. Music not only recalls past experiences, however, given its

---

[32]   Finnegan, *The Hidden Musicians*.

[33]   Ruth Finnegan, 'Music, Performance and Enactment', in Hugh MacKay (ed.), *Consumption and Everyday Life* (London, 1997), p. 137.

[34]   Finnegan, *The Hidden Musicians*, p. 123.

[35]   Ruth Finnegan, 'Music, Experience, and the Anthropology of Emotion', in Martin Clayton et al. (eds), *The Cultural Study of Music: A Critical Introduction* (London, 2003), p. 188.

[36]   DeNora, 'Music as a Technology', p. 35.

[37]   DeNora, ibid., p. 37.

[38]   DeNora, ibid., p. 46.

more immediate role in public places. As DeNora and Belcher show, music in retail clothing stores plays an important role in how staff and customers become emotionally involved in the everyday practice of shopping.[39] For example, music serves an atmospheric function in helping shoppers to imagine how they would feel wearing different clothes in social contexts such as restaurants.

DeNora's everyday and local approach to popular music audiences is both sociological and, to a lesser extent, psychological. It acknowledges work in the social psychology of music, which has emerged as a significant area of research in Britain.[40] One such study by Mark Tarrant et al., finds that young consumers nurture strong identities with particular music styles both through interpersonal (self with others) and intergroup (peer group with other 'out-groups') relations.[41] Further, music identities help young people to form positive social identities. Far from having antisocial effects, young people's music tastes would appear to afford pro-social benefits. For example, music was used by Tarrant et al.'s teenage respondents in everyday contexts such as school playgrounds to manage impressions of themselves formed by others, as well as facilitating how they formed impressions of their peers. This social-psychological perspective on the everyday and local approach has an advantage over other approaches in its capacity to contextualize individual uses and needs. It might be argued, however, that too much focus on individual and local peculiarities avoids consideration of wider political and economic structures (determined by global music industry infrastructures) in which ideas about individual choice and local creativity are invariably stifled.

The Media Studies Approach

An alternative to the everyday and local approach is that which treats popular music audiences predominantly as consumers of global media products and technologies. There is some overlapping between the two approaches – particularly given the everydayness of media communications – but they remain distinct because music productions are regarded, on the one hand, as *localized* or *individualized* cultural resources, and on the other hand, as *globalized* mediums. The media

---

[39]   Tia DeNora and Sophie Belcher, '"When You're Trying Something On You Picture Yourself in a Place Where They Are Playing This Kind of Music" – Musically Sponsored Agency in the British Clothing Retail Sector', *The Sociological Review*, 48/1 (2000): pp. 80–101.

[40]   See for example David J. Hargreaves and Adrian C. North, *The Social Psychology of Music* (Oxford, 1997); John A. Sloboda and Susan A. O'Neill, 'Emotions in Everyday Listening to Music', in Patrik N. Juslin and John A. Sloboda (eds), *Music and Emotion: Theory and Research* (Oxford, 2001).

[41]   Mark Tarrant et al., 'Youth Identity and Music', in A. Raymond and R. MacDonald et al. (eds), *Musical Identities* (Oxford, 2002).

studies approach to popular music audiences also differs in this respect from the subcultural approach, which avoids media analysis on the assumption that mass-produced, commercial music is of no interest to youth subcultures. However, there are closer connections between the media studies and club cultures approaches. Thornton's 1995 study,[42] for example, argues that club and rave cultures in the late 1980s actively publicized themselves via mass media channels – such as tabloid newspapers – to boost their 'street' credibility. As well as mass media, Thornton identifies two other types of media associated with clubbing audiences. First, micro media such as flyers, fanzines and low-budget websites are narrowly targeted at specific groups of music consumers (e.g. partakers in the London club scene). Located somewhere between mass and micro media, though, are a second type of niche media in the form of consumer magazines such as *The Face*. Niche media are considered by Thornton to be integral to the creation of subcultural capital. In this sense, *The Face* not only reports about clubbing and raves – it helps to construct the alternativeness of these club cultural pursuits.

On a sceptical note, though, it is easy to become suspicious of claims about certain consumer lifestyle magazines playing a lead in the formation of underground club cultures when it is these exact same claims that the magazines make in their marketing campaigns to increase sales. The club cultural approach also tends to assume that music media are used intensively by consumers as a means to acquire subcultural capital. By contrast, a media studies approach is equally concerned with less intense (i.e. casual) audiences for popular music. Unfortunately, in Britain at least, studies of casual music media consumption are in short supply. Sian Lincoln's zoning model[43] attempts to capture processes in which several media technologies often compete for attention in teenage bedroom culture. Typically, a television set might be operating in the background whilst another zone of the bedroom – governed by, say, the CD player – takes precedence, although the fading out of one zone in order to bring another zone to the fore is a frequent feat of teenage consumer agency. Moreover, listening to music on the radio is commonly a technique of background zoning, 'associated with "doing other things"' such as homework.[44] Zoning techniques also help to carve a mediated 'pathway out of the private sphere of the bedroom and into the public sphere of the city' for teenagers as they prepare to go out at night.[45] Importantly, Lincoln demonstrates how even casual, functional music media use requires sophisticated user agency and should not be dismissed as inferior use.

My own research also takes seriously the casual consumption of music media.[46] Ethnographic interviews with young people in the Greater Manchester

---

[42] Thornton, *Club Cultures*.

[43] Sian Lincoln, 'Feeling the Noise: Teenagers, Bedrooms and Music', *Leisure Studies*, 24/4 (2005): pp. 399–414.

[44] Lincoln, 'Feeling the Noise', p. 408.

[45] Lincoln, ibid., p. 409.

[46] Laughey, *Music and Youth Culture*.

area revealed the regularity of everyday contexts – schools, cafes, shops, gyms and so on, as well as domestic settings – in which mediated music played a background role. Music on radio and television served as 'soundtrack' media for other personal and social activities. Moreover, mainstream music media provided a previewing function for young consumers. Many of my respondents would preview the latest pop releases on radio or television, and then decide whether or not to purchase them in record shops or online. Indeed, what I categorize as 'drifters' – consumers who invest little involvement in mediated music and rarely access public music venues – would almost solely rely on 'previewing media', except on the rare occasions when they would actually purchase music.[47] Drifters constituted a significant group among my research sample. This finding alone explodes the myth of a monolithic young generation – or 'youth culture' – equally absorbed in intense popular music activity. Sadly, studies of subcultures, club cultures and pop music fandom have kept this myth alive.

Of course, within the media studies approach there is also research on intensive music consumption. Interestingly, Michael Bull's work on personal stereo and iPod use in public places[48] explodes another common myth – that media technologies are consumed mostly in domestic, private settings.[49] The roots of this myth are relatively straightforward to identify. Television has been the most researched medium in academia and it also happens to be probably the most domesticated media technology ever invented. But portable television devices have yet to find a 'killer application' because it is far easier to listen to music or radio 'on the move' than to watch television. On the contrary, Bull shows that music media technologies facilitate use in public as well as private or domestic contexts, particularly the more advanced forms: 'iPod users often refer to the magical nature of carrying their entire music collection with them wherever they go, thus giving them an unprecedented amount of choice of music to listen to.'[50] Moreover, personal devices such as iPods can alter the sensual experience of, for example, moving around cityscapes: 'iPods are used both as a mundane accompaniment to the everyday and as a way of aestheticizing and controlling that very experience … one strategy of the iPod user is to create their own personal movie out of the scene they pass through.'[51] For Bull, personal music media help to 'reorganize the sounds of the city',[52] although the sinister, Adorno-esque implication is that these technologies effectively dull users' awareness of their oppressed, workaday existence in late capitalist societies.

---

[47]   Laughey, ibid., pp. 175–6.

[48]   Michael Bull, *Sounding Out the City: Personal Stereos and the Management of Everyday Life* (Oxford, 2000); Michael Bull, 'No Dead Air! The iPod and the Culture of Mobile Listening', *Leisure Studies*, 24/4 (2005): pp. 343–55.

[49]   See also Laughey, *Music and Youth Culture*, pp.139–45.

[50]   Bull, 'No Dead Air!', p. 344.

[51]   Bull, ibid., p. 350.

[52]   Bull, ibid., p. 352.

Intensive use of music media in public, social networks has been examined recently by Marshall in relation to bootleg[53] and by Hayes in relation to vinyl[54] record collectors. According to the former study, 'the individuals who collect bootlegs are in general the most committed fans that an artist has' and 'it is *fans* rather than casual consumers who are the market for bootleg records'.[55] Marshall's interviews with bootleg record collectors depict a network of highly committed individuals who are fanatic about owning entire collections of every recording that was ever produced – legally or illegally – in the name of a particular artist. For example, Dylan collectors demonstrate extremely intensive media use by typically owning the same albums on various formats (vinyl, cassette, CDs and so on). In the latter study, a small network of youth consumers exhibit 'engagement in the listening process'[56] through intensive use of vinyl records as a means of accessing rare music of past times. They demonstrate this intensive use by 'their active involvement in negotiating the pops, skips, and crackles endemic to most second-hand records'.[57] This contrasts with the lack of physical participation required in operating a CD player with a remote control device. Hayes argues that these young vinyl collectors used their LP records to regain a level of agency in resisting the 'ideal consumer' type favoured by a profit-driven global music industry. He continues: 'Sadly, many of their peers have yet to develop this degree of autonomy, quickly embracing each new singing sensation simply because MTV has his or her video in heavy rotation.'[58] The vinyl record is perhaps the most alternative music medium in existence today precisely because it continues to be regarded by record companies as a minor (indeed, almost extinct) sector of the commercial marketplace.

The media studies approach contributes most tellingly, however, to research on the internet – now a commonplace medium for popular music audiences in Britain since the recent rise of online music distribution. In its early years, though, downloading of MP3 (compressed digital music) files via the internet was considered to be a subversive – even subcultural – practice, not least by the major record companies who filed law suits against 'large-scale uploaders'. Peer-to-peer (P2P) file-sharing software enabled users to search out unprecedented libraries of music on sites such as – most notoriously – Napster, in order to download tracks free of charge and without restriction given that copyright laws had been flouted. Internet music piracy had become a widespread, alternative use of new media technology by the turn of the century. Unlike previous music piracy

---

[53]   Lee Marshall, 'The Effects of Piracy Upon the Music Industry: A Case Study of Bootlegging', *Media, Culture and Society*, 26/2 (2004): pp. 163–81.

[54]   David Hayes, '"Take Those Old Records Off the Shelf": Youth and Music Consumption in the Postmodern Age', *Popular Music and Society*, 29/1 (2006): pp. 51–68.

[55]   Marshall 'The Effects of Piracy', pp. 166–7.

[56]   Hayes, 'Take Those Old Records Off the Shelf', p. 52.

[57]   Hayes, ibid., p. 58.

[58]   Hayes, ibid., p. 67.

activities that operated in criminal circles within developing countries,[59] internet piracy spread firstly in North America and Western Europe, therefore hitting the major record companies in their core markets.[60] Britain and France are among 16 nations where file-sharing practices have been targeted by intelligence services, and Britain has been home to some of the worst piracy offenders: 'more than £140,000 in compensation has been paid to the British Phonographic Industry by 71 individuals'.[61]

However, the successful duopoly between Apple's iPod and iTunes services has thrust internet music into mainstream commercial culture. From 2007, the British popular music charts have monitored sales of online downloads in addition to traditional formats such as CDs. Use of P2P software, although still often far from lawful, has become normalized and is perceived, on the whole, to be less 'alternative' than before. As such, online music use in all its intricate ways 'introduces the level of innovative flexibility and choice to the *consumption* of popular music that previously were obtained only in its *production*'.[62] Furthermore, MP3 file-sharing can be seen to 'weaken[s] the traditional divide between the producer and the consumer, the licit and the illicit, since options of opportunistic reproduction and exchange are vastly multiplied'.[63] The media studies approach to popular music audiences generally accords with this perspective, although Bull offers a less optimistic view. Notably, internet music audiences are now almost all conformists and – in stark contrast to subcultures – they have tended to embrace the 'mainstreaming' of online music distribution by corporate interests, so long as opportunities for new kinds of consumer experiences remain accessible. Given the almost impossible task of policing internet music distribution, this state of affairs should persist for some considerable time.

Summary

The three approaches outlined here capture the diverse social, cultural and economic changes that have occurred in British popular music since the 1950s. Interestingly, approaches to popular music audiences have moved from a subcultural perspective – in which mediated music is dismissed as a product of dominant commercial culture – to a media studies perspective devoted to analysis of such music. As

---

[59]   See Dave Laing, 'The Music Industry and the "Cultural Imperialism" Thesis', *Media, Culture and Society*, 8 (1986): pp. 331–41.

[60]   See Andrew Leyshon et al., 'On the Reproduction of the Musical Economy After the Internet', *Media, Culture and Society*, 27/2 (2005): pp. 177–209.

[61]   BBC Online, 'Legal Fight Hits "Music Pirates"', 15 November 2005, http://news.bbc.co.uk/1/hi/entertainment/-music/4438324.stm.

[62]   Chris Rojek, 'P2P Leisure Exchange: Net Banditry and the Policing of Intellectual Property', *Leisure Studies*, 24/4 (2005): pp. 357–69.

[63]   Rojek, ibid., p. 364.

stated previously, these three approaches should not be regarded as mutually exclusive ways of analysing popular music consumption. The everyday and local approach, for instance, is inseparable to some work within the media studies approach. Furthermore, media studies of subversive or highly committed music audiences, such as illegal online file-sharers or vinyl record collectors, retain elements of the subcultural or club cultural approach. Research in the near future within the British context is likely to shift between the everyday and media studies approaches, focusing less on local or live music audiences, but more on bridging the relationship between mediated music producer and consumer practices. However, further research and funding of some magnitude is needed. Funding for popular music research is difficult to secure in Britain, because cultural and media studies sit uneasily between the different concerns of the Economic and Social Research Council (ESRC) and the Arts and Humanities Research Council (AHRC). This situation is awkward and must change if government money is to reflect the social importance of cultural and media resources in people's everyday life contexts. It seems sensible, in this respect, to begin by overcoming the myth that popular music remains essentially a youth cultural pursuit in Britain. This may have had some truth for 'subcultural moments' of the 1960s and 1970s – although I have argued that 1930s British youth enacted subversive music practices akin to post-war subcultures.[64] But as Finnegan has observed and several other authors argue more lately,[65] British popular music audiences today are more diverse – and, I would add, more unpredictable – than ever before.

---

[64]   Laughey, *Music and Youth Culture*.

[65]   Hesmondhalgh, 'Subcultures, Scenes or Tribes?'; Rupa Huq, *Beyond Subculture: Pop, Youth and Identity in a Postcolonial World* (London, 2006).

Chapter 13
Music Audiences, Cultural Hierarchies and State Interventionism: A Typically French Model?

Philippe Le Guern

Whilst research into the audiences, reception and uses of culture has over the last 20 years undergone substantial development in France, some sectors have, however, been ignored by such progress in theory: knowledge about popular music audiences[1] has for instance suffered from lack of attention, when compared to the much stimulating research undertaken on literature or, more recently, on television and cinema. To take some examples, it is essentially analysis of television and its viewers which has informed contemporary rereadings of ideas from the School of Frankfurt, or enabled Bourdieu's legitimacy theory to be placed into perspective and allowed a redefinition of 'popular' audiences.[2] In contrast, whilst music is a particularly appropriate subject for analysis of the industrial production of cultural products and their reception, it has to be noted that it has barely assumed such a role. Consequently, to comment on the standardization of cultural products or the effects of mass culture on audiences, academic authors have generally resorted to alternative fields of the media. When Armand Mattelart and Jean-Marie Piemme defined mass culture as a 'means of social control', they used television as their example, not music:[3] and it is symptomatic that research into commercial strategies in music, whether radio programming or targeting of audiences by record labels, is rare, or even non-existent in France.

---

[1] By convention, and because there is no scope here for a full discussion, we shall use the term 'popular' to describe a body of musics which are in reality heteregenous in styles, types of audience, and social or political stakes of their production. On the issue of musical categories used specifically in France – popular, rock, amplified, current etc – see Simon Frith and Philippe Le Guern (eds), 'Sociologies des musiques populaires', special number of *Réseaux*, 25/141–2 (2007).

[2] Precisions moreover that, in a symmetrical interchange with Anglo-Saxon countries for which Bourdieu or de Certeau were able to constitute new sources for inspiration, the contribution of cultural studies has had a significant role in renewing French paradigms.

[3] Armand Mattelart and Jean-Marie Piemme, *Télévision: enjeux sans frontières* (Grenoble, 1980), p. 24.

On a methodological level, the question of knowing how audiences of culture can be understood – and what is the pertinence but also the limitations of statistical or ethnographic approaches – has also produced much writing: but once more, it must be noted that studies into the cultural life of French people have favoured television,[4] cinema,[5] or cultural events such as the Cannes film festival or the Avignon theatre festival.[6] Comparatively, knowing 'how people listen to music' has rarely been discussed: whereas functionalist approaches on television have multiplied, analysing the role attributed to television by viewers,[7] nothing comparable or of such scale can be found on music.

Perhaps it is necessary to question this increased interest in television occurring at the time that music was the poor relation in French academia. A generational effect caused by the age of researchers? Caused by Anglo-Saxon paradigms imported by a handful of authors more familiar with television than with rock? Due perhaps to a particularly low legitimacy of such music in French academia, which until very recently limited the number of theses submitted on this type of subject? Perhaps it was due to inability to understand such a complex entity as the audiences of this music, which elude statistical or difficult-to-implement ethnographic studies in the space and time of concerts? Finally, was it was perhaps due to perceptions of television as a threat to written culture and reading, which thrust it to the forefront of debate?[8] It was not until recent years that the study of popular music found its – admittedly modest – place in the French academic field, notably through the work of a new generation of researchers, many of whom have strong direct ties with musical practice.[9]

The fact remains that the study of music audiences, and in particular the social construction of musical tastes, has constituted a major element in the critique of the dominant theory in France for the last 30 years, namely the sociology of cultural legitimacy. In this chapter on popular music audiences, we shall demonstrate how the primary paradigms and themes of study in this field closely rely on the wider

---

[4]   Michel Souchon, 'Le vieux canon de 75'. L'apport des méthodes quantitatives à la connaissance du public de la télévision', *Hermès*, 11/12 (1993): pp. 233–45.

[5]   Jean-Michel Guy, *La Culture cinématographique des Français* (Paris, 2000).

[6]   Emmanuel Ethis (ed.), *Aux marches du palais. Le festival de Cannes sous le regard des sciences sociales* (Paris, 2001).

[7]   For example, Dominique Boullier, *La Conversation télé* (Rennes, 1987); Jean Bianchi, 'La promesse du feuilleton', *Réseaux*, 39 (1990); Dominique Pasquier, *La Culture des sentiments* (Paris, 1999).

[8]   This is the hypothesis outlined by Olivier Donnat, *Les Pratiques culturelles des Français. Enquête 1997* (Paris, 1998), p. 310.

[9]   See Philippe Le Guern (ed.), 'Musiciens-sociologues. Usages de la réflexivité en sociologie de la culture', special number on 'Autour des musiques populaires', *Copyright Volume!*, 4/1 (2005).

context of analysis of cultural audiences.[10] On the one hand, we will focus on research based upon the theory of cultural legitimacy produced by Pierre Bourdieu to illustrate this reliance, or, inversely, to underline its disjunctions, looking in particular at research on the sociology of taste and of fans. On the other hand, using data from government studies and others undertaken by actors involved in music broadcasting, we shall illustrate how the issue of popular music audiences is central in cultural policy – established in France on the principle of democratization, that is, the accessibility of creation for the masses – and its analysis.

Alienated Taste Versus Attachment of Fans?

'How can we understand the enormous backwardness – almost two decades – of French research compared with that in the English-speaking world? This cannot be explained without looking at the actual beginnings of research into the sociology of culture during the 1960s and 1970s, when Bourdieu's cultural legitimacy theories gradually established themselves', remark Daniel Cefaï and Dominique Pasquier. These theories did in fact 'literally block the development of research into media audiences, considering them within a theory of deficiency which left no room for other analysis'.[11] In other words, what we are talking about here is a conception of the reception of cultural products based almost exclusively on a well-known theory of alienation: intermediate audiences ('petits-bourgeois' to borrow Bourdieu's term) and working class audiences ('the dominated') have no choice but to suffer dominant forms of legitimate culture imposed by elements of the population best-equipped in different types of cultural capital, and consequently best-able to impose their own cultural hierarchies on society. This 'upper-class' culture, according to Bourdieu, spreads all the more efficiently since it is taken as 'a given' by alienated consciences.[12]

In reaction to this in France, in the last 20 years or so there has arisen a series of research works focusing primarily on Anglo-Saxon authors in order to offer an alternative vision of ways in which cultural works are received, and in which the relationship between popular audiences and the media and their content is unquestionably more active, more autonomous, and always less alienated. From this point of view, it is difficult to say to what extent the theory of domination, distinction and symbolic violence has played in the field of popular music study either an inhibitive or a structuring role. This is perhaps because popular music was always understood in its most 'vulgar' form by Bourdieu, that is, variety music,

---

[10]   Of course, in this chapter is not dealing with radio listeners, a subject which is analysed by Hervé Glevarec in this book.

[11]   Daniel Cefaï and Dominique Pasquier (eds), *Les Sens du public. Publics politiques, publics médiatiques* (Paris, 2003), p. 37.

[12]   See Eric Maigret, 'Pierre Bourdieu, la culture populaire et le long remords de la sociologie de la distinction culturelle', *Esprit* (2002): pp. 170–78.

and even when studied has only been treated summarily, ignoring the subtler and richer relationship that the 'general public' entertain with this genre of music, as demonstrated, for example, by Edgar Morin in his discussion of the 'yé-yé' movement in the 1960s.[13]

It is perhaps the work of Antoine Hennion that represents, in France, the most radical and detailed critique of Bourdieu's determinism as transposed into the musical field.[14] To summarize, Antoine Hennion's research aims at not considering musical experience merely as a direct relationship between a creation and its audience, but at taking into consideration everything that intervenes before and after, between the music and the market. These 'interventions' are described by Hennion via the concept of 'mediation',[15] – anything through which music exists as such, and not merely as an object in itself detached from the material, practical and aesthetic conditions of its broadcasting and reception: for example, listening, instruments, records, radios, sleeve notes, musicians, technical just as much as human or institutional mechanisms. Mediation rejects the objectivist vision of music (and audiences), and is rather conceived as the result of a collective operation where audiences, musicians, the scene or stage and instruments come together. Resultantly, this theory of mediation produces an autonomous interpretation of audiences, which are not merely obliged to adopt, more or less successfully or with more or less relevance, a previously defined meaning of the music. Thus, for Hennion, liking music cannot be reduced to social determinism: his notions of 'attachment' and 'fan' aim specifically at surpassing the theory of socially conditioned taste and the portrayal of fans as liking without knowing what it is they like, as well as a hierarchy of tastes against which Hennion proposes 'formats of different tastes'.[16] The notion of attachment also describes the fact of sharing a 'collective' love for music and dependence on other people's taste. Finally, the representation of the fan as self-questioning – do I like the same thing as other

---

[13]   Edgar Morin, 'Salut les copains: le yé-yé' and 'Salut les copains: une nouvelle classe d'âge', *Le Monde*, 6 and 7 July 1963. On this issue refer to Philippe Le Guern, 'En arrière la musique! Sociologie des musiques populaires en France. La genèse d'un champ', in Philippe Le Guern and Simon Frith (eds), 'Sociologies des musiques populaires', *Réseaux*, 141–2 (2007): pp. 24–6.

[14]   'I must undertake a task of rationalisation, of struggling with bibliographies, of positioning in relation to the dominant sociology. Notably, it is the sociology outlined by Bourdieu which is dominant, particularly in terms of culture', cited in Pierre Floux and Olivier Schinz, 'Engager son propre goût. Entretien autour de la sociologie pragmatique d'Antoine Hennion', *Ethnographiques.org*, 3, (2003): p. 6. One can however wonder whether this critique, albeit rather stimulating, of Bourdieu's determinism has not paradoxically hampered research into popular music, by resulting in a bi-polarized conflict, of being either 'for or against' Bourdieu.

[15]   Antoine Hennion, *La Passion musicale. Une sociologie de la médiation* (Paris, 1993).

[16]   Antoine Hennion, Sophie Maisonneuve, Emile Gomart, *Figures de l'amateur. Formes, objets, pratiques de l'amour de la musique aujourd'hui* (Paris, 2000), p. 251.

people? For the same reasons? Is what I like really good? Does it have real worth? – distances our understanding from that of the sociology of alienated audiences. On the contrary, Hennion portrays *competent* fans, attentive to what they like, prepared to doubt their own tastes and to discuss them. In other terms, 'this is another impasse in Bourdieu's work on culture: it analyses modes of consumption and life styles without giving mention to their associated experiences'.[17]

This idea of audiences which actively appropriate creativity spread across France through the reading of authors such as Michel de Certeau[18] or Richard Hoggart.[19] If at first glance the relationship between artists and their publics is assymmetrical – to the extent that producers impose forms of use and of reading – the true position of audiences can actually be restored by considering that readers are entitled to make their own interpretations of texts, and to invent unexpected, subversive uses. In popular music analysis, this conception notably fed into a series of works on fans, a particularly favourable ground for analysing the issue of 'popular taste' in terms of both music and collective experience of attachment to music.

One of the earliest texts explicitly devoted to music fans was published in an edited volume bringing together specialists in religion and cult events: by observing the cult of Claude François – one of the most famous variety singers of the 1960s–70s in France – Marie-Christine Pouchelle worked with analogies between saints and stars.[20] A dominant paradigm can be found in the study of fans: namely the comparison between fans' activities and ritual activities, which was a dimension of research initiated by Edgar Morin as early as the late 1950s[21] and encouraged in the 1990s through the reading of one of the few 'Anglo-Saxon' texts about fans available to French researchers.[22] Yet, as Eric Maigret has shown, whilst the hypothesis of equivalence between religious cults and media cults is appealing, it is nonetheless imperfect because fans are thereby linked to 'fanaticism' and the particularities of groups of fans are blurred by the religious metaphor, without considering that it is easy to find something of the religious in anything or to see in fans and their rituals so-called expressions of the secularization at work in

---

[17]   Cefaï and Pasquier (eds), *Les Sens du public*, p. 39.

[18]   Michel De Certeau, *L'Invention du quotidien* (Paris, 1980).

[19]   Richard Hoggart, *La Culture du pauvre* (Paris, trans. 1970).

[20]   Marie-Christine Pouchelle, 'Sentiment religieux et show-business: Claude François, objet de dévotion populaire', in Jean-Claude Schmitt (ed.), *Les Saints et les stars. Le texte hagiographique dans la culture populaire* (Paris, 1983), pp. 277–97.

[21]   Edgard Morin, *Les Stars* (Paris, 1957).

[22]   Lisa A. Lewis (ed.), *The Adoring Audience* (London, 1992). Another particularly influential work for those interested in fan culture in France is Henry Jenkins, *Textual Poachers. Television Fans and Participatory Culture* (London, 1992) whose many references to French authors show how one can discover or re-discover French authors in France, re-imported by American researchers!

our societies.[23] An apt example of this 'religious' reading of the fan movement is to be found in the work of Gabriel Segré. In observing fans of Elvis Presley in Paris and Memphis, and particularly in Graceland, he questions contemporary reconfigurations of the religious,[24] through an analysis of conditions behind the construction of the Presley myth, notably rationalization of the cult for commercial purposes by Elvis Presley Enterprises.

A completely contrasting approach to fans is presented by Christian Le Bart regarding French fans of the Beatles.[25] On the one hand, he shows how these fans are in some ways predisposed to like the Beatles: parents, siblings, school friends are always found behind a passion which is born during adolescence, and which is experienced as something mystical. Even though the first hearing of a Beatles song is described as an instant love affair or a revelation, there are undeniable transmission mechanisms which lead to the Beatles and make possible the conditions for first hearing their music and a passion for the group: 'Contrary to what the enchantment model suggests, in postulating an ignorant, indifferent or even hostile receptor, suddenly overcome by an overwhelming force, these expressions show a desire to like, a disposition and a receptivity which guarantees that the music performed by the Beatles meets at least a favourable reception.'[26] Le Bart also demonstrates how fans are always in a dialectic relationship with the subject of their passion: fans must find a place between the assertion of singularity (in the sense of 'what I like distinguishes me from the next person, my passion is exclusive') and the discovery of others like themselves which allows them perspective on their singularity whilst also allowing them to enter into the community of fans and become part of a shared taste. In fact, the malleability of the Beatles as an object of passion enables fans to work on their identities: one can be a policeman-fan, a catholic-fan and so-on. Challenging determinist sociologies, Le Bart tries to reconcile two opposing theoretical positions: the way in which fans love the Beatles expresses both a position within social space, but also shows a constructed identity, little by little self-built around musical taste.

A final perspective on music fans is my own work on fans of the Eurovision song contest: this research forms part of a wider analysis of fandom – my initial observations dealt with the fan-club of a television series[27] – revealing new trends

---

[23]   Eric Maigret, 'Du mythe au culte … ou de Charybde en Scylla. Le problème de l'importation des concepts religieux dans l'étude des publics des médias', in Philippe Le Guern (ed.), *Les Cultes médiatiques. Culture fan et œuvres cultes* (Rennes, 2002), pp. 97–110.

[24]   Gabriel Segré, *Le Culte Presley* (Paris, 2003).

[25]   Christian Le Bart, *Les Fans des Beatles. Sociologie d'une passion* (Rennes, 2000).

[26]   Le Bart, *Les Fans des Beatles*, p. 33.

[27]   Philippe Le Guern, 'En être ou pas. Le fan-club de la série Le Prisonnier, une enquête par observation', in Le Guern, *Les Cultes médiatiques*, pp. 177–215.

of eclecticism in cultural consumption,[28] that is to say, the *heterogeneity* of genres and tastes of single individuals, who may simultaneously appreciate Mozart as well as a variety singer. In my research into Eurovision based on ethnographic observations of members of the French fan-club, and more particularly observations of preparations for and of the running of a competition, I focused on an untouched aspect, namely the preponderance of homosexuals in the fan-club. But more significant was understanding the taste of these fans for a music termed *kitsch* playing cleverly on the codes and clichés of international variety music. Initially, it was appealing to adopt *Queer* theories, which make an object such as Eurovision a pool of *kitsch* signs reminding homosexuals of their dominated position and inviting them to practice irony and the subversion of cultural codes. However, this reading seemed questionable as it completely excluded the fact that people can 'seriously' like the most commercial or sentimental forms of culture: the majority of fans I met had an intense passion for the Eurovision songs. Some fans – clearly cultivated individuals collecting variety records by the thousand as well as operatic pieces – seemed to invalidate completely hypotheses of homology between social situations and life-styles. Overall I underlined the heterogeneity of an alleged homosexual 'community' and highlighted that forms of social domination were not absent, as attitudes appeared not autonomous of class status: the study of the origins and social paths of these fans who were members of the Eurovision fan club seemed to show that this largely constituted a means of being themselves for homosexuals from modest, provincial social backgrounds, having met with problems of acceptance.

Music and Cultural Democratization

One of the most striking characteristics of French cultural life is perhaps the existence of State-run policies favouring arts and culture since at least the end of the nineteenth century. The ideal of 'democratization' which was behind the establishment of the Ministry for Cultural Affairs under André Malraux in 1959, and which can be summarized as the objective of allowing culture to be accessed by the masses,[29] has left a mark in people's minds. This dimension of State policy did not fail, subsequently, to be extended to so-called 'contemporary' music,[30] a specific or, more precisely, hybrid sector inasmuch as it intersects cultural and socio-cultural perspectives, where public interests must permanently negotiate

---

[28]   The issue of cultural eclecticism, which adds to without rebutting the legitimacy theory of Bourdieu, was notably considered by Bernard Lahire, *La Culture des individus. Dissonances culturelles et distinction de soi* (Paris, 2004).

[29]   See Philippe Urfalino, *L'Invention de la politique culturelle* (Paris, 2004).

[30]   See Philippe Teillet, 'Éléments pour une histoire des politiques publiques en faveur des musiques amplifiées', in Philippe Poirrier (ed.), *Les Collectivités locales et la culture. Les formes de l'institutionnalisation, xixe et xxe siècles* (Paris, 2002), pp. 361–93.

with private interests (labels, tour managers etc.), and where funding comes primarily from the State (subsidies). As Philippe Teillet demonstrated regarding the dependence of this sector on the State and on regional authorities, 'all of this has led actors in the contemporary music sector to envisage the future for themselves and for their "sector" within the framework of State policies. The anti-institutional mood of the early 1980s has nowadays been replaced by a strong demand for intervention … even if people do not believe in the imminent achievement of democratising "culture" …'.[31]

In this context, public authorities have tried to acquire tools enabling the impact of their policies on audiences to be assessed. In 1963, the Studies and Research Department (SER) of the Ministry for Cultural Affairs was established by Augustin Girard, which would carry out some of the major studies into cultural practices in France which, since 1973, the Ministry for Cultural Affairs has chosen to undertake (1973, 1981, 1989, and 1997). The general findings of these studies have tended, even for those undertaking them, to prove the ineffectiveness of cultural policies: briefly put, cultural practices and consumption seem to remain primarily tied to the situations and social trajectories of individuals, and thus State intervention rather paradoxically contributes to reinforcing elitist access to culture. In other words, increased attendance of cultural events consists primarily of people who have a pre-existing interest in culture.[32] It could in theory be believed that popular music escaped this cumulative pattern and concerned a widening social audience for culture.

However, the relative rarity of research in France describing the profile of fans of this music must be underlined.[33] Essentially, we can refer to two sources, the DEPS studies previously mentioned, and studies – albeit few in number and often questionable methodologically – administered by the performance venues themselves.[34] DEPS studies allowed the description of music fans to be improved; they also underlined developments in people's relationships to popular music, focusing notably on the gradual hybridization of popular and cultured tastes. In fact, the majority of research undertaken in the 1970s–80s in France had reduced this music to the expression of one particular group, youth, which was grist to the mill of State cultural policies when in the early 1980s, they were (re-)established

---

[31]   Philippe Teillet, 'Le "secteur" des musiques actuelles. De l'innovation à la normalisation … et retour?', in Frith and Le Guern, *Sociologies:* pp. 271–96.

[32]   Olivier Donnat, 'La stratification sociale des pratiques culturelles et son évolution 1973–1997', *Revue française de sociologie*, XL/L (1999): pp. 111–19.

[33]   See 'Le public, cet obscur objet du désir', *La Scène*, 42, September 2006.

[34]   Recent meetings with agents in the sector have shown that the issue of audiences has become a recurring concern, difficult to investigate through studies. It can be supposed that this growing Interest for audiences has been arisen because of a perceived need to 'give account' to local authorities granting subsidies, itself something to be seen in the context of the new framework law on finance which will impose evaluation on the basis of results rather than merely project management.

on behalf of young people.[35] Whilst, admittedly, it can be hypothesized that there is some synchrony between the history of rock and youth protest movements,[36] it is not sufficient to conclude that 'contemporary' music is only for young people. DEPS studies show that young people represent a particular group for whom music plays a specific role, and where age plays a determining factor in the choice of music to listen to: in the 1990s, 15–19-year-olds favoured rock and Anglo-Saxon hits, whereas 20–34 year olds preferred jazz, 35–45-year-olds listened quantitatively more to classical music than the other age brackets and 55–65 year olds preferred ballroom dance music and operetta. *Chanson* held a privileged place in this list as it came top in the musical styles mentioned by every age bracket, except for 15–19 year olds. It is also apparent that international variety is the main preference for 15–24 year olds, a genre theoretically situated at the opposite extreme of rock due to its commercialism. In reality, Olivier Donnat shows in the DEPS studies that the 'age-group' variable has no meaning unless linked to gender, or social background, which are further variables displaying strong internal disparities within the grouping of 'young people'.[37] In fact, on reading these findings, it is difficult not to be struck by the rapid development in tastes, since it is not certain that operetta is nowadays such a favoured genre for 55–65 year olds. On this point, Olivier Donnat correctly indicates that rock (in the widest sense of the term) is not so much the music of a specific age bracket (young people) as it is the music which – in constantly renewed forms – has successively accompanied different generations. Increased recent interest in former legends such as Deep Purple, 1980s–90s groups like Queens of the Stone Age, or the success of amateur groups made up of rock 'veterans' reveals a 'more elderly' audience, whose purchasing power has doubtless not excaped the interest of the music industry. An example of this is the case – *inter alia* – of the Zimmers, a British rock group whose eldest member is almost 100 years old, and who made a name for themselves with a cover of the Who's 'My Generation' (1965), which quickly broke into the Top 30.

Furthermore, whilst it might be expected that contemporary music might not follow the model of cultural participation where practice rises according to social grouping – which holds so strongly for all forms of participation in cultural life – this is not at all the case. Even in the case of activities deemed less elitist such as rock concerts, managerial classes top the list for some age brackets. This observation is clearly noted by Donnat: '… Attendance at rock festivals – the comment is particularly valid for adults – produces disparities both geographical and social which are clearly more accentuated than those seen in record sales:

---

[35]   See Philippe Teillet, 'Publics et politiques des musiques actuelles', in Olivier Donnat and Paul Tolila, *Le(s) Public(s) de la culture* (Paris, 2003), pp. 155–80.

[36]   See for example Paul Yonnet, *Jeux, modes et masses. La société française et le moderne, 1945–1985* (Paris, 1985).

[37]   In terms of the variable 'age group' in the study of audiences of culture, see Vincent Caradec and Hervé Glevarec, 'Présentation', in *Réseaux*, 'Âge et usages des médias', 119 (2003): pp. 9–23.

attending a rock concert (especially when it is not a one-off) is a particular feature of cultured social backgrounds, notably in the Paris area. ... managerial classes and higher intellectual socio-professional categories attend concerts the most, and are – but to a lesser extent – regular listeners: unquestionably, rock fans come from cultured classes and urban areas ...'.[38]

These findings confirming the massive increase in people listening to music over the last three decades – which has developed from being a one-off activity reserved to a minority of music lovers in the 1950s to a daily activity, notably for younger generations – cannot but show the impact of technological developments on ways in which music is disseminated and received. In this perspective, studies published by DEPS to date have not been able to consider the Internet and mobile telephony, web sites, blogs, myspace, download platforms and MP3s: it is, therefore, possible that analyses published almost a decade ago need to be redone; it may, for instance, be necessary to verify whether music – notably for young audiences – is experienced more in exchange of audio files than by attending concerts (distinction between concert-going and festival attendance also needing to be made) or what is the impact of illegal downloads and free music on attitudes to paying for music formats which are obsolete (CDs). More generally, it is perhaps the symbolic value of music for young people which should be recconsidered; for example, is the idea that music is the primary vector for constructing the identity of young people today demolished or in need of revision? Additionally, because of the growth of music creation by amateurs, should we not reconsider the relationship between audience and artistic creator?

A second series of studies into concert-going audiences is formed by surveys undertaken by performance venues themselves. Understanding audiences is indeed one way of responding to questions regarding the use of public funding. We can take three examples here, each representing studies undertaken in venues of different capacities and at different dates. The first is of a pioneering study led between 1995 and 1996 in five venues scattered across France, the second study is that of *Le Réservoir* in Périgueux, and the last that of *La Cartonnerie* in Reims. Each of these illustrates the difficulty of producing a typology of audiences. Led by the GEMA (Amplified Music Study Group), the first study[39] invalidates the idea that the audience of amplified music is homogenous by showing firstly, that irrespective of musical genre, one third of concertgoers are women, secondly, that concert goers are not necessarily young, since the average age varies considerably depending on the musical genres performed and, thirdly, audiences are fairly evenly balanced between schoolchildren, secondary school and university students (46 per cent) on the one hand, and people of working age (54 per cent), white-collar workers and intermediary professions here occupying

[38]   Olivier Donnat, *Les Français face à la culture. De l'exclusion à l'éclectisme* (Paris, 1994), p. 227.

[39]   Gema, 'Les publics des concerts de musiques amplifiées', *Développement Culturel*, ministère de la Culture et de la Communication, 122, June 1998.

the greater share. Finally, the study shows that audiences are primarily from the local area, this criterion playing an essential role in the choice of concerts. In the study led on *Le Réservoir* in 2005,[40] it can be observed that whereas most concert goers are 18–24, dominant age ranges vary according to musical genre, with some concerts attracting primarily 35–49 year olds. Similarly, the socio-professional make-up of the audience varies for different concerts, even if secondary school students often represent the majority share of the audience, this needing to be considered in conjunction with the dominant age range. During certain concerts, managerial classes and members of the higher intellectual professions represented more than 23 per cent of attenders. When the 'age-group' variable is taken on its own, it can be observed that a supposed male monopoly on concert-going is debatable, as some concerts attract majorities of women (up to 63 per cent). Finally, most concerts attract audiences made up of musicians, but once more the proportion of musicians varies with genre and group performing. Overall, once again, we can note an image of an audience reasonably different from that of the stereotypical 'young male audience' supposedly characteristic of amplified music. The 2006 study of *La Cartonnerie*[41] presents some differing and complementary findings to previous studies but does not invalidate their main conclusions. For example, students only represent 25 per cent of the total audience, whereas wage earners represent 65 per cent and unemployed 6 per cent. Season-subscribers (one audience member in five) come, more so than any others, from the 20–29 bracket (49 per cent), a figure which decreases as age increases (22 per cent for 30–39 year olds). Finally, two in three audience members describe themselves as regular attendees.

More generally, this deconstruction of stereotypes regarding concert-going audiences goes together with observations of increased eclecticism of taste. As shown by Philippe Coulangeon from an INSEE study undertaken in 2003,[42] of 100 senior managerial class individuals claiming to mostly listen to variety music, 37 per cent also listened to opera, an indication of the increasing repertoire of tastes. However, this eclecticism certainly does not indicate the end of the distinguishing power of these kinds of music, but rather a redefinition of the frontiers of cultural legitimacy where that which is valued nowadays is the plurality of tastes: '… eclecticism as displayed by members of higher social classes is rarely indiscriminate. While "informed" eclecticism, which is more often than not a product of measured incursion in the domain of arts which are "undergoing legitimization", does in fact constitute a particular method of aesthetic refinement, "indistinct eclecticism" on the other hand constitutes the most radical disqualification of competence and "good taste"'.[43]

---

[40]   The study into audiences of *Le Réservoir* can be consulted at the following site: http://www.sans-reserve.org/sansresreve/telechargements.php.

[41]   *Enquêtes, chiffres et bilan* (Reims, 2006).

[42]   Philippe Coulangeon, *Sociologie des pratiques culturelles* (Paris, 2005).

[43]   Coulangeon, *Sociologie*, p. 61.

In contrast to statistical studies undertaken into concert-going audiences in venues themselves, we also find studies undertaken via observation during outdoor concerts, such as techno music gatherings, sound system parties and raves, and their 'rituals', have provided an alternate view of audiences understood through a perspective of 'tribalism' largely inspired by the works of Michel Maffesoli. Lionel Pourtau,[44] Sandy Queudrus[45] and Emmanuel Grynszpan,[46] amongst others, have thus set out to describe raves as communal experiences organized by deviant culture. Whilst drug use or the meaning of trances or secrecy for example are the subject of much discussion, analyses are also undertaken into the social and generational composition of these audiences often composed in large proportion of middle class young people originally from working class backgrounds, having abandoned education and now in work, who identify in the techno lifestyle 'a manner of once more taking control of their youth for themselves and acquiring a certain distance from the world of work typical of the students that they have never been ..., the final step in a deviant career [which] consists of entering into an organised sub-cultural group offering a shared future'.[47]

Conclusion: Failed Democratisation Policies and Success of the Internet. Rethinking Popular Music Audiences?

As we have seen, the tradition of French research on music audiences has been distinguished, in France, by the influence of the legitimacy model established by Pierre Bourdieu, sometimes modernized by the description of new forms of classification and distinction, and at other times by the suggestion of more active and less determined depictions of audiences. But it is far from certain that these two approaches are the most appropriate in analysing new forms of people's relationships with music; it can be thought that the far-reaching changes nowadays shaking up the music landscape, brought about by the internet and new methods of creation (low-cost digital recording), promotion (podcast, blogs, community web sites etc.) and broadcasting (download platforms, peer to peer networks) have had a decisive effect on the nature of audiences, the methods of receiving music and types of use, in new and influential ways. Consequently, the 'musical boom' discussed by Donnat in describing the importance music has assumed during

---

[44]   Lionel Pourtau, 'Le risque comme adjuvant, le cas des free-parties', *Sociétés*, 76 (2002).

[45]   Sandy Queudrus, *Un maquis techno. Modes d'engagement et pratiques sociales dans la free party* (Paris, 2000).

[46]   Emmanuel Grynszpan, *Bruyante techno. Réflexion sur le son de la free party* (Paris, 1999).

[47]   Lionel Pourtau, 'Les *sound systems* technoïdes. Une expérience de la vie en communauté', in Béatrice Mabilon-Bonfils (ed.), *La Fête techno. Tout seul et tous ensemble* (Paris, 2004), pp. 100–14.

the last 30 years, is no longer adequate in describing current transformations of cultural practices as the internet establishes its leading role in French people's consumer habits and induces new economic models. Piracy and the drop in record sales for example, or new forms of online social networking, or even the removal of barriers between creators and consumers – all of these are phenomena which require a renewed understanding of music audiences.[48] Moreover, in terms of live music audiences, the failure of typically French democratization policies – perhaps due to their inherent weaknesses?[49] – calls for reflection on the limitations of the institutional mechanisms which foster the transmission of contemporary music, and reconsideration of the role of citizens in the public cultural sphere. At the polar opposite of cultural *laisser-faire* this typically French interventionism also demonstrates limitations: the increased interest stimulated by the idea of a 'non public'[50] as an expression of cultural policies' loss of confidence in their ambition to prescribe culture to audiences who have not asked for anything, and whose ways of participating in culture are unorthodox and varied.

---

[48] See notably Nicolas Curien and François Moreau, *L'Industrie du disque* (Paris, 2006); Bernard Miège, *La Société conquise par la communication – 3: les TIC entre innovation technique et ancrage social* (Grenoble, 2007).

[49] To use the expression of Doc Kasimir Bisou, in 'Le médiateur culturel: héros malheureux de la culture universelle ou hardi négociateur dans la société de diversité culturelle?', speech given during the symposium entitled *Médiations, médiateurs, médias* organized by the 'Salon du livre et de la presse jeunesse', 27 April 2006, consultable on the Irma website (www.irma.asso.fr).

[50] Pascale Ancele and Alain Pessin (eds), *Les Non Publics: les arts en réception* (Paris, 2004). The expression 'non-audience' – 'a human immensity made up of all those people who have no access to nor any chance of accessing the cultural phenomenon anytime soon' – was conceptualized in 1968 with the Villeurbanne manifesto written by François Jeanson, published in his *L'Action culturelle dans la cité* (Paris, 1973).

Chapter 14
Is it Different for Girls? Unpacking Sheffield's 'Scene'

Josie Robson

Two landmark ethnographic studies provided the inspiration for this ten-year feminist ethnography of music making in Sheffield: Ruth Finnegan's *The Hidden Musicians: Music Making in an English Town,* and Sara Cohen's *Rock Culture in Liverpool: Popular Music in the Making.*[1] Both texts highlight the benefits of studying local music and related activities as 'social practice and process',[2] providing detailed empirical insights into the specific conditions that facilitate different kinds of social and musical networks. Crucially, both writers also note the lack of women in the rock and pop 'worlds' of Milton Keynes and Merseyside, an absence that Cohen defines as 'structural exclusion'.[3]

Building on notions of 'hidden' musicianship, exclusion *and* access, this chapter uses Sheffield's rock and pop 'scene' as a lens to explore the ways in which women negotiate place-specific and more widely established barriers to participate in musical practice. It draws on data generated through interview and participant observation of 27 functional bands and their audiences, selected to reflect a diversity of participants and experiences.[4] This chapter also examines the influence of the city's industrial heritage on local cultural policy initiatives and the much-debated concept of a 'Sheffield sound', in order to assess how narratives of 'Sheffieldness' and localized pathways have shaped conditions and perceptions of the city and its 'scene'.

---

[1] Sara Cohen, *Rock Culture in Liverpool: Popular Music in the Making* (Oxford, 1991) and Ruth Finnegan, *The Hidden Musicians: Music Making in an English Town* (Cambridge, 1989).

[2] Sara Cohen, 'Ethnography and Popular Music Studies', *Popular Music*, 12/2 (1993): pp. 123–8.

[3] Sara Cohen, *Rock Culture in Liverpool*.

[4] Robert Burgess, *In the Field: An Introduction to Field Research* (London, 1984). The sample is one all-female, seventeen all-male and nine mixed-gender bands.

Meanings of Scene

> People were generally interested in what everyone was doing creatively and that, in essence, distils what a scene is, doesn't it?'[5]

> Sheffield's never had a scene really ... It's never had a big record company like other cities. Manchester had Factory, Newcastle had Kitchenware, Glasgow had Postcard, but we never had that really ... And it was the only major city that never had a TV station based in it ... we had to go to Leeds ... I hated Leeds because of that.[6]

> We were like kings of the jungle then and we were very close to the Stones. It was like a men's smoking club, just a very good scene.[7]

The above quotations illustrate three of the characteristic ways in which a scene is variously perceived. Academic writers have embraced the concept as a flexible analytical tool for mapping the dynamic relationships between spaces, sounds, structures and social groups. Musicians tend to collapse these dimensions in order to define *their* sites and networks of musical activity as the scene. Martyn Ware's comment is a case in point. He is referring to a specific historical period, the late 1970s and early 1980s, when a number of groups including Cabaret Voltaire, Heaven 17, ABC and the Human League, were gaining commercial and/or critical success. This exposure helped to construct a 'blue-print' for a 'Sheffield sound',[8] melding a particular coalition of spatial, social and aesthetic factors through a distinctive sub-genre: post-punk electronica. My focus on the broader but equally 'elusive'[9] pathways of rock and pop inevitably considers the impact of electronica, but to reduce the scene to a handful of acts symbolized by analogue synthesizers obscures the diversity of music and music makers that co-exist in the locale. In order to demonstrate the flexible, overlapping and historically conditional trajectory of Sheffield's multiple pathways, I consequently refer to scene/s as a plural concept.

The second quotation illustrates the fundamental role of music infrastructure in supporting and stimulating musical productivity. What is of equal interest is the 'regional sense of grievance' this particular musician draws upon to highlight unequal perceptions of opportunity,[10] expressed through the filter of 'local structures

---

[5]   Martyn Ware, *Made in Sheffield* (Slackjawfilm, 2002).

[6]   Ogy McGrath from mid-80s band Dig Vis Drill, cited in Mark Sturdy, *Truth and Beauty: The Story of Pulp* (London, 2003), p. 106.

[7]   John Lennon cited in Simon Frith, *Sound Effects: Youth, Leisure and the Politics of Rock'n'Roll* (London, 1983), p. 79.

[8]   Alexis Petridis, *The Guardian*, 3/5/02.

[9]   Finnegan, *The Hidden Musicians*.

[10]   Ian R. Taylor, Karen Evans and Penny Fraser, *A Tale of Two Cities: Global Change, Local Feeling and Everyday Life in the North of England* (London, 1996, p. 10). They also

of feeling' that are inextricably linked to the material conditions and mythologized characteristics of a particular place (ibid.). I will examine these interconnected themes in the context of Sheffield's industrial past and so-called post-industrial present, for the legacy of Sheffield's 'dual economy' of steel and cutlery have furnished masculinist narratives of 'Sheffieldness' that shape the ways in which local music is produced, consumed and understood.

The subsequent collapse of traditional industry has had an equally profound effect on – for the purposes of this study – two critical areas. Firstly, the success of the above groups helped to facilitate an ideological shift from constructing music as play to music as work, thus placing 'culture' at the centre of policies of economic and urban regeneration.[11] Secondly, the crisis of de-industrialization, coupled with 'the dominant, enterprise model of creativity',[12] has been shown to accentuate relations of gender inequality,[13] producing a paradoxical nexus of increased opportunities and constraints for women that is highlighted in the third quotation.

John Lennon's construct of a 'men's club' underscores the gendered dimensions of access and exclusion in 'translocal' scene narratives, for he is not referring to the entrenched male-ness of Liverpool music detailed by Sara Cohen, but rather, to an exclusive clique of rock acts that the Beatles allied with in the early 1960s. Sheffield is host to similar cliques and I examine some of the local cultural industries to assess how contemporary 'men's clubs' are forged. I also consider the role of local media in constructing a sense of scene, focusing especially on the 'free monthly music magazine' *Sandman*, and the ways in which a group of women attempted to problematize hegemonic masculinity through the counterpart, *Sandlady*. In sum, this chapter aims to map some of the significant features of Sheffield's scene/s to illustrate how the interaction of place, policy, and musical practice produces contrasting perceptions and material conditions within which gendered musical practices are both constructed and contested.

Narratives of Sheffieldness

Sheffield's industrial identity, landlocked topography, stable demographic and 'enclave mentality' have all served to shape the music 'made in Sheffield'.[14] Building on Taylor et al.'s concept, 'local structures of feeling', I now examine

---

note 'angry local comment' that regional news is produced in the 'rival' city of Leeds.

[11]   Simon Frith, 'Popular Music and the Local State', in Tony Bennett et al. (eds), *Rock and Popular Music* (London: Routledge, 1993).

[12]   Elly Tams, *The Gendering of Work in Sheffield's Cultural Industries Quarter (CIQ)* (unpublished Ph.D. Thesis, Sheffield Hallam University, 2003).

[13]   Taylor et al., *A Tale of Two Cities*; Sue Yeandle et al., *Gender Profile of South Yorkshire's Labour Market 2000* (produced for South Yorkshire Objective 1, 2004).

[14]   John Firminger and Martin Lilleker, *Not Like a Proper Job: The Story of Popular Music in Sheffield 1955–1975* (Sheffield, 2001), p. 7.

the ways in which narratives of place or 'Sheffieldness' have influenced the city's musical trends in order to address a key question posed by Frith: 'what is the Sheffieldness of Sheffield bands?'.[15]

Taylor et al. apply John Urry's 1981 theory of a 'local class structure' to demonstrate how relations of production, particular occupations and trade union activity are shaped by distinctive industrial conditions.[16] These conditions are inextricably linked to the local cultural structure – marked by particular institutions such as working mens' clubs and pubs – which produce, developing Raymond Williams' oft-used phrase, '*local* structures of feeling' (emphasis added). By this, they mean the processes through which knowledge and folklore associated with a particular place and the people who live there is translated into 'commonsense talk', simultaneously circulated *by* the people who live there.

Frequently referred to as 'the largest village in England',[17] the cliquey facets of the city's musical scene/s are habitual complaints: 'Sheffield is the only city that thinks it's a town with a village in-look' as one artist manager put it. On the other hand, it is suggested that the city's topography and parochialism provides a fertile training ground for 'outsiders' – 'it's a place where you can actually experiment'.[18] Another performer extends this rationale, describing Sheffield as a 'DIY city, full of independent spirit'.[19] Competing interpretations of an 'enclave mentality' continue to provoke controversy.

In her documentary 'Made In Sheffield' (Slackjaw Film, 2002), Eve Wood draws on another emotive strand of Sheffieldness, that of quality. Imprinted on a range of metalwork exports, the brand 'Made In Sheffield' signifies a place-specific marker of value that she appropriates to emphasize the 'unique' cluster of acts involved in 'the birth of electronic pop'.[20] Belonging and familiarity are related recurring themes: 'I ... love this city, which is why I stay here. I were born here, all my family's here, my roots are here.'[21] Equally common however, is the perception that there are better scenes, with better facilities or opportunities, happening elsewhere.

Bemoaning regional inequality also serves an underlying compensatory function for the vast majority who do not 'make it'. Thus, local bands are typically defined as 'insular', 'independent' and 'self-supporting'.[22] Stereotypes of down-to-earth masculinity characterized by 'a blunt, no-shit type of personality',[23] locate these narratives within a masculinist framework. Even the success of the celebrated

---

[15]   Frith, 'Popular Music and the Local State', p. 22.
[16]   Taylor et al., *A Tale of Two Cities*.
[17]   Taylor et al., *A Tale of Two Cities*, p. 28.
[18]   Martyn Ware on *Calendar Goes Pop*, YTV, 1998.
[19]   Sandlady in *Sandman*, August 2004.
[20]   www.sheffieldvision.com.
[21]   Richard Hawley, *The Guardian*, 13/2/03.
[22]   Sturdy, *Truth and Beauty*, p. 18.
[23]   *Sandman*, May 2003.

few are storied within the context of tenacious Northern grit, with 'Sheffield's famous five', Pulp, setting the 1990s' benchmark for 'resilience, perseverance and belief'.[24] In sum, each of these perceived traits – insularity, individuality, sociability, quality, familiarity, inequity, tenacity and masculinity – serve to shape the city's 'sound, look and story'[25] and the 'Sheffieldness of Sheffield bands'.

Music City

The collapse of Sheffield's traditional industries and consequent devastating job losses – almost 75 per cent of those working in steel and metals production between 1981 and 1991 – advanced a process of 're-imaging' in a bid to construct a post-industrial identity founded on culture, leisure and tourism.[26] Encouraged by the achievements of the Human League et al., popular music was identified as a key motor for economic and urban regeneration. As legend has it, the impetus for the rise of electronica stems back to a gig at Sheffield University's Lower Refectory on 26 June 1978, when Cabaret Voltaire supported Kraftwerk on their Trans Europe Express tour. According to one of those present, 'there were only 17 or 18 people there and [we] all formed bands. That was the key, it unlocked the Sheffield thing'.[27]

Cabaret Voltaire were certainly an influential force on those acts who would become the pioneers of 'synth-pop' in the early 1980s, not least because they owned only one of two commercial recording studios in Sheffield at that time. Places to play and the infrastructure needed to disseminate music were similarly scarce, although in line with the DIY ethic, several bands released independent records before acquiring major deals. Due to the lack of competitive facilities, the 'drift to London' was inevitable for signed bands.[28] The Human League's Phil Oakey, amongst others, aimed to reverse this trend by suggesting ways in which successful acts could invest in a 'local' music industry. The resulting initiative was founded on two interlinking aims: to provide increased community access to the resources needed to develop local talent, whilst simultaneously promoting economic growth and employment.[29] Sheffield's post-industrial vision was therefore globally

---

[24]   'How Pulp Gained Overnight Stardom in Just 12 years', *The Star*, 29 December 1994.

[25]   Michael Jones, *Organising Pop: Why So Few Pop Acts Make Pop Music* (unpublished Ph.D. Thesis, Institute of Popular Music, Liverpool University, 1997).

[26]   Adam Brown, et al., 'Local Music Policies Within a Global Music Industry: Cultural Quarters in Manchester and Sheffield', in Toru Mitsui (ed.), *Popular Music: Intercultural Interpretations* (Kanazawa: Kanazawa University Press, 1998).

[27]   Jamie Fry, *World of Twist*, cited in 'Forged in the City of Steel' (www.timesonline.co.uk 23/4/04).

[28]   Brown et al., 'Local Music Policies'.

[29]   Brown et al., ibid.

determined – shifting demand and markets for steel; multinational advances; US record sales – and locally framed.

The first phase incorporated all four municipal areas of investment identified by John Street and Michael Stanley: recording studios, venues, concert promotion and training provision.[30] Initially opened as an arts centre (circa 1978), the Leadmill became the first council-owned performance space in the UK. Training, recording and rehearsal facilities were established on two further sites – Darnall's 'Music Factory' and the city centre flagship, Red Tape Studios. Launched in 1986, Red Tape was the founding venture underpinning a wider strategy of creative enterprise – the Cultural Industries Quarter (CIQ) – that has since developed managed workspaces for a range of cultural producers. Thus, in opposition to Adorno's negative construction of the 'Culture Industry',[31] the small-scale production of symbolic goods, from records to computer games, is now heralded as an affirmative 'model for 21st Century Working'.[32] My concern here is not primarily with specific policy but rather with the tensions municipal intervention and investment gives rise to. In short, how do 'local structures of feeling' interact with narratives of entrepreneurship and community to facilitate – or indeed constrain – access?

'This isn't the Spirit of Rock'n'Roll, this is Sheffield City Council'[33]

Economic subsidies enabled the Human League and members of the Comsat Angels to build commercial recording studios within the Audio Visual Enterprise Centre (AVEC) where Red Tape was already established. Financed by the proceeds of local band Chakk's recording contract with MCA, FON recording studios added to AVEC's burgeoning roster, producing an eponymous record label (FON). Tensions emerged early however, as these perceived enclaves of power became branded the 'Sheffield Music Mafia'.[34] The major complaint was that the powerful few had the ear of London A&R, restricting access – even thwarting opportunities – for those outside the 'men's club.' Indeed, several employees at Red Tape subsequently (and in one case, simultaneously) worked as A&R 'scouts'. Thus, narratives of 'regional grievance' became locally focused.

On the other hand, council policy meshed fortuitously with Sheffield's growing prominence as a centre of dance music production, encouraging entrepreneurs like those behind the independent record label, Wau! Mr Modo, to relocate. The city's 'unique' associations with left-field electronica were also developed by local labels such as Warp. Collectively, these labels generated a 3.2 per cent share of British

---

[30]   Frith, 'Popular Music and the Local State', p. 15.

[31]   Theodor Adorno, 'On Popular Music', in Simon Frith and Andrew Goodwin (eds), *On Record: Rock, Pop and the Written Word* (London, 1990).

[32]   www.ciq.org.uk; Milestone and Richards, 2000).

[33]   From *23.59*, by Nicola Baldwin, the Crucible theatre's millennium play about a fictional Sheffield 'scene'.

[34]   Sturdy, *Truth and Beauty*, p. 193.

singles sales in 1990, leading to claims that 'the City is on target to register as a major music production centre, increasingly recognised as such by the Media and Record Industry'.[35] Despite Wau! Mr Modo's subsequent bankruptcy[36] and Warp's move away from the CIQ, the internationally renowned Gatecrasher phenomenon at the Republic nightclub served to underline the city's post-industrial success during the mid to late 1990s.

Whilst 'difficult to define', the 'Cultural Industries' were an expanding sector, with a 10 per cent growth in employment between 1997 and 1999. Not surprisingly, the council literature capitalized on these real and perceived achievements: 'what was once a sceptic's field day is fast becoming the envy of the nation'.[37] Other commentators were more measured, emphasizing the local council's own concern that the CIQ was somehow still a 'hidden Sheffield', unknown to many Sheffielders.[38]

This notion of a 'hidden Sheffield' was confirmed in Brown, O'Connor and Cohen's 1998 comparative study of Liverpool, Manchester and Sheffield's cultural industries.[39] They found that production facilities had been prioritized at the expense of complementary amenities such as bars, cafes and shops that would attract people into the area. The lack of 'soft infrastructure', vital to encouraging new social pathways, also resulted in cultural producers and community arts projects outside the CIQ feeling excluded.[40] Brown et al. therefore challenge the policy focus, stating: 'Quarters are complex clusters of activities – they are networks embedded in a particular place ... it is these "scenes", "milieus", "happening places", which are the real context for a local music industry rather than facilities'.[41]

I would argue that the musical strand of Sheffield's cultural policy was founded on the assumption that music production generates consistent economic growth. Thus, 'community access' became subordinate to the 'buoyant expectations'[42] of free market enterprise, arguably impacting on the eventual downfall of Sheffield's popular music 'museum', the National Centre for Popular Music (NCPM). Opening on 1 March 1999, only 65,500 paying visitors were recorded in the first six months. Despite many redundancies, the NCPM continued to trade at a massive loss, accruing over £13 million debts. When it finally closed to visitors

---

[35]   Frith, 'Popular Music and the Local State', p. 17.

[36]   In part, due to the lack of sector-specific 'back-up'. 'There are no club promoters, no clubs, no cutting places, no pluggers. There are no marketing companies ... so it's quite difficult. You have to be willing to spend a lot of time travelling to London' (Adam Morris, 4 June 1993).

[37]   *Dirty Stopouts Guide*, 1998/99.

[38]   *Sheffield Telegraph*, 15 October 1999.

[39]   Brown et al., 'Local Music Policies'.

[40]   Ibid.; Tams, *The Gendering of Work*.

[41]   Brown et al., 'Local Music Policies', p. 256.

[42]   Marcus Breen, 'Making Music Local', in Bennett et al., *Rock and Popular Music*.

in June 2000, its spectacular, highly newsworthy collapse contributed to negative perceptions of the city and its scene/s.

Failure to address the 'spatial politics'[43] also had a profound impact on the gendered use of the area, as illustrated by the changing fortunes of two sites at the heart of the CIQ. Firstly, the demise of the Women's Cultural Club – one of the many community oriented casualties of what Elly Tams, in her doctoral research investigating the gender imbalance of the CIQ, has coined 'the dominant, enterprise model of creativity'.[44] Secondly, the transformation of the nightclub, Brown Street, into a so-called 'gentlemen's club' (December 2002) – part of the Spearmint Rhino chain – initially provoking fierce opposition, followed by 'avoidance'.[45] My own experience bears this out.

Whilst working at Red Tape (2000–2004), I found that the sexualized pathways to the 'gentleman's club' generated a heightened sense of threat after dark. Personal safety has been a primary consideration for almost every woman I have talked to over the last decade – there were only a handful that felt confident going to venues or pubs alone. Women's mobility is therefore restricted by the perceived and actual dangers of urban city spaces,[46] particularly those 'zones' that are manifestly 'sex-typed'.[47] In short, the CIQ has become another 'overwhelmingly male place' which limits women's access to the cultural facilities in the area such as Red Tape. The continued male-domination of this training provider also deserves further consideration, in order to shed light on the exclusionary practices that contribute to gender inequalities on the wider 'scene'.

From the Little Mester to the Music Maker

For four years, I ran the Band Development Programme (BDP) at Red Tape during which time 46 acts – 32 bands, one vocal harmony group and 13 solo artists – completed the programme, totalling 140 music makers. Only 17 (12 per cent) of these were women. With the exception of four 'black' men, all the musicians were white. There are potential problems when generalizing from this sample however. Many established, functional bands in and around the Sheffield area are too *developed* to consider a training programme of this kind, and the exclusive and exclusionary reputation of Red Tape, coupled with subsidized but potentially substantial course fees, undoubtedly deters other aspirant music makers – as does the council tag.[48] With these provisos in mind, the above statistics, building on

---

43   Brown et al., 'Local Music Policies', p. 256.
44   Tams, *The Gendering of Work*.
45   Taylor et al., *A Tale of Two Cities*.
46   Doreen Massey, *Space, Place and Gender* (Minneapolis, 1994).
47   Taylor et al., *A Tale of Two Cities*.
48   Brown et al., 'Local Music Policies'.

my ethnographic sample (see below), uphold Cohen's findings that band culture overwhelmingly produces 'whiteness' and masculinity.[49]

The vast majority of 'rock' bands on the BDP developed their skills collectively, within the fraternity of an all-male group founded upon an ideological allegiance to the process and practice of making music that simultaneously defined them as musicians. This social practice reinforces the masculinity of its participants, a fragile construct that, as Bayton argues, 'is only preserved by the exclusion of girls'.[50] Even those in mixed-gender bands were subject to a range of deterrents, from direct sexual harassment to more subtle means of exclusion, such as in-jokes. In short, many bands within Sheffield's scene/s operate as micro 'men's clubs'. Despite the best efforts of many staff, Red Tape has failed (thus far) to tackle the imbalance of access effectively, particularly in the light of original policy aims to 'develop new skills and extend and increase opportunities for finding work for both adults and young people, both black and white, male and female, and make use of the new and interesting job opportunities available locally and nationally in an industry with growth potential'.[51]

According to Yeandle et al., 'girls and boys [in South Yorkshire] are underachieving in all age groups compared to pupils in England as a whole'.[52] Furthermore, that there is a marked tendency for girls – and boys from BME groups – to 'opt out' of the design and technology curriculum (ibid.). It is therefore hardly surprising that the white male hegemony of Red Tape is most acutely pronounced in the technology courses.[53] Many prominent 'cultural intermediaries' working in local venues, recording studios or training providers, initially trained as sound engineers at Red Tape. Thus, the training cycle perpetuates the masculinism of Sheffield's scene/s.

Whilst the stainless steel drums of the 'National Centre of Regional Embarrassment' became a blot on Sheffield's contemporary 'scenescape',[54] a more organic meld of the city's dual identities can be traced through the gradual re-appropriation – from the 1960s onwards – of cutlery and finishing works into affordable rehearsal spaces and associated cultural industries. Many of these works have been demolished over the last two decades, with the most notable remaining ones concentrated in a few streets opposite Sheffield United's football ground,

---

[49]   Cohen, *Rock Culture in Liverpool*; 'Men Making a Scene: Rock Music and the Production of Gender', in Sheila Whiteley (ed.), *Sexing the Groove: Popular Music and Gender* (London, 1997) and 'Popular Music, Gender and Sexuality', in Simon Frith et al. (eds), *The Cambridge Companion to Pop and Rock* (Cambridge, 2001).

[50]   Mavis Bayton, *Frock Rock* (Oxford, 1998), p. 41.

[51]   Cited in Frith, 'Popular Music and the Local State', p. 16.

[52]   Sue Yeandle et al., *Gender Profile of South Yorkshire's Labour Market 2000*, p. 7.

[53]   Bayton, *Frock Rock*; Anne-Marie Marshall, *Gender Balance within the South Yorkshire Music Industry*, (unpublished research report funded by the Yorkshire Arts Board, Research and Development Grant, 2003).

[54]   Cohen, 'Men Making a Scene'.

just outside the city centre. A symbiotic relationship has consequently developed between music and metal workers in the area, with one collective at Stag Works housing silversmiths, precious metalworkers and pewterers.

Stag Works is also host to the largest concentration of micro music businesses representing various strands of Sheffield's overlapping scene/s, including the Juju club specializing in 'global dance'; Headcharge – 'legendary Sheffield club with international DJs and very, very late nights'; rehearsal facilities for numerous bands; record labels and recording studios. In an attempt to attract funding to develop the facilities, the entrepreneurs fronting the initiative drew on 'local structures of feeling' to explicitly link the music maker to the 'Little Mester'. *Sandman* disseminated their theory as follows: 'There is a strong and interesting argument that the independent nature of Sheffield's musicians is a direct result of these small businesses which, unlike the huge corporations that dominated the workforce of other Northern cities ... lead to competition within the city itself.'[55]

This nostalgic vision of enterprise culture represents a 'celebration of masculinity'.[56] According to Tams, the 'creative entrepreneur' is constructed as a 'masculinised ideal', blurring the boundaries between work and play in a living embodiment of the creative consumer-turned-producer.[57] The Stag Works' account reinforces this ideal in a bid for self-sufficiency apart from the CIQ – thus 're-imaging' entrepreneurship through the enduring filters of individuality, insularity and competitiveness. In sum, narratives of Sheffieldness shape those of entrepreneurship in ways that naturalize the masculinity of creativity. The homosocial norms of rock and pop are potentially disrupted when mixed-gender or all-women bands perform however and the following section returns to the initial fieldwork to examine some of the key strategies developed by women music makers in Sheffield.

Gendered Strategies of Inclusion

Out of the 27 acts selected, there were nine mixed-gender groups and one all-women band, Treacle. Six women were in their teens; four under the age of 25, with the other ten ranging between late 20s and mid 30s. Thirteen were either lead or backing vocalists, confirming the typicality of these 'gender-influenced roles'.[58] They also challenge the gendered hierarchy of creativity proposed by Green,[59] engaging in multiple activities as songwriters and/or instrumentalists, along with promotion and business negotiation. I have yet to meet *just* a singer.

---

[55]   www.sandman.co.uk, 26 November 2004.

[56]   Cohen, 'Popular Music, Gender and Sexuality'.

[57]   Tams, *Gendered Strategies of Working*.

[58]   Finnegan, *The Hidden Musicians*.

[59]   Lucy Green, *Music, Gender, Education* (Cambridge, 1997). Green establishes a gendered hierarchy of creativity by claiming that singers 'affirm', instrumentalists 'interrupt', and composers 'threaten' patriarchal constructs of femininity.

The range of instruments was equally diverse, including: one clarinet player; one trumpeter; two electric guitarists; one keyboard player and two drummers. Treacle played the full range of rock instruments – bass, electric guitar and drums. Developing competences and the cultural capital appropriate to their divergent pathways is a key legitimating strategy for all players, but a particularly crucial one for female musicians who frequently state, as do women in other masculine spheres, that they have to be 'exceptional' in order to gain a grudging acceptance: 'you're alright for a girl'.[60] Velodrome 2000 problematized notions of excellence however, by embracing the 'purposeful' style of 'musical incompetence',[61] swapping instruments and sharing lead vocals.

Finding like-minded/tasted others to play with is a further critical 'hurdle'.[62] Three of the mixed-gender groups had only one female player. The Human League, Reaction and Velodrome 2000 contained two or more women members who were firm friends. The most striking feature for the remaining four was the level of family involvement. EKM, Belief and Derrick each contained two women members who were sisters. There were two sets of sisters in Treacle, and one father had taken on the role of manager. Belief were also managed by the sisters' father – Derrick's by their mother. Belief and EKM's memberships consisted almost entirely of extended family members, including brothers, partners and husbands. This strategy of collectivism is a common, pragmatic practice also adopted by all-male groups, who draw on accessible social networks to collaborate and develop corresponding social pathways. Playing with family and friends takes on additional significance for women, due to considerations of safety and confidence,[63] paradoxically creating the potential for additional constraints.

The third ideal strategy is that of commitment. All the women featured in this study displayed an intensely 'intrinsic' commitment to *their* music.[64] For those working in bands, personal commitment to the music needed to be translated into an extrinsic set of group practices that were both specific to the group and commonly understood.[65] Notions of commitment were shaped by varying narratives of 'making it'. Pulp, the Human League and Speedy were already signed, with several others harbouring 'romantic' aspirations of 'getting a deal'. As two of the oldest 'amateur' bands, members of Reaction and EKM had previously worked within the mainstream music industry, forming new bands for the collective and

---

[60]   Cited in Green, ibid., p. 74).

[61]   Cohen, *Rock Culture in Liverpool*; Rob Strachan, *Industry, Ideology, Aesthetics and Micro Independent Record Labels in the UK* (unpublished Ph.D. Thesis, Institute of Popular Music, Liverpool University, 2004).

[62]   Bayton, *Frock Rock*.

[63]   Mavis Bayton, 'Women and the Electric Guitar', in Sheila Whiteley (ed), *Sexing the Groove: Popular Music and Gender* (London, 1997).

[64]   J.A. Sloboda et al, 'Is Everyone Musical?', *The Psychologist*, 7/8, (1994): pp. 349–54.

[65]   Punctuality for example, became synonymous with professionalism for Red Tape's trainee sound engineers and managers.

creative pleasures of the group experience whereas the 'DIY aesthetic'[66] of punk-pop encouraged Velodrome 2000 to set up their own label. Supporting Strachan, I would argue that each 'making it' narrative is ideologically constructed because they serve to shape the aesthetic practice of musical groups. EKM's story illustrates this point.

The four black members of the six-strong band were from the same family, who had grown up under the paternal influence of the Darnall Congregationalist gospel church. Described as 'the most important ... setting that Black people control',[67] the church represented a social, spiritual and musical training ground. Initially known as Eliakim, they formed in the early 1980s, playing a mixture of gospel standards and original material on the 'circuit': 'Manchester, Birmingham, Leeds, Nottingham, London ... the network of churches is country-wide.'[68]

Much to the consternation of their minister, Eliakim began performing at local pubs and clubs in the mid-1980s, generating tensions that were still apparent at one of the sister's weddings over a decade later.

Gospel remained the touchstone for their symbolic creativity. They released an independent single, *I'm a Christian Warrior*, in 1988,[69] an explicitly ideological remit that continued to inform their love and logic of live: 'for those of you who have never been inside a black gospel church, then we're going to bring it to you'.[70] Although EKM were a highly visible presence in predominantly white, male 'scene' settings, their professionalism and passionate zeal moved audiences, however momentarily, to imagine different kinds of Sheffieldness. As local journalist Martin Lilleker enthused: 'EKM, the impressive new line-up which has emerged from one of Sheffield's finest bands of the mid-eighties ... still featur[es] those superb vocalists, sisters Sharon and Jacqui.'[71] To summarize, gendered strategies of inclusion are variously reworked according to the aesthetic and ideological values informing particular pathways which are, in turn, shaped by 'extra-local' scene narratives of exclusion and access. I will now investigate the role of the media in this process.

Mediated Scenes

National media play a vital role in the construction, circulation and 'fetishization' of a 'scene' outside its locale.[72] To invert Smith's 1994 phrase, geography has

---

    66   Strachan, *Industry, Ideology, Aesthetics*.

    67   Cheryl Townsend Gilkes cited in S. Reinharz, *Feminist Methods in Social Research*, Oxford, 1992), p. 12.

    68   Personal communication, 1997.

    69   Funded by self-declared fan, Phil Oakey.

    70   The Slug and Fiddle, 21 April 1997.

    71   *Sheffield Telegraph*, 18 April 1997.

    72   Thornton, *Club Cultures*; Tony Mitchell, *Popular Music and Local Identity. Rock, Pop and Rap in Europe and Oceania* (Leicester, 1996).

become 'integral to the musical imagination'. This is particularly evident for places associated with particular sounds such as Seattle, Bristol, Manchester, Liverpool and Sheffield: 'music seems to "express" a locality in some way'.[73] Consequently, the Human League were the only act to win a Q Award in 2004 to be identified in terms of both place and genre, as 'Sheffield's premier synth-pop trio'.[74] Local media functions in similar ways, for whilst 'local structures of feeling' about the 'scene' are contradictory, the pronoun 'our' is frequently used to distinguish acts that hail from the region, fostering a sense of inclusion and place identity. 'We're proud you're from Sheffield and we're proud you've stayed.'[75]

Sheffield media consists of two newspapers, the daily *Star* and weekly *Sheffield Telegraph*, along with two FM radio stations, BBC Radio Sheffield and Hallam FM. Launched in 1974, Hallam FM provided a platform for local music throughout the 1970s and 1980s, producing and broadcasting live sessions on the weekly 'New Age Muzak', along with live roadshows. Subsequent takeovers by the Metro Radio Group and more recently, EMAP (1995), resulted in a generic streamlining of playlists and content. On the other hand, BBC Radio Sheffield has a policy of supporting local music, from the 1980s' 'amateur' 'ROTT' to BBC South Yorkshire's 'Raw Talent' (2001). This weekly Thursday night programme provides a combination of live sessions, unsigned demos and music industry features, supplemented by a website featuring a directory of bands throughout Yorkshire and Humberside.

There are two digital radio stations currently supporting 'local' music: SheffieldLive! and Radio 2XS. The internet represents a significant channel for 'lively scenelike exchange', with a proliferation of chatrooms and websites such as www.sheffieldscene.co.uk.[76] Many bands have also developed websites, providing virtual 'links' between their local and translocal networks. For instance, one act 'ensuring Sheffield's legacy of groundbreaking industrial electropop is safe'[77] is Hiem – whose recommended websites include Kraftwerk, Stereolab and *Sandman*. Launched in October 2002 with a circulation of 10,000 (August 2004), *Sandman* was one of the most recent additions to a consistent culture of fanzines, rapidly becoming a key symbol of Sheffield's contemporary scene/s.[78]

---

[73]   Brown et al., 'Local Music Policies', p. 259.

[74]   *Q magazine*, December, 2004.

[75]   As proclaimed by BBC Look North in an interview with the Human League, 1 December 2004.

[76]   Richard A. Peterson and Andy Bennett, 'Introducing Music Scenes', in Andy Bennett and Richard A. Peterson (eds), *Music Scenes: Local, Translocal and Virtual* (Nashville, 2004), p. 6.

[77]   From *The Sunday Times*, cited on www.hiem.co.uk/press.asp (accessed 22 December 2004).

[78]   Including 'NMX' (Martin Lacey) in the 1970s, Russell Senior's 'Bath Bankers', and 'Sheffield City Press' in the 1980s. Three additional fanzines were launched in 2004 (www.L2SB.co.uk, December 2004).

Sheffield Telegraph's 'listings' presents the most detailed map of the city's multiple pathways, organized around the following subheadings: Clubbing; Rock/ Pop; Jazz; Folk/Roots; Country; Opera and Concerts/Recitals, which includes information about an array of musical projects, from community brass bands to cathedral choirs. Diverse musical activities are consequently grouped into discrete categories relating to genre. It is striking how closely these categories correlate with the musical 'worlds' of Milton Keynes.[79] They also overlap in similar ways, with 'folk/roots' events often duplicated in the 'rock/pop' section. As the most prolific local pathways, the first two categories typically generate the most coverage, structuring the week in terms of which bands/artists/DJs are appearing at which venues on a particular night. Similarly, *The Star* and *Sandman* contain 'What's On' guides. All three also preview and review selected gigs and events, thus acting as key tastemakers in the process of discrimination.

Knowing who is playing where and what is happening to whom, provides an important source of cultural capital for both music makers and listeners. One member of the band Saxon describes *The Star* as 'a musicians' bible,' recalling that: 'All musicians bought it ... because there were three or four advertising columns in the back – I used to know the numbers off by heart – Instruments For Sale, Musicians Wanted and Bands. We'd all look at those columns. I still buy it today and still look at them just out of habit.'[80] Prior to its demise in 2008/20099, *Sandman* was central to the scene, mediating relations between those seeking personnel and services – musicians, demos, 'enthusiastic flyerers' – and those supplying commodities and skills: 'string arranger available'; 'affordable website design'; 'free rehearsal room, come and do us a gig in return'; 'bass for sale'.[81]

Although *Sandman* drew on a wide pool of freelance, unpaid writers, some of whom were women, the majority of those working in 'professional' media-related fields are male. This male domination perpetuates a homosocial network that, when coupled with the proliferation of aspirant bands, inevitably leads to the 'discursive exclusion'[82] of many music makers. The absence of women, emphasized by the typical inequalities of these interdependent scene roles, accentuates the gendered power dynamics at play.

---

[79]   Finnegan, *The Hidden Musicians*.

[80]   Cited in Firminger and Lilleker, *Not Like a Proper Job*, p. 105.

[81]   *Sandman*, August 2004, p. 18.

[82]   Simon Frith, 'The Cultural Study of Popular Music', in Lawrence Grossberg et al., (eds), *Cultural Studies* (London, 1992).

Local Women: The Absent Presence

Women working in male dominated environments are said to adopt 'blind eyes and deaf ears'[83] to preserve the *status quo*, whilst those attempting to draw attention to gendered iniquities are frequently censured. Consequently, the claim that it is 'harder for women than men to get respect in the music business', elicited the following response: 'perhaps calling your record label Slappa isn't the best of starts'.[84] This paradox – what I have called the *absent presence* of women[85] – was challenged by an 'anonymous' female collective 'taking over the centre pages of Sandman'. As the opening paragraphs explained:

> Now I can almost hear what you're thinking saying or shouting, why do women NEED a magazine devoted to them … surely that's patronizing, unnecessary, sexist etc?! Well we take your point and, believe me, it's been the subject of hot debate since we decided to go ahead with it. *Sandman*, and we love it, does a damn fine job of writing about and promoting Sheffield's musicians and bands (and Leed's and Hull's). But how many women have they had on the front cover and how many women are featured inside? Not as many as the men. Are we whinging? Nah, we just thought that *Sandman* needed more women in it. And come to mention it, so does the Sheffield music scene in general … We don't profess to want to be popstars … but if we did, I think we'd be more inspired to go for it if we saw local women playing out … So that's what this magazine's for … a magazine where we don't have to scour through the pages desperately seeking women. It'll be a bit of fun and also highlight a serious issue.[86]

The main feature, 'Queens of Club', presented a selection of significant role models, including the Leadmill's general manager and live music manager at Sheffield University. In addition, there was a review of the *Sandlady* launch gig, features on two artists, and an interview with a woman bouncer by regular Headcharge DJ, Ann D – 'Sheffield's turntable diva'. *Sandlady*'s aim was therefore laudable, but the underlying dialectic – 'a bit of fun' versus 'a serious issue' – is tellingly highlighted through the 'stop press' announcement: 'the winking fanny … coming soon … Sheffield gossip … things you NEED to know', and competition. 'No one knows who the Sandladies are. Are they young? Are they old? Are they sweet and lovely or a malevolent manifestation of the Sandmen's worst nightmares? Send us an artist's impression of how you see them.'

---

[83] Carol Gilligan, 'Getting Civilised', in Ann Oakley and Juliet Mitchell (eds), *Who's Afraid of Feminism? Seeing Through the Backlash* (London, 1998).

[84] *Sheffield Telegraph*, 26 February 1998.

[85] Drawing on Finnegan's (1989) notion of 'hidden' musicians and Cohen's (1997) observation that 'women were very much present, despite their absence'.

[86] Sandlady in *Sandman*, August 2004.

Through foregrounding stereotypical attributes of femininity – how do we look? how do we feel? – within the malestream magazine, these 'adaptive strategies' undermined their intent to raise local women's profiles in a credible, equitable context. In short, by 'doing femininity', 'masculinity' is simultaneously restated[87] given that, as Cohen argues, gender is a relational category.[88] In the final section, I examine a further range of tensions and characteristics shaping gendered musical practices.

Band Culture Revisited

The dynamics of band culture are shaped by local conditions such as performance opportunities and existing pathways that are simultaneously influenced by wider industry trends and tastes. The year 1964 consequently heralded an 'explosion' (over 300) of aspirant Sheffield bands, due to a combination of Dave Berry's chart success, the proliferation of beat clubs, and Anglo-American construction of teenage consumers and markets.[89] It is difficult to quantify the exact number of functional bands during the ethnographic time frame of this research however, for groups of popular music makers are rarely stable, taking on new members and shedding others, often disbanding completely. Thus, out of the 27 bands in the 1996–97 sample, many had broken-up or metamorphosed beyond recognition four years later. As Finnegan notes, 'trying to make an exact count of an ill-defined and variegated field is not altogether productive'.[90]

Treacle, Reaction and Derrick split up within the year, the latter because of A-level pressures, one of the many significant 'turning points' identified by Finnegan, along with marriage and parenthood.[91] A further three bands changed their names. Fine became Redder, Fruit became Seafruit and Belief developed dual (and conflicting) identities, playing working men's clubs as Rumours, Sisters T and then Live From Earth. Seafruit secured a recording deal whilst the Longpigs and Speedy were 'dropped' and later disbanded. Speedy's guitarist subsequently joined Seafruit, who also recruited EKM's keyboard player for their 1999 tour. EKM split up in 1998 due to membership problems when their drummer, after touring with another band, decided to stay in Spain. Velodrome 2000 instigated a gender split to form two new bands, GG Action and the Motherfuckers, who then toured together. Pulp's line-up also changed as Russell Senior left in 1997, forming another local group, Venini, who announced their break-up in 2001. Pulp, too, have finally 'retired'. All of these changes illustrate a culture in constant flux

---

[87]   Candace West and Don Zimmerman, 'Doing Gender', in Judith Lorber and Susan Farrell (eds), *The Social Construction of Gender* (Newbury Park, Calif., 1991).

[88]   Cohen, 'Popular Music, Gender and Sexuality'.

[89]   Firminger and Lilleker, *Not Like a Proper Job*.

[90]   Finnegan, *The Hidden Musicians*, p. 298.

[91]   Ibid., p. 257.

yet, simultaneously, displaying some stable and widely recognized characteristics. Firstly, collaboration and social networking are core features of local musical activity for 'amateur' and professional groups alike. Pulp enlisted guitarist Richard Hawley (formerly of the Longpigs) when touring, whilst the Human League employed Hiem's 'session' guitarist for their 2004 winter tour. Secondly, competitiveness and rivalry are equally evident. Bands compete for limited resources, whether they are audiences, gigs, drummers or record deals, and the rapid turnover of members precipitates further inter and intra-group conflict. Thus, endorsing Cohen's findings, Sheffield's musical networks are sustained through the relational filters of cooperation and competition.

One member of the now defunct Seafruit has since established 2-Fly Studios in Stag Works, reinforcing the third characteristic identified by Cohen and Finnegan: for many Sheffield musicians, making music and related cultural activities have become 'a way of life'. The continued success of the Human League for example,[92] entirely refutes Oakey's claim that 'the concept of the group [is] obsolete'.[93] Along with production, artist management provides a complementary role for ex-musicians. Seafruit's previous lead singer co-manages the Arctic Monkeys, whilst the Comsat Angels' Stephen Fellows 'discovered' Gomez when working at the independent record shop, Record Collector, which has been run by the same entrepreneur for over 25 years.

Sound engineering, promotion and music journalism are equally well-trodden routes: Martin Lilleker began working on rival paper, *The Star*, in 1976. Penny from Velodrome 2000's story further illustrates how musical pathways can become 'a framework for living'.[94] Along with her band involvement, Penny hosted DJ nights and ran an independent record store, before becoming Live Events Manager at Sheffield University's Union of Students in 2002. Her very presence provokes 'negative responses' however:

> Every single day of my professional life I battle against being patronised and scolded for the fact that I've got the nerve to be a woman and to have got so far in the music industry ... every job I've ever done is a job I shouldn't be doing as a girl.[95]

---

[92]   The Human League are currently working on their tenth album after signing a worldwide deal with Wall of Sound (musicweek online, 11 January 2010).

[93]   Cited in Andrew Goodwin, 'Rationalization and Democratization in the New Technologies of Popular Music', in J. Lull (ed.), *Popular Music and Communication* (Newbury Park, Calif., 1992), p. 95.

[94]   Finnegan, *The Hidden Musicians*, p. 324.

[95]   Penny, personal interview, 2003.

This statement underlines the fourth widely recognized feature of 'local' rock and pop: the vast majority of music makers and associated cultural intermediaries are male, reflecting the white, male dominance of the 'mainstream' music industry.[96]

However, in contrast to Liverpool's 'indie scene', Sheffield's multiple pathways allowed for more flexibility and by 1998, I had observed an increase in mixed-gender bands. There are two potential reasons for this increase: firstly, chart success. Successful acts marketed in terms of their place identity serve to raise the profile of that locality, stimulating local productivity and wider interest from national media and record companies. Chart success therefore fuels romanticized myths of 'making it', encouraging aspirant music makers to join and form bands. This cycle – what Abigail Gilmore refers to as a 'feedback loop'[97] – is crucial to the mobility of scene/s,[98] and following the exposure of 'Sheffield' acts such as Pulp, Babybird, Gomez[99] and the Longpigs in the mid-1990s, there was a notable rise in the number of groups and musicians performing in the city – some of whom were women.

This observation also raises interesting methodological issues. As people became aware of my gender focus, they would highlight acts I didn't know about, occasionally helpfully but, even more frequently, to dispute my argument that local music was male dominated. Bayton found a similar tendency to 'exaggerate' women's participation due to the increasing visibility of women in the charts or on our TV screens. Thus, when conducting her Sheffield interviews, one of Treacle's guitarists claimed there were 'hundreds … loads' of teenage girls playing guitar.[100] Conversely, *Sandman*'s 2003 database listed over 300 local bands, but only 13 female players.[101]

The second factor concerns genre. Successful groups – counting those noted above, along with a cluster of electronica acts over three decades, ranging from Hula's 'white funky sound' (www.soureden.com) to The Lovers' 'avant electropop'

---

[96]   Although at the music industry conference, *In The City 2003*, BMG provided statistics generated from within the company to demonstrate how employment opportunities for under-represented groups are improving. Women constituted 48 per cent of the BMG workforce (although typically, in more 'low status' positions); ethnic minorities, 17.5 per cent (cited by BMG's Rosie Belfield on the panel, 'We don't need no education', ITC, 15 September 2003).

[97]   Abigail Gilmore, 'City Beats: Local Popular Music and Cultural Policy', *International Journal of Urban Labour and Leisure*, 3/1 (2001), http://www.ijull.co.uk/vol3/1/000018.htm.

[98]   Mark Olson, 'Everybody Loves Our Town': Scenes, Spatiality, Migrancy', in Thom Swiss et al. (eds), *Mapping the Beat: Popular Music and Contemporary Theory* (Oxford, 1998).

[99]   Gomez formed during their time at Sheffield Hallam University and were referred to in *The Guardian* (20/2/01) as 'a Sheffield product'.

[100]   Bayton, *Frock Rock*, p. 22.

[101]   Marshall, *Gender Balance within the South Yorkshire Music Industry*.

(www.voilathelovers.com) – also include the bluesy rock of Joe Cocker; stadium rock of Def Leppard; 'indie' rock of the Arctic Monkeys and Pink Grease's 'arty punk pop'. As their singer usefully puts it, 'the great thing about pop is that it never sticks to one genre'.[102] Even at the height of first wave electronica, a four-track EP released on Stephen Singleton's Neutron label – *1980: The First 15 Minutes* – demonstrates the breadth of music being produced. It features the quirky synth-pop of Vice Versa; 'Sheffield's leading punk band' the Stunt Kites; the industrial funk of Clock DVA and post-punk, female-led, I'm So Hollow.

The Stunk Kites' former manager claims that '[it] was ... quite an important record at the time because it ... defined the different strands of Sheffield'.[103] Russell Senior agrees, stating that 'there has never been a Sheffield sound, there's always been that experimental edge to it'.[104] According to Frith, this highlights a fundamental 'contradiction' between local practice and council policy, predicated on the notion of a geographically specific music making 'community' 'with a distinctive language and history'.[105] Although narratives of Sheffieldness serve to promote individualism and difference, the emphasis on experimentalism rather than genre allows highly differentiated 'communities' to co-exist, enabling women to enter marginalized pathways such as folk and punk-pop, or occasionally 're-territorialize'[106] the more chart friendly, homosocial pathways of indie rock and electronica. These two factors contribute to a more flexible and contested cultural terrain than that detailed by Cohen.[107]

Finnegan's study challenged many commonsense assumptions about 'rock' including its intimate associations with youth: 'playing and listening to rock music ... was *not* the preserve only of the young'.[108] Whilst the above examples reinforce this position, the following highlight the gender issues at stake. When the Stunt Kites reformed in 1998 for instance, their singer proffered this reason for playing again: 'Well we were always friends and we thought, why not? It's what we always did and I suppose as well, it's about us carrying on our youth.'[109] In contrast, 30-something live music enthusiast, Caroline, queries her continued involvement in local music:

---

[102] *The Telegraph*, 12 June 2004.

[103] Martin Lacey, 8 June 1993.

[104] Venini interview (27 November 1999), from their (now defunct) website on www.sheffieldscene.co.uk.

[105] Frith, 'Popular Music and the Local State', p. 22.

[106] Norma Coates, 'Can't We Just Talk About Music? Rock and Gender on the Internet', in Thom Swiss et al. (eds), *Mapping the Beat: Popular Music and Contemporary Theory* (Oxford, 1998).

[107] The Long Blondes, who won the *NME*'s 'one to watch' award (2006), typify a number of contemporary local mixed gender bands treading similar indie/pop/electro pathways. They cite Jarvis Cocker as a key influence, as do The Lovers.

[108] Finnegan, *The Hidden Musicians*, p. 123.

[109] Personal communication, The Lescar pub, 1 May 1998).

I like just going out and meeting people and being a part of that scene and I fear for the point – when will that end? … when do you not go to the Leadmill or to the Grapes or whatever? … And I was talking about this … with some women friends [who] said … that we like to 'muscle in' … on [youth] culture cos we don't want to grow old … that it's their culture and we should let them get on with it, we should bow out.[110]

Many of the women interviewed in Milestone and Richards' study[111] echo Caroline's fears, setting an age-limit for their participation in Manchester's cultural industries. Although many men also 'bow out' due to domestic and/or work commitments, older women are further disadvantaged by a Western ideological framework that fetishises youthfulness. On the other hand, 'ideals of masculinity become increasingly realisable and cumulative with age'.[112] In sum, the 'ageing-out'[113] process is more prevalent for women involved in scene activities, including those who participate as music listeners, as part of the live audience.

Conclusion

Using the notion of scene as a metaphor of access and exclusion, this chapter has investigated the ways in which gendered musical practices are constructed and contested through Sheffield's worlds of rock and pop. Taylor et al.'s concept of 'local structures of feeling'[114] has provided a useful framework for identifying specific narratives of 'Sheffieldness' that shape perceptions of access and exclusion for a range of 'scene' participants. They also contribute to the masculinist characteristics ascribed to music makers, for as Massey confirms: 'particular ways of thinking about space and place are tied up with, both directly and indirectly, particular social constructions of gender relations'.[115] Building on the work of Cohen and Finnegan, I have identified many factors that construct Sheffield's scene/s as male, from the circulation and celebration of 'Sheffieldness', to the ways in which band culture restricts women's participation. I have also noted several ideal strategies and material conditions through which the homosocial cultural norms and boundaries of local rock and pop are challenged.

---

[110]   Caroline, personal communication, 1996.
[111]   Katie Milestone and Nicola Richards, 'What Difference Does it Make? Women's Pop Cultural Production and Consumption in Manchester', in *Sociological Research Online* (www.socresonline.org.uk, 2000).
[112]   Jackie Stacey, *Star Gazing: Hollywood Cinema and Female Spectatorship* (London, 1994), p. 226.
[113]   Thornton, *Club Cultures*, p. 3.
[114]   Taylor et al., *A Tale of Two Cities*.
[115]   Massey, *Space, Place and Gender*, p. 2.

For those women who struggled to circumnavigate widespread 'mechanisms of exclusion',[116] the desire to 'make it' was a powerful motivational force. Success also stimulates local productivity by raising the profile of a geographically based 'scene'. This 'feedback loop'[117] was particularly evident in the mid-to-late 1990s in Sheffield and is equally apparent in the wake of the Arctic Monkey's success. And yet wider patterns in pop production, illustrated by the renaissance of the band, serve to normalize the masculinism of music making within the chart friendly pathway of 'indie' rock.

On the other hand, women were more prevalent in the 'highly particularistic'[118] pathway of punk-pop in late-1990s Sheffield, and members of Velodrome 2000 have since become a significant force in its promotion and extension. Yet the 'ageing out' process cuts across all genres or pathways, representing a key barrier for female music makers and listeners. Thus, the 'ideal' gendered strategies of inclusion I propose are simultaneously constrained by spatial politics and complex sets of inter and intra-group gender relations, relations which are socially constructed within music scenes to embody difference and inequality.[119] Even so, whilst there are striking similarities between Cohen and Finnegan's empirical findings and the construction of Sheffield's scene/s as male, 'hidden' case studies are vital for disrupting the commonsense homosocial and heterosexist meanings of scene.

In line with Massey (1994) and Olson (1998),[120] I therefore conclude that local scenes are not passive spaces but productive places that shape particular forms of musical activity, identities and social relations. They are simultaneously constructed through media exposure[121] and the research process itself. Scenes can thus be described as 'fictional realities'[122] with aesthetic and performative 'logics',[123] representing a complex and contradictory site of imagined freedoms and material and ideological constraints which serve to obscure more 'hidden' gendered musical practices, pathways, relationships and agentic constructs of scene.

---

[116]   Norma Coates, '(R)evolution Now? Rock and the Political Potential of Gender', in Sheila Whitely (ed.), *Sexing the Groove: Popular Music and Gender* (London, 1997).

[117]   Gilmore, 'City Beats'.

[118]   Finnegan, *The Hidden Musicians.*

[119]   Cohen, 'Popular Music, Gender and Sexuality'.

[120]   Massey, *Space, Place and Gender*; Olson, 'Everybody Loves our Town'.

[121]   Thornton, *Club Cultures*.

[122]   Shaun Moores, 'Broadcasting and its Audience', in Hugh Mackay, *Consumption and Everyday Life* (London, 1997).

[123]   Will Straw, 'Communities and Scenes in Popular Music', in Ken Gelder and Sarah Thornton (eds), *The Subcultures Reader* (London, 1997); Cohen, 'Men Making a Scene'; Strachan, *Industry, Ideology, Aesthetics.*

Chapter 15
Local Music Scenes in France: Definitions, Stakes, Particularities

Gérôme Guibert

Introduction: From Festivals to Music Scenes

With the increased dematerialization of commercial practices and uses related to sound recordings, it is now commonplace to say that the economic and creative potential of music depends on more than just the CD sector. For some, it is the internet which is the leading influence, whilst many others suggest that it is primarily on music scenes (what is often referred to in France as 'live performance') that study should be focused. Since the beginning of the current century, there have, moreover, been countless articles on audiences' increased interest in concerts,[1] in addition to articles on the usefulness of festivals as symptoms of the triumph of 'authenticity' represented by concerts compared to recorded music. From this perspective, the summer of 2007 was particularly unusual. Attendance at rock festivals in France appeared, unusually, to be rather unpredictable. For the first time, festivals which never failed to sell out (for example, *Vieilles Charrues* in Carhaix, Brittany, *Rock en Scène* at Domaine de Saint Cloud in Paris or, on a smaller scale, *Microcosm* at la Roche-sur-Yon) saw attendance figures fall despite scheduling many headline acts. Why?

Some blamed bad weather, pointing the finger at persistent summer rain. Others, more aware of the economic functioning of the music industry, underlined the increasing standardization of headline acts, accusing tour managers of having absolute control over scheduling and creating a relative standardization of the supply of acts. What can be said with certainty however is that there had never been so many festivals organized in France,[2] which inevitably led to a relative fall in financial subsidies allocated to them individually;[3] competition between festivals was particularly strong, and it could be said that saturation point had been reached. Thus, it seems reasonable to suggest that the potential audience of such events,

---

[1]   For example Benjamin Bibas, 'L'avenir du disque, c'est la scène?', *Rézo international – magazine de l'AFAA,* 13, (2004): pp. 29–38.

[2]   CNV, *Éléments statistiques sur la diffusion des spectacles de variétés et de musiques actuelles en 2006. Présentation des données et éléments d'évolution 2005–2006* (Paris, 2007).

[3]   Fédurok, *Enquête tour de France, résultats 2001 et 2003,* www.la_fedurok.org.

overly solicited, was smaller than the supply of entertainment. The unique aspect of an event such as a festival no longer exists when they become so widespread.

Reflecting upon the exponential growth of festivals since the 1990s[4] leads us to the question of 'music scenes' because, behind a unity of time, festivals are characterized by a unity of place. Over the last 15 years many local authorities have seen, in the use of subsidies for festivals, a means of generating positive effects on the localities under their responsibility, whether from a cultural, tourism and/or economic development perspective. Local authorities[5] realized that through their 'impact' as events, festivals could have effects in terms of communication (publicizing a town or area), symbolically (demonstrating the dynamism of an area and aiding it to forge a visible identity), and economically (generating business for local firms). It was thus that, at the end of the 1990s, the multiplier effect of economic activity calculated by impact studies became a frequent justification,[6] prior to the adoption early in this century of the notion of sustainable development – often linked to specific localities – by festival stakeholders.[7] More pragmatically, the private stakeholders in the world of music who are often described as 'mediators' (tour managers, producers, artistic promoters), also grasped festivals as a means of asserting their brands (for example, 'Les Jeux' as undertaken by the promotions company Olympic Tour or the 'Reggae festival' from the producer Garance Production). Amidst this mass of events, it was, understandably, those which developed a consistency in musical styles or other specific characteristics and linked them to a local area who met with the most success (for example, emphasis on 'emerging artists' at the Transmusicales de Rennes festival).[8] The piling high of scheduled artists – however high their record sales or their media visibility[9] – was in itself insufficient to ensure a festival's success in the medium term. The festival as a kind of musical 'Mecca'[10] and its

---

[4]   Luc Benito, *Les Festivals en France. Marchés, enjeux et alchimie* (Paris, 2001).

[5]   Local and Departmental councils chiefly, but also Regional councils or communities of villages and cities, if we take as a basis our field study into festivals, commissioned for the cooperation cluster of contemporary music stakeholders in the Pays-de-la-Loire region in 2007.

[6]   Joëlle Farchy and Dominique Sagot-Duvauroux, *Économie des politiques culturelles* (Paris, 1994) and Yann Nicolas, *L'analyse d'impact économique de la culture. Principes et limites* (Paris, 2006).

[7]   Stéphanie Loup and Marion Polge, 'Quel entrepreneuriat pour quel développement durable? Le cas du terroir', in *Actes du congrès de l'AIMS*, 2003, http://www.strategie-aims.com/dd03/comdd/polgeloup.pdf and Mathias Milliard, 'Agenda 21 : un moyen de repenser la production des festivals?', www.cij.irma.asso.fr.

[8]   Jean-Marie Lucas, *Rock et politique culturelle: l'exemple de Rennes, 1976–1983* (Paris, 1984).

[9]   On this subject refer to the article by Bruno Lesprit, 'Malgré Björk, bilan mitigé pour Rock en Seine', *Le Monde,* 28 August 2007 and letters from readers of *Rock & Folk,* October 2007.

[10]   Bernard Debarbieux, 'Du haut lieu en général et du mont-Blanc en particulier', *L'Espace géographique*, 1 (1993): pp. 5–13.

status as a not-to-miss event, is progressively constructed beyond what it simply is, building on what it represents and the image it forges for itself. It could, therefore, be said that festivals – seen through the perspective of regional development – raise the question of the geographical location of 'current music'.

The Concept of a Music Scene

To study the way in which musical practices operate in relation to geographical areas, French researchers are beginning to talk about 'music scenes'.[11] In so doing, they are following research from Anglophone countries which began in the 1990s.[12] It is interesting to note that the foundations of research in English-speaking countries came in part from concepts elaborated by French researchers, foremost among whom is Henri Lefebvre.[13] However, here just as in England or America, the term 'music scene' was already used by journalists before being adopted by academics.[14] The notion appeared useful prior to being theorized by social science research, doubtless because it allowed the question of musical cultures in relation to geographical areas to be readdressed, whilst however avoiding several pitfalls. The first of these was of research questions designed in too essentialist a manner concerning the aesthetics of amplified musical genres and their contemporary folklore in terms of appearances, mythologies, instruments used or the sounds generated. The next pitfall was that of research questions defining music within closed social spaces (for example, from the perspective of music belonging to particular communities or music as belonging to the 'world of art').

In sociology, and more widely in intellectual society, amplified music – seen without historical depth[15] – was for a long time considered without truly taking into account regional particularities surrounding its production. Admittedly, this analytical short-sightedness can, at least in part, now be explained by the concentration of cultural industries in Paris, which could, until the 1980s, be considered as monopolistic. In Paris, there were music industry professionals and, everywhere else in France, consumers, as if music came from 'the top' to reach the 'receiving' listeners at the end of the chain. With supply looming over a somehow spatially undifferentiated demand, it was social differentiation which enabled

---

[11] Here I shall refer to my own PhD thesis, *Scènes locales, scène globale. Contribution à une sociologie économique des producteurs de musiques amplifiées en France*, université de Nantes, Sociology department (2004).

[12] See notably Will Straw, 'Community and Scene in Popular Music' and Sarah Cohen, 'Scene', in Bruce Horner and Thom Swiss, *Key Terms in Popular Music and Culture* (Oxford, 1999).

[13] Notably the books *La Vie quotidienne dans le monde moderne* (Paris, 1968); *La Révolution urbaine* (Paris, 1970); *La Production de l'espace* (Paris, 1974).

[14] Max Well and François Poulain, *Scènes de rock en France* (Paris, 1994).

[15] This is one of the criticisms made of the term 'current musics'.

explanation of the diversity of existing musical genres. This holistic and macro-sociological approach worked particularly well in France where, for a long time, a Jacobin, Republican and centralist tradition existed, just as much in practice as in discourses:[16] given that all citizens were equal, there had been no reason to highlight the specific diversities existing in different geographical areas. Following an implicit evolutionist logic, it was considered that Paris – as a forerunner and generator – experienced, particularly for music, and several years early, trends that would later spread to 'the regions'.

The increase in the supply of culture coming from almost everywhere in France finally undermined this debatable notion. For new musical trends, rather than a chain linking producers to listeners (the music industry), what was important was what was happening by and through 'the fan', listening and making music right up to the home production of music (the 'underground'). This meant that to properly understand new popular musical phenomena, they had to be seen as more than mere products of the cultural industries (see Figure 15.1).

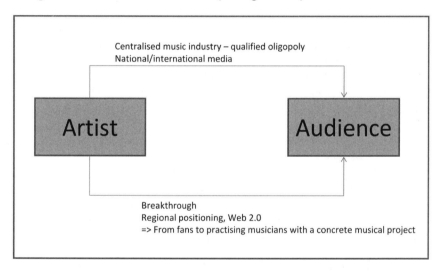

Figure 15.1   The two economic branches of the music industry

What is a Music Scene?

From the second half of the 1980s, social science field research began to analyse the group dynamics at work in rock, and more widely in amplified music.[17] The

---

16   Mona Ozouf and Jacques Ozouf, *La République des instituteurs* (Paris, 1989).

17   See for example Jean-Marie Seca, *Vocations rock* (Paris, 1988), Catherine Doublé-Dutheil, 'Les groupes de rock nantais', in Patrick Mignon. and Antoine Hennion (eds),

ties between locally emerging groups and local audiences who support them by attending their concerts (the 'following') can, according to Patrick Mignon, be explained following two perspectives. It could be 'feelings of strong local identity, such as the feeling of isolation which sets people from Le Havre apart from Normandy and from France as a whole. Elsewhere, such as in France's overseas islands, it's an issue of musical style'.[18]

Local identity or stylistic identity: these two major concepts can both refer to the notion of the musical scene, as used in social sciences. The first, which can be described as interactionist, following Goffman, refers to the dramaturgy of the social world. Behaviour, body techniques and positions adopted are all linked to musical genres by an ensemble of values, found in spaces where people who share an interest in a particular musical genre meet, such as cafés, concert venues or festivals. The second concept is the more widespread. It views the notion of a music scene on a wider scale, as a tool allowing both for the explanation of ways in which musical dynamics develop or are lived locally, and also a way of shedding light on their relations with the translocal (in other words between music scenes) or the global.

A music scene appears for itself and for the outside world through a merging of these understandings, through individual stories which collectively incorporate the paths of people involved in its music.[19] A music scene is strengthened from the moment collective activity becomes visible (the repeated performance of artists linked to local events) and once it is taken up by agents (what economists call the Penguin effect).[20] The scene increases in density if real connections exist in terms of concrete projects, beyond mere geographic proximity, but also if agents are involved in various interrelated and interdependent activities (the network effect).

These encouraging effects can then be confirmed by the media – local then national – which may designate a geographical area – more often than not a city – as being a sort of musical 'trademark': the Versailles music scene and its *French Touch* in the mid-1990s is an example of this.[21] Just as much as realities of musical practices, it is the spotlight cast upon particular locations which amplifies the strength of a music scene. From the multiple and interstitial relations between agents, competition develops during a given space and time and is amplified performatively by the media and public policies.

Rock. De l'histoire au mythe (Paris, 1991), pp. 147–58.

[18] Patrick Mignon, 'Paris, Givors. Le rock local', in Mignon and Hennion, *Rock, de l'histoire au mythe*.

[19] Bruno Latour, 'Pourquoi viens-tu si Tarde?', in Bruno Latour, *Chroniques d'un amateur de science* (Paris, 2006).

[20] Raphael Suire, 'Formation et stabilité des *clusters* d'activité TIC : questions à la politique des pôles de compétitivité', in Pierre-Noel Favennec (ed.), *Communications et territoires* (Paris, 2006).

[21] With artists such as Air, Phoenix, Alex Gopher, Étienne De Crecy, etc.

Examples: Contexts – Geographical Areas – Networks

These few theoretical works discussed above can be considered in relation to music in various local geographical contexts. In the discussion that follows this will be done using data gathered from field studies undertaken in the west of France.

Contexts

Local scenes first appeared in France at the beginning of the 1980s.[22] Several factors came together to create the conditions required for these scenes to emerge. Firstly, the agents involved had become numerous enough to reach critical mass and even numerous enough to be specialized in musical sub-genres created by newer generations of fans. Rock'n'roll had been present in France for 20 years and those born post-1945 had become familiar with its electric instruments, with listening to its records, with rock'n'roll dances and at the very least some recent artists. For the most part self-taught, people involved in music during this period had adopted what Marc Touché termed 'the potentiometer culture',[23] using amplification systems and its various sound effects when performing music on stage or in the studio.

Moreover, they were usually the composers of the music which they performed. This factor was significant because it challenged the hierarchical understanding of the music industry, at least in as much as it was represented. Until then, within classical music, just as in variety or town band music, this hierarchical understanding did indeed seem to make sense when describing music from the 'conceptual' summit (professional composers linked to copyright companies) which filtered down to the 'executive' base (professional and amateur musicians across France).

While the amount of time available for music – freely chosen or imposed – had grown for younger generations (extended education, time spent unemployed), the use of new technologies, and the self-made items and innovations which resulted from them were made possible by falling relative prices of new equipment. After vinyl records at the end of the 1950s, the audio cassette in the mid-1960s and then the twin tape recorder in the 1970s allowed people to record, allowing in other words for musical creation to be captured. From the early 1980s, audio cassette multitrack recorders were sold, and these devices allowed groups to make demos at home, such recordings then constituting musical visiting cards – a necessary tool in canvassing concert organizers and record companies.

Where people played – from places of study (high school through to university) to bars via youth clubs, rehearsal rooms, record stores or nightclubs – local

---

[22]   Gérôme Guibert, 'Les musiques amplifiées en France. Phénomènes de surface et dynamiques invisibles', *Réseaux*, 25/141–2 (2007): pp. 297–324.

[23]   Marc Touché, 'La culture du potentiomètre est-elle soluble dans les clichés?', *Fusibles,* 4 (1996): pp. 6–7.

music scenes were in part created through the different audiences attracted to the music and its fashions. Whereas the musical genres at the time were wide-ranging, at the turn of the 1980s, the variety of styles claiming an influence from punk (often called post-punk) were particular catalysts because they promoted a do-it-yourself (DIY) approach to music, favouring autonomy, initiative and spontaneity rather than professional production with a commercial outlet. They allowed the emergence of relatively autonomous 'simplified circuits of music production'. This 'buzz' allowed musical recordings to circulate as well as enabling beginner musicians to play on stage.

Many local music labels supporting groups from their local area or city thus began to appear. The majority were established by fans, with the legal status of an association. Recording a record on vinyl became affordable (from the second half of the 1980s, 500 vinyl record singles could be produced for less than the then monthly minimum wage), with cassettes even more inexpensive. In post-punk thinking, music labels offered records known as splits (different groups on each side) or compilations which were to a certain extent labels' artistic manifestos.[24] Record producers could, therefore, offer records to mailing lists (printed or photocopied), which are nowadays often complemented by web-lists. The better-organized labels, those whose organizers were hoping to become professional, themselves sought out distributors who could channel their productions towards retail music stores so as to reach anyone who might be interested.[25]

In the 1980s, the creation of several independent distributors from local post-punk scenes (such as Danceteria in Lille or New Rose in Paris) offered many independent labels the chance to become known. This bypassing of showbusiness had never been seen before at this level of the industry and contributed towards the national and international image of French music scenes. The growth of alternative musical press (fanzines) available in record stores or by mail order was similarly encouraged through the availability of photocopiers and DIY attitudes in music. Furthermore, the early 1980s fostered alternative local media in France after the legalization of free radio broadcasting in 1981, which led to a marked proliferation of programmes broadcasting the widest variety of music and which paid heed to local musical initiatives, whether or not they were taken up on a national level and whatever their precise technical form. Current development of websites and blogs, webzines and web-radios on the internet, to a certain extent nowadays perpetuates this way of working.

---

[24] For N. Heinich, 'a manifesto is a text which demonstrates the minimum form of an event presented by a band, or a group of artists …, this allows a group to exist in the public domain. An artistic strand of music thus requires on the one hand a band or a group, and on the other hand a programme or manifesto'. See Nathalie Heinich, *Être Artiste* (Paris, 1996), pp. 44–5.

[25] During the 2000s, this model was taken up on the internet by the '*agrégateurs*' who allowed for a critical mass to be reached in terms of back catalogues on offer, as well as a referencing system by search engines.

Geographical Areas

The particular characteristics of different locations determine the development of individual music scenes. By comparing the local music scenes in the city of Nantes (in the Loire-Atlantique region) and the town of Montaigu (in the Vendée), it can for example be observed that the sociability and the workings of associations are very different in rural and urban areas. Whilst in the urban milieu, concert organizing associations, fanzines or webzines are run by a small hardcore of enthusiasts highly specialized in a 'cutting edge' musical niche, in rural areas, associations frequently bring together dozens or even hundreds of supporters during unifying events which cover various musical genres.

Alongside this structural variable, other factors linked to the history and geography of music scenes often explain some of their features. One such example is Rouen, whose garage-punk scene was a much noted phenomenon in France during the later 1970s. This music scene emerged around an independent specialist record dealer (Mélodie Massacre) – a fan of 'garage' – who established a record label and signed local groups formed by customers with whom he shared a passion for the genre; some of these, such as *les Dogs*, began rehearsing in his cellar. Other labels of similar musical genres then emerged (Closer, Teenage Records). In this process, it must be understood that the location of the city was itself significant. Situated in Normandy, close to holiday destinations frequented by Parisians during vacations and also close to the UK, the city was able, long before many other French towns, to stage rock concerts given by renowned foreign or Parisian groups. Furthermore, from the 1960s, people in Rouen had been able to tune into pirate English radio stations broadcasting from the Channel, just as the nearby port town of Le Havre – Rouen's fraternal enemy – was able to attract many groups and agents from the music sector who were competitors but also aesthetically close to those forming the music scene in Rouen.

Regional cultures and diasporas should not be neglected in understanding the constitution of local scenes. A city such as Nantes, whose Breton identity is largely debated, was at the very forefront of the wave of folk music in the 1970s (with the group Tri Yann an Naoned) before a new wave of celtic groups affiliated with 'world music' appeared in the 1990s (a number of associations were in existence as well as labels such as Dastum or events such as the *Naoned Breizh Fever*). Equally, diasporas play a part in the development of music scenes. For example, during my own ethnographic study conducted in 2001 in the Vendée, I realized that many musicians of African origin (Togo, Côte d'Ivoire and Senegal notably) who were performing in the reggae roots music scene between La Roche-sur-Yon (Vendée) and Nantes were linked in one way or another with the group Apartheid Not, a forerunner reggae outfit in the region from the mid-1980s.[26] This group was one of the first French reggae groups to record an album and its roots can be

---

[26]   Such was the case for Natural Expression, Wailing Natty Roots, Unity Reggae Style, Ossoffo, Yaoundé or Jade. Moreover, I was able to identify, in addition to musicians,

traced back to the first wave of African immigrants who sought employment in the Vendée region.[27] Unravelling the threads of inter-agent connections in this reggae roots scene proves particularly informative regarding the forces at work in the dynamics of local music.

Networks

As a local scene is created, fans of a particular group who travel to another city create an image of that local scene on the outside. Similarly, when fanzines interview groups who are foreign to a particular music scene as they are in concert in a city, or associative radio broadcasts specializing in any given musical genre, the strong aesthetic or geographical identity of music labels allows ties to be visualized between recorded groups. These ties are today magnified by the development of the internet, and more particularly by what is termed web 2.0, where content is developed by agents themselves. The same applies for webzines or sites like MySpace and, more generally, web forums. Although some groups limit their activities strictly to the internet (seeking to promote their images and sounds), most musicians hope to have an impact in 'the real world' (through record sales or increased attendance at concerts).

Moreover, individual recognition of an artist or group when considered alone does not enable the artist to enjoy the positive effects of a scene, which is by definition a collective phenomenon. Geographical ties – whether real or virtual – or even an aesthetic identity are not sufficient to allow groups to benefit from a music scene, in the same manner as self-produced records do not allow for alternative networks to be used.

The mere juxtaposition of many groups in a geographical area and a shared musical genre may indeed lead to a music scene (the 'penguin effect' of economists) but such a scene remains fragile, often relying on the image of a key group – such as the Thugs in the Angers music scene for the latter 1980s. For a music scene to impose itself, and therefore have positive effects on its members, closely interlinked and jointly interdependent networks are required. Recording studios or key sound engineers can constitute examples of this 'network effect'.

To be even more specific, the emergence of a collective movement where musicians outline various artistic projects in common is another factor allowing music scenes to develop. This jazz-based method of organization is notable within post-rock genres. In Nantes, the new indie-pop scene which was established around

---

associations promoting 'African culture' in an ecumenical manner such as Kori (La Roche-sur-Yon) as well as activists behind the Maison des Rastas (Nantes – Olivettes District).

[27]   A monograph on Apartheid Not remains to be undertaken. According to some accounts which I gathered in 2001, the group was offered a residency and financially supported by the local council in La Roche-sur-Yon around 1983 as an arrangement with an African footballer who agreed to play for the local club provided his family and friends, including the band members, were assisted by the local council.

the Effervescence collective operates in such a manner: when a musician aims to release a record of his/her own compositions, other members of the collective are called upon, a method again mirrored when musicians go on tour, which enables the majority of artists concerned to qualify for the Social Security regime as an 'intermittent du spectacle'.[28] In this way a dozen musicians circulate in an equal number of groups who release recordings on various local labels (Effervescence but also Kithybong, Autres Directions In Music, Labo lofi). Moreover, to supplement their incomes, musicians employ their know-how in other roles, for instance in graphic design and/or concert organization in cafés, as well as tours and promoting groups for the company Muraille Médias belonging to the Effervescence label. Thus, the contacts established by any one of the members can benefit the others.

These features enable the establishment of a central core whose organization is not necessarily immediately visible from outside, but which can lay the foundations of a local music scene in a specific geographical area known for a specific musical aesthetic. If local audiences identify themselves with such a collective, and if nationally, media and audiences establish a link between place of origin and musical style, a local scene becomes identifiable. There are, however, two factors which are critical for the crystallization of a local music scene. It is firstly necessary for musicians themselves to emphasize their (regional) origins, which is rarely done in France,[29] and secondly, it is necessary for the local or regional authorities representing the geographical area to make use of the image created by the music scene to favour the local economy by using it in tourism policy for example, which is also rarely done in France in the 'contemporary music sector' although in England this type of opportunity is already widely seized upon.[30] Today such strategies are only beginning to be noticeable. To take Nantes as an example, since 2007 the spotlight has been on the local music scene as part of an annual one-off event where dozens of artists are scheduled – by genres – to perform at the Zénith venue, attracting over 6,000 concert goers. The issue here is to clearly demonstrate the importance of the city's creativity through the organization of a well-attended

---

[28] On this subject refer to Dimitri Della Faille, 'Espaces de solidarités, de divergences et de conflits dans la musique montréalaise émergente', *Copyright Volume!*, 4/2 (2005): pp. 61–74.

[29] Thus, in the early 1990s, in Nantes, the local music scene *chanson*/pop had failed to work properly as the agents involved (Dominique A, Katerine, Little Rabbits, Perio, Françoiz Breut or Elliot *alias* Pierre Bondu) with organizations such as the music label Lithium, the association Karen, the club Le Floride and record stores (successively Fuzz to Black et Noir) were not interested in this local affiliation, although they had recognized the importance of networking. We can suggest that their unwillingness – less common today in popular music – to espouse this type of categorization was linked to the French concern for music to be 'art for art's sake'. However, for an illustration of such discourse, see Sylvain Chantal, 'Billet d'humeur ', *Magic*, 110 (2007): p. 3.

[30] For example, Andy Bennett, 'Music, Media and Urban Mythscapes: A Study of the "Canterbury Sound"', *Media, Culture and Society*, 24 (2002): pp. 87–100.

large-scale event hosting emerging artists coming from parallel cultural networks to which more traditional local references are thus attached. It is this very same idea which led in 2007 to the May Cooperative movement in Clermont-Ferrand, uniting local artists on a Velvet Underground cover album sold as a vinyl record before an advertising campaign allowed the project to roll out nationally.[31]

Whereas the economic dimension of centres of cultural competitiveness has long been underestimated in France, what really exemplifies the ways in which the music scenes here have been transformed compared to other countries is the role of public cultural policies. These policies have gained in scale since the 1980s, primarily being State-led – via the intermediary of the Drac primarily – before local authorities took over, notably at the level of towns and regions. Cultural policies have considerably modified the appearance of local music scenes, because they have formally recognized the creation of music in which we have an interest as culture, but also because they have contributed to the professionalization of a number of agents involved in these scenes.

A Specifically French Feature: Public Policy and its Effects

French State intervention inherited from its Jacobin tradition is a well known specificity. As early as the Third French Republic, alongside education, the town band movement allowed a certain central idea of what popular music should be to spread through France. Although the emergence of teen culture in the 1960s began to qualify the influence of the public sector – as a superstructure – the emergence of local music scenes, from the late 1970s, was in part enabled through the use of youth clubs and other socio-cultural facilities which were products of an ambitious government policy for young people. Whilst they had not been intended for this kind of activity, local youth clubs and other community and arts centres played host to many groups for rehearsals or concerts. But State involvement was to radically transform the manner in which local music scenes operated following the arrival of socialist governments into power in the 1980s. It was subsequently a more pragmatic and also anthropological vision of culture which was to be adopted. After a more general national policy (including the Zénith concert venue programme, the establishment of a special tax funding for live performance or the establishment of the *Fonds pour la création musicale*), this culminated, via the Culture Ministry, in the recognition of subsidies provided to the principal local agents involved in the musical domain (designated festivals and performance venues). With regional centres for contemporary music, this vision would, at the turn of this century,

---

[31]   In 2006, the attempt to construct a Parisian rock scene from the media buzz kick-started by the magazine *Rock & Folk* (BB Brunes, Naast, Plasticines, Les Shades, etc.) was also symptomatic of a turnaround in the French perception of the phenomenon of a 'music scene'.

be adopted at devolved level, thereby accentuating interconnections between initiatives resulting from policy and those resulting from actors in the scenes.

Three Local Music Scenes

To conclude this chapter, we can take the examples of three local scenes studied in the west of France – Angers, Montaigu and Périgueux[32] – providing a summary of their development in terms of government intervention. In these three towns, artistic creativity linked to the emergence of alternative rock groups developed during the 1980s and was relayed by local media (radio stations and fanzines), record shops and independent record producers, and performances took place in cafés and on wasteland. Following initial measures presented at national level by the Minister for Culture (festivals organized in Rennes, Lille, Bourgues, États du rock in Montpellier etc.), local agents, musicians or otherwise, campaigned to obtain support from local government. It is interesting to note that in these three towns – as in many others – at various times in the 1990s, those agents involved in the local music scene acted collectively in the form of legally constituted associations. As well as symbolic recognition of the cultural value of their musical styles, they requested construction of rehearsal studios, and particularly concert venues, and thus the possession of a specific performance venue, or a 'place to perform' as people from Angers and Montaigu would say. The Fédurok network established in the 1990s united these new venues of hybrid economics (public/private/reciprocity) which resulted from the demands of agents and the reactions to these demands by various local authorities, such as in Angers (Le Chabada) and in Périgueux (Le Réservoir).

In many towns, it was after a period of campaigning that collaboration and teamwork led to the construction of facilities subsequently 'approved' by the Ministry for Culture. Together with rising professionalism and the establishment of a legal framework for this sector, these facilities permanently transformed the identity of music scenes and their functioning. After professionalization, these facilities tended to reproduce previously criticized modes of operating of the cultural infrastructures which had preceded them, notably music scenes at national level.[33] Consequently there was a large fall in participation by agents who had previously worked in local scenes, whether this was bands or associations of stakeholders in local live performance. With the introduction of government subsidies, many local scenes seemed to be transformed, and to have developed specific stylistic

---

[32]   For details of the local scenes of the first two cities, see Gérôme Guibert, *La Production de la culture. Le cas des musiques amplifiées en France* (Paris, 2007). For Périgueux, see Carole Le Rendu-Lizée and Gérôme Guibert, *Gestion prévisionnelle des emplois et compétences au sein du Rama* (Bordeaux, 2007).

[33]   Philippe Teillet, 'Le "secteur" des musiques actuelles. De l'innovation à la normalisation ... Et retour?', *Réseaux*, 25/141–2 (2007): pp. 269–96.

identities moving towards musical ecumenicalism and a weakened core where the numbers of genres represented had increased. Furthermore, with increased legal regulation, the decreasing number of *café concerts* led to a concentration of the supply of music in these new facilities which had an increasingly strong influence on the local music field and in ways more societal and communitarian, to use the distinction proposed by Tönnies.

In the three towns studied, the situation in terms of government intervention was identical until the late 1980s: local authorities were initially ill-prepared and contact with musical associations began with conflict (protests, features in the local written press, campaign leafleting, impromptu concerts etc.), but subsequently, reaction of the local authorities diverged in each of the three towns.

In Angers, the association (established 1988) adopted the title *Adrama* (association for the development of rock and other music in Angers). The town hall, followed by other local and regional authorities, opened negotiations with this grouping leading to the construction of rehearsal premises (La Cerclère, 1990) followed by a licensed venue with two performance halls (le Chabada 1994) managed by *Adrama*, which had in the meantime repeatedly changed leadership. With the legal status of an association, le Chabada operated with around ten employees but some volunteer members did not feel their views counted and the local scene often came into conflict with the small professional team running the venue. Moreover, the licensed bar, open every evening for the first few years, was later only open for concerts. The team sought to work alongside local associations to co-produce concerts but met with obstacles. Éric Source from Angers – guitarist with the Thugs (the most important group in the music scene until the early 2000s) and also chairman of *Adrama* – stated, before resigning:

> The beginning of the 1990s was a pivotal period ..., it was at then that the Fédurok network began. 1990 was the time when everything became institutionalised within the sector ... it became difficult for groups to perform in bars etc. Until then people had great fun. There were some crazy record labels, notably Gougnaf, Bondage etc. There was a swarm of activity, loads of associations organising concerts. Later, after the late 1990s, people began playing in big venues with anonymous organisers. There was a completely different mindset. In the 1980s things were rough and ready, amateurish, not professional, but still it was a million times better than what we saw afterwards.[34]

By bringing together all of the stakeholders, *Adrama* became the sole point of contact in Angers for local government and thus found itself in a difficult position. This position was rendered even more difficult with the construction of the Chabada venue, the increase in subsidies and the creation of permanent posts. The fact that employees at the Chabada were primarily former local musical activists

---

[34] Éric Source interview in Arno Rudeboy, *Nyark nyark! Fragment des scènes punk et rock alternatif en France. 1976–1989* (Paris, 2007).

led to envy, and for others not sharing this specific background, the Chabada was deemed to be the symbolic property of a wider grouping of activists (the Angers music scene), in reality not in charge of its activities. In some cases, *Adrama* was criticized for stifling all other musical initiatives, and conversely, the Chabada employees and management underline the difficulties they encounter with people who 'continue to think in outdated ways'.

In Périgueux (Dordogne), it was the association 'Collectif24' which initially brought together the demands of the local scene in the early 1990s. A project undertaken in collaboration with the local council then followed, leading to the construction of rehearsal rooms and subsequently a concert venue (Le Réservoir). Initially however, members of the association wanting it to retain leadership of the project imposed elements of participative democracy in the running of the *Sans Réserve* grouping created to manage the venue. The management board includes three representative committees of the agents involved; 'musicians', 'associations' and 'audience', and the neighbouring town of Boulazac was also a stakeholder in the project. The mission statement indicates that the manager of the venue must offer musical genres which are not campaigned for or representative of local music associations. Scheduling of acts is not understood as the artistic choice of a single individual with informed artistic tastes (as is the case in many venues having adopted a typical 'national music scene' culture). Furthermore, the venue has to encourage co-productions with local volunteer associations (under favourable conditions for the latter). According to the chair of the association *Sans Réserve*, 'the plus point is that the underground associations have networks and contacts which we do not and which can allow us to host key bands at a reasonable rate'.[35] When the venue opened in the late 1990s, the local council demanded the recruitment of a manager from an outside town so as not to create local 'jealousy', even if it advised the new manager to hire local figures involved in the amplified music scene to form part of the team. Today, Le Réservoir is well recognized by local stakeholders, even though, according to the manager (who is paid and heads a team of five paid employees), 'some decisions are taken undemocratically outside of the board, but we still ensure all stakeholders are informally consulted'. However, the various stakeholders do talk to each other, and there is a respected record dealer who is a member of the association in the town and some cafés organizing concerts. The association *Some Product*, for example, specializing in independent rock and hardcore-punk, schedules concerts both in bars as well as at Le Réservoir.

Finally, in Montaigu (Vendée), where the local music scene is dense and well-recognized, despite the small size of the town, *Icroacao* (which unites seven associations involved in the amplified music sector) began organizing concerts in various venues (former rail station, youth centre, bars, etc.) in 1990 and since the 1950s has been demanding a 'performance venue'. But the local town authorities,

---

[35]   Interview March 2007.

led by a predominantly MPF[36] mayor has turned a deaf ear to these appeals, claiming that the music in question cannot be defined as culture and that such activities should be managed by the private sector. From the late 1990s, initiatives led by *Icroacao* intensified (unofficial concerts, disturbance of one stage of the Tour de France, presentation of a 'protest party' list for the 2001 municipal elections which received 11 per cent of votes in the first round) but there was no solution to the conflict. Unlike in Angers however, *Icroacao* still today works with a large number of heavily involved volunteers and there are deep-rooted interpersonal and intergenerational networks in place. As early as the mid-1990s, musicians created their own self-managed rehearsal venue (the owner of one of the café-concerts – himself a musician – held the keys); there have been many low-budget concerts given in a wide variety of locations and musicians usually paid cash-in-hand.

Whilst several members of the music scene found employment in professional concert venues in other towns (La Roche-sur-Yon, Saint-Nazaire), many agents of the Montaigu association have simply given up, whereas others are prepared to take more 'extreme' measures in protest against the formalities for authorizing concert venues which thwart numerous initiatives.[37] The legendary 'underground' music scene in Montaigu, focused on resistance, remains small-scale and does not have the resources to develop. The sole paid employment within the association no longer exists as the employment contract, created by the Youth Employment Policy, is currently expired and the main links with local authorities have been severed. It could be said that whilst the national context has evolved, in Montaigu the music scene has retained old methods of functioning, characterized by a vast gulf between those involved in music and cultural policies, as well as by an economics of solidarity based on the short-term and on informal financial transactions.

Conclusion

This brief overview has shown how local music scenes represent an interface between different worlds: the old and the new, but also between public and private spheres, diverse musical cultures, amateurs and professionals. Today in France, maintaining and conserving creative dynamism is a real challenge within an increasingly complex and rationalized legal framework (copyrights, employment law, health and safety, sound pollution, etc.). Possessing financial resources in proportion to the volume of activities is often the sole guarantee of respecting legal requirements. This is why subsidized musical venues – which are the hub of musical activity in France – are amongst the rare organizations able to consistently ensure long-term continuity in this brief to preserve creativity (which is particularly difficult since it includes performance, rehearsal, support etc). Doing so requires

---

[36]   Right-wing conservative political party led by Philippe de Villiers.

[37]   For example, up until 2007, successive refusals by security inspectors prevented the association from repeating the annual festival which attracted 7,000 people in 2000.

active involvement of a number of heterogeneous stakeholders (users, members, professionals, volunteer managers, local authorities) so as to jointly construct in a given location an area for democratic exchange and activity. But barely has this project been defined than new relationships between stakeholders have begun to develop: following major record labels, it is now mobile telephone operators and telecommunication groups such as Clear Channel who are adroitly moving their business model towards diversified musical activities which generate profit (sometimes incorrectly called '360 degrees'). They have made a noticeable entry into a market where cultural industries had not yet ventured, namely live performance: SFR is developing its own performance venue in Paris and has signed a partnership agreement with La Cigale concert venue, whilst at the Saint-Malo Route du Rock festival, Le Palais du Grand Large has been renamed the Sony Ericsson venue. Clear Channel is a multinational maintaining its business of urban street advertising and bicycle transport systems while its performance arm Live Nation signs exclusive contracts with internationally recognized artists and organizes high-ticket-price festivals in Europe of exclusive performances by numbers of internationally recognized musicians. Will such a new deregulation lead to a new musical order? The impact this will have on local music scenes remains to be explained by future research.

Bibliography

Abbé-Decarroux, F., 'Demande artistique et préférences endogènes', *Revue économique* 46/3 (1995): pp. 983–92.

Abbé-Decarroux, F., 'La demande de services culturels: une analyse économique', unpublished PhD thesis (1990), *Université de Genève*.

Abt, Dean, 'Music Video: Impact of the Visual Dimension', in James Lull (ed.), *Popular Music and Communication* (London: Sage, 1987).

Actes de l'Université d'été, *Les Musiques des Jeunes*, Rennes, 7–11 juillet 1986 (Paris: Cenam, 1987).

Adem-Florida, *Politiques publiques et musiques amplifiées*, actes des premières rencontres nationales (Paris: GEMA,1997).

Adorno, Theodor, 'On Popular Music', in Simon Frith and Andrew Goodwin (eds), *On Record: Rock, Pop and the Written Word* (London: Routledge, 1990).

Advisory Committee on Pop Festivals, *Report and Code of Practice* (London: HMSO, 1973).

Ahlkvist, Jarl A. and Faulkner, Robert, 'Will This Record Work For Us? Managing Music Formats in Commercial Radio', *Qualitative Sociology*, 25/2 (2002): 189–215.

Ambroise, Jean-Charles and Christian Le Bart, *Les fans des Beatles. Sociologie d'une passion* (Rennes: PUR, 2000).

Ancel, Pascal and Pessin, Alain (eds), *Les non-publics: les arts en réception* (Paris: L'Harmattan, 2004).

Anon., 'Politiques publiques et musiques amplifiées/actuelles', *La Scène*, special edition, avril (1999).

Aquatias, Sylvain, 'Les consommations de produits psychoactifs dans les milieux festifs de la culture rock', *Observatoire français des drogues et des toxicomanies*, 27 (2002): http://www.drogues.gouv.fr.

Assayas, Michka (ed.), *Dictionnaire du Rock* (Paris: Robert Laffont, 2000).

Attali, Jacques, *Bruits, Essai sur l'Economie Politique de la Musique* (Paris: Fayard, 1978).

Aubert, Augustin, Casimiro de San Leandro, Marc, Milliot, Virginie, *Je texte termine, Anthologie de textes rap* (Vénissieux, Paroles d'aube/La Camarilla, coll. Noces, 1998).

Autrement, 'La fête techno. Tout seul et tous ensemble', 231 (2004).

Bachmann, Christian, Basier, Luc, 'Junior s'entraîne très fort ou le smurf comme mobilisation symbolique', *Langage et Société*, 34 (1985): 58–68.

Baker, Joséphine and Jo Bouillon, *Joséphine* (Paris: Robert Laffont, 1976).

Bannister, Matthew, *White Boys, White Noise: Masculinities in 1980s Indie Guitar Rock* (Aldershot: Ashgate, 2006).

Baptiste, Eric, *Rapport du groupe de travail sur les relations entre les radios et la filière musicale* (2002).

Barnard, Stephen, *On the Radio: Music Radio in Britain* (Milton Keynes: Open University, 1989).

Barnard, Stephen, *Studying Radio* (London: Arnold, 2000).

Barthes, Roland, *Mythologies* (London: Vintage, 1993).

Baumol, W. and Bowen, W., *Performing Arts, the Economic Dilemma* (New York: Twentieth Century Fund, 1966).

Bayton, Mavis, *Frock Rock* (Oxford: Oxford University Press, 1998).

Bayton, Mavis, 'Women and the Electric Guitar', in Sheila Whiteley (ed.), *Sexing the Groove: Popular Music and Gender* (London: Routledge, 1997).

Bazin, Hugues, *La culture hip-hop* (Paris: Desclée de Brouwer, 1995).

BBC Online, 'Legal Fight Hits "Music Pirates"', 15 November 2005, http://news.bbc.co.uk/1/hi/-entertainment/music/4438324.stm.

BBC, Annual Report and Accounts 2006/2007: The BBC Executive's Review and Assessment (London: BBC, 2007).

Becker, G., 'A Note on Restaurant Pricing and Other Examples of Social Influences on Price', *Journal of Political Economy*, 99/5 (1991): 1109–16.

Becker, Howard S., *Les mondes de l'art* (Paris: Flammarion, 1988).

Benetollo, Anne, *Rock et politique: Censure, Opposition, Intégration* (Paris: L'Harmattan, 1999).

Benetollo, Anne and Le Goff, Yann, 'Historique du rock', in Gourdon, Anne–Marie (ed.), *Le rock, Aspects esthétiques, culturels et sociaux* (Paris: CNRS Éditions, 1994).

Benghozi, P.J., and Sagot-Duvauroux, D. 'Les économies de la culture', *Réseaux*, nov–déc. (1994): 107–30.

Benhamou, F., 'Ce que révèle l'économie des musiques actuelles', in Dos Santos, L. (ed.), *Valoriser les musiques actuelles* (Paris: Charbonnières, 2003).

Benhamou, F., *Economie du Star System* (Paris: Odile Jacob, 2002).

Benhamou, F., *Essai d'analyse économique d'une pratique culturelle: l'achat et la lecture de livres*, unpublished PhD thesis, (1985). Université de Paris 1.

Benhamou, F., 'L'analyse économique de la musique enregistrée. Qui connaît la chanson ?', *Revue de la Bibliothèque nationale*, 16 (2004): pp. 54–6.

Benhamou, Françoise, *L'économie de la culture* (Paris: La Découverte, 2004).

Benhamou, F., *Les dérèglements de l'exception culturelle, plaidoyer pour une perspective européenne* (Paris: Seuil, 2006).

Benhamou, F., and Farchy J., 'Droit d'auteur et copyright' (Paris: la Découverte, 2007).

Benhamou, F., and Sagot-Duvauroux, D., 'La place du droit d'auteur dans la rémunération de la création artistique, une synthèse', *Culture Études,* 16 (2007–2008). (Paris: Documentation française/*Ministère de la Culture et de la Communication*, 2008).

Benhamou, Françoise, and Stéphanie Peltier, 'Une méthode multicritère d'évaluation de la diversité culturelle: application à l'édition de livres en

France' in Xavier Greffe (ed.), *Création et diversité au miroir des industries culturelles* (Paris: La Documentation française, 2006).

Benito, Luc, *Les Festivals en France. Marchés, Enjeux et Alchimie* (Paris: L'Harmattan, 2001).

Bennett, Andy, 'Music, Media and Urban Mythscapes: A Study of the "Canterbury Sound"', *Media, Culture and Society*, 24 (2002): 87–100.

Bennett, Andy, *Popular Music and Youth Culture: Music, Identity and Place* (Basingstoke: Palgrave, 2000).

Bennett, Andy and Kahn-Harris, Keith (eds), *After Subculture: Critical Studies in Contemporary Youth Culture* (Basingstoke: Palgrave, 2004).

Bennett, Tony, Lawrence Grossberg and Meaghan Morris (eds), *New Keywords: A Revised Vocabulary of Culture and Society* (Oxford: Blackwell, 2005).

Berland, Jody, 'Radio, Space and Industrial Time: The Case of Music Formats', in Bennett, Tony, et al., *Rock and Popular Music: Politics, Policies, Institutions* (London: Routledge, 1993).

Bernard, Yvonne, 'La chanson, phénomène social', *Revue Française de Sociologie*, 5/2 (1964): 166–74.

Berthod, Michel and Weber, Anita, *Rapport sur le soutien de l'Etat aux musiques dites actuelles* (Paris: Ministère de la Culture et de la Communication, 2006).

Béthune, Christian, *Le rap, Une esthétique hors la loi* (Paris: Autrement, 2003).

Bianchi, Jean, 'La promesse du feuilleton', *Réseaux*, 39 (1990).

Bianchini, Franco, and Parkinson, Michael (eds), *Cultural Policy and Urban Regeneration* (Manchester: Manchester University Press, 1993).

Bibas, Benjamin, 'L'Avenir du Disque, c'est la Scène ?', *Rézo international – Magazine de l'AFAA*, 13 (2004): 29–38.

BIPE, *L'économie du domaine musical en France* (Paris: la Documentation française, 1984).

Bipe/Deps, *Approche générationnelle des pratiques culturelles et médiatiques* (Paris: DEPS, ministère de la Culture et de la Communication, 2007).

Björnberg, Alf, 'Structural Relationships of Music and Images in Music Video', in Middleton, Richard (ed.), *Reading Pop: Approaches to Textual Analysis in Popular Music* (Oxford: Oxford University Press, 2000).

Blair, Tony, 'Britain can re-make it', *Guardian*, 22 July 1997: 17.

Blake, Andrew, *The Land Without Music*: *Music, Culture and Society in Twentieth Century Britain* (Manchester, MUP, 1997).

Bomsel, O., *Gratuit, du déploiement de l'économie numérique* (Paris: *Editions Gallimard*, 2007).

Bomsel, O., Geoffroy, A.G., and Le Blanc, G., *When Internet Meets Entertainment – the Economics of Digital Media Industries* (Paris: Presses de l'école des mines, 2006).

Bonnell, R., *Le cinéma exploité* (Paris: Seuil, 1978).

Bonnell, R., *L'initiative culturelle en économie de marché: l'exemple du cinéma français depuis 1945*, unpublished PhD thesis (1976). Université Paris 1.

Bonniol, Marie-Pierre, 'Sonic Youth, du style au geste ou la prétention esthétique d'un groupe de rock', *Copyright Volume!*, 1/1 (2002): 61–80.

Bordes, Véronique, *Le rap est dans la place ou du bon usage du rap par les institutions locales et les jeunes, Étude des relations entre des sociabilités juvéniles et des politiques locales de la jeunesse* (Université de Paris 10, Nanterre: unpublished PhD, 2005).

Borthwick, Stuart and Ron Moy, *Popular Music Genres* (Edinburgh: Edinburgh University Press, 2004).

Boucher, Manuel, Rap, *Expression des lascars, Significations et enjeux du rap dans la société française* (Paris: L'Harmattan, 1998).

Bougain, Roland and Bruno Rotival, *Photo Music, Lyon 1975–76* (Lyon: Auto-Edition, 1976).

Boullier, Dominique, *La conversation télé* (Rennes: Lares, 1987).

Bourdieu, Pierre, *La Distinction* (Paris: Minuit, 1979).

Bourdieu, Pierre, 'Vous avez dit "populaire"?', *Actes de la Recherche en Sciences Sociales*, 46 (1983): 98–105.

Bourreau, M. and Labarthe-Piol, B., 'Le peer to peer et la crise de l'industrie du disque: une perspective historique', *Réseaux* 22/125 (2004): 17–54.

Bourreau, M., Gensollen M., Moreau F. 'Musique enregistrée et numérique: quels scénarios d'évolution de la filière?', *Culture Prospective* 1 (2007): 16.

Bradley, Dick, *Understanding Rock 'n' Roll* (Milton Keynes: Open University Press, 1992).

Brault, Christophe, *1978–1988: 10 ans de Rock à Rennes* (Rennes: Auto-Edition, 1988).

Braverman, H., Foster, J.B., 'Labor and Monopoly Capitalism: The Degradation of Work in the Twentieth Century', *New York, Monthly Review Press*, 1999, cited in Koch, G. *Sexual Representation: Introduction, Jump Cut*, 35/April (1990): 16 at http://www.ejumpcut.org/archive/-onlinessays/JC35folder/SexualRepnIntro.html.

Breen, Marcus, 'Making Music Local', in Tony Bennett et al. (eds), *Rock and Popular Music* (London: Routledge, 1993).

Briggs, Asa, *The History of Broadcasting in the United Kingdom* (Vols. 1–5, Oxford: Oxford University Press, 1995).

British Invisibles, *The Overseas Earnings of the Music Industry* (London: British Invisibles, 1995).

Brousseau, E. and Feledziack, B., *Étude sur l'Economie des Droits d'Auteurs dans le domaine de la Musique, Rapport au Ministère de la Culture et de la Communication* (Paris: Département des Études, de la Prospective et de la Statistique, 2007).

Brown, Adam, O'Connor, Justin and Cohen, Sara, 'Local music policies within a global music industry: cultural quarters in Manchester and Sheffield', *Geoforum*, 31 (1998): 437–51.

Brownrigg, Mark and Meech, Peter, 'From Fanfare to Funfair: The Changing Sound World of UK Television Idents', *Popular Music*, 21/3, (2002): 345–55.

Bull, Michael, 'No Dead Air! The iPod and the Culture of Mobile Listening', *Leisure Studies*, 24/4 (2005): 343–55.

Bull, Michael, *Sounding Out the City: Personal Stereos and the Management of Everyday Life* (Oxford: Berg, 2000).

Bureau, M., Gomel, B., and Schmidt, N., 'Les associations de musiques actuelles, partenaires du programme Nouveaux services – emplois jeunes. Contribution à un état des lieux', *CEE* 04/02 (2004): 117.

Burgess, Robert, *In the Field: An Introduction to Field Research* (London: George Allen and Unwin, 1984).

Butler, David and Kavanagh, David, *The British General Election of 1997* (Basingstoke: Macmillan, 1997).

Buxton, David, *Le rock, star-système et société de consommation* (Grenoble: La Pensée Sauvage, 1985).

Cahiers Jeunesses et Sociétés, 'Jeunes et musique', 10 (1988).

Callahan, Caroline, Martin, Andy and Piece, Anna, *Licensing Act 2003* (London: DCMS, 2006).

Campos, Rémy et al. (eds), 'Musique et Sciences Humaines. Rendez-Vous Manqués?', special number of *Revue d'Histoire des Sciences Humaines*, 14 (2006).

Cannon, Steve, 'Globalization, Americanization and hip hop in France', in Hugh Dauncey and Steve Cannon (eds), *Popular Music in France from Chanson to Techno* (Aldershot: Ashgate, 2003).

Caradec, Vincent and Glevarec, Hervé, 'Présentation', in *Réseaux* 119 (2003): 9–23.

Carasso, Jean-Gabriel, *Nos enfants ont-ils droit à l'art et à la culture?: Manifeste pour une politique de l'éducation artistique et culturelle* (Toulouse: Editions de l'Attribut, 2005).

Carles, Philippe and Jean-Louis Comolli, *Free Jazz, Black Power* (Paris: Folio Gallimard, 2000).

Castagnac, G., 'L'économie phonographique: de filières en filiales', in Perret J. and Saez G. (eds), *Institutions et vie culturelles* (Paris: la Documentation française, 1996).

Caune, Jean, *La culture en action. De Vilar à Lang: le sens perdu* (Grenoble: PUG, 1991).

Caves, R., *Creative Industries: Contracts Between Art and Commerce* (Harvard: Harvard University Press, 2000).

Cavignac, Julie, 'Nécrologie d'un bar rock, In memoriam luxoris, ou du vécu comme source du travail ethnologique', *Cahiers ethnologiques,* 9 (1988): 49–65.

Cayla, Véronique and Anne Durupty, *Relations entre télédiffuseurs et filière musicale* (Paris: Ministère de la culture/la Documentation française, 2005).

Cefaï, Daniel and Pasquier, Dominique (eds), *Les sens du public. Publics,. politiques publics médiatiques* (Paris: PUF, 2003).

Certeau, Michel, *L'invention du quotidien* (Paris: 10/18, 1980).

Chambers, Iain, *Urban Rhythms* (Basingstoke: Macmillan, 1985).

Chanan, Michael, *Repeated Takes: A Short History of Recording and its Effects on Music* (London: Verso, 1995).

Chantal, Sylvain, 'Billet d'Humeur', *Magic*, 110 (2007): 3.

Chantepie P., and Le Diberder A., *Révolution numérique et industries culturelles* (Paris: la Découverte, 2005).

Chapman, Robert, *Selling the Sixties: The Pirates and Pop Music Radio* (London: Routledge, 1992).

Charliot, Laurent, *La fabuleuse histoire du Rock nantais de 1960 à nos jours* (Sainte Florence: Imprimédia, 2003).

Chartier, Roger, *Au Bord de la falaise: l'histoire entre certitudes et inquiétude* (Paris: Albin Michel, 1998).

Chartier, Roger, Bourdieu, Pierre and Robert Damton, *Pratiques de la lecture* (Paris: Payot, 2003).

Chaudoir, Philippe and de Maillard, Jacques (eds), *Culture et politique de la ville* (La Tour d'Aigues: éditions de l'Aube, 2004).

Cheval, Jean-Jacques, 'Le public des radios locales privées: évolution nationale et exemples aquitains' in Michèle de Bussière, Méadel, Cécile and Mauriat, Caroline (eds), *Histoire des publics à la radio et à la télévision. Actes de la journée du 20 mars 1992* (Paris: Comité d'Histoire de la Radio, Comité d'Histoire de la Télévision et GEHRA, 1994).

Cheval, Jean-Jacques, *Les radios en France. Histoire, état et enjeux* (Rennes: Editions Apogée, 1997).

Cheyronnaud, Jacques, 'Ethnologie et musique: l'objet en question', *Ethnologie Française*, 27/3 (1997): 382–93.

Cheyronnaud, Jacques, *Musique, politique, religion. De quelques menus objets de culture* (Paris: L'Harmattan, 2002).

Chiapello, Eve, *Artistes versus Managers* (Paris: Métailié, 1998).

Clarke, Gary, 'Defending Ski-jumpers: A Critique of Theories of Youth Subcultures', in Simon Frith and Andrew Goodwin (eds), *On Record: Rock, Pop, and the Written Word* (London: Routledge, 1990).

Cloonan, Martin, *Banned! Censorship of Popular Music in Britain; 1967–1992* (Aldershot: Arena, 1996).

Cloonan, Martin, 'Popular Music and the Nation-State: Towards a Theorisation', *Popular Music*, 18/2 (1999): 193–207.

Cloonan, Martin, *Popular Music and the State in the UK* (Aldershot/Birmingham USA: Ashgate, 2007).

Cloonan, Martin, 'State of the Nation: "Englishness", Pop and Politics in the mid-1990s', *Popular Music and Society*, 21/2 (1997): 47–70.

Cloonan, Martin and Street, John, 'Rock The Vote: Popular Culture and Politics', *Politics*, 18/1 (1998): 33–8.

CNV, *Eléments Statistiques sur la Diffusion des Spectacles de Variétés et de Musiques Actuelles en 2006. Présentation des Données et Eléments d'Evolution 2005–2006* (Paris: CNV, 2007).

Coates, Norma, 'Can't We Just Talk About Music? Rock and Gender on the Internet', in Thom Swiss et al. (ed), *Mapping the Beat: Popular Music and Contemporary Theory* (Oxford: Blackwell, 1998).

Coates, Norma, '(R)evolution Now? Rock and the Political Potential of Gender', in Sheila Whitely (ed.), *Sexing the Groove: Popular Music and Gender* (London: Routledge, 1997).

Coghe, Jean-Noël, *Autant en emporte le rock: 1960–2000* (Paris: EPM/Le Castor Astral, 2001).

Cohen, Phil, 'Subcultural Conflict and Working-class Community', in Stuart Hall et al. (eds), *Culture, Media, Language: Working Papers in Cultural Studies 1972–79* (London: Routledge, 1992).

Cohen, Sara, *Beyond the Beatles. Decline, Renewal and the City in Popular Music Cultures* (Aldershot: Ashgate, 2007).

Cohen, Sara, 'Ethnography and Popular Music Studies', *Popular Music*, 12/2 (1993): 123–8.

Cohen, Sara, 'Men Making a Scene: Rock Music and the Production of Gender', in Sheila Whiteley (ed.), *Sexing the Groove: Popular Music and Gender* (London: Routledge, 1997).

Cohen, Sara, 'Popular Music and Urban Regeneration: The Music Industries of Merseyside', *Cultural Studies*, 5/3 (1991): 332–46.

Cohen, Sara, 'Popular Music, Gender and Sexuality', in Simon Frith et al. (ed), *The Cambridge Companion to Pop and Rock* (Cambridge: Cambridge University Press, 2001).

Cohen, Sara, *Rock Culture in Liverpool: Popular Music in the Making* (Oxford: Clarendon Press, 1991).

Cohen, Sarah, 'Scene', in Bruce Horner and Thomas Swiss (eds), *Key Terms in Popular Music and Culture* (Oxford: Blackwell, 1999).

Cohen, Stanley, *Folk Devils and Moral Panics* (London: McGibbon and Kee, 1973).

Colin, Bruno, 'Vers une économie solidaire du spectacle vivant ?' in Adem-Florida, *Politiques publiques et musiques amplifiées*, actes des premières rencontres nationales (Paris: GEMA,1997).

Colling, Daniel and Philippe Magnier, *Le Printemps de Bourges: scènes, rues et coulisses* (Paris: Ed. du Garde Temps, 2003).

Collins English Dictionary (London: Collins, 1988 and 1998).

Colombié, Thierry, Lalam, Nacer, Schiray, Michel, *Drogue et techno, Les trafiquants de rave* (Paris: Stock, 2000).

Copyright Volume!, special number on 'La presse musicale alternative au 21ème siècle', 5/1 (2006).

Copyright Volume!, special number on 'Les musiques metal. Sciences sociales et pratiques culturelles radicales', 5/2 (2007).

Copyright Volume!, special number on 'Sonorités du hip-hop. Logiques globales et hexagonales', 3/2 (2004).

Corner, John, 'Sounds Real: Music and Documentary', *Popular Music*, 21(3), (2002): 357–66.

Cotro, Vincent, *Champs libres: le free jazz en France, 1960–1975* (Paris: Outre mesure, 2000).

Coulangeon, Philippe, *Sociologie des pratiques culturelles*, (Paris: La Découverte, 2005).

Coutinet, Nathalie and Dominique Sagot-Duvauroux, *Economie des fusions et acquisitions* (Paris: La Découverte, 2003).

Couturier, Brice, *Une Scène-Jeunesse* (Paris: Autrement, 1983).

Crisell, Andrew, *An Introductory History of British Broadcasting* (Abingdon: Routledge, 2nd edition 2002).

Crook, Tim, *International Radio Journalism: History, Theory and Practice* (London: Routledge, 1998).

Crook, Tim, *Radio Drama: Theory and Practice* (London: Routledge, 1999).

Crossley, Neil, 'Survey Success', *The Musician*, Spring 2007: 20–21.

Curien, Nicolas and François Moreau, 'L'industrie du disque à l'heure de la convergence télécoms/médias/internet' in Xavier Greffe (ed.) *Création et diversité au miroir des industries culturelles* (Paris: La Documentation française, 2006).

Curien, Nicolas and Moreau, François, *L'industrie du disque* (Paris: La Découverte, 2006).

Danchin, Sébastian, *Elvis Presley ou la revanche du Sud* (Paris: Fayard, 2004).

D'Angelo, M., *La renaissance du disque*, Notes et Etudes Documentaires (Paris: La Documentation française, 1989).

D'Angelo, M., *Socio-économie de la musique en France, Diagnostic d'un système vulnérable* (Paris: la Documentation française, 1997).

D'Arcy, Doug and Brindley, Paul, *Make or Break: Supporting UK Music in the USA* (London: British Council, 2002).

Daufouy, Philippe and Jean-Pierre Sartron, *Pop Music Rock* (Paris: Champ Libre, 1972).

Dauncey, Hugh, 'The French Music Industry: Structures, Challenges and Responses', in Hugh Dauncey and Steve Cannon (eds), *Popular Music in France from* Chanson *to Techno: Culture, Identity and Society* (Aldershot: Ashgate, 2003).

Dauncey, Hugh and Philippe Le Guern, (eds) *Stéréo. Sociologie comparée des musiques populaires France / G.–B.* (Paris: Irma/Seteun, 2008).

Davet, Stéphane and Frank Tenaille, *Le Printemps de Bourges: chroniques des musiques d'aujourd'hui* (Paris: Gallimard, 1996).

De Coster, M., *Le disque, art ou affaires* (Grenoble: PUG, 1976).

Debarbieux, Bernard, 'Du Haut Lieu en Général et du Mont Blanc en Particulier', *L'Espace Géographique*, 1 (1993): 5–13.

DeCurtis, Anthony and James Henke (eds), *The Rolling Stone Illustrated History of Rock & Roll* (New York: Random House, 1992).

Della Faille, Dimitri, 'Espaces de Solidarités, de Divergences et de Conflits dans la Musique Montréalaise Emergente', *Copyright Volume!*, 4 (2005): 61–74.

DeNora, Tia, 'Music as a Technology of the Self', *Poetics*, 24 (1999): 31–56.

Denora, Tia, *Music in Everyday Life* (Cambridge: Cambridge University Press 2000).

DeNora, Tia and Belcher, Sophie, '"When You're Trying Something On You Picture Yourself in a Place Where They Are Playing This Kind of Music" – Musically Sponsored Agency in the British Clothing Retail Sector', *The Sociological Review*, 48/1 (2000): 80–101.

Denselow, Robin, *When The Music's Over* (London: Faber and Faber, 1989).

Department for Culture, Media and Sport (DCMS), *Consumers Call The Tune*: *The Impact of New Technologies on the Music Industry* (London: DCMS, 2000).

Department for Culture, Media and Sport, *Creative Industries Mapping Document 1998* (London: DCMS, 1998).

Department for Culture, Media and Sport, *Creative Industries Mapping Document 2001* (London: DCMS, 2001).

Dingo Association, *10 ans de Musiques Amplifiées à Angoulême* (Angoulême: Auto-Edition, 1998).

Donin, Nicolas and Stiegler, Bernard, 'Le Tournant machinique de la sensibilité musicale', *Cahiers de Médiologie,* 18 (2004): 7–17.

Donnat, Olivier, 'La stratification sociale des pratiques culturelles et son évolution 1973–1997', *Revue Française de Sociologie*, XL/L (1999): 111–119.

Donnat, Olivier, *Les Français face à la culture: de l'exclusion à l'éclectisme* (Paris: La Découverte, 1994).

Donnat, Olivier, *Les Pratiques culturelles des Français* (Paris: La documentation Française, 1997).

Donnat, Olivier, *Les pratiques culturelles des Français* (Paris: La Documentation française, 1998).

Donnat, Olivier, (ed.), *Regards croisés sur les pratiques culturelles* (Paris: La Documentation Française, 2003).

Donnat, Olivier, and Octobre, Sylvie, (eds), *Les publics des équipements culturels* (Paris: Ministère de la Culture et de la Communication, 2001).

Doublé-Dutheil, Catherine, 'Le Rock est-il une musique populaire ?', in Joëlle Deniot and Catherine Doublé-Dutheil, (eds), *Métamorphoses Ouvrières* (Paris: L'Harmattan, 1994).

Doublé-Dutheil, Catherine, 'Les groupes de rock nantais', in Mignon, Patrick, and Hennion, Antoine (eds), *Rock, De l'histoire au mythe* (Paris: Anthropos, 1991).

Dubois, Vincent, 'Action culturelle/action sociale: les limites d'une frontière', *Revue Française des Affaires Sociales*, 48/2 (1994): 27–42.

Dubois, Vincent, *La politique culturelle – Genèse d'une catégorie d'intervention publique* (Paris: Belin, 1999).

Dubois, Vincent and Laborier, Pascale, 'Le "social" dans l'institutionnalisation des politiques culturelles locales en France et en Allemagne', in Richard Balme,

Alain Faure, Albert Mabileau (eds), *Les nouvelles politiques locales* (Paris: Presses de Sciences Po, 1999).

Dupuis, X., *Essai sur les pratiques culturelles de l'État: l'exemple de la musique*, unpublished PhD thesis, (1981). Université de Paris XIII.

Dupuis, X., 'La gestion des institutions musicales ou comment gérer l'ingérable', in Wangermee, R., (ed), *Les malheurs d'Orphée* (Bruxelles: Mardaga, 1990).

Dupuis, X., 'La surqualité: le spectacle vivant malade de la bureaucratie?', *Revue Economique*, November (1983).

Durafour, Antoine, *Le milieu gothique. Sa construction sociale à travers la dimension esthétique* (Paris: Le Manuscrit, 2005).

Ethis, Emmanuel, *Aux marches du palais. Le festival de Cannes sous le regard des sciences sociales* (Paris: La Documentation française, 2001).

Eudeline, Christian, *Anti Yé-Yé. Une autre histoire des Sixties* (Paris: Denoël X-trême, 2006).

Eudeline, Christian, *Nos Années punk, 1972–1978* (Paris: Denoël X-trême, 2002).

Farchy, J., *Internet et le droit d'auteur, la culture Napster* (Paris: CNRS Editions, 2003).

Farchy, J., *La fin de l'exception culturelle* (Paris: CNRS Editions, 1999).

Farchy, J. *Le cinéma français sous influence: De la concurrence audiovisuelle à la différentiation des produits cinématographiques*, unpublished PhD thesis (1989). Université Paris 1.

Farchy, Joëlle, and Dominique Sagot-Duvauroux, *Economie des Politiques Culturelles* (Paris: PUF, 1994).

Farmer, Frances, *Will There Really Be a Morning?* (London: Allison & Busby, 1973).

Favre, Pierre and Christian Pirot, *Bourges, Histoire d'un Printemps 1977–1986* (Paris: Christian Pirot, 1986).

Fédurok, Enquête Tour de France, *Résultats 2001 et 2003* (Nantes: Fédurok, 2004).

Fine, Gary Alan, and Kleinman, Sheryl, 'Rethinking Subculture: An Interactionist Analysis', *American Journal of Sociology* 85/1 (1979): 1–20.

Finkielkraut, Alain, *La défaite de la pensée* (Paris: Gallimard, 1987).

Finnegan, Ruth, 'Music, Experience, and the Anthropology of Emotion', in Martin Clayton et al. (eds), *The Cultural Study of Music: A Critical Introduction* (London: Routledge, 2003).

Finnegan, Ruth, 'Music, Performance and Enactment', in Hugh MacKay (ed.), *Consumption and Everyday Life* (London: Sage, 1997).

Finnegan, Ruth, *The Hidden Musicians: Music Making in an English Town* (Cambridge: Cambridge University Press, 1989).

Firminger, John and Lilleker, Martin, *Not Like a Proper Job: The Story of Popular Music in Sheffield 1955–1975* (Sheffield: Juma, 2001).

Flichy, P., *Les industries de l'imaginaire* (Grenoble: PUG, 1980).

Floux, Pierre and Schinz, Olivier, 'Engager son propre goût. Entretien autour de la sociologie pragmatique d'Antoine Hennion', *Ethnographiques.org* (April 2003).

Fondation Cartier pour l'Art Contemporain, *Rock'n Roll 39–59* (Paris: Xavier Barral, 2007).

Fontaine, Astrid, and Fontana, Caroline, *Raver* (Paris: Economica, 1996).

Fornatale, Peter, and Joshua Mills, *Radio in the Television Age* (Woodstock, N.Y.: Overlook Press, 1980).

Fraser, Nancy, *Qu'est-ce que la justice sociale ? Reconnaissance et redistribution* (Paris: La Découverte, 2005).

Friedberg, Erhard, and Urfalino, Philippe, *Le jeu du catalogue* (Paris: La Documentation Française, 1984).

Frith, Simon, 'Look! Hear! The Uneasy Relationship of Music and Television', *Popular Music*, 21(3) (2002): 277–90.

Frith, Simon, 'Music and Everyday Life', in Martin Clayton et al. (eds), *The Cultural Study of Music: A Critical Introduction* (London: Routledge, 2003).

Frith, Simon, *Performing Rites: On the Value of Popular Music* (Oxford: Oxford University Press, 1996).

Frith, Simon, 'Popular Music and the Local State', in Tony Bennett et al. (eds), *Rock and Popular Music* (London: Routledge, 1993).

Frith, Simon, *Sound Effects: Youth, Leisure and the Politics of Rock 'n' Roll* (London: Constable, 1983).

Frith, Simon, 'The Cultural Study of Popular Music', in Lawrence Grossberg et al. (eds), *Cultural Studies* (London: Routledge, 1992).

Frith, Simon, 'The Popular Music Industry', in Frith, Simon, Straw, Will and Street, John, (eds), *The Cambridge Companion to Pop and Rock* (Cambridge: Cambridge University Press, 2001).

Frith, Simon, *The Sociology of Rock* (London: Constable, 1978).

Frith, Simon, 'Video Pop', in Frith, Simon (ed.), *Facing the Music* (London: Mandarin, 1988).

Frith, Simon, and Andrew Goodwin (eds), *On Record: Pop, Rock and the Written Word* (London: Routledge, 1990).

Frith, Simon, and Le Guern, Philippe (eds), *Sociologie des musiques populaires* (Paris: Réseaux, 25/141–2 (2007).

Frith, Simon and Philippe Le Guern (eds), 'Sociologie des Musiques Populaires', special number of *Réseaux*, 25 (2007).

Frith, Simon, John Street, and Will Straw (eds), *The Cambridge Companion to Pop and Rock* (Cambridge University Press, 2001).

Fryer, Paul, '"Everybody's on Top of the Pops": Popular Music on British television 1960–1985', *Popular Music and Society*, 21/3 (1997): 153–71.

Fumaroli, Marc, *L'Etat culturel* (Paris: de Fallois, 1991).

Gabszewicz, Jean and Nathalie Sonnac, 'Concentration des industries de contenu et diversité des préférences' in Xavier Greffe (ed.), *Création et diversité au miroir des industries culturelles* (Paris: La Documentation française, 2006).

Gabzewicz, J., and Sonnac, N., *L'industrie des médias* (Paris: la Découverte, 2006).

Garner, Ken, *In Session Tonight* (London: BBC Books, 1993).

Gasquet-Cyrus, Médéric, Kosmicki, Guillaume, Van Den den Avenne, Cécile (ed.), *Paroles et musiques à Marseille, Les voix d'une ville* (Paris: L'Harmattan, 1999).

GEMA, 'Les publics des concerts de musiques amplifiées', in *Développement culturel*, 122 (Paris: Ministère de la Culture et de la Communication, 1998).

Gensane, Bernard, *La pop music 1955–1970: existence, essence et fonction* (Université de Paris 8: unpublished PhD thesis, 1973).

Ghosn, Joseph, 'Du "Raver" au "Sampler": vers une sociologie de la techno', *L'Homme et la Société*, 126 (1997): 89.

Gibson, Chris, and Homan, Shane, 'Urban redevelopment, live music and public space', *International Journal of Cultural Policy*, 10/1 (2004): 67–84.

Gillett, Charlie, *The Sound of the City* (London: Souvenir Press, 1983).

Gillett, Charlie, *The Sound of the City. Histoire du Rock'n'Roll* (Paris: Albin Michel, 1986).

Gilligan, Carol, 'Getting Civilised', in Ann Oakley and Juliet Mitchell (eds), *Who's Afraid of Feminism? Seeing Through the Backlash* (London: Penguin, 1998).

Gilmore, Abigail, 'City Beats: Local Popular Music and Cultural Policy', *International Journal of Urban Labour and Leisure*, 3/1 (2001): http://www.ijull.co.uk/vol3/1/000018.htm.

Glevarec, Hervé, 'La fin du modèle classique de la légitimité culturelle. Hétérogénéisation des ordres de légitimité et régime contemporain de justice culturelle. L'exemple du champ musical', in Eric Maigret and Macé, Eric (eds), *Penser les médiacultures. Nouvelles pratiques et nouvelles approches de la représentation du monde* (Paris: Colin/INA, 2005).

Glevarec, Hervé, 'Les producteurs de radio à France Culture, "Journalistes", "Intellectuels" ou "Créateurs"?: de la Définition de soi à l'Interaction radiophonique', *Réseaux*, 86 (1997): 13–38.

Glevarec, Hervé and Michel Pinet, 'L'écoute de la radio en France. Hétérogénéité des pratiques et spécialisation des auditoires', *Questions de communication*, 12 (2007): 279–310.

Glevarec, Hervé, and Michel Pinet, 'From Liberalization to Fragmentation: A Sociology of French Radio Audiences Since the 1990s and the Consequences for Cultural Industries Theory', *Media, Culture and Society*, 30/2 (2008): 215–38.

Goodwin, Andrew, 'Rationalization and Democratization in the New Technologies of Popular Music', in J. Lull (ed.), *Popular Music and Communication* (Newbury Park, Calif.: Sage, 1992).

Gourdon, Anne-Marie (ed.), *Le Rock. Aspects esthétiques, culturels et sociaux* (Paris: CNRS Editions, 1994).

Gowers, Andrew, *Gowers Review of Intellectual Property* (London: The Stationery Office 2006).

Green, Lucy, *Music, Gender, Education* (Cambridge: Cambridge University Press, 1997).

Greffe, Xavier, *Analyse économique de la bureaucratie* (Paris: Economica, 1981).

Greffe, Xavier (ed.), *Création et diversité au miroir des industries culturelles. Actes des Journées d'économie de la culture 2006* (Paris: La Documentation française, 2006).

Greffe, Xavier, Pflieger, S., and Rouet, F., *Socio-économie de la culture: Livre, musique* (Paris: Economica, 1990).

Grignon, Claude and Jean-Claude Passeron, *Le Savant et le Populaire* (Paris: Le Seuil, 1985).

Grynszpan, Emmanuel, *Bruyante techno. Réflexion sur le son de la free party* (Nantes: Mélanie Seteun, 1999).

Guibert, Gérôme, 'Is the French Word "Chanson" Equivalent to the English Term "Popular Music"?' in Geoff Stahl (ed.), Rome 2005 IASPM International Conference Proceedings (Rome: IASPM, 2008).

Guibert, Gérôme, *La production de la culture, Le cas des musiques amplifiées en France, Genèses, structurations, industries, alternatives* (Nantes: Mélanie Séteun/Irma, 2006).

Guibert, Gérôme, 'Les Musiques Amplifiées en France. Phénomènes de Surface et Dynamiques Invisibles', *Réseaux*, 25 (2007): 297–324.

Guibert, Gérôme, *Scènes Locales, Scène Globale. Contribution à une Sociologie Economique des Producteurs de Musiques Amplifiées en France* (Nantes: Université de Nantes, 2004).

Guibert, Gérôme and Fabien Hein, 'Les Scènes Metal, Sciences Sociales et Pratiques Culturelles Radicales', special issue of *Copyright Volume!*, 5/2 (2006).

Guiu, Claire (ed.), 'Géographie et Musiques', special issue of *Géographie et Cultures*, 59 (2007).

Guy, Jean-Michel, *La culture cinématographique des Français* (Paris: La Documentation française, 2000).

Hall, Stuart, and Jefferson, Tony (eds), *Resistance Through Rituals: Youth Subcultures in Post-war Britain* (London: Routledge, 1975).

Hall, Stuart, and Whannel, Paddy, *The Popular Arts* (London: Hutchinson, 1964).

Hampartzoumian, Stéphane, *Effervescence techno ou la communauté trans(e)cendantale* (Paris: L'Harmattan, 2004).

Hargreaves, David J., and North, Adrian C., *The Social Psychology of Music* (Oxford: Oxford University Press, 1997).

Harker, Dave, *One For The Money* (London: Hutchinson, 1980).

Harris, John, *The Last Party: Britpop, Blair and the Demise of English Rock* (London, Fourth Estate, 2003).

Harrison, S., *Fan-Based Funding for New Bands: Alamo Records as an Alternative Business Model* (University of Liverpool, unpublished MA Dissertation, 2007).

Hawes, Steve, 'I Was There: Putting Punk on Television', in Andre Blake (ed.), *Living Through Pop* (London: Routledge, 1999).

Hawkins, Peter, Chanson. *The French Singer-Songwriter from Aristide Bruand to the Present Day* (Aldershot: Ashgate, 2000).

Hawkins, Stan, *Settling the Pop Score: Pop Texts and Identity Politics* (Aldershot: Ashgate, 2002).

Hayes, David, '"Take Those Old Records Off the Shelf": Youth and Music Consumption in the Postmodern Age', *Popular Music and Society*, 29/1 (2006): 51–68.

Hebdige, Dick, *Subculture: The Meaning of Style* (London: Methuen, 1979).

Hein, Fabien, *Hard Rock, Heavy Metal, Metal. Histoire, cultures et pratiquants* (Paris: Mélanie Séteun/Irma, 2003.

Hein, Fabien, 'Le critique rock, le fanzine et le magazine: Ça s'en va et ça revient', *Copyright Volume!*, 5/1 (2006): 83–105.

Hein, Fabien, *Le monde du rock. Ethnographie du réel* (Paris: Mélanie Séteun/ Irma, 2006).

Hein, Fabien and Gérôme Guibert, 'Metal. Une culture de la transgression sonore, Entretien avec Marc Touché', *Copyright Volume!*, 5/2 (2006): 137–52.

Heinich, Nathalie, *Etre Artiste* (Paris: Klincksieck, 1996).

Heinich, Nathalie, *Le triple jeu de l'art contemporain* (Paris: Minuit, 1998).

Hendy, David, 'Pop Music Radio in the Public Service: BBC Radio 1 and New Music in the 1990s', *Media, Culture and Society* 22/6 (2000): 743–61.

Hennion, Antoine, 'Affaires de goût. Se rendre sensible aux choses' in Michel Peroni and Roux, Jacques (eds), *Sensibiliser. La sociologie dans le vif du monde* (La Tour d'Aigues: Éd de l'Aube, 2006).

Hennion, Antoine, *La Passion musicale. Une sociologie de la médiation* (Paris: Métailié, 1993).

Hennion, Antoine, Maisonneuve, Sophie, and Gomart, Emilie, *Figures de l'amateur. Formes, objets, pratiques de l'amour de la musique aujourd'hui*, (Paris: La Documentation française, 2000).

Hennion, Antoine and Cécile Méadel, 'Programming Music: Radio as a Mediator', *Media, Culture and Society*, 8/3 (1986): 281–303.

Hercovici, A., 'Analyse économique des modes de production et de diffusion de la musique moderne', in Wangermee, R. (ed), *Les malheurs d'Orphée* (Bruxelles: Mardaga, 1990).

Hercovici, A., *Essai sur l'économie de la musique moderne*, unpublished PhD thesis (1983). Université de Paris 1.

Hermes, Joke, *Reading Women's Magazines: An Analysis of Everyday Media Use* (Cambridge: Polity Press, 1995).

Herzhaft, Gérard, *Le blues* (Paris: PUF, 1981).

Herzog, Amy, 'Discordant Visions: The Peculiar Musical Images of the Soundies Jukebox Film', *American Music*, 22/1 (2004): 27–39.

Hesmondhalgh, David, 'Indie: The Aesthetics and Institutional Politics of a Popular Music Genre', *Cultural Studies*, 13/1 (1999): 34–61.

Hesmondhalgh, David, 'Subcultures, Scenes or Tribes? None of the Above', *Journal of Youth Studies*, 8/1 (2005): 21–40.

Hewitt, Paolo, *Paul Weller. The Changing Man* (London: Bantam, 2007).

Hill, John, 'Television and Pop: The Case of the 1950s', in Corner, John (ed.), *Popular Television in Britain* (London: BFI, 1991).

Hirsch, Paul, 'Processing Fads and Fashions: An Organization-Set Analysis of Cultural Industry Systems', *American Journal of Sociology*, 77/4 (1972): 639–59.

Hirsh, Thomas and Grégory Tuban, *Perpignan Rock: 1960–2000* (Perpignan: Trabucaire, 2000).

Hodkinson, Paul, *Goth: Identity, Style and Subculture* (Oxford: Berg, 2002).

Hoggart, Richard, *La culture du pauvre* (Paris: Editions de Minuit, 1970).

Honneth, Axel, *La lutte pour la reconnaissance* (Paris: Cerf, 2002).

House of Commons Trade and Industry Committee, *Marketing UK plc – UKTI's five-year strategy*, sixth report of Session 2006–2007, Report together with formal minutes, p. 17.

Hull, Geoffrey P., *The Recording Industry* (London: Routledge, 2nd ed. 2004).

Huq, Rupa, *Beyond Subculture: Pop, Youth and Identity in a Postcolonial World* (London: Routledge, 2006).

Hurstel, Jean, *Jeunes au Bistrot, cultures sur macadam* (Paris: Syros, 1984).

Hutton, W, O'Keefe, A., Schneider, P., Andari, R., and Bakhshi, H., *Staying Ahead: The Economic Performance of the UK's Creative Industries* (London: The Work Foundation, 2007), Chapter 5: p. 2.

Jenkins, Henry, *Textual Poachers: Television Fans and Participatory Culture* (New York: Routledge, 1992).

Jobert, Bruno and Muller, Pierre, *L'Etat en action* (Paris: PUF, 1987).

Jones, Michael, *Organising Pop: Why So Few Pop Acts Make Pop Music* (Unpublished Ph.D. Thesis, Institute of Popular Music, Liverpool University, 1997).

Jones, Mike, 'Changing Slides – Labour's Music Industry Policy under the Microscope', *Critical Quarterly*, 41/1 (1999): 22–31.

Jones, Steve (ed.), *Pop Music and the Press* (Philadelphia: Temple University Press, 2002).

Jones, Steve, 'The Intro: Popular Music, Media and the Written Word', in Steve Jones (ed.), *Pop Music and the Press* (Philadelphia: Temple University Press, 2002).

Jones, Steve and Featherly, Kevin, 'Re-viewing Rock Writing: Narratives of Popular Music Criticism', in Jones, Steve (ed.) *Pop Music and the Press* (Philadelphia: Temple University Press, 2002).

Jouffa, François, *La Culture Pop des Années 70. Réédition des 'Pop-notes' de la revue Pop Music 1970–1972* (Paris: Europe 1/Spengler, 1994).

Jouffa, François and Jacques Barsamian, *Vinyl Fraise: Les Années 60* (Paris: Michel Lafon, 1993).

Jouvenet, Morgan, *Rap, techno, electro ... Le musicien entre travail artistique et critique sociale* (Paris: Éditions de la Maison des sciences de l'homme, 2006).

Kalifa, Dominique, *La Culture de Masse en France, 1860–1930* (Paris: La Découverte, 2001).

Kane, Pat 'Don't Rock the Vote', *Guardian*, 19 January 1996, part two: 13.

Kaplan, E. Ann, *Rocking Around the Clock: Music Television, Postmodernism and Consumer Culture* (London: Routledge, 1987).

Karanfilovic, Nathalie, *Les implications sociopolitiques du rap afro-américain: de l'engagement new school au nihilisme gangsta* (Université de Metz: unpublished PhD, 2004).

Karsenty-Ricard, Thomas, *Dylan, l'authenticité et l'imprévu* (Paris: L'Harmattan, 2005).

Kopp, Pierre, *Télévisions en concurrence* (Paris: Anthropos, 1990).

Kosmicki, Guillaume, 'Analyse de "Let's Play" de Crystal Distortion: les paradoxes d'un "tube" de la Free Party', *Musurgia*, 9/2, (2002): 85–101.

Kruse, Holly, 'Abandoning the Absolute: Transcendence and Gender in Popular Music Discourse', in Labadie, F., and Rouet, F., 'Régulation du travail artistique', *Culture Prospective*, 4 (2007): 20.

Labadie, F., and Rouet, F., *Travail artistique et économie de la création* (Paris: la Documentation française, 2008).

Labarthe-Piol, B., *L'impact d'Internet sur l'industrie du disque: vers un nouveau régime de croissance*, unpublished PhD thesis (2005). Université Paris-Dauphine.

Lafargue de Grangeneuve, Loïc, *Fonctionnaliser la culture? Action publique et culture hip-hop* (École Normale Supérieure, Cachan: unpublished PhD, 2004).

Lafargue de Grangeneuve, Loïc, 'L'ambivalence des usages politiques de l'art. Action publique et culture hip-hop', *Revue Française de Science Politique*, 56/3 (2006): 457–77.

Lafargue de Grangeneuve, Loïc, 'L'opéra de Bordeaux, la danse hip hop et ses publics', in Paul Tolila and Olivier Donnat (eds), *Le(s) public(s) de la culture* (Paris: Presses de Sciences Po, 2003).

Lafargue de Grangeneuve, Loïc, 'Une sociologie des fêtes techno clandestines', *Mouvements*, 42 (2005): 143.

Lagrée, Jean-Charles, *Les jeunes chantent leurs cultures* (Paris: L'Harmattan, 1982).

Lahire, Bernard, *La culture des individus. Dissonances culturelles et distinction de soi* (Paris: La Découverte, 2004).

Laing, Dave, 'Music Video: Industrial Product, Cultural Form', *Screen*, 26(1) (1985).

Laing, Dave, 'The Music Industry and the "Cultural Imperialism" Thesis', *Media, Culture and Society*, 8 (1986): 331–41.

Lange, A., 'Le nouveau tempo de l'industrie de la musique', in Wangermee, R. (ed), *Les malheurs d'Orphée* (Bruxelles: Mardaga, 1990).

Lange, A., *Stratégies de la musique* (Bruxelles: Mardaga, 1987).

Lapassade, Georges, and Rousselot, Philippe, *Le rap ou la fureur de dire* (Paris: Loris Talmart, 1990).

Lash, Scott, and Lury, Celia, *Global Culture Industry* (Cambridge: Polity, 2007).

Latour, Bruno, 'Pourquoi viens tu si Tarde ?', in Bruno Latour (ed.), *Chroniques d'un amateur de science* (Paris: Editions de l'Ecole des Mines, 2006).

Laughey, Dan, *Music and Youth Culture* (Edinburgh: Edinburgh University Press, 2006).

Laurie, Peter, *The Teenage Revolution* (London: Anthony Bland, 1965).

Le Bart, Christian, and Ambroise, Jean-Charles, *Les fans des Beatles, Sociologie d'une passion* (Rennes: Presses Universitaires de Rennes, 2000).

Le Diberder, A., 'La formation du profit dans les industries culturelles', in François Rouet (ed), *Economie et culture. Tome III, les industries culturelles* (Paris: la Documentation française, 1990).

Le Diberder, A. and Pflieger, S., *Crise et mutation du domaine musical* (Paris: la Documentation française, 1987).

Le Galès, Patrick, *Le retour des villes en Europe* (Paris: Presses de Sciences Po., 2003).

Le Guern, Philippe, 'En arrière la musique! Sociologies des musiques populaires en France. La genèse d'un champ', *Réseaux*, 141/2 (2007): 15–45.

Le Guern, Philippe, 'En être ou pas. Le fan club de la série *Le Prisonnier*. Une enquête par observation', in Philippe Le Guern (ed.), *Les cultes médiatiques. Culture fan et oeuvres cultes* (Rennes: PUR, 2002).

Le Guern, Philippe (ed.), *Les cultes médiatiques. Culture fan et œuvres cultes* (Rennes: PUR, 2002).

Le Guern, Philippe, 'Quand le sociologue se raconte en musicien. Remarques sur la valeur sociologique de l'autobiographie', *Copyright Volume!*, 4/1 (2005): 25–55.

Le Guern, Philippe (ed.), 'Sociologues et Musiciens: Usages de la Réflexivité en Sociologie de la Culture', *Copyright Volume!*, 4/1 (2005).

Le Guern, Philippe, 'The Study of Popular Music Between Sociology and Aesthetics – a Survey of Current Research in France', in Hugh Dauncey and Steve Cannon, *Popular Music in France from* Chanson *to* Techno: Culture, Identity and Society (Aldershot: Ashgate, 2003).

Le Rendu-Lizée, Carole, and Gérôme Guibert, Gestion Prévisionnelle des Emplois et Compétences au sein du RAMA – Réseau Aquitain des Musiques Actuelles (Bordeaux: RAMA-CRESS, 2007).

Le temps des médias, L'essentiel. *Les comportements médias et les pratiques multimédias des Français, dans leurs contextes*, Médiamétrie, 2005.

Lebrun, Barbara, 'A Case Study of Zebda: Republicanism, Métissage and Authenticity in Contemporary France', *Copyright Volume!*, 1/2 (2002): 59–69.

Lebrun, Barbara, 'Charity and Political Protest in French Popular Music', *Modern and Contemporary France*, 13/4 (2005): 435–47.

Lebrun, Barbara (ed.), *Corps de chanteurs. Performance et présence dans la chanson française et francophone* (Paris: forthcoming L'Harmattan, 2011).

Lebrun, Barbara, 'Le bruit et l'odeur ... du succès': Contestation et contradictions dans le rock métis de Zebda', *Modern and Contemporary France*, 15/3 (2007): 325–37.

Lebrun, Barbara, 'Mind over Matter. The Under-performance of the Body and Gender in French Rock Music of the 1990s', *French Cultural Studies*, 16/2 (2005): 205–21.

Lebrun, Barbara, 'René, Ginette, Louise et les autres: nostalgie et authenticité dans la chanson néo-réaliste', *French Politics, Culture and Society,* 27/4 (2009): 47–62.

Lefèbvre, Henri, *La production de l'espace* (Paris: Anthropos, 1974).

Lefèbvre, Henri, *La révolution urbaine* (Paris: Gallimard, 1970).

Lefèbvre, Henri, *La vie quotidienne dans le monde moderne* (Paris: Gallimard, 1968).

Lemery, Denys, 'Musique Contemporaine, Pop-Music et Free-Jazz, Convergences et Divergences', *Musique en Jeu*, 2 (1971): 80–86.

Leonard, Marion, '"We're in it for the art, but we'd like to see it chart in the Billboard Hot 100": Promoting UK music in the US', paper presented at 12th International IASPM conference, Montreal, 2003.

Leroy, D., *Economie des arts du spectacle vivant, essai sur la relation entre l'économique et l'esthétique* (Paris: Economica, 1980).

Lescop, Gildas, '"Honnie soit la Oi!": naissance, émergence et déliquescence d'une forme de protestation sociale et musicale', *Copyright Volume!,* 2/1 (2003): 109–28.

Lesprit, Bruno, 'Malgré Björk, bilan mitigé pour Rock en Seine', *Le Monde*, 21 June 2007.

Lévy-Garboua, L. and Montmarquette, C., 'A Microeconometric Study of Theatre Demand', *Journal of Cultural Economics*, 20/1 (1996): 25–50.

Lévy-Garboua, L. and Montmarquette, C., 'Demand', in Towse, R., (ed.), *A Handbook of Cultural Economics* (Cheltenham: Edward Elgar, 2003).

Lewis, Lisa A. (ed.), *The Adoring Audience. Fan Culture and Popular Media* (London: Routledge, 1992).

Lewis, Peter M. and Booth, Jerry, *The Invisible Medium: Public, Commercial and Community Radio* (Basingstoke: MacMillan Education, 1989).

Leyshan, Andrew et al., 'On the Reproduction of the Musical Economy after the Internet', *Media, Culture and Society*, 27/2 (2005): 177–209.

Liesenfeld, Thierry, *Le Temps des Copains, Rock Twist. Alsace Années 60* (Turckheim: Editions de la Nuée Bleu, 1996).

Lincoln, Sian, 'Feeling the Noise: Teenagers, Bedrooms and Music', *Leisure Studies*, 24/4 (2005): 399–414.

Lindberg, L., G. Gudmundsson, M. Michelsen and H. Weisehaunet (eds), *Rock Criticism from the Beginning* (Oxford: Peter Lang., 2005).

Llewellyn-Smith, Caspar, 'Editor's Letter', *Observer Music Monthly*, 1 (September 2003).

Longhurst, Brian, *Popular Music and Society* (Cambridge: Polity, 1995, 2nd edition 2007).

Looseley, David, 'Back to the Future: Rethinking French Cultural Policy, 1997–2002', *International Journal of Cultural Policy*, 9/2, July 2003: 227–34.

Looseley, David, 'Conceptualising Youth Culture in Postwar France', special issue 'Youth Cultures in the Fifth Republic', Chris Tinker and Wendy Michallat (eds), *Modern and Contemporary France*, 15/3 (2007): 261–75.

Looseley, David, 'Cultural Democratisation and Popular Music', in David Looseley and Phil Dine (eds), 'Cultural Practices and Policies: Democratisation Reassessed', special issue of *Modern and Contemporary France*, 11 (February 2003): 45–55.

Looseley, David, 'Fabricating Johnny: French Popular Music and National Culture', *French Cultural Studies*, 16/2 (June 2005): 191–203.

Looseley, David, 'Frères ennemis'? French Discourse on Jazz, Chanson and Pop', special number on 'Jazz Adventures in French Culture' (eds), J. Dutton and C. Nettelbeck, *Nottingham French Studies*, 43 (Spring 2004): 72–9.

Looseley, David, 'In from the Margins: Chanson, Pop and Cultural Legitimacy', in Hugh Dauncey and Steve Cannon (eds), *Popular Music in France from Chanson to Techno* (Aldershot: Ashgate, 2003).

Looseley, David, 'Intellectuals and Cultural Policy in France: Antoine Hennion and the Sociology of Music', *International Journal of Cultural Policy*, November (2006): 341–54.

Looseley, David, 'Naming the Popular: Youth Music, Politics and Nation in Contemporary France', in J. Marks and E. McCaffrey (eds), *French Cultural Debates* (Newark, University of Delaware Press, 2001), pp. 109–20.

Looseley, David, *Popular Music in Contemporary France: Authenticity, Politics* (Oxford: Berg, 2003).

Looseley, David, 'The Development of a Social Exclusion Agenda in French Cultural Policy', *Cultural Trends*, 13/2 (2004): 15–27.

Looseley, David, *The Politics of Fun: Cultural Policy and Debate in Contemporary France* (Oxford: Berg, 1995).

Looseley, David, 'Thinking Postcolonially about French Cultural Policy', *International Journal of Cultural Policy*, 11/2 (2005): 145–55.

Louapre, Richard, *Les Années Rock en Haute-Normandie: 1958–1968* (Rouen: PTC Normandie, 2002).

Loup, Stéphanie and Marion Polge, 'Quel entrepreneuriat pour quel développement durable ? Le cas du terroir', *Actes du Congrès de l'AIMS* (2003). [http://www. strategie-aims.com/dd03/comdd/-polgeloup.pdf].

Lucas, Jean-Michel, *Culture universelle et diversité culturelle: reconstruire la politique culturelle* (Paris: Apogée, forthcoming).

Lucas, Jean-Michel, *Rock et Politique Culturelle: l'exemple de Rennes. 1976– 1983* (Paris: SER-Ministère de la Culture, 1984).

Lull, James, (ed.), *Popular Music and Communication* (London: Sage, 1987).

Lury, Karen, *British Youth Television* (Oxford: Oxford University Press, 2001).

Machill, M., 'Musique as Opposed to Music: Background and Impact of Quotas for French Songs on French Radio', *The Journal of Media Economics*, 9/3 (1996): 21–36.

Maconie, Stuart, 'The Golden Age of Pop', *Times Online*, January 11 2008.

Maigret, Eric, 'Du mythe au culte ... ou de Charybde en Scylla ? Le problème de l'importation des concepts religieux dans l'étude des publics des médias', in Philippe Le Guern (ed.), *Les cultes médiatiques. Culture fan et oeuvres cultes* (Rennes: PUR, 2002).

Maigret, Eric, 'Pierre Bourdieu, la culture populaire et le long remords de la sociologie de la distinction culturelle', Esprit (2002): 170–78.

Maigret, Eric, *Sociologie de la Communication et des Médias* (Paris: Armand Colin, 2001).

Maigret, Eric, and Macé, Eric (eds), *Penser les médiacultures* (Paris: Armand Colin, 2005).

Maisonneuve, Sophie, 'De la "Machine Parlante" à l'auditeur: le disque et la naisssance d'une culture musicale nouvelle dans les années 1920 et 1930', *Terrain*, 37 (2001): 11–28.

Maisonneuve, Sophie, 'Du Disque comme médium musical', in *Cahiers de Médiologie*, 18 (2004): 35–43.

Maisonneuve, Sophie, 'La Constitution d'une culture et d'une écoute musicale nouvelles: le disque et ses sociabilités comme agents de changement culturel dans les années 1920 et 1930', *Revue de musicologie*, 102 (2002): 43–66.

Malbon, Ben, 'Clubbing: Consumption, Identity and the Spatial Practices of Every-night Life', in Tracey Skelton and Gill Valentine (eds), *Cool Places: Geographies of Youth Cultures* (London: Routledge, 1998).

Malbon, Ben, *Clubbing: Dancing, Ecstacy and Vitality* (London: Routledge, 1999).

Mansier, Thomas, *Identité du rock et presse spécialisée, Évolution d'une culture et de son discours critique dans les magazines français des années 90* (Université de Lyon 2: unpublished PhD thesis, 2004).

Marie, Dominique, 'La Férarock', *Musique Info Hebdo*, 19/1 (1998): 1.

Marquis, Simon, 'Commercial Radio's Evangelist', *The Guardian*, 27 August 2007.

Marshall, Ann Marie, *Gender Balance within the South Yorkshire Music Industry* (Unpublished research report funded by the Yorkshire Arts Board, Research and Development Grant, 2003).

Marshall, Lee, 'The Effects of Piracy Upon the Music Industry: A Case Study of Bootlegging', *Media, Culture and Society*, 26/2 (2004): 163–81.

Martel, Frédéric, *De la culture en Amérique* (Paris: Gallimard, 2006).

Martin, Beatrice, *A Sociology of Contemporary Cultural Change* (Oxford: Blackwell, 1981).

Martin, Denis-Constant et Olivier Roueff, *La France du jazz. Musique, modernité et identité dans la première moitié du xxe siècle* (Marseille: Parenthèses, 2002).

Martin, George, *Making Music* (London: Frederick Muller, 1983).

Marty, Laurent, 'De la Chanson ouvrière du XIXe siècle au rock. Une Approche socio-anthropologique de l'histoire de la chanson française', in Dietmar Rieger (ed.), *La Chanson française et son histoire (*Tubingen: GNV, 1988).

Massey, Doreen, *Space, Place and Gender* (Minneapolis: University of Minnesota Press, 1994).

Mattelart, Armand, *Diversité culturelle et mondialisation* (Paris: la Découverte, 2005).

Mattelart, Armand, and Piemme, Jean-Marie, *Télévision: enjeux sans frontières* (Grenoble: PUG, 1980).

Matthews, Jacob Thomas, *Communication d'une star: Jim Morrison* (Paris: L'Harmattan, 2003).

Mauger, Gérard, *Hippies, loubards, zoulous. Jeunes marginaux de 1968 à aujourd'hui* (Paris: la Documentation Française, 1992).

Mauger, Gérard, *Hippies, zoulous, loubards: jeunes marginaux de 1968 à aujourd'hui* (Paris: La Documentation Française, 1998).

Mayol, Pierre, *Les Pratiques musicales des jeunes* (Paris: DEP-Ministère de la Culture, 1991).

McLeish, Kenneth (ed.), *Guide to Human Thought: Ideas that Shaped the World* (London: Bloomsbury, 1993).

McLeod, Kembrew, 'MP3s are Killing Home Taping: The Rise of Internet Distribution and its Challenge to the Major Label Music Monopoly', *Popular Music and Society*, 28/4 (2005): 521–31.

Méadel, Cécile, *Histoire de la radio des années Trente. De l'auditeur au sans-fili*ste (Paris: Economica-Anthropos, 1994).

MediaTel, *ABC (Audit Bureau of Circulation) consumer magazine round-up: music magazine circulation*, January–June 2007. http://www.mediatel.co.uk/ abcroundup/2007/08/article08.cfm. (Accessed 21 August 2007.)

Ménard, Marc, *Eléments pour une économie des industries culturelles* (Montréal: SODEC, 2004).

Menger, P.-M., *Portrait de l'artiste en travailleur* (Paris: Seuil, 2002).

Menger, P.-M., 'Rationalité et incertitude de la vie d'artiste', *L'année sociologique* 39 (1989).

Middleton, Richard, *Reading Pop: Approaches to Textual Analysis in Popular Music* (Oxford: Oxford University Press, 2000).

Middleton, Richard, *Studying Popular Music* (Milton Keynes: Open University, 1990).

Miège, Bernard (ed.), *Capitalisme et industrie culturelle* (Grenoble: PUG, 1978).

Miège, Bernard, *La société conquise par la communication: Les TIC entre innovation technique et ancrage social* (Grenoble: PUG, 2007).

Mignon, Patrick, 'Evolution de la prise en compte des musiques amplifiées par les politiques publiques', GEMA/ADEM-FLORIDA (ed.), *Politiques Publiques et Musiques Amplifiées* (Agen: Gema, 1997).

Mignon Patrick, *La Production sociale du rock* (Paris: EHESS, PhD thesis, 1996).

Mignon, Patrick, 'Les jeunesses du rock', in Actes de l'Université d'été, *Les Musiques des Jeunes, Rennes*, 7–11 juillet 1986 (Paris: Cenam, 1987): 27–33.

Mignon, Patrick, 'Paris, Givors. Le rock local', in Patrick Mignon and Antoine Hennion, *Rock, de l'histoire au mythe* (Paris: Anthropos, 1991).

Mignon, Patrick, 'Rock et alcool', *Sociétés & Représentations, Les Cahiers du CREDHESS*, 1 (1995): 103–10.

Mignon, Patrick, and Hennion, Antoine (eds), *Rock, De l'histoire au mythe* (Paris: Anthropos, 1991).

Milestone, Katie and Richards, Nicola, 'What Difference Does it Make? Women's Pop Cultural Production and Consumption in Manchester', in *Sociological Research Online* (www.socresonline.-org.uk, 2000).

Milliard, Mathias, 'Musique, Développement Durable et Solidarité', (2007). [http://www.irma.-asso.fr/MUSIQUES-DEVELOPPEMENT-DURABLE-ET].

Milliot, Virginie, 'Culture, cultures et redéfinition de l'espace commun: approche anthropologique des déclinaisons contemporaines de l'action culturelle', in Jean Métral (ed.), *Cultures en ville ou de l'art et du citadin* (La Tour d'Aigues: de l'Aube, 2000).

Milliot-Belmadani, Virginie, *Les Fleurs sauvages de la ville et de l'art, Analyse anthropologique de l'émergence et de la sédimentation du mouvement hip-hop lyonnais* (Lyon II: unpublished PhD thesis, 1997).

Miquel, Pierre, *Histoire de la radio et de la télévision* (Paris: Richelieu, 1972).

Mitchell, Tony, *Popular Music and Local Identity. Rock, Pop and Rap in Europe and Oceania* (Leicester: Leicester University Press, 1996).

Monopolies and Mergers Commission, *The Supply of Recorded Music* (London: HMSO, 1994).

Moore, Allan, *Rock: The Primary Text – Developing a Musicology of Rock* (Aldershot: Ashgate, 2nd edition 2001).

Moores, Shaun, 'Broadcasting and its Audience', in Hugh Mackay, *Consumption and Everyday Life* (London: Sage, 1997).

MORI, *A Survey of Live Music Staged in England and Wales in 2003/4* (London: MORI, 2004).

Morin, Edgar, *Journal de Californie* (Paris: Seuil, 1970).

Morin, Edgar, *Les stars* (Paris: Seuil, 1957).

Morin, Edgar, 'Salut les copains: le yé-yé', *Le Monde* (6 juillet 1963).

Morin, Edgar, 'Salut les copains: une nouvelle classe d'âge', *Le Monde* (7 juillet 1963).

Morris, Steven, 'Song Promises to Stop Flyposting after Court Threat', *Guardian*, 15 June 2004.

Moulin, Raymonde, *L'artiste, l'institution et le marché* (Paris: Flammarion, 1997).

Moureau, Nicolas and Dominique Sagot-Duvauroux, *Le marché de l'art contemporain* (Paris: la Découverte, 2006).

Mouvements, 'Hip-hop. Les pratiques, le marché, la politique', 11 (2000).

Mouvements, 'Techno. Des corps et des machines', 42 (2005).

Mucchielli, Laurent, 'Le rap de la jeunesse des quartiers relégués, Un univers de représentations structuré par des sentiments d'injustice et de victimation collectives', in Boucher, Manuel, and Vulbeau, Alain (eds), *Émergences culturelles et jeunesse populaire, Turbulences ou médiations?* (Paris: L'Harmattan, 2003).

Muggleton, David, *Inside Subculture: The Postmodern Meaning of Style* (Oxford: Berg, 2000).

National Heritage Committee, *The Price of Compact Discs Volume I* (London: HMSO, 1993a).

National Heritage Committee, *The Price of Compact Discs Volume II* (London: HMSO, 1993b).

Naudin, Marie, *Evolution parallèle de la poésie et de la musique en France. Rôle unificateur de la chanson* (Paris: Nizet, 1968).

Negus, Keith, 'Music Divisions: The Recording Industry and the Social Mediation of Popular Music', in J. Curran (ed.), *Media Organisations in Society* (London: Arnold, 2000).

Negus, Keith, 'Plugging and Programming: Pop Radio and Record Promotion in Britain and the United States', *Popular Music*, 12/1 (1993): 57–68.

Negus, Keith, *Popular Music in Theory* (Cambridge: Polity, 1996).

Nicolas, André, *Baromètre des investissements publicitaires du secteur des éditions musicales en radio et télévision. Année 2005* (Observatoire de la musique: Cité de la musique, 2006).

Nicolas, André, *Indicateurs de la diversité musicale dans le paysage radiophonique, Rapport annuel 2006* (Paris: Observatoire de la musique: Cité de la musique, 2007).

Nicolas, André, 'La diversité musicale dans le paysage radiophonique' (Paris: Observatoire de la musique, 2004).

Nicolas, André, *Le Jazz dans le paysage radiophonique Edition 2004* (Paris: Observatoire de la musique/Cité de la musique, 2004).

Nicolas, André, *Les marchés de la musique enregistrée – Rapport 2005* (Paris: Observatoire de la musique, 2006).

Nicolas, André, *Les marchés du support musical* (Paris: Observatoire de la musique, 2006).

Nicolas, André and Conradsson, V., *Les marchés numériques de la musique* (Paris: Observatoire des usages numériques culturels, 2005).

Nicolas, Yann, *L'Analyse d'Impact Economique de la Culture. Principes et Limites* (Paris: DEPS-Ministère de la Culture, 2006).

Nott, James, *Music for the People. Popular Music and Dance in Interwar Britain* (Oxford: Oxford University Press, 2002).

Oates, John, 'London council clamps down on Sony and BMG', *The Register*, 3 June 2004.

Ofcom (Office of Communications) *Communications in the Next Decade.* http://www.ofcom.org.uk/-research/commsdecade (2007a) (Accessed 15 July 2007).

Ofcom (Office of Communications) *The Communications Market 2007.* http://www.ofcom.org.uk/-research/cm/cmr07/cm07_print (2007b) (Accessed 18 August 2007).

O'Hagan, Sean, 'Labour's Love Lost', *Guardian*, 13 March 1998, part two: 12–13.

Olson, Mark, '"Everybody Loves Our Town": Scenes, Spatiality, Migrancy', in Thom Swiss et al. (eds), *Mapping the Beat: Popular Music and Contemporary Theory* (Oxford: Blackwell, 1998).

Osborne, Richard, 'The Label', *Reseaux* 25 (2007): 67–96.

Ostroff, David H., Smith, F. Leslie and Wright, John W., *Perspectives on Radio and Television: Telecommunication in the United States* (Mahwah, NJ: Lawrence Erlbaum, 4th edition 1998).

Ozouf, Mona and Jacques Ozouf, *La République des Instituteurs* (Paris: Gallimard, 1989).

Palmer, Robert, *Dancing in the Street: A Rock and Roll History* (London: BBC, 1996).

Panassié, Hugues, *Le Jazz Hot* (Paris: Ed. Corrêa, 1934).

Pasquier, Dominique, *La culture des sentiments* (Paris: EMSH, 1999).

Passeron, Jean-Claude, *Le raisonnement sociologique* (Paris: Nathan, 1991).

Pattison, Robert, *The Triumph of Vulgarity: Rock Music in the Mirror of Romanticism* (Oxford: Oxford University Press, 1987).

Pecqueux, Anthony, *La politique incarnée du rap, socio-anthropologie de la communication et de l'appropriation chansonnières* (EHESS, Marseille: unpublished PhD, 2003).

Pépin, Rémi, Rebelles. *Une Histoire du rock alternatif* (Paris: Hugodoc, 2007).

Péralva, Angelina, 'Skinhead: une identité politique?' in CERI Amiens/CURAPP, *L'identité politique* (Paris: PUF, 1994).

Péron, René, Cottereau, Jacques and Armel Huet, 'Le Disque', in CNRS, *La Marchandise culturelle* (Paris: CNRS, Actions Thématiques Programmées, 1978).

Perrenoud, Marc, *Les musicos: enquête sur des musiciens ordinaires* (Paris: La Découverte, 2007).

Peterson, Richard, and David Berger, 'Cycles in Symbol Production: The Case of Popular Music', *American Sociological Review*, 40/2 (1975): 158–73.

Peterson, Richard A. and Bennett, Andy, 'Introducing Music Scenes', in Andy Bennett and Richard A. Peterson (eds), *Music Scenes: Local, Translocal and Virtual* (Nashville: Vanderbilt University Press, 2004).

Petiau, Anne, *Musiques et musiciens électroniques, Contribution à une sociologie des musiques populaires* (Université de Paris 5: unpublished PhD, 2006).

Pierson, Paul, 'Path Dependence, Increasing Returns, and the Study of Politics', *American Political Science Review*, 94/2 (2000): 251–67.

Pistone, Danièle, 'De l'Histoire sociale de la musique à la sociologie musicale: bilans et perspectives', in Green, Anne-Marie (ed.), *Musique et sociologie. Enjeux méthodologiques et approches empiriques* (Paris: L'Harmattan, 2000).

Poirrier, Philippe, *Etat et Culture en France au XXè siècle* (Paris: Livre de Poche, 2000).

Pouchelle, Marie-Christine, 'Sentiments religieux et show-business: Claude François, objet de dévotion populaire', in Schmitt, Jean-Claude (ed.), *Les saints et les stars, Le texte hagiographique dans la culture populaire* (Paris: Beauchesne, 1983).

Pourtau, Loïc, *Frères de son, Les socialités et les sociabilités des Sound System technoïdes* (Université de Paris 5, unpublished PhD, 2005).

Pourtau, Lionel, 'Le risque comme adjuvant. Le cas des free-parties', *Sociétés*, 76 (2002): 69–81.

Pourtau, Loïc, 'La subculture technoïde, entre déviance et rupture du pacte hobbesien', *Sociétés*, 90 (2005): 78.

Pourtau, Lionel, 'Les sound systems technoïdes. Une expérience de la vie en communauté', in Béatrice Mabilon-Bonfils (ed.), *La fête techno. Tout seul et tous ensemble* (Paris: Autrement, 2004).

Prévos, André, 'Le business du rap en France', *The French Review*, 74/5, (2001): 900–921.

Privat, Jean-Marie (ed.), *Chroniques de Folklore d'Arnold Van Gennep. Recueil de textes parus dans le Mercure de France 1905–1949* (Paris: CTHS, 2001).

Psychotropes, 'Fêtes sous influences', 9/3–4 (2003).

PWC, *Music Collection Societies: Evolution or Regulation* (London: PWC, 2006).

Queudrus, Sandy, *Un maquis techno. Modes d'engagement et pratiques sociales dans le free party*, (Nantes: Mélanie Seteun, 2000).

Quillien, Christophe, *Génération Rock&Folk. 40 Ans de Culture Rock* (Paris: Flammarion, 2006).

RAJAR (Radio Joint Audience Research) http://www.rajar.co.uk/listening/quarterly_listening.php (2007) (Accessed 15 August 2007).

Redhead, Steve, 'Rave off: Youth, Subcultures and the Law', *Social Studies Review,* January 1991: 92–4.

Regev, B, 'Producing Artistic Value. The Case of Rock Music', *Sociological Quarterly*, 35/1 (1994): 85–102.

Regourd, S., *L'exception culturelle* (Paris: PUF, 2002).

Reinharz, S., *Feminist Methods in Social Research* (Oxford: Oxford University Press, 1992).

Reynolds, Simon, *Rip It Up and Start Again: Post-punk 1978–1984* (London: Faber, 2005).

Reynolds, Simon and Joy Press, *The Sex Revolts: Gender, Rebellion and Rock'n'Roll* (New York: Serpent's Tail, 1995).

Ribac, François, *L'Avaleur de rock* (Paris: La Dispute, 2004).

Richards, Chris, *Teen Spirits: Music and Identity in Media Education* (London: UCL Press, 1998).

Rietveld, Hillegonda, 'Living the Dream', in Steve Redhead (ed.), *Rave Off: Politics and Deviance in Contemporary Youth Culture* (Aldershot: Avebury, 1993).

Rigaud, Jacques, *Rapport pour la refondation de la politique culturelle de l'Etat* (Paris: La Documentation Française, 1996).

Rigby, Brian, 'La "culture populaire" en France et en Angleterre: la traduction française de *The Uses of Literacy*' in Jean-Claude Passeron (ed.), *Richard Hoggart en France* (Paris: BPI, 1999).

Rigby, Brian, *Popular Culture in Modern France: A Study of Cultural Discourse* (London: Routledge, 1991).

Rigby, Brian, 'The Hidden Selves of Scholars and Teachers', *French Cultural Studies*, 10 (1999): 241–53.

Ritaine, Evelyne, *Les stratèges de la culture* (Paris: Presses de la FNSP, 1983).

Rochelandet, F., *Propriété intellectuelle et changement technologique, la mise en œuvre du droit d'auteur dans les industries culturelles*, unpublished PhD thesis (2000). Université Paris 1.

Rodger, Gillian, 'Drag, Camp and Gender Subversion in the Music Videos of Annie Lennox', *Popular Music*, 24/1 (2004): 17–30.

Rojek, Chris, 'P2P Leisure Exchange: Net Banditry and the Policing of Intellectual Property', *Leisure Studies*, 24/4 (2005): 357–69.

Rosen, S., 'The Economics of Superstar', *Journal of Political Economy* 71 (1981): 845–57.

Ross, Peter, 'The Invincible Band', *Sunday Herald*, 11 September 2005, magazine: 10–17.

Roueff, Olivier, 'L'Ethnologie musicale selon André Schaeffner: entre musée et performance', *Revue d'Histoire des Sciences Humaines*, 14 (2006): 71–100.

Rudeboy Arno, *Nyark nyark! Fragment des Scènes Punk et Rock Alternatif en France, 1976–1989* (Paris: FZM, 2007).

Rudeboy, Arno, *Nyark-Nyark. Rock alternatif 1976–1989* (Paris: FZM, 2007).

Russell, Derek, *Popular Music in England 1840–1914. A Social History* (Manchester: Manchester University Press, 1987).

Rutten, Paul, 'Popular Music Policy: A Contested Area – The Dutch experience', in Tony Bennett et al. (ed.), *Rock and Popular Music* (New York: Routledge, 1993).

Sabatier, Marc, Grenet, Stanislas, Touché, Marc and Marie-Claire Lory, *Guitares Jacobacci, un Atelier de Lutherie à Paris, 1924–1994* (Paris: Somogy, 2007).

Sablon, Jean, *De France ou bien d'Ailleurs...* (Paris: Robert Laffont, 1979).

Saez, Guy (ed.), *Institutions et vie culturelles* (Paris: La Documentation Française, 2004).

Saez, Guy, 'Le modèle culturel français face à la mondialisation', in Saez Guy (ed.), *Institutions et vie culturelles* (Paris: La Documentation Française, 2004).

Saez, Guy, 'La politique culturelle des villes', in Saez Guy (ed.), *Institutions et vie culturelles* (Paris: La Documentation Française, 2004).

Saez, Guy, 'Les politiques de la culture', in Leca, Jean and Grawitz, Madeleine (ed.), *Traité de Science Politique* (4 vols), (Paris: PUF, 1985).

Sagot-Duvauroux, D., 'La propriété intellectuelle, c'est le vol!' Le débat sur le droit d'auteur au milieu du XIXeme siècle', *L'Economie Politique*, 22 (avril 2004): 34–52.

Sagot-Duvauroux, D., *La propriété intellectuelle, c'est le vol!' Les majorats littéraires de Proudhon et autres textes* (Dijon: Les Presses du réel, 2002).

Sagot-Duvauroux, D., 'Quel modèle économique pour les scènes de musiques actuelles', *Copyright Volume!*, 2 (2005): 15–24.

Sagot-Duvauroux, D., *Structure de financement et organisation d'un système, l'exemple du théâtre*, unpublished PhD thesis, (1985). Université de Paris 1.

Salewicz, Chris, 'Thorpe: victim of the curse of rock 'n' roll?', *NME*, 19 February 1977: 11.

Sandbrook, Dominic, *Never Had It So Good* (London: Little Brown, 2005).

Sandbrook, Dominic, *White Heat* (London: Little Brown, 2006).

Savage, Jon, Sleeve notes, *Pop Justice: 100% Solid Pop Music*, CD (Fascination B000JCESCU, 2006).

Savev, Marc, 'Deux Exemples de presse musicale jeune en France, de 1966 à 1969: *Salut Les Copains* et *Rock & Folk*', *Copyright Volume!*, 3/1 (2004): 5–30.

Sberna, Béatrice, *Le rap, à Marseille* (EHESS, Paris: unpublished PhD, 2005).

Scannell, Paddy and Cardiff, David, *A Social History of British Broadcasting* (Vol. 1, Oxford: Basil Blackwell, 1991).

Scannell, Paddy, 'Public Service Broadcasting and Modern Life', *Media, Culture and Society*, 11/2 (1989): 135–66.

Schaeffner, André, *Le Jazz (*Paris: Jean Michel Place, 1988 [1926]).

Schaeffner, André, *Origine des instruments de musique. Introduction ethnologique à l'histoire de la musique instrumentale* (Paris: Payot, 1936).

Schneider, Michel, *La comédie de la culture* (Paris: Le Seuil, 1993).

Scott, Derek. *The Singing Bourgeois. Songs of the Victorian Dining Room and Parlour* (Milton Keynes: Open University Press, 1989).

Seca, Jean-Marie, *L'Etat acide. Analyse pyscho-sociale des minorités rock* (Paris: Paris V–La Sorbonne, PhD thesis, 1987).

Seca, Jean-Marie (ed.), *Musiques populaires underground et représentations du politique* (Paris: Cortil-Wodon, InterCommunications/EME, 2007).

Seca, Jean-Marie, *Vocations rock* (Paris: Méridiens Klincksieck, 1988).

Segré, Gabriel, *Le culte Presley* (Paris: PUF, 2003).

Sermet, Vincent, *Les musiques soul et funk, La France qui groove des années 1960 à nos jours* (Paris: L'Harmattan, 2008).

Sevin, Jean-Christophe, 'Hétérotopie techno', *Ethnographiques.org*, 3 (2003): http://www.ethnographiques.org/2003/Sevin.html.

Sexton, Paul, *Music* (London: Foreign and Commonwealth Office, 2002).

Shapiro, H.R., *Economie de l'information, guide stratégique de l'économie des réseaux* (Bruxelles: de Boeck université presses, 1999).

Shuker, Roy, *Key Concepts in Popular Music* (London: Routledge, 1998).

Shuker, Roy, *Understanding Popular Music* (London: Routledge, 1994, 2nd edition 2001).

Sirinelli, Jean-François, *Les Baby-Boomers. Une Génération, 1945–1969* (Paris: Fayard, 2003).

Sklower, Jedediah, *La Catastrophe féconde. Une histoire du monde éclaté du Jazz en France 1960–1982* (Paris: L'Harmattan, 2007).

Sloboda, J.A. et al., 'Is Everyone Musical?', *The Psychologist*, 7/8, (1994): 349–54.

Sloboda, John A. and O'Neill, Susan A., 'Emotions in Everyday Listening to Music', in Patrik N. Juslin and John A. Sloboda (eds), *Music and Emotion: Theory and Research* (Oxford: OUP, 2001).

Smith, Chris, *Creative Britain* (London: Faber, 1998).

Sociétés, 'Effervescence techno', 65 (1999).

Sociétés, 'La religion metal', 88 (2005).

Souchon, Michel, '"Le vieux canon de 75". L'apport des méthodes quantitatives à la connaissance du public de la télévision', *Hermès*, 11/12 (1993): 233–45.

Spence, Neil, 'Britpop's Morning Glory', *Observer*, 30 June 1996: 15.

Stacey, Jackie, *Star Gazing: Hollywood Cinema and Female Spectatorship* (London: Routledge, 1994).

Steiner, Peter, 'Program Patterns and Preferences, and the Workability of Competition in Radio Broadcasting', *The Quarterly Journal of Economics*, 66 (1952): 194–223.

Stigler, George J. and Gary S. Becker, 'De Gustibus Non Est Disputandum', *American Economic Review*, 67/2 (March 1977): 76–90.

Stokes, Jane C. and Reading, Anna (eds), *The Media in Britain* (Basingstoke: Macmillan, 1999).

Storey, John, *An Introduction to Cultural Theory & Popular Culture* (Hemel Hempstead: Prentice Hall/Harvester Wheatsheaf, 1993).

Strachan, Rob, *Industry, Ideology, Aesthetics and Micro Independent Record Labels in the UK* (Unpublished Ph.D. Thesis, Institute of Popular Music, Liverpool University, 2004).

Straw, Will, 'Communities and Scenes in Popular Music', in Ken Gelder and Sarah Thornton (eds), *The Subcultures Reader* (London: Routledge, 1997).

Straw, Will, 'Systems of Articulation, Logics of Change: Community and Scene in Popular Music', *Cultural Studies*, 20 (1991): 368–88.

Street, John, 'Making Fun: The Local Politics of Popular Music', paper presented at Political Studies Association conference, York, 1995.

Street, John, *Politics and Popular Culture* (Cambridge: Polity Press, 1993).

Sturdy, Mark, *Truth and Beauty: The Story of Pulp* (Omnibus Press, 2003).

Suire, Raphaël, 'Formation et Stabilité des Clusters d'Activité TIC: Questions à la Politique des Pôles de Compétitivité' in Pierre-Noël Favennec (ed.), *Communications et Territoires* (Paris: Lavoisier, 2006).

Tacchi, Jo, 'The Need for Radio Theory in the Digital Age', *International Journal of Cultural Studies*, 3/2 (2000): 289–98.

Tams, Elly, *The Gendering of Work in Sheffield's Cultural Industries Quarter (CIQ)* (Unpublished Ph.D. Thesis, Sheffield Hallam University, 2003).

Tarrant, Mark et al., 'Youth identity and Music', in Raymond A., R. MacDonald et al. (eds), *Musical Identities* (Oxford: Oxford University Press, 2002).

Tassin, Damien, *Rock et production de soi. Une sociologie de l'ordinaire des groupes et des musiciens* (Paris: L'Harmattan, 2004).

Taylor, Charles, *Multiculturalisme, différence et démocratie* (Paris: Flammarion, 1994).

Taylor, Ian R., Evans, Karen and Fraser, Penny, *A Tale of Two Cities: Global Change, Local Feeling and Everyday Life in the North of England* (London: Routledge, 1996).

Teillet, Philippe, 'Artistes et politiques', *L'Observatoire*, 26 (2004): 4–7.

Teillet, Philippe, 'Demandez le programme', *L'Observatoire*, 31 (2007): 9–13.

Teillet, Philippe, 'Éléments pour une histoire des politiques publiques en faveur des "musiques amplifiées"', in Poirrier, Philippe (ed.), *Les collectivités locales et la culture. Les formes de l'institutionnalisation, XIXè et XXè siècles* (Paris: Comité d'Histoire de Ministère de la Culture, La Documentation Française, 2002).

Teillet, Philippe, 'La politique des politiques culturelles', *L'Observatoire*, 25 (2003): 4–10.

Teillet, Philippe, 'Le secteur des musiques actuelles. De l'innovation à la normalisation ... et retour ?', in Simon Frith and Philippe Le Guern (eds), *Sociologie des musiques populaires*, *Réseaux* 25/141–2, (2007): 269–96.

Teillet, Philippe, 'Les cultes musicaux. La contribution de l'appareil de commentaires à la construction de cultres; l'exemple de la presse rock' in Philippe Le Guern (ed.), *Les cultes médiatiques. Culture fan et et œuvres cultes* (Rennes: PUR, 2002).

Teillet, Philippe, 'Publics et politiques des musiques actuelles', in Olivier Donnat and Paul Tolila, *Le(s) Public(s) de la culture* (Paris: Presses de Science–Po, 2003).

Teillet, Philippe, 'Sur une transgression: la naissance de la politique du rock', *L'Aquarium*, 11–12 (1993): 73–85.

Teillet, Philippe, 'Une politique culturelle du rock?', in Mignon, Patrick and Hennion, Antoine (eds), *Rock. De l'histoire au mythe* (Paris: Anthropos, 1991).

Thornton, Sarah, *Club Cultures: Music, Media and Subcultural Capital* (Cambridge: Polity Press, 1995).

Thornton, Sarah, 'Strategies for Reconstructing the Popular Past', *Popular Music* 9 (1990): 87–95.

Tinker, Chris, *Georges Brassens and Jacques Brel: Personal and Social Narratives In Post–war Chanson* (Liverpool: Liverpool University Press, 2006).

Tinker, Chris, 'Jacques Brel is Alive and Well: Anglophone Adaptations of French Chanson', *French Cultural Studies*, 16/2 (2005): 179–90.

Tinker, Chris, 'Salut les copains' (1962–76) *Interrogating Culture and Youth* (Peter Lang, forthcoming, 2010).

Tinker, Chris, 'Shaping Youth in *Salut Les Copains*', *Modern and Contemporary France*, 15/3 (2007): 293–308.

Tolila, Paul and Donnat, Olivier (eds), *Le(s) public(s) de la culture* (Paris: Presses de Sciences Po, 2003).

Tolson, Andrew, *Mediations: Text and Discourse in Media Studies* (London: Arnold, 1996).

Touché, Marc, *Connaissance de l'environnement sonore urbain. L'exemple des lieux de répétition* (Vaucresson: Rapport de recherche CRIV-CNRS, 1994).

Touché, Marc, *Ethno-sociologie des musiciens utilisant des instruments électroamplifiés* (Montluçon: Catalogue de l'exposition 'Guitares, guitaristes et bassistes électrique', Musée des musiques populaires de Montluçon, 1998).

Touché, Marc, 'La Culture du potentiomètre est-elle soluble dans les Clichés?', *Fusibles*, 4 (1996): 6–7.

Touché, Marc, 'Les lieux de répétition de musiques amplifiées, défaut d'équipement et malentendus sociaux', *Les Annales de la Recherche Urbaine*, 70 (1996): 58–67.

Touché, Marc, *Mémoire Vive* (Annecy: CNRS, MNATP, Le Brise Glace, 1998).

Touché, Marc, 'Muséographier les "musiques électro-amplifiées", Pour une socio-histoire du sonore', *Réseaux* 141/2 (2007): 97–141.

Touché, Marc, 'Musique, vous avez dit musiques?', in Pierre Quay-Thévenon (ed.), *Les Rencontres du Grand Zebrock, A propos des musiques actuelles* (Noisy-le-Sec: Chroma, 1998).

Tournès, Ludovic, 'Jalons pour une histoire internationale de l'Industrie du disque: expansion, déclin et absorption de la branche phonographique de Pathé (1894–1936)', in *Histoire des Industries Culturelles en France XIX et XXe siècles* (ADHE: 2002).

Tournès, Ludovic (ed.), 'L'Enregistrement Sonore', special number of *XXe Siècle*, 92 (2006).

Tournès, Ludovic, *New Orleans sur Seine Histoire de Jazz en France, 1917–1992* (Paris: Fayard, 1999).

Toynbee, Jason, *Bob Marley* (Cambridge: Polity, 2007).

Toynbee, Jason, *Making Popular Music: Musicians, Creativity and Institutions* (London: Arnold, 2000).

Urfalino, Philippe, 'Après Lang et Malraux, une autre politique culturelle est-elle possible ?', *Esprit*, 304/5 (2004): 55–72.

Urfalino, Philippe, 'De l'anti-impérialisme américain à la dissolution de la politique culturelle', *Revue Française de Science Politique*, 43/5 (1993): 823–49.

Urfalino, Philippe, *L'invention de la politique culturelle* (Paris: Hachette, 2004).

Urfalino, Philippe, 'Les politiques culturelles: mécénat caché et académies invisibles', *L'Année sociologique* (1989): 81–109.

Urfalino, Philippe, *Quatre voix pour un opéra* (Paris: Métailié, 1991).

Valero, Valérie, 'Le festival de rock, entre passion et désenchantement', *Copyright Volume!*, 1/1 (2002): 113–23.

Various authors, 'Trente ans de rock et de folk', *Rock&Folk*, special issue (1996).

Verlant, Gilles, 'Interview Jean-Marie Perrier par Gilles Verlant', in Fabrice Ferment (ed.), *40 Ans de Tubes, 1960–2000, les meilleures ventes de 45 Tours et CD singles* (Paris: Larivière, 2002).

Verlant, Gilles (ed.), *Le Rock et la plume, le Rock raconté par les meilleurs journalistes 1960–1975* (Paris: Hors Collection, 2000).

Vernallis, Carol, 'The Aesthetics of Music Video: An Analysis of Madonna's "Cherish"', *Popular Music*, 17/2 (1998): 153–85.

Verret, Michel, *La Culture ouvrière* (Saint-Sébastien: ACL, 1988).

Vicherat, Mathias, *Pour une analyse textuelle du rap français* (Paris: L'Harmattan, 2003).

Victor, Christian and Julien Regoli, *Vingt ans de Rock français* (Paris: Albin Michel, 1978).

Wangermee, R. (ed), *Les malheurs d'Orphée* (Bruxelles: Mardaga, 1990).

Warner, Simon, *Rockspeak: The Language of Pop and Rock* (London: Blandford, 1996).

Well, Max and François Poulain, *Scènes de Rock en France* (Paris: Syros Alternatives, 1994).

West, Candace and Zimmerman, Don, 'Doing Gender', in Judith Lorber and Susan Farrell (eds), *The Social Construction of Gender* (Newbury Park, Calif.: Sage, 1991).

Whitcomb, Ian, *After The Ball* (New York: Limelight, 2nd edition, 1994).

Wicke, Peter and Sheperd, John, 'The Cabaret is Dead': Rock Culture as State Enterprise – The Political Organization of Rock in East Germany', in Tony Bennett et al. (ed.), *Rock and Popular Music* (New York: Routledge, 1993).

Widdicombe, Sue and Woffitt, Robin, *The Language of Youth Subcultures: Social Identity in Action* (Hemel Hempstead, Harvester Wheatsheaf, 1995).

Wieviorka, Michel, 'Culture, société et démocratie', in Michel Wieviorka (ed.), *Une société fragmentée?* (Paris: La Découverte / Poche, 1997).

Willey, Mireille, 'Le rock à travers la presse spécialisée', in Anne-Marie Gourdon (ed.), *Le rock, Aspects esthétiques, culturels et sociaux* (Paris: CNRS Éditions, 1994).

Williams, Patrick, 'Un héritage sans transmission: le jazz manouche', *Ethnologie Française*, 30/3 (2000): 409–22.

Williams, Raymond, *Keywords: A Vocabulary of Culture and Society* (London: Fontana Press, 1988).

Williams, Zoë, 'The New Listeners', *The Guardian*, 24 August 2007.

Williamson, John and Cloonan, Martin, 'Rethinking the Music Industry', *Popular Music*, 26/2 (2007): 305–22.

Willis, Paul E., *Profane Culture* (London: Routledge & Kegan Paul, 1978).

Willis, Paul E., 'Symbolism and Practice: The Social Meaning of Pop Music', *CCCS Stencilled Paper No. 13* (Birmingham: University of Birmingham, 1972).

Wilson, Nicolas, Stokes, David and Blackburn, Robert, *Banking on a Hit*: *The Funding Dilemma for Britain's Music Business* (London: DCMS, 2001).

Working Group on Pop Festivals, *Free Festivals* (London: HMSO, 1976).

Working Group on Pop Festivals, *Pop Festivals and Their Problems* (London: HMSO, 1978).

Wyatt, Robert O. and Hull, Geoffrey P., 'The Music Critic in the American Press: A Nationwide Survey of Newspapers and Magazine', *Mass Communication Review*, 17/3 (1988): 38–43, cited in Yeandle, Sue et al., *Gender Profile of South Yorkshire's Labour Market 2000* (produced for South Yorkshire Objective 1, 2004).

Yonnet, Paul, *Jeux, modes et masses. La société française et le moderne, 1945–1985* (Paris: Gallimard, 1985).

Index